79.95

D1710488

Antique
Swords & Daggers

Mircea Veleanu

Schiffer Publishing Ltd

4880 Lower Valley Road, Atglen, PA 19310 USA

Dedication

This book is dedicated to my life partner Nadia, who encouraged and stimulated me to write another book requiring, again, formidable physical and intellectual effort. Also, I dedicate this book to my children, Iris, Guy, and Leor, with the wish that one day they will fall in love with collecting antiques and enjoy this as much or more than I ever did.

Other Schiffer Books by Mircea Veleanu
Jade: 5000 B.C. to 1912 A.D.

Other Schiffer Books on Related Subjects
German Swords of World War II – A Photographic Reference, Volumes 1-3, by Thomas M. Johnson
German Daggers of World War II, Volumes 1-4, by Thomas M. Johnson
Officer Swords of the German Navy 1806-1945, by Claus P. Stefanski and Dirk Stefanski

Designed by Mark David Bowyer
Type set in New Baskerville BT / Arrus BT

ISBN: 0-7643-2506-X
Printed in China
1 2 3 4

Published by Schiffer Publishing Ltd.
4880 Lower Valley Road
Atglen, PA 19310
Phone: (610) 593-1777; Fax: (610) 593-2002
E-mail: Info@schifferbooks.com

For the largest selection of fine reference books on this and related subjects, please visit our web site at
www.schifferbooks.com
We are always looking for people to write books on new and related subjects. If you have an idea for a book please contact us at the above address.

This book may be purchased from the publisher.
Include $3.95 for shipping.
Please try your bookstore first.
You may write for a free catalog.

In Europe, Schiffer books are distributed by
Bushwood Books
6 Marksbury Ave.
Kew Gardens
Surrey TW9 4JF England
Phone: 44 (0) 20 8392-8585; Fax: 44 (0) 20 8392-9876
E-mail: info@bushwoodbooks.co.uk
Website: www.bushwoodbooks.co.uk
Free postage in the U.K., Europe; air mail at cost.

Contents

Acknowledgments

I want to express my appreciation and thanks to Tina Skinner, who assisted with the preparation of this book as well as my first collector book on antique jade. I am deeply grateful to Donna Baker, for the excellent and dedicated work of editing my previous book on collecting jade and this book as well. Last, and certainly not least, my thanks are directed to Bruce Waters, who took on the big task of shooting most of the photographs exhibited in this book.

Introduction

Writing a book for collectors is a tremendous challenge, requiring intellectual stimulation sometimes to the level of exhaustion. Checking the reference books does not always elucidate matters; instead, it can generate confusion created by divergent opinions from authors and a plethora of nomenclature terms. With regard to this book's subject matter, authors frequently use the indigenous terminology of swords and daggers, sometimes interchanged with international nomenclature. Nowhere does this hold more true than with the description of Japanese and Indonesian edged weapons. If you are familiar with the Japanese language, or are an avid collector of Japanese swords and daggers, then the description of a Japanese edged weapon will not be especially problematic. However, for beginning collectors of Japanese edged weapons, the description of a Japanese sword or dagger invariably necessitates the use of a Japanese sword collectors' dictionary or glossary. The same applies to the description of an Indonesian kris dagger. While English language synonyms are present, it appears that the use of foreign descriptive terms is considered barbarism or a tendency to "show off" the erudite knowledge of the author. For this book, I have no choice other than presenting the foreign language terminology at the beginning of a chapter and thereafter trying to use the English terminology for most of the items.

In contrast to most private sword collections that focus primarily on one category, the collection showcased in this book is very eclectic—including representatives from stone age and ancient times, European and Asiatic examples, plus tribal, ceremonial, and presentation edged weapons. The collection features many Indonesian krises and Borneo "headhunter" swords, due to my special interest in these edged weapons. A diversity of very rare Tibetan and Indian edged weapons is also displayed in their respective chapters.

My personal sword collection was acquired over a period of thirty-eight years by purchasing swords and daggers at antique shows, antique shops, antique auctions, and through a continuous process of buying abroad while visiting countries around the world. While thirty-eight years may seem a considerable time period, in contrast, most of the famous sword collections were accumulated over a span of several generations. It is highly unusual to encounter a very comprehensive collection of swords and daggers, even when the owner was quite eclectic in his manner of collecting edged weapons. Most European royal and aristocratic collections, as well as the majority of European museums, contain primarily a rather mono-representation of western world weaponry from medieval times to the end of the chivalry period. As an example, the Metropolitan Museum in New York exhibits in their medieval section a sizable collection of European medieval edged weapons, but only a couple of Chinese medieval swords and only a few Japanese edged weapons.

Availability and Rarity

It can be especially challenging for the serious collector to gather edged weapons, mostly due to a lack of availability on the collectors' market. For example, although military swords were produced in large quantities, they have experienced significant attrition over the centuries; wear of the weapons in the battlefield, corrosion of the metal, and degrading of the organic, non-metal parts led to low survival of these weapons. Given high standards of collecting, metal corrosion and decomposition of organic parts such as ornaments, hilts, scabbards, and pommels cause decreased interest in such pieces. Accordingly, high quality antique swords and daggers with minimal wear are not only very rare, but out of the budget of the average collector. In addition, the demand for these antique edged weapons has created a large market of reproductions flooding the Internet.

The use of firearms also had an impact on availability, as they essentially made edged weapons obsolete. However, while firearms were more effective in the battlefields, swords and daggers remained functional until the modern era, mostly due to the romanticism attached to these weapons. Military traditions continued to use edged weapons in ceremonial roles and for the ornamentation of military dress uniforms. Ceremonial rituals used by Masonic organizations also perpetuated the survival of swords and daggers.

The rarity of antique swords and daggers is additionally affected by restrictions imposed by many countries prohibiting export of native antiques labeled as national patrimony, or national treasures. It is not quite clear what items are "national patrimony" and therefore prohibited from export, as opposed to more ordinary or common antiques that are not rare. This kind of confusion might create problems for travelers acquiring daggers and swords in Malaysia, Russia, Eastern European countries, India, and other countries as well. A pleasure trip abroad could become a nightmare when the treasures purchased are confiscated at the departing country's customs! Keep in mind that the old red Chinese seal actually certified that an antique item was more than one hundred years old. The newer Chinese yellow customs seals, however, only certify that an antique could be exported. China prohibits the export of antiques that are not verified by the government and sealed with a wax stamped seal. However, this regulation is on paper only, as China is very liberal with the export of the antiques that bring an influx of foreign currency.

A positive aspect of collecting antiques from present day China is the availability of very rare Chinese antiques that were pilfered during the Cultural Revolution and now are resurfacing and being imported to Western countries. As the Red Guards destroyed the most valuable Chinese antiques during the Cultural Revolution, it is a blessing that many antiques were saved by stashing them in hiding places. The damage done was irreparable and most collectors have no compunction about buying anything related to the past. Since it is impossible to return these antiques to the original owners, inheritors, or places where they once were exhibited, their acquisition may represent the best possible outcome for an avid collector.

Conversely, in the past few years, inexpensive antique and semi-antique swords and daggers have been imported from China in large quantities, mostly from arsenals in Manchuria and Chinese Inner Mongolia, dating from the end of the 19th century up to World War II. The Manchurian swords were also produced prior to 1940 during the Japanese occupation. Some of these swords and daggers have a Chinese style appearance, while many others were destined for Japanese military forces stationed in China. After accumulating dust for the past sixty plus years, these Manchurian swords and daggers began appearing on the market, depressing the prices. Such antique and semi-antique swords and daggers should not be confused with modern reproductions that also concomitantly flood the market, mostly due to Internet sales directly from Chinese dealers.

Another trend appearing in the last few years is one that threatens the stability of the antique market in general and edged weapons in particular. Many countries have requested that antiques or antiquities be returned to their country of origin. It seems unlikely to me that the major museums of the world are going to return treasures accumulated over the centuries to the originating country. Nevertheless, many antiques that were stolen during World War II, or even more recently, have been identified by the original owners or heirs as their property, and as a result, civil suits have been filed requesting the return of such property to the original owner(s).

Determining Age and Provenance

Attributing specific ages to swords or daggers where the provenance is obscure was one of the challenges I faced in writing this book. During the cataloging of my collection, I found that many of the swords and daggers had poor attributions or none at all. The amount of wear on a sword or dagger does not necessarily mean that specific item is older than another one with less damage, corrosion, oxidation of metal parts, or wear of organic parts. Rather, the attribution of age is made by using one's experience in handling innumerable swords and daggers, comparing each one with similar weapons where the age

is known, and noting specific styles and decorations peculiar to a time period, amongst other characteristics. Faced with a suspected fake or reproduction, the above knowledge, combined with a special "feel" that only an advanced collector might acquire by seeing and handling many weapons, can provide the clues needed for making a final decision of authenticity. Telltale signs of a fake or reproduction include an unusual style or decorations not ever seen with similar weapons of the period, intentional "aging" of an object, mismatches of decorations, color, relief, etc.

Building a Collection

Due to their rarity, collections of swords and daggers appear infrequently for sale and the pedigreed swords and daggers sold by major auction houses fetch high prices. In order to build a collection of these weapons, it is necessary to have the patience for acquiring items gradually at reasonable prices—unless, of course, a collector has the desire and ability to spend large amounts of money for faster build-up of a collection.

Given this scarcity of collector items and their high prices, my advice to novice collectors is to acquire knowledge by reading reference books, visiting major museums around the world where large collections of swords and daggers are exhibited, reviewing sword collection catalogs with plenty of photographs, and consulting with a trusted dealer prior to purchasing antique edged weapons, especially when the desired item is expensive. Some novice collectors who enjoy bargain hunting and venture into buying at non vetted auctions or Internet auctions may be greatly disappointed to learn that a prized "antique" item purchased is actually a modern reproduction and practically valueless. The expertise and honesty of a specialized dealer is invaluable in building a collection of antique swords.

Most antiques and antiquities available for sale on the collectors' market have no known provenance. Accordingly, the collecting of antiques and antiquities represents a series of acquisitions made with bona fide assurance given by the seller to the buyer that the objects offered for sale have a known line of previous owners. *Absolute* assurance that items acquisitioned legitimately over a long period of time have such a known origin is a rather impossible task, however, as it is unlikely that the entire provenance spanning all previous owners would be very well known. Even the large auction houses occasionally place for sale antiques and antiquities of unknown origin. Of course, an antique or antiquity with a strong, verified provenance will command a premium price in the marketplace.

A differentiation should be made between weapons and collectors' items. In my opinion, antique swords and daggers were weapons at one time in their history. At the present time, however, they should not be considered weapons, as the intent of collectors purchasing them is to enjoy them as collector items, rather than use them as weapons. Be aware that several countries have laws restricting the import of swords and daggers that are considered weapons. One of these is Germany, where the import of swords and daggers is prohibited, regardless of whether they are antiques or not. Because the U.S. Postal Service uses Germany as an intermediary for all packages destined to other European countries, no edged weapons should be mailed to Europe using the U.S. Post Service.

If each antique piece for sale could tell its own story of historical events occurring since its creation, I believe some collectors might become alarmed and ultimately dissuaded from the purchase. After all, any Japanese sword buyer should be aware that these antique swords were tested by cuts taken on human beings, so those with feeble hearts should ignore or stay away from collecting edged weapons at all!

Reproductions and Fakes

It is not uncommon for naive beginning collectors to purchase over-priced, brand new imitation swords and daggers. These imitations are mass-produced and sold over the Internet as antique items, without being disclosed as imitations or reproductions. This is seen mostly in the sale of Japanese swords and knives, which are in high demand by collectors. Most of these imitation Japanese edged weapons are newly manufactured in China and misrepresented as antiques by unscrupulous dealers.

A sword or dagger sold as a reproduction or copy is perfectly acceptable but consequently the price should reflect such transaction. A fake is different than a copy or reproduction as the fake is manufactured to appear old and made with the intent to deceive a potential buyer. An artificial patina of the metal in a shade of bright green should be an immediate warning sign. Added inscriptions on a tang or blade are another deliberate attempt to deceive a buyer. Suspicion should also arise when evidence of metal scraping or polishing with artificial retoning is detected.

It is recognized that parts of a sword made from organic matter might deteriorate much faster than the metal parts. Consequently, a need for replacement of such parts as the hilt or scabbard can be necessary. For such reasons, many antique swords and daggers may not be composed of the original parts. For example, the antique kris daggers almost invariably have coexistent very old blades with much more newer replacement parts. A similar situation is encountered with antique samurai swords that have interchangeable parts. However, the most important part is the original blade—that needs to be present in order to maintain the value of the item.

Values

As previously mentioned, the collection of edged weapons seen in this book was gathered over a span of thirty-eight years through purchase from reputable dealers and auction houses, travels around the world, and private sales. Determining a current value for each item poses a tremendous challenge. It is important to remember that the condition of each piece will influence the pricing. I have tried to refrain from fads or buying trends that might influence values due to an immediate rise in price of a specific item or items, followed by a complete disinterest in this same item(s) when demand diminishes. Over the years, I have witnessed such trends; the most significant was probably the tremendous rise in prices for Japanese samurai swords, followed by a precipitous drop in those prices, most likely due to fakes flooding the market. Occasionally, a single collector may cause fluctuation of the market prices due to an artificial increased demand associated with the spending of unlimited funds.

Another factor contributing to increased prices of edged weapons is the progressive decrease in the value of the U.S. dollar in comparison with the Euro dollar or other currencies, as well as the high inflation in Europe. Oddly enough, we are witnessing a reverse process where foreign collectors can buy swords and daggers in the United States at prices well below the prices existing in their own countries. Conversely, an antique Turkish yataghan can be purchased in New York at a price well below what one would pay to procure it at the Grand Bazaar in Istanbul.

Without any doubt, the price of antique swords and daggers is constantly increasing due to vanishing supplies and increased demand from collectors. The pricing shown here is not an absolute guide for buying and the rarity of specific items can be tested when excessive demands come face to face with a limited availability market. Collectors should know that besides the pleasure obtained from owning antique swords and daggers, the possibility of an increase in value over the years is very realistic. Nonetheless, any antique sword or dagger collection should be viewed as a pleasurable hobby, not as investment speculation.

Terminology

In this book, the international terms for labeling an object antique, ancient, or archaic have been used. In order to be classified as antique, an object needs to be more than one hundred years old. Medieval objects are those that were created between 700 CE and 1500 CE. Objects classified as ancient were created between 500 BCE and 700 CE. Finally, objects classified as archaic were created prior 500 BCE.

Chapter One

Anatomy of Edged Weapons

Any edged weapon has at least two components, the handle and the blade. The third component, the scabbard, is optional but important, as it deals with protection of the blade from inclement weather and possible damage and wear.

The *blade* is the most important component and may have one edge or a double edge. In the great majority of cases, the blade is uniform; some exotic blades may be serrated. The back of a single-edged blade weapon may be reinforced with thickened back blade or encompassed in an ornamental envelope. Occasionally, the lower part of the back edge has a true edge that facilitates cutting, withdrawing, and back slashing, as is in the case of koummiya, the Moroccan dagger.

The term *shoulder of the blade* applies to the proximal portion of the blade near the hilt that is unsharpened. The distal end of the blade is called the *point* and can be triangular in shape when penetration (thrusting) is the desirable feature, or rounded in shape when cutting or slashing is the requested task. When armor piercing is desired, a thickening of the blade toward the point is an important feature of the weapon. Where slippage of the hand is not possible, as with rapiers or basket-hilted swords, the shoulder is non-existent. The term *forte* is applied to the upper part of the blade, where its strength prevents blade breakage. Longitudinal channel(s) usually located in the center or toward the back of the blade are called *fullers*, or "blood grooves." Rather than facilitating blood drainage as the name implies, they make the blade lighter in weight for easier handling and increased power of penetration. The great majority of blades curve upward in the lower third and, less frequently, downward. Inscriptions, ornaments, or inlaid metals might decorate the blade, usually in the upper third near the hilt. Forging of the blade by folding the steel and incorporating ashes (carbon) through a repeated process of heating, hammering, and water cooling increases the strength and durability of the blade.

The *ricasso* is a flat or concave metal plate with a central slot for blade passage, whose role is to reinforce the blade. The blade extension inside the handle is called the *tang* and its role is to provide stability of the blade and prevent breakage. Perforations in the center of the tang allow attachment to the handle through rivets. The *pommel* is the extension of the tang in the proximal end and serves as a hand support and reinforcer of the tang. In most cases, however, the pommel is just an elaborate terminal ornament.

The *hilt* is the handle of the sword or dagger and covers the tang located within. To prevent slipping of the sword, a cover for the hilt (called the *grip*) is made from leather, metal wire, rattan, reptilian or shark skin, as well as any other non-slippery material. Protection for the hand can be achieved by using a *knuckle-guard* that extends upward from the cross-guard. The *cross-guard* is a cruciform, lateral metal extension arising from the end portion of the hilt and linking to the knuckle-guard. Obviously, the cross-guard is built to prevent the slippage of the hand over the blade during a blow. The bulbous extensions of the cross-guard are called *quillons*. They are represented by a divided cross-guard with an arm curved upward extending to the pommel and forming the *counter-guard*, and a downward arm extension above the blade.

The third component of swords or daggers is the *scabbard*, which consists of a cover made from wood, metal, leather, or other material that protects the blade from contact with the environment. Better preservation of a blade is assured when a scabbard prevents inadvertent mishaps or direct contact with water, corrosive organic materials containing acid, or any other chemicals deleterious to the metal. Besides the protection role assigned to scabbards, they also offer the possibility of decorating edged weapons with carvings, incisions, inlaid materials, and attachments for the esthetic pleasure of the owner. Suspension rings usually located on the scabbard facilitate hanging the sword or carrying it around by attaching to a belt or shoulder band (baldric). The distal part of the scabbard is called the *chape* and serves mostly as a decorative part and end-protector of the scabbard.

Chapter Two

Historical Background

Edged stone knives were the first weapons used by human beings. Sharpened stones were used in the Paleolithic period between 19,000 and 10,000 BCE. The stones were chosen for their strength and durability and consequently, flint and black obsidian were the favorites. The stones were sharpened using another stone for chiseling and a heavy, bulky stone as a hammer. These sharpened edged weapons in the shape of knives, axes, and scrapers were used for hunting animals and probably as defensive or offensive weapons against other rival clans. Arrow points were preferred over knives as weapons, because the distance between the hunter and the prey assured safety for the individual hunter. The stone axes and knives were used in cases of close contact when the hunted animal counter-attacked and for skinning and dismembering of the prey.

The bronze age, which extended from 3000 BCE to 500 BCE, saw marked improvements in the evolution of edged weapons. Gold and silver were used as early as 3500 BCE in Mesopotamia (present day Iraq), but were too soft to be used as edged weapons; instead they were used as decorative implements. Copper had been mined in Timna (an early settlement in the Negev dessert near the Red Sea) since the Solomon kingdom. While copper was also too soft to be used for sword blades, the alloy made with tin (and known as bronze) allowed for the development of longer blades that were strong and less likely to break or bend during use. About 2000 BCE, the first swords, axes, and bronze knives were introduced and the early history of warfare is tied to the development and perfection of these edged weapons. Casting of bronze weapons made it easier to manufacture swords and daggers in large quantity and was used extensively by migratory tribes originating in Caucasus that eventually settled in Eastern and Central Europe, mostly in the Balkan region.

The iron age, which began in the 5th century BCE, also brought significant advancements in the use of edged weapons. Durability of sword blades was augmented through the use of different alloys, but most importantly, iron allowed increased flexibility of the blade without breakage. It is believed that the Hittite civilization, which developed in Asia Minor (also known as Anatolia and the site of present day Turkey), introduced iron usage in the Middle East. Archeological diggings at the La Tene site, France, revealed extensive use of iron blade weapons about 500 BCE. The Roman legions used a short sword (gladius), which appeared to be superior in close combat due to a stable hilt. Nomadic tribes that originated in Central Asia

and invaded Europe favored long curved swords that were used while riding a horse. These swords provided superior advantage in slashing and thrusting, rather than penetrating and cutting, and in fact marked the end of the Roman Empire.

Medieval European swords signified the chivalry period, identified by a horseman warrior armed with a sword. European swords and daggers from this era are renowned for their intricate ornaments, with inlaid gold, silver, and precious stones decorating the weapons of aristocrats. The fact that iron blades corroded rapidly in contact with atmospheric humidity made mandatory the use of scabbards for blade protection. Wood, leather, tin, brass, or silver were used for scabbard construction. Suspension of the sword was facilitated by attaching the scabbard to the belt or baldric (a band or belt over the shoulder) and placing the sword at the side.

Extraordinary power was attributed to swords, and ritual ceremonies involving elaborate procedures were utilized starting in ancient times. As royalties were crowned, a ceremonial sword was handed to them, usually by a high priest. The symbols of monarchy were represented through the crown and sword, which were carried from one generation to the next, or from one dynasty to the next. When royal power was usurped, the most important trophy object to be obtained was the sword, which granted royal power to the usurper. In certain civilizations, some swords or daggers were even credited with having magical or spiritual powers conferring to the owner a feeling of invincibility and the help of divine power. Royalties in Europe were crowned by the pope and nobility titles were given by country rulers in ceremonies where the sword played a major role. The nobility of European countries in the age of chivalry gave the sword an aura of romantic allure that stimulated poets, book writers, and bards to glorify the possession and use of this noblest of all arms. Even more, the Christian church attributed to the sword the third highest rank in royal ceremonies, preceded only by the scepter that represented the king's power and the orb that signified the royal justice. In addition, knighthood was conferred by touching with the sword the head of the kneeled person destined to be a knight.

In the battlefield, swords symbolized the cross through the union of the hilt with the quillons; in this way, swords represented the fight for the right cause against an enemy that represented evil power. Not surprisingly, the symbol of Christian cross conferred comfort and support to the wounded or dying. The legend of "Excalibur," King Arthur's sword, is famous for its tale of the sword being passed to Tancred of Sicily and finally reaching the possession of Richard Coeur de Lion, who fought the emir Saladin (owner of another famous sword, a scimitar allegedly given by the prophet Muhammad himself).

Being precious possessions of the highest degree, swords and daggers became one of the most attractive art objects created during the medieval epoch. Gold, silver, precious and semi-precious stones, and carved ivory embellished the swords. Sword-smiths were skilled artisans who kept trade secrets in their families, transferring knowledge and skills from father to son.

Very few centers of sword production existed in Europe between 1400 and 1700. These centers involved mass production of edged weapons by several craftsmen, each specializing in a certain step of the process. The blacksmith would forge the iron blades, the damascener and gilder would decorate the blade, the iron chiseler and engraver would ornate the hilt or scabbard, and the ivory or wood carver would further embellish the hilt or scabbard. The most famous centers for blade production were Solingen, Passau, and Munich in Germany, Toledo in Spain, and Milan in Italy. The cost of manufacturing the most expensive swords was so great that only the richest rulers who were art supporters could afford this luxury. In the Orient, Ottoman sultans of immense wealth commissioned swords and daggers of unsurpassed beauty—at colossal costs. Gold, precious and semi-precious stones, diamonds, pearls, ivory, and carved mother-of-pearl, as well as enamel and lacquer, were used to decorate the best pieces destined for a ruler's possession. A special treat for art lovers is a visit to the Topkapi Museum in Istanbul, where a priceless collection of Ottoman swords and daggers is exhibited. Swords and daggers of the most famous sultans, as well as swords of the prophet Muhammad, are displayed in the treasury of Topkapi Palace.

The process of decorating with gold and silver was extremely laborious, requiring great skill and patience. Working with gold decorations could be very hazardous, as the goldsmith had to apply an amalgam of gold and mercury on the metal surface that was specially prepared for gilding. Applying heat caused the liquid mercury to evaporate and the gold became permanently bonded to the surface. "Fuming off" the mercury was extremely dangerous, as inhalation of the mercury vapors caused mercury poisoning. Gilding with gold leaf, an alternative process, was not hazardous to the health of the goldsmith's apprentices, but the gold's adherence to the metal surface was not permanent; it eventually rubbed off due to age and usage. The least expensive method of gilding involved the use of gold powder dissolved in a lacquer or varnish and applied to the metal surface. More laborious and costly was a method in which gold or silver filament was applied on a metal surface that had been previously roughened using elaborate decorative patterns. This method is called koftgari in India, or shallow damascening. In contrast, inlaid damascening required chiseling and channeling the metal surface for inlaid application of gold or silver wire in the formed grooves, which were designed with intricate decorative designs. In a similar way, cloisonné decorations were achieved by affixing silver, gold, copper, or brass wires to the metal and filling the spaces (cells) in between with translucent polychrome enamel, or applying precious or semi-precious stones.

These methods of ornamentation were brought to Europe mostly by Sephardic Jews involved in the Levantine trade and skilled in precious metal workmanship. The old master European painters were well acquainted with swords and daggers and their paintings provide an accurate rendition of the edged weapons contemporary to the period in which they lived. Renaissance artists designed or featured daggers or swords in their paintings. An example is Hans Holbein the Younger, who designed trousse knives decorated with elaborate allegorical subjects. These trousses continued to be manufactured until the 17th century. The trousse knife contained (in attached compartments) a small knife and a sharpening rod, probably imitating the earlier Chinese knives that contained two ivory chopsticks in addition to the knife.

Spears and halberds had only simple ornamentation, as these edged weapons were in the arsenal of foot soldiers and not used by officers of the army, knights, or royal court nobility. Such weapons remained in existence up to the modern era—limited, however, to ceremonial functions, such as the Swiss guards' arms of the pope at the Vatican.

Fig. 2/1. China. Neolithic period large green jade axe with surface calcination in several areas and mottled appearance. The suspension hole (hao) was drilled unevenly from both sides, typical for Neolithic jade. Evidently, this axe was used for ceremonial, rather than utilitarian purposes. Dimensions: 10.8" (27.2 cm.) x 12" (30 cm.). Estimated value: $2,500-3,500.

Fig. 2/2. China. Neolithic period (ca.5000 BCE) long green jade axe. The suspension hole (hao) was drilled in the typical Neolithic fashion, unevenly carved from both sides. Small areas of surface calcification and large brown veins crate a mottled green color. This large jade axe was used in religious ceremonial rituals and had no utilitarian use. Dimensions: 14.5" (37 cm.) x 7.8" (19.5 cm.). Hao: 2" (5 cm.) diameter. Estimated value: $2,500-3,500.

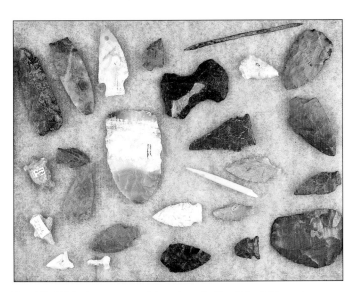

Fig. 2/3. USA. Assortment of American Indian Paleolithic and Neolithic stone knives, scrapers, axes, and points that were discovered in Missouri. Size varies from 1" to 7". Estimated value: $2,000-2,500 for the set.

Fig. 2/4. USA. American Indian Neolithic stone axes and spear points ranging in size from 2" to 6". All collected in Missouri. Estimated value: $1,000-1,200 for the set.

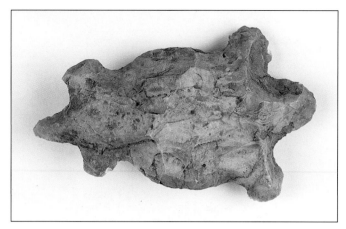

Fig. 2/5. Paleolithic American Indian turtle shaped flint stone. Size: 2" x 1.25" (5 cm. x 3 cm.). Estimated value: $300-$400.

Fig. 2/8. USA. Cedar County, Missouri. Tri-color large spearhead stone (gray, white, and pink). Initially, the attributed age was ca. 500 CE, however new research attributes the age to be at least 12,000 years earlier in the Paleolithic period. The stone has sharp edges that were chiseled with another stone. Dimensions: 4.5" x 2.5" (11.5 cm. x 6.5 cm.). Provenance: Harmer-Rooke Galleries, NYC. Estimated value: $500.

Fig. 2/6. USA. Paleolithic American Indian pointed scraper. Size: 3.5" x 1.5" (9 cm. x 4 cm.). Estimated value: $400-450.

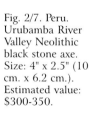

Fig. 2/7. Peru. Urubamba River Valley Neolithic black stone axe. Size: 4" x 2.5" (10 cm. x 6.2 cm.). Estimated value: $300-350.

Fig. 2/9. USA. Cedar County, Missouri. Large brown stone chisel with sharp edges. The reverse side is concave and has no chisel marks. The age was believed to be 500-1000 CE, however new paleontology research revealed the age to be at least 12,000 years earlier. Dimensions: 3.5" x 2.8" (9 cm. x 7 cm.). Provenance: Harmer-Rooke Galleries, NYC. Estimated value: $400.

Fig. 2/10. USA. Cedar County, Missouri. Black stone spear-point with triangular shape and sharp edges. The age was believed to be 500-1000 CE, however new paleontology research points toward a much earlier period of 10,000-17,000. Dimensions: 4.2" x 1.5" (11 cm. x 4 cm.). Provenance: Harmer-Rooke Galleries, NYC. Estimated value: $450.

Fig. 2/13. USA. Cedar County, Missouri. Black basalt stone spear-point with chipped point indicating a prior use. Its age was estimated to 500-1000 CE, however new paleontology research pinpoints toward an actual age of 12,000-15,000 BCE. Dimensions: 3.1" x 1.5" (8 cm. x 4 cm.). Provenance: Harmer- Rooke Galleries, NYC. Estimated value: $450.

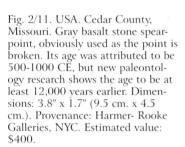

Fig. 2/11. USA. Cedar County, Missouri. Gray basalt stone spear-point, obviously used as the point is broken. Its age was attributed to be 500-1000 CE, but new paleontology research shows the age to be at least 12,000 years earlier. Dimensions: 3.8" x 1.7" (9.5 cm. x 4.5 cm.). Provenance: Harmer- Rooke Galleries, NYC. Estimated value: $400.

Fig. 2/14. USA. Cedar County, Missouri. Black stone double head axe with convex obverse side tapering toward edges. The age was estimated to be 500-1000 CE, however new paleontology research points toward an age as early as 12,000 BCE. Dimensions: 3.3" x 2.2" (8.5 cm. x 6 cm.). Provenance: Harmer-Rooke Galleries, NYC. Estimated value: $450.

Fig. 2/12. USA. Cedar County, Missouri. Gray basalt stone spear-point thinning toward the edges that are sharp. The age was estimated to be 1000 CE, however new paleontology research revealed the age to be 12,000 BCE or more. Dimensions: 3.1" x 1.8" (8 cm. x 4.5 cm.). Provenance: Harmer-Rooke Galleries, NYC. Estimated value: $450.

Fig. 2/15. USA. Cedar County, Missouri. White flint-stone spear-point with sharp edges. The age was attributed to 500-1000 CE, however, modern paleontology research revealed the age to be at least 12,000 BCE. Length: 2.5" (6.5 cm.). Dimensions: 3" x 1.1" (7.5 cm. x 3 cm.). Provenance: Harmer-Rooke Galleries, NYC. Estimated value: $500.

Fig. 2/16. USA. Cedar County, Missouri. Black stone spearpoint with a triangular shape and sharp edges and point. Attributed age was 500-1000 CE, however new paleontology research points to an earlier age of 12,000 BCE. Provenance: Harmer-Rooke Galleries, NYC. Estimated value: $475.

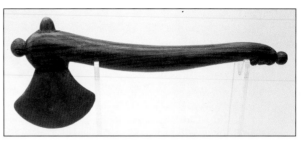

Fig. 2/18. Indonesia, Bali. Rounded sharp edge Neolithic axe dating to circa 5000-BCE. It was placed in a wooden handle in the 20th century. The handle has an anthropomorphic carving at the end. Dimensions: 5.5" x 4" (14 cm. x 10 cm.). Handle's length: 13" (33 cm.). Estimated value: $500-$700.

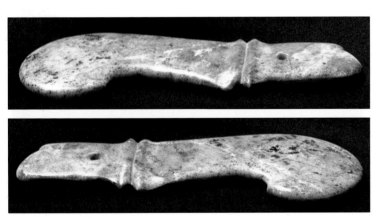

Fig. 2/17. China. Neolithic period, circa 5000 BCE. Large jade carving in the shape of a curved wide blade sword. The hilt has a conic perforation drilled from both sides in typical Neolithic fashion. Obviously this jade sword was used for ceremonial purposes. Length: 12.5" (32 cm.). Estimated value: $1,500-1,800.

Fig. 2/19. China. Neolithic period, circa 5000 BCE. Jade axe with round suspension hole carved from both sides in a typical Neolithic fashion with uneven edges. Dimensions: 8.2" x 4.2" (21 cm. x 11 cm.). Estimated value: $800-$1,000.

Chapter Three

Western World Edged Weapons

The early development of Western world edged weapons has already been described in the previous chapter on history. For the sword and dagger collector, the most exciting period constitutes the medieval era, or chivalry period. European medieval feudal society was based on division of the kingdoms in vassal regional provinces governed by a feudal landlord residing in a fortified citadel surrounded by defense walls. This regional division was necessary in order to defend against barbarian invaders, court rivalries, and attempts to seize or consolidate power by different clans.

Swords from the 10th century had cross-shaped quillons with a short hilt ending in a round pommel. Those from the 14th century had triangular shape blades with a ridge along the center of the blade. Their use was mostly for thrusting rather than slashing. This period was known as the birth of fencing, a sport that is still practiced today. The first manual for teaching fencing was written by Hans Thalhofer and published in Nuremberg, Germany, in 1467.

It is believed that the ornamentation of European swords and daggers imitated and derived from the Islamic swords of Turkmen origin. Damascus in Syria was well known in the middle ages for the high quality of steel blades forged in specialized workshops. These swords were known for their flexible strength, sharpness, and magnificent decorations. Inlaid gold and silver and precious and semi-precious stone decorations made these swords and daggers very famous. They were usually obtained as war trophies during the crusades or used as gift presentations to the rulers. Stable handling of the sword was crucial for survival, as the warrior knights were riding horses and losing one's grip on the sword would most likely result in death. Two-handed swords were used to add more power to the sword blow, for enemy hacking, and also for the unlikely event of losing the grip of the hilt during blow administration. The romantic aura of chivalry persisted until modern times and was widely represented in books or movies of the 20th century.

Central and Eastern European rulers used the two-handed sword for its effective power in delivering an overhead blow. The length of the hilt allowed for gripping with both hands, doubling the power of the strike. European double-handed swords are much rarer in comparison to Japanese and Chinese two-handed swords of the same period. A rarer type of medieval European sword is the execution sword. This type of sword usually has a double edge and rounded point. The importance of cutting and completely ignoring the thrusting (penetrability) is well represented in the executioner swords.

During the late medieval period, crusaders came in contact with the advanced metallurgy of Islamic swords and daggers, and imitation Islamic swords were created by sword-smiths with knowledge of Islamic sword manufacture. As contact with the Islamic world was limited, European rulers used goldsmiths and sword-smiths. Sephardic Jews as, for example, Ercole the Believer at the Medici's court, and other talented and skilled mastercraftsmen, were converted to Christianity and created masterworks of damascene swords with the highest level of ornamentation.

Western World Swords

The *Roman gladius* was a short sword (average length 24 inches or 60 cm.), with a wide, double-edged blade and a sharp point. The efficacy of gladii was proven in close quarters battles, where discipline, courage, and stamina, in addition to planned strategy, were superior to the rival combatant armies. The preponderance of gladii in battles ended with the nomadic barbarian invasions. These nomadic tribes used cavalry for superior mobility and the advantage of unpredictable strikes to the flank and rear of the Roman legions. Even more, the gladii were no match for the barbarians' long swords. Collectors' specimens of gladii, when available, are very unattractive due to fragmentation and corrosion caused by underground burial. They are also overpriced due to their rarity.

Scottish *claymore* swords were double-handed and characterized by a very heavy and long blade. The name "claymore" originates from the Gaelic name "claidheanh mor," which means large sword. This type of sword was unadorned as it was used exclusively in battle, rather than as a nobleman's garment decoration. The only additions to the hilt were purely functional rather than ornamental and consisted of large quillons that prevented the hands from slipping on the sharp edges of the blade. Claymore swords were widely used in the 15th and 16th centuries, however they appear very rarely on the collectors' market today.

Bastard sword is another edged weapon used in the late medieval period, very popular in the 15th century due to its versatility. It is known as a "hand and a half" sword, as the size of the hilt increases gradually toward the pommel, allowing the hands to overlap and deliver an increased power blow. Its odd name probably derives from the ability to change the grip of the hilt from a one hand wield to an overlapping hands wield.

Landesknecht sword is a type of broadsword widely used in Central Europe at the end of medieval period in the 15th century. It has a double-edged blade that is broad and straight. A German slang word for this sword is "katzbalger" deriving from the way cats scratch with their foreleg claws.

An *épée* is the forerunner of the modern fencing sword. It appeared at the end of the 15th century and was a very long sword (43 to 45 inches) with a peculiar triangular shape blade when viewed in cross-section. Another feature of the épée was its considerable weight (27 oz., or 750 gm.). Nevertheless, this sword was very inefficient on the battlefield, due to the minor wound infliction it might cause—except when striking a vital organ. These features were probably considered very attractive for the duel invented at the beginning of 16th century in Italy. The movements were well choreographed in the book "Il duello" published in Bologna, Italy in 1517 by Achille Marozzo. Later, toward the middle of the 16th century, a version of épée became popular in Germany. These swords, named "schlagers" (in translation, "popular theme"), had heavy double-edged blades efficient not only in thrusting, but in slashing as well.

The *rapier* was a favorite sword in 16th and 17th century Western Europe, not because of its military merits on the battlefield, but rather for its appeal to the aristocratic class as a costume embellishment. The rapier has a rather long, double-edged blade and was used both for cutting and thrusting. Adornments of silver, gold, and skilled chiseling added esthetic pleasure for the owners, many derived from the "nouveau riche" of developing bourgeoisie. Rapiers appear on the collectors' market more frequently but usually command high prices.

Broadswords originated in the Middle Ages and were widely used in most European countries during the 18th and 19th centuries, when they became the standard weapon of cavalry and infantry. Frequently, the broadsword had a basket hilt and, when owned by an aristocrat, featured intricate decorations. The *backsword* is a variant of the broadsword, deriving its name from the practice of carrying it attached to the back. While the backsword was the most used weapon in the Orient, it never became popular in Europe.

Smallswords are related to rapiers and became widely used in the 18th century. The smallsword was mostly used as a complement to the uniform, rather than as a battlefield sword. Consequently, elaborate decorations adorn the smallsword. Silver wire mixed with gold wire wound around the hilt's grip, allowed for a better grasp. The pommel as well as the quillons had incised decorations, enamel cloisonné in silver or gold. The blade had a rhomboidal appearance in cross section and was rather narrow, double edged with a sharp point. Characteristic for the smallsword was a double ring just below the quillon, allowing the insertion of the index and middle finger for a stable grip. A ricasso below offered protection for the hand knuckles.

Saber was the ultimate weapon of the cavalry armies in the 18th and 19th century. It has a single edge, slightly curved blade.

The *hanger* sword, so popular because of its use by the pirates, gets it name because it hangs from the belt of the wearer. Some collector books in this field associate this type of sword with naval swords, due to the shell decorations present on the hanger sword. The blade is usually narrow, single edged and slightly curved. The hanger swords are short (24-27 inches, or 60-70 cm.).

In contrast to the hanger sword, which was modest and poorly decorated, the *hunting* sword was lavishly adorned with silver and gold, fine chasing, and a high quality blade that was even shorter than a hanger sword's blade (20 inches, or 50 cm.). The length of the hilt was the same as the hanger's hilt (6 inches, or 15 cm.). In the 18th century, hunting swords were used by nobility and the very rich. The most beautiful swords are of this type and are highly sought by collectors.

The first *naval* swords appeared in the 18th century and represented a version of the smallswords, followed by the hanger swords type in the second half of the 18th century. The so called "*fighting* sword" is a British Royal Navy officer sword with grooved bone hilt and straight quillon. This type of sword has a single edge, narrow and quite long (as long as 30 inches, or 75 cm.). A revised version of the naval swords appeared after 1770 with a reduced length of the sword to 24 inches, or 60 cm..

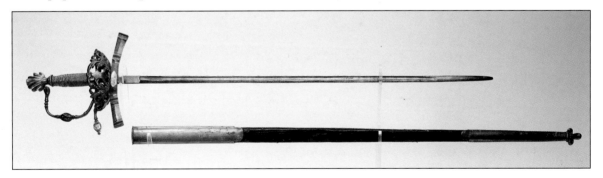

Fig. 3/1. Late medieval German sword. It has a pas d'ane (a guard below the quillons). This particular pas d'ane is in the shape of a basket formed by four decorated panels. The pas d'ane allows for grasping of quillons and holding onto the ricasso. It is marked on the blade "F. Horster, Solingen." Wooden scabbard is covered with leather in the mid-portion and has metal extremities. Wooden hilt is covered with silver wire for an excellent grip. The quillons are straight and have shell decorations, as does the hand-guard. Peculiar for this sword is a downward curved quillon that appeared flattened on the sagittal view, or like a double row of quillons. Estimated value: $4,500.

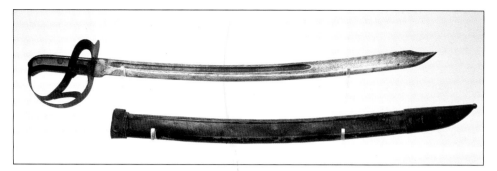

Fig. 3/2. European falchion dating to the 16th century. The blade is quite wide, slightly curved, widest near the point where the back joins in a concave curve, very sharp, and has one fuller. The hand-guard is of a basket type with three bands. The hilt is made from black horn with three rivets for the attachment to the tang. Brown leather covers the scabbard with steel chape and scabbard's mouth. Blade's length: 25.2" (64 cm.). Sword's length: 30.5" (77.5 cm.). Estimated value: $3,500.

Fig. 3/3. 17th century Spanish rapier with wire bound hilt. One quillon is oriented downward while the other is oriented upward, following the curvature of the counter-guard. A hemispherical cup is located below the quillon. The scabbard is made from leather with metallic ends. A "frog" is present on the upper part of the scabbard for attachment to the belt. Blade's length: 32" (81.5 cm.). Sword's length: 42.5" (1108 cm.). Estimated value: $4,500.

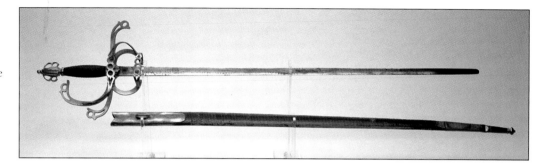

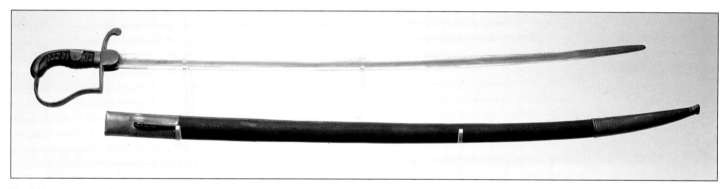

Fig. 3/4. American saber, circa 1775, with leather hilt bound with silver wire strings. The scabbard is made from black leather with brass endings. A "frog" is present on the upper part of the scabbard for attachment to the belt. Blade's length: 34.5" (87.5 cm.). Sword's length: 41.5" (105.5 cm.). Estimated value: $3,000.

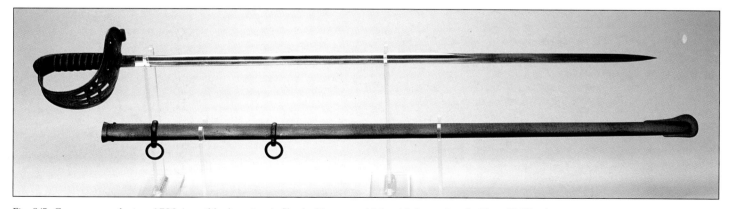

Fig. 3/5. German sword, circa 1790 (possibly American). Shark skin covered hilt with brass rings holders. Half-basket hand-guard with pierced open-work design. Sharp, single-edged blade inscribed "Solingen" and with the initials of the sword-smith, "AA." In a semi-circle is inscribed the name of the owner, "Schnitzler." Brass scabbard with two suspension rings. Blade's length: 33.5" (85 cm.). Sword's length: 41.2" (105 cm.). Estimated value: $2,500.

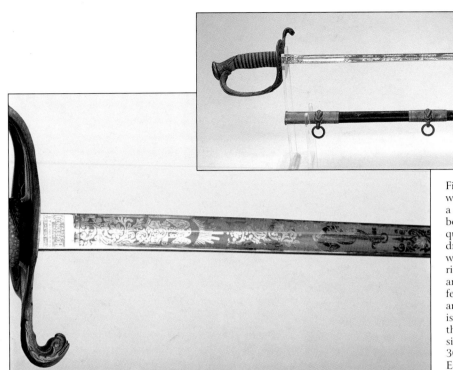

Fig. 3/6. US naval officer sword. The blade is engraved with a gilded design featuring thirteen stars and USN in a decorated engraved panel. USN also appears on the bottom of the hand-guard, which ends in an incurved quillon in the shape of a dragon's head and has another dragon at the attachment to the hilt. The hilt is covered with shark skin and bands of metal wire. The blade's ricasso is engraved "Trade conqueror mark," "stainless," and "NS Meyer Inc Germany." The reverse of the ricasso features a Star of David and ".. oved" inscribed. Leather and brass adorn the scabbard. A zoomorphic decoration is present on the chape. The pommel has an eagle and thirteen stars. We could not locate in the literature a similar sword from this sword-smith. Blade's length: 30.5" (77.5 cm.). Sword's length: 36.3" (92.2 cm.). Estimated value: $3,500.

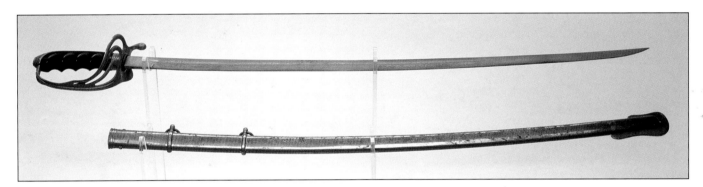

Fig. 3/7. 19th century US Army sword with ebony grip hilt. The scabbard is made of white metal and has two rings for the attachment. The blade is engraved "US E Pluribus Unum" with an eagle holding banner and the owner's initials, "LN." Marked on the ricasso, "MC Lilley Co Columbus O." This type of sword was used extensively in the Civil War by both the Union and Confederate armies. Blade's length: 30" (76 cm.). Sword's length: 36.5" (92.7 cm.). Estimated value: $2,000-$2,500.

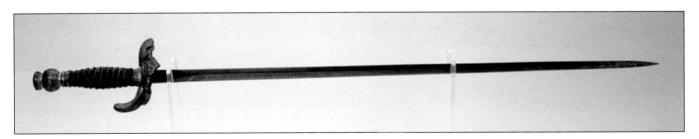

Fig. 3/8. Antique American bronze d'orè sword inscribed on the blade with the owner's name, "Rudolph Schmerda." On the ricasso appears the manufacturer's name, "Cincinnati Regalia Co. Cincinnati O." Gilded pommel and hand-guard. The hilt is covered with black leather and retaining gilded wire. Double-edged blade. Blade's length: 28" (71 cm.). Sword's length: 34" (86.5 cm.). Estimated value: $1,000.

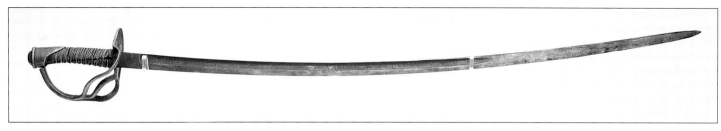

Fig. 3/9. USA. Civil War sword pattern 1840 Union cavalry. Wooden hilt with encircling wire. White metal handguard with three bands converging into the knuckle-guard that is linked to the pommel. Single-edged blade with one fuller. Blade's length: 33.8" (86 cm.). Sword's length: 39.3" (100 cm.). Estimated value: $800-$1,000.

Fig. 3/10. Russia. 18th-19th century shashka sword originating from Chechnya, Caucasus. The scabbard is made from black leather decorated with a chiseled brass band and low grade silver in the lower third. Silver hilt with chiseled decorations on the back edge extending over the blade's back in a cruciform pattern. The pommel is made from dark, aged horn. Very heavy single-edged straight blade. Typically, the scabbard admits the hilt up until the pommel with an easy draw of the sword. Blade's length: 22.3" (57 cm.). Sword's length: 33.5" (85 cm.). Estimated value: $3,500-4,000.

Fig. 3/11. Russia. Caucasian shashka broadsword dated on the upper part of the quillon "1897" and with the initials "AB" in monogram. Single-edged blade, slightly curved and very heavy, displays light pitting. Brass hilt. Blade's length: 19.2" (49 cm.). Sword's length: 24.8" (63 cm.). Estimated value: $2,000-$2,500.

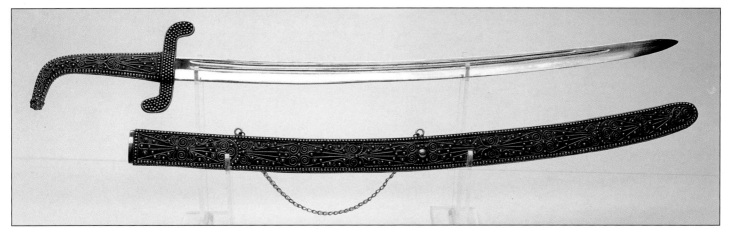

Fig. 3/12. Gruzia (Georgia). 19th-20th century silver sword. The hilt and scabbard are made from solid silver decorated with filigree silver forming an intricate pattern. Silver knobs dot the margins and also mix with the filigree silver wire design, forming a complex pattern. The quillons are decorated with silver knobs and are pointing in different directions. The upper part of the hilt is curved in right angle with the round pommel as well. The scabbard has a two eyelet hanger that holds the suspension silver chain. Both sides of the sword are decorated with the complex filigree design. Curved blade with two fullers. This type of sword was common in Turkey and the Russian Caucasus as well. Blade's length: 26.4" (67 cm.). Sword's length: 35.5" (90 cm.). Estimated value: $5,000.

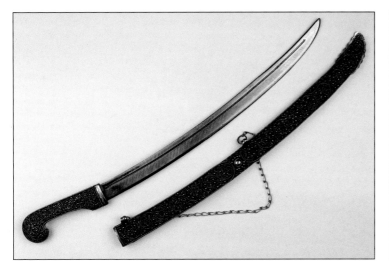

Fig. 3/13. Gruzia (Georgia). 19th-20th century silver sword. The hilt and scabbard are made from solid silver covered with intricate filigree decorations on the obverse side. The reverse side has incised simple decorations in the silver. A stylized bird's head forms the sword's pommel. Single-edged curved blade with one fuller. A silver chain held by two hangers on the scabbard allows for suspension of the sword. Blade's length: 17" (43 cm.). Sword's length: 25.5" (65 cm.). Estimated value: $3,500-$4,000.

Fig. 3/14. 1796 English infantry officer's sword with brass hilt and pommel decorated with relief ornaments that appear to be chased and hammered rather than cast. Bi-lobate knuckle-guard with one bulbous quillon. Other than the single stubby quillon with leaf design, what is peculiar about this sword is the ability to fold one leaf of the hand-guard in order to facilitate the holding and carrying of the sword. Single-edged blade with one deep fuller that continues close to the point. Elaborate etching decorations are present on both sides of the blade. The scabbard is made from brass and black leather. At the proximal end, on the ricasso, the blade is marked "Solingen Iwald Cleff." Instead of the second quillon, the knuckle-guard emerges and continues up to below the pommel and also carries leaf decorations. Silver wire covers the hilt to facilitate the grip and also to provide decoration. Blade's length: 32.2" (82 cm.). Sword's length: 38.5" (98 cm.). Estimated value: $2,000-$2,500.

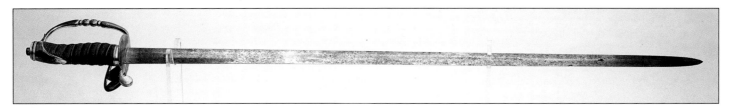

Fig. 3/15. 1845 French infantry officer sword. Shark skin hilt cover retained by brass wire. Elaborate brass hand-guard, with artillery shell explosion decoration, continues to the pommel and forms the knuckle-guard. Double-edged blade bears some indentations pointing toward a previous use in battle. Blade's length: 31" (79 cm.). Sword's length: 35.5" (90 cm.). Estimated value: $800.

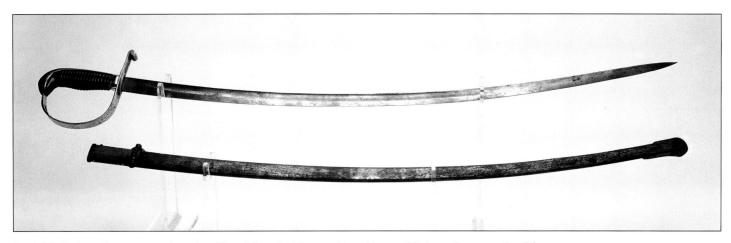

Fig. 3/16. Antique European cavalry saber. Horn hilt and white metal knuckle-guard links to the pommel and forms the hand-guard. Single-edged blade with one fuller. On the ricasso there is a mark of two opposing seated bears. The blade is etched with decorations and inscription on a scroll (in trene). Metal scabbard with one ring for suspension. Blade's length: 33" (84 cm.). Sword's length: 39" (99 cm.). Estimated value: $1,000.

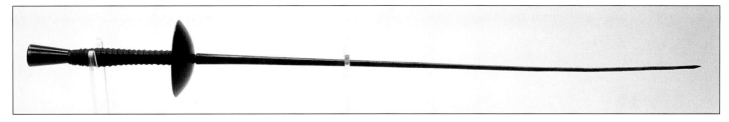

Fig. 3/17. 19th-20th century fencing sword. The blade is rectangular and has a very sharp point. Engraved on the blade is "Solingen, Made in Germany." Also inscribed near the round hand-guard, "J.H. Lau & Co. New York." The hilt is covered with leather and silver or white metal filigree wire. Conic shaped pommel made from wood. Blade's length: 23.2" (59 cm.). Sword's length: 31.5" (80 cm.). Estimated value: $500.

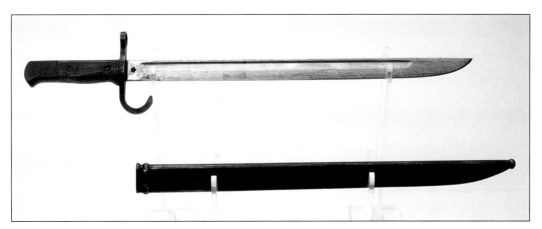

Fig. 3/18. 19th-20th century bayonet. Wooden hilt with two retaining pins. One quillon is oriented downward, while the other has a central perforation. Single-edged blade with five-pointed star in the proximal end. The blade has a single wide fuller. Metal scabbard without ornaments. Blade's length: 15.5" (39.5 cm.). Bayonet's length: 21" (53.5 cm.). Estimated value: $450.

Fig. 3/19. 19th-20th century British or American bayonet. The scabbard is made from black leather with metal endings. Single fuller blade inscribed "artill." and two crossed swords. On the reverse side is inscribed "76004." Blade's length: 15.6" (39.5 cm.). Bayonet's length: 21.5" (54.5 cm.). Estimated value: $550-$600.

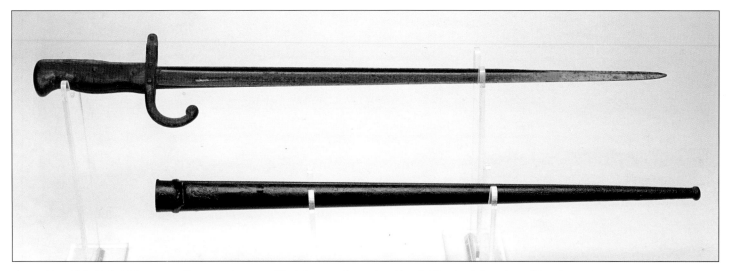

Fig. 3/20. 19th-20th century European bayonet. Black lacquered metal scabbard. Wooden hilt and small hand-guard with one quillon curved downward. Single-edged blade tapering toward the point. Blade's length: 20.5" (52 cm.). Bayonet's length: 26" (66.5 cm.). Estimated value: $450.

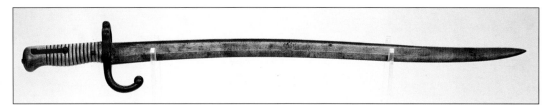

Fig. 3/21. France. Lebel pattern 1886 bayonet with down curved quillon. Brass hilt with horizontal striations allowing use as a hand-held sword. Single-edged blade with one fuller. Blade's length: 22.7" (57.5 cm.). Bayonet's length: 27.5" (70 cm.). Estimated value: $600.

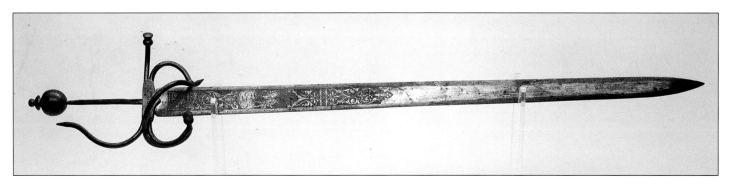

Fig. 3/22. 17th century rapier. The hilt is missing, probably due to disintegration of the organic material, but the tang is present. Round, bulbous pommel. The hand-guard is horizontal, with quillons oriented downward. Double-edged blade with elaborate engraving. Curved knuckle-guard that does not reach the pommel. Blade's length: 32" (81.5 cm.). Sword's length: 43" (109 cm.). Estimated value: $2,750.

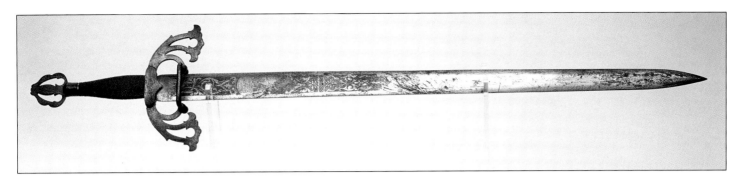

Fig. 3/23. Spain. Sword with bound wire hilt. Blade carries the inscription "Colada del Cid." On the obverse side, the blade features a horseman El Cid. and the factory name, Toledo, as well as floral decorations. Double-edged blade with sharp point. Blade's length: 25.5: (65 cm.). Sword's length: 32.2" (82 cm.). Estimated value: $1,500.

Western World Daggers and Knives

Since Paleolithic times (20,000 BCE) and extending into the bronze age, stone knives and axes were used in Europe and Asia. Documented archeological findings from Scandinavia, the Americas, China, and Persia point toward vast usage of stone implements for hunting and defense against other clans. Obsidian knives (black volcanic hard rock) were used in Mexico by the Aztecs. During the Dolktid period in Scandinavia, brown or black flint and white quartzite were used for knife manufacture. A much stronger and durable stone was used in China in the Neolithic period since 5000 BCE. Interestingly, during the Neolithic period, jade axes and knives were manufactured only in China—even though jade was found in other locations around the world. The only plausible explanation is that the Chinese craftsmen developed the skills to work with such an extremely hard stone, despite the use of very rudimentary tools. Unlimited patience combined with specialized skill artisans, who transmitted their knowledge from one generation to the other, brought the development of jade axes and knives. Later on, improved metallurgic technology, progressing chronologically from copper to bronze to iron, allowed for the production of short weapons with effective thrusting and cutting abilities.

Types of Western World Daggers and Knives

The *scramasax* was a knife widely used by the Vikings since the 8th century CE, and originating from the barbarian Frank and German hordes that invaded Western Europe in the 4th and 5th century CE. The scramasax was a single-edged knife with a triangular blade, averaging in length about 10 inches (25 cm.). Leather or wood was used to cover the grip portion and the hilt was riveted to the tang.

The *cinquedea* is a dagger with a broad blade progressively tapering toward the point. It has a central rib and adjacent blood grooves (fullers). It originated in Northern Italy and the name derives from "five fingers," as the width of the blade at the shoulder is the size of five fingers. Two downward pointed quillons frequently decorated with elaborate ornaments are present on this type of dagger.

The *dirk* originated from a medieval Scottish knife used as early as the 11th century CE. The name is widely used for a multitude of knives and daggers from all over the Europe and occasionally, from around the world. The dirk is a double-edged blade weapon hung from a belt and carried between the thighs. A leather scabbard envelops this dagger, occasionally embossed with intricate decorations. Conversely, the hilt and the pommel have elaborate ornaments with carvings in horn, ivory, and stag-horn.

Hauswehren are derivatives of dirks and, as the name implies, were used for home protection. This cutting knife was used throughout Europe and looks more like a butcher knife due to its single-edged blade.

Roundel daggers and *eared daggers* are related in shape, the sole difference being the appearance of the pommel.

The ear dagger has a split pommel in two converging disks and the thumb is placed between the disks for added power and efficiency. From the upraised wielding hand, the strike was carried downward. There is a strong resemblance between the Turkish yataghan hilt and pommel and the ear dagger's hilt and pommel. Lavish decorations adorn better quality ear daggers that obviously belonged to European royalty and nobility. Oddly, ear daggers were favorite weapons of the assassins and hired killers in Europe. The roundel daggers have a disk shaped pommel and another disk used as a hand-guard.

Ring daggers were favorite weapons of the medieval knights and European nobility. The name derives from the ring-shaped pommel that served as a suspension facility for the sword's attachment to a belt. This dagger is also known as a *quillon* and is actually a miniature sword.

A *stiletto* is a small knife used for thrusting only, due to the triangular shape of the blade. It was widely used as a concealed weapon due to the ease of hiding this small knife in clothes, pockets, or inside hollow staffs or canes. Stilettos that were used by privileged aristocrats or medieval rulers are attractively decorated with precious and semi-precious stones, gold, silver, or ivory. On the other hand, stilettos were also used by assassins.

Swiss daggers, also known as *Holbeins* (portrayed in paintings by the old master painter Holbein the Younger), are profusely decorated daggers used by medieval nobility. Silver and inlaid gold with allegorical decorations ornate the hilt, pommel, and quillons of this type of dagger.

Navaja was a medieval Spanish switch-blade knife whose blade was folded within the handle. Switch blade knives were not used by the aristocracy and were considered weapons of the lower class. Consequently, navaja knives had no spectacular decorations that would be of interest to collectors.

Left hand daggers (main gauche) were used for left hand wield as an auxiliary weapon to rapiers in the 16th and 17th centuries, and not necessarily as a weapon for left handed persons. Intricate decorations usually ornate the hilt, pommel, and scabbard of these daggers.

The *Baselard* is actually a small sword whose name originates from the city of Basel in Switzerland. Characteristic of this long dagger is the convex shape of the lower part of the pommel, as well as the upper part of the hand-guard forming a medieval calligraphic capital I. This dagger has a double-edged blade that tapers gradually toward the point.

The *Bowie knife* is a traditional American fighting knife, despite being initially intended for the skinning and disemboweling of hunted animals. Its name originates from Colonel Jim Bowie of Kentucky, who designed this knife and had it manufactured by a blacksmith from Arizona named James Black. An alternative name is the *Arkansas Toothpick*, due to its slender shape. As a result of their popularity and high demand, most of the Bowie knives were produced in England by Sheffield in the late 19th century, rather than in the U.S. The name of the original owner could be found inscribed on the shoulder of the blade, or back, near the handle. These knives have a single-edged blade whose length is 10 inches or shorter.

A *bayonet* is a dagger or knife mounted to a rifle and used solely for close quarters combat. The popularity of this weapon decreased after World War I, and in our modern times it is used only for public exhibits of honor guards or for marches. History points toward invention of the bayonet in Spain and it was practically used by the French Army in 1640. The earliest bayonet had a triangular blade plugged into the muzzle of the gun; later, it was side-fitted to the barrel and used as a pike in close combat. Except for India in 18th century, bayonets were never used in the Eastern world. While bayonets were shown in the sword section, two are shown in the dagger section as well, mostly because of their diminutive size.

Fig. 3/24. Russia. 18th-19th century Caucasian dagger from Chechen (Chechnya•region). The hilt is saddle shaped on top and decorated with silver niello technique. An Islamic inscription is present on one side of the blade. The scabbard has repoussé floral design decorations in silver on velvet background. Blade's length: 4.5" (11.5 cm.). Dagger's length: 9.5" (24 cm.). Estimated value: $1,000-$2,500.

Fig. 3/25. Imperial Russia. 18th-19th century signed dagger. Double-edged blade inscribed "Postawshik Imperat Tzestva works" with the czar's emblem. Signed "Egor Samsonov, Bitula." The hilt is made from criss-cross incised black wood. Leather and black metal form the scabbard. Blade's length: 9.8" (24.7 cm.). Dagger's length: 16" (40.6 cm.). Estimated value: $3,000.

Fig. 3/26. Imperial Russia. 18th century dagger. The hilt is made from wood with ivory ends and a small metal pommel. Single-edged blade with wide central fuller. The scabbard is covered with black leather and decorated with filigree silver and terminal ivory. Two rings are attached to the back of the scabbard for suspension purposes. Blade's length: 8.5" (21.5 cm.). Dagger's length: 17" (43 cm.). Estimated value: $3,000-$3,500.

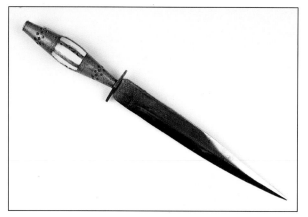

Fig. 3/28. Antique Spanish dagger with strong Moorish influence. The blade is dated 1567 and signed "Albacen"(?); on the reverse is inscribed "Abia." The blade is single-edged for 2/3 of the length, then becomes double-edged with a central rib for re-enforcement. Floral decorations are incised on the back of the blade. The hilt is made from brass and ivory and vertical brass striations. Simple perforations decorate the hilt. Obviously, the dagger is influenced in its design by the Islamic Moorish design. Blade's length: 8.2" (21 cm.). Dagger's length: 12.3" (31.5 cm.). Estimated value: $1,000.

Fig. 3/27. 17th century or much earlier Transylvanian stiletto made by a master craftsman for a prince or grof. Silver stiletto decorated with precious and semi-precious stones: rubies, agate, turquoise, agate, jasper, coral, and pearls. The pommel has a jasper end decoration. Chiseled silver along with precious and semi-precious stones decorate the hilt. The quillons are curved, one upward and the other downward, and made from chased silver and inlaid rubies, turquoise, and pearls. Green lizard skin decorates the scabbard. One side of the blade has a stylized and inlaid copper dragon along the blade's length (the emblem of Vlad the Impaler-Dracul, or Dracula!). Blade's length: 4.5" (11.5 cm.). Stiletto's length: 9.4" (24 cm.). Estimated value: $15,000.

Fig. 3/29. Italy. 18th-19th century stiletto with exceptional artistic decoration. The hilt is in the shape of a nude man; above, the Goddess of Justice holds the balance. A tourmaline stone forms the pommel. The quillons are in the shape of gargoyle heads united in the center by a skull. A serpent coiled around a tree lavishly decorates the scabbard. The blade is decorated with a coiled serpent around a pole and two fenestrations. It appears to me that this stiletto allegorically represents the vendetta and, used for this purpose, self imposed revenge and justice widely represented in Italy during this period of time. Estimated value: $2,500.

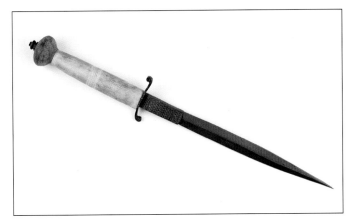

Fig. 3/30. Southern Europe. 19th-20th century dagger. Ivory hilt with simple decorations. Round wooden pommel. Double-edged blade with incised decorations on the proximal part. Blade's length: 8.7" (22 cm.). Dagger's length: 14" (36 cm.). Estimated value: $400.

Fig. 3/31. 18th-19th century Italian stiletto. The hilt is made from silver with a central portion made from ivory. A round carnelian stone forms the pommel. Rhomboid shape blade tapers toward the point. Silver scabbard with ball end chape. Blade's length: 4.6" (12 cm.). Stiletto's length: 8.8" (22.5 cm.). Estimated value: $900.

Fig. 3/32. Bayonet with the inscription "W G" near the hilt. The handguard is engraved "4508" and the scabbard's hook is engraved "Y&N." Blade's length: 9.5" (24 cm.). Bayonet's length: 14.5" (37 cm.). Estimated value: $375.

Fig. 3/33. 20th century European bayonet with leather scabbard. Metal hilt with button attachment to the rifle. The scabbard is embossed "SC Arema 1935" and has polished brass at the ends. Single-edged blade with a deep fuller. "TA" and a royal crown are incised in the ricasso. Blade's length: 9.2" (23.5 cm.). Bayonet's length: 15.5" (39.5 cm.). Estimated value: $400.

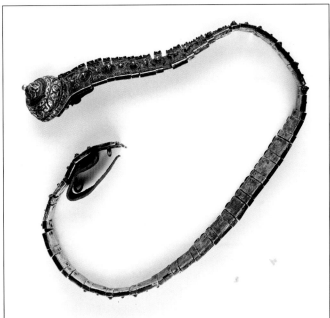

Fig. 3/34. Russia, Caucasus. 18th-19th century silver belt made from rectangular silver segments decorated with chiseled ornaments, all marked with imperial mark "84" for silver. The belt was used to carry a dagger. Length: 33" (84 cm.). Estimated value: $850.

Ceremonial and Presentation Swords and Daggers

Presentation swords are very rare and difficult to acquire for the average collector. These swords were awarded for bravery in war or as a sign of appreciation for services provided to the royal court by a noble person or commander of the army. Lavish decorations and inscriptions on the blade are typical of presentation swords. Recognition of distinguished political or military service allowed the monarch to reward a military leader or nobleman with a highly decorated sword, usually manufactured by royal court recognized sword-smiths, top jewelers, and engravers.

A *bearing* sword is one variety of presentation sword used since Byzantine times. This large sword was used for ceremonial events such as royal weddings or funerals. The bearing sword was held unsheathed and pointing upward, as testimony of the royal power under God. The scabbard of a bearing sword is usually covered with red velvet and decorated with expensive ornaments. This type of sword is found in the treasury of royal palaces or in museums.

A *coronation* sword is another type of ceremonial sword symbolizing the authority of royal power. The coronation sword is probably the most magnificent sword created by European craftsmen and truly an art object to be respected by the nation the monarch belonged to.

A *papal* sword is a ceremonial sword awarded by popes to heads of states, usually monarchs honored for their loyalty to the pontiff. The papal swords were awarded from the 11th century until the 19th century and the recipients were royal military leaders considered by the pontiffs to be the defenders of the faith. These swords attest to the immense power exercised by the pope through the centuries and the involvement of the pontiffs in the western Europe politics.

Masonic swords and daggers are used for ceremonial purposes in Masonic clubs or fraternal societies, frequently denoting the rank and name of the person who possesses the sword. These swords are the only ceremonial swords that could be procured by collectors and several are shown here.

Fig. 3/36. USA. Masonic sword of the Knights of Pythias order. The scabbard carries a relief decoration inscribed "FCB" on an obverse plaque. There is a cruciform hand-guard representing opposing relief design of a bird. A central plate bears the inscription UR (Uniform Rank). Below FCB is a relief decoration representing a man with shackled feet carrying a scroll in each hand. The hilt is covered with leather held in place by spiral wire. A helmeted knight with a lion on his helmet forms the highly decorative pommel. The blade has etching on both sides and the name of the owner, "William H. Brown," is inscribed on the obverse. On the reverse side the sword's manufacturer, "Horstmann Philadelphia," is etched in a cartouche on the ricasso, close to the hilt. Blade's length: 27.1" (69 cm.). Sword's length: 35" (89 cm.). Estimated value: $800-1,000.

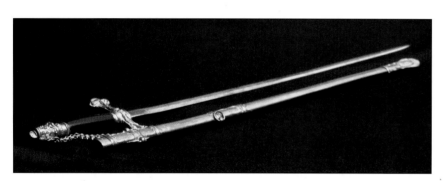

Fig. 3/35. USA. Odd Fellows Society sword dating to circa 1850. The scabbard has decorations in high relief on gilded brass representing a crusade officer in a friendly facing with a Muslim officer. In a cartouche below, Moses carrying the tables of the law is shown in high relief. The blade has etching and gilt engravings featuring the owner's name, Geo Whipple, and the manufacturer, M.C. Lilley & Co., Columbus, Ohio. This is a very rare fraternal organization sword. Blade's length: 31" (79 cm.). Sword's length: 39.6" (101 cm.). Estimated value: $1,500-$2,000.

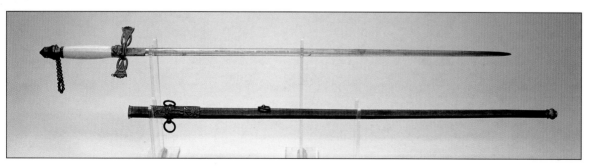

Fig. 3/37. USA. 19th century masonry ceremonial sword with bone hilt. Solingen blade with etched decorations. Marked "Horstmann Philadelphia." The ricasso is marked with the manufacturer's name, "W Glauberg Solingen." The name of the owner, "Guoof," is incised in the scabbard. Blade's length: 28.2" (71.7 cm.). Sword's length: 36" (91.5 cm.). Estimated value: $900.

Chapter Four

Middle Eastern and Islamic Edged Weapons

One of my favorite collecting categories of swords and daggers are those so-called "swords of Islam" that originate from a very broad geographic area—starting from Central Asia, all over the Middle East, and extending to North Africa. Due to the vast territory where these edged weapons could be found, it is easy to understand the multitude of shapes and decorations that characterize them.

Better quality Islamic edged weapons are typified by a high degree of decorating skills and advanced knowledge of the metallurgic process involved in creating the weapon. While Islamic swords and daggers are generally believed to have curved blades, the early Islamic edged weapons were straight and rather wide. Turkmen invaders from Mongolian steppes, mostly from Altai high plateau, were nomadic tribes of horsemen warriors. The cavalry sword was used for cutting and slashing rather than thrusting and penetrating, and this explains the extensive use of curved swords, designed primarily for slashing; since cavalry attacks were carried out from a horse-mounted position that was far from the combatant, the need for thrusting was eliminated. Also, the horsemen would have had difficulty carrying a straight sword, unless it was mounted to the back, rather than attached to the belt.

Pre-Islamic Middle Eastern swords (prior to the 7th century CE) are very rare and usually seen only in specialized museum collections. The bronze age swords originating from Luristan (present day Iran) are the exception, and plenty of examples are available on the market. Luristan swords and daggers were known to exist as early as 2 millennia prior to the Islamic period. The Sassanid dynasty, which ruled Persia between the 3rd to 8th century CE, was known for creating broad, straight swords, similar to Byzantine swords of the same period. Unfortunately, due to the high iron content of the blades, corrosion damaged most of these early swords, including the ancient Egyptian swords. The earlier bronze Egyptian edged weapons of more than 3000 years ago had a better survival rate, especially in dry climates.

Early Islamic swords are also extremely rare and generally not available for collectors. One of the reasons for this scarcity was the tendency of medieval blacksmiths to recycle swords that got damaged in battles. Some swords were shortened when the point was damaged, others completely recycled for the use of all metal scraps. Gold and silver were shaved off, melted, and reused, as were semi-precious stones, inlaid ivory, mother-of-pearl, etc.

During the early Islamic medieval era, the city of Damascus, Syria, was known as the main center for pro-duction of high quality blades for edged weapons. Due to its geographic location at the crossroads of the Middle East, Damascus became a center of trading with the West (European countries), as well as with the East (Damascus being one of the end points of the Silk Road). I speculate that advanced metallurgic knowledge of the Tang period in China influenced the production of watered steel blades in Damascus. In fact, the Damascus blade became a standard for the finest watered steel blade, also named damascene. Damascus was also known as a center of trade for edged weapon blades manufactured in other countries, such as India and Yemen, amongst others.

A lack of protective gear for the hand-guard is typical of Islamic swords. Since battles were carried out while mounted on a horse—with the enemy at a relatively safe distance—having a protective hand-guard was not a priority. The only hand-guard device existing was in a cruciform shape, to avoid the hand slipping on the sharp blade. Occasionally, the hand-guard on one of these swords will have longets extending downward—their sole purpose being to protect the hand from slipping on the cutting edge during a strike.

Nothing is more important for an advanced Islamic sword collector than a visit to the Topkapi Palace and museum in Istanbul, Turkey. The Palace has a magnificent view of Bosphorus and is home to the most important collection of Islamic swords and daggers in the world. The Treasury of the Palace contains swords and daggers accumulated over the centuries by various sultans. For example, it contains the famous "Topkapi dagger," once featured in an adventure movie. This dagger has giant emerald embellishments on the hilt, making it very distinguished. Also on display is the famous sword of Soleyman the Magnificent, who ruled half of Europe. The sword is dated 1526/7 and signed on the back of the blade by the sword-smith, Ahmed Tekelü. Inlaid gold decorations in relief with dragons and an inscription in praise of the sultan ornate the blade. Another famous sword housed at Topkapi's Treasury is the sword of Mehmet the Conqueror (the conqueror of Constantinople in the 15th century), which features an inlaid gold inscription along the blade's length. These swords are vivid representations of the peak of late medieval Ottoman art.

Persia was another region famous for the production of high quality Islamic swords. The tradition of manufacturing fine edged weapons in Persia extends well into the ancient pre-Islamic era. Forging the steel in repeat sequences produced the highest quality of watered steel blade on Persian swords. Many of these swords were manufactured in the Northern part of India under the Moghul empire and it is practically impossible to distinguish the Indian Moghul swords from those manufactured in Persia. Specific for these high end swords and daggers named Indo-Persian is the excellent quality of watered steel blades and the light green, inclusions-free nephrite used to make the hilt.

Types of Islamic Edged Weapons

Typical of Ottoman swords is the *yataghan*, a curved sword with a blade that widens gradually in the lower third and a hilt with a double ears end that also forms the pommel. The high quality yataghans have ivory, rhinoceros, gold, silver, or jade hilts and scabbards decorated with repoussé or filigree silver, coral, turquoise, precious or semi-precious stones, and inlaid gold.

A *kard* is a Persian knife with a single-edged straight blade and very sharp point made to penetrate the steel mail. Better kards have ivory hilts and silver or gold koftgari (superficially inlaid as a metal wash).

A variant of the kard is the Turkish dagger, *bichaq*. It is only 7-8 inches long and has a watered single-edged blade. The scabbard is made from chiseled and embossed silver or brass. Two ivory or bone plates riveted to the tang form the hilt.

Another type of Persian sword is a saber called a *shamshir* or *scimitar*. The shamshir has a markedly curved, narrow blade, usually made from watered steel. Peculiar for the shamshir is the pistol shaped hilt with the grip at an angle with the pommel. It has a short hand-guard with short quillons, sometimes oriented downward along the blade. Better quality shamshirs have an ivory hilt and inlaid decorations. The Syrian scimitars (shamshirs) usually have watered blades and gold or silver ornaments inlaid in the blade.

A *tulwar* (talwar) is an Indian saber with marked curvature that is related to the shamshir. For this reason, the tulwar is also called an Indo-Persian sword. The hilt is bulbous and ends with a disk shaped pommel. Inlaid silver or niello decorations frequently ornate the hilt and pommel of this sword. Often, the hand-guard links to the pommel, but occasionally it may end side by side to the pommel or below. The tulwar was the most common Indian sword, frequently used by the Sikh warriors.

A *pulomar* sword is a variation of the tulwar. Its characteristic feature is the markedly curved blade with no counter-guard. The quillons are stubby and downward oriented toward the edges of the blade. Typically, the pommel is hemispheric, with the roundness oriented toward the hilt.

A *khanjar* is a very common Indian dagger, also used in different Muslim countries. It has a curved double-edged blade and a peculiar pommel oriented in sharp angle to the hilt as a pistol grip. Khanjars of high quality have jade, ivory, or rhinoceros horn carved hilts and are decorated with filigree gold, silver, semi-precious or precious stones. Fine forging of the blade complements the beauty of these daggers.

A *jambiya* is the most common dagger used in Arabic language countries. Some of the most expensive jambiyas were owned by royal families or aristocrats in the royal Islamic courts. Those jambiyas had ivory or rhinoceros horn hilts embellished with gold threads. Elaborate decorations on the scabbard made from filigree gold or silver, coral, turquoise, jade, agate, or precious stones such as rubies, emeralds or sapphires ornate these exquisite daggers.

The Moroccan type of jambiyas are much better known in the Western world, but much less elaborately decorated. These Moroccan jambiyas are called *koummiya* (*koumiya*) and were created for the tourist trade or for utilitarian use; therefore, most are lacking any significant artistic value. They are made from wood with brass or copper decorations. Simple steel blades lacking the watering and gold or silver damascening are typically seen in these less expensive koummiya. The collection here features high quality Moroccan koummiya created by master craftsmen. These are called Berber daggers or swords and are found in the northern part of Morocco. The scabbards of these daggers are covered with chiseled silver in high relief (sometimes low relief as an engraving) and also filigree silver. The daggers usually have a wooden or rhinoceros hilt with decorated silver ends matching the scabbard, and occasionally a flattened pommel like a rooster crest or three lobes with elaborate silver decorations. The blades of these high end daggers lack watering or gold or silver damascening. My own belief is that since the blade was not visible unless the dagger was withdrawn from the scabbard, no effort was made to make these blades more attractive. Even more, indigent blades were crudely manufactured with depressions in the metal due to uneven forging. Many koummiyas were made from recycled European daggers and swords, mostly of Spanish origin. These daggers typically have a shiny, smooth blade apparently containing a high percentage of chrome and zinc and occasionally bearing Spanish inscriptions with a trademark emblem. Most of the high quality koummiyas were made by skilled Jewish Moroccan artisans and are characterized by one or more Stars of David engraved or incised in the silver scabbard, hilt, or both. Another mark seen is that featuring a goat's head, attributed to King Hassan I, who ruled during the 19th century. Some of these daggers or swords are fantasy edged weapons, as they represent unique prototypes for daggers or swords that were not made for mass production but were probably created instead as custom made edged weapons for the royal court or Moroccan aristocracy.

The Sahara desert region features a different type of edged weapon, Touareg (Tuareg) knives and swords. The swords are called *takouba* and feature a straight double-edged blade with crude indigenous forged iron manufacture as previously described. Brown leather covers the hand-guard as well as the hilt. The scabbard is usually made from leather with green or red inlaid decorative leather strips. Takoubas of better quality have silver scabbards and hilt ends. The silver has a few marks attributed to a Tuareg alphabet but I have not found any description of these Tuareg letters in the literature. All pieces I acquired while exploring different regions of the Moroccan northern Sahara desert carry these marks, appearing as alphabet letters and resembling the Ethiopian alphabet. Takouba swords are related to *kaskara*, also a Saharan sword, which has a double edge and straight blade with cruciform hand-guard. The kaskara originated in Sudan.

A *kilij* (or *kilich*) is a Turkish sword related to the shamshir. This sword is very long with a broad blade widening toward the point and ending in a cusp. Due to marked widening in the distal third, the scabbard that accommodates the blade has a slot along the back edge covered with a spring cover. This allows withdrawal of the blade and simultaneous closure of the opening slot after the blade's withdrawal. Despite such an ingenious device, marked dexterity is required to achieve a quick drawing of this type of sword. I feel sure that warriors kept the sword unsheathed in anticipation of needing it, rather than drawing it on impulse.

Russian Islamic Swords and Daggers

The most common dagger and knife used in Caucasus is the *kindjal*. It has a broad, double-edged blade that narrows in the distal third, sometimes in a triangular fashion, having a very sharp point. Without doubt, the most attractive part of the kindjal is the scabbard, frequently made from a decorated sheet of silver with niello work, or filigree silver. Wood or horn riveted to the tang form the hilt, which ends in a semi-circular, horn type shape.

A *shashka* is a Russian Caucasian sword that is related to the Turkish yataghan. The shashka's blade is slightly curved and single-edged. The most attractive part of the shashka is the hilt, which is usually made from solid silver or inlaid silver with intricate niello motifs and gilding. Wood or leather is the material of choice for the scabbard. Particular to shashkas with leather scabbards is the way the blade and the hilt up to the pommel are inserted into the scabbard, this due to the fact that there is no hand-guard at all. Because of the efficacy and prestige of this type of sword, the Russian Red Army also included them in its armament. Russian shashkas are illustrated in Chapter Three.

Indian Swords and Daggers

Some description of Indian swords has already been included above, however greater detail will be provided in this section. The 16th and 17th century Indian swords and daggers were manufactured from an indigenous steel named wootz. Repeat folding by hammering and cooling created visible blade patterns as parallel stripes along the blade, called "prophet's ladder" or kirk narduban (40 steps). Another watering blade pattern is in the form of scattered small islands called bidr and qum (gravel). Extensive polishing of the blade will exhibit the watered steel of blades rivaling the famous Damascus blades produced earlier in 15th century Syria. The blades have an inlaid gold square called bedouh. The bedouh is divided into four quarters bearing the Arabic numerals for 2, 4, 6, and 8, believed to bring good luck to the owner. Two cartouches with circumvallated inlaid gold lines carry invocations from the Koran to Allah and Ali. The best made blades have a small cartouche with the sword-smith's signature in inlaid gold located on the blade near the hilt. A decoration that is common to many Indian swords and daggers is bidri, a combination of black stained pewter contrasting with inlaid shiny silver. The bidri decorations originated in the city of Bider, northwest of Hiderabad, where these hilt decorations were created.

The typical Indian talwar has a disc pommel with a central linear dome and upward drawn edges. Some talwars have a knuckle-guard that originates from the ventral quillon and curves upward in an S form, touching the pommel but not soldered to it. The quillons are globulous at the ends and the central part of the of the hand-guard projects downward toward the blade, forming the longets. Leather or carved wood form the scabbard, which is frequently covered with colorful velvet fabric. Talwars are Islamic swords, but Hindu talwars were described as having zoomorphic or Hindu god decorations chiseled on the blade. These talwars are extremely rare and, as a matter of fact, I have never seen one! The talwars are suspended on a baldric or belt sling around the left shoulder.

An interesting Indian sword is the *pata*, a long, straight blade sword of European origin. The pata's hilt is a rigid half gauntlet with a long cuff occasionally exhibiting inlaid gold and silver decorations of koftgari type. Interestingly, the hand holds a cross bar inside the gauntlet, thus allowing a strong grip. The gauntlet extends upward along the forearm, reinforcing the grip and exacerbating the strength of the blow. Pata swords were favorite weapons of Hindu Southern India Mahrattas, who challenged the extension of the Moghul Empire over the centuries.

The *firangi* is another Mahratta weapon, originating from the southern part of India. This sword has a narrow, straight blade, usually made from imported European blades and usually decorated with koftgari inlaid gold or silver. The blade is reinforced by a back fold-over rib. Characteristic of firangi is a disc shaped pommel with a long spike used for a two-handed blow. Koftgari ornaments frequently decorate the hilt and the pommel with its spike. The basket type hilt is padded with embroidered silk or colorful velvet.

The *khanda* is another Indian Hindu sword considered to be the oldest known Indian sword. It has a wide straight blade, widening toward the point that could be round or triangular in shape. The hilt and pommel are similar to firangi swords, and in addition, this sword has a wide knuckle-guard. The khanda also has a double rib that reinforces the strength of the blade near the hilt. A bigger rib along the back of the sword is longer than the rib along the cutting edge, the second having the role of strengthening the thinner and lighter weight blade. It is believed that the spiked pommel had a double role. In battle, the pommel was used as a double handed grip; when the sword was in the scabbard, the pommel served as a hand rest.

The *bichwa* is an interesting Indian Mahratta dagger that originally had a buffalo horn hilt. Due to its double curvature, it appears similar to a scorpion sting, from which the name derives. It is double edged with a central raised rib portion and usually has an ornate hilt and knuckle-guard. Frequently, bichwas are combined with a *bagh nakh*, an Indian concealed weapon that has four or five curved blades used as claws and attached to a central bar held in the palm. The name in Hindi means tiger's claw, clearly describing this weapon that is usually used by assassins. The ends of the bar have rings for inserting two distal fingers. Sivaji, the founder of the Mahratta Empire, used a bagh nakh to kill Afzal Khan, commander of the Bijapur army.

The *chilanum* Indian dagger closely resembles the bichwa. It also has a double-edged and double curved blade. Some chilanums have a forked blade point that is characteristic of this small dagger. The chilanum is made from one piece of metal, including the pommel, hilt, and blade.

The *katar* is a weapon found only in India and has the ability to inflict devastating injury to an opponent. The katar resembles the pata in that the weapon is held with a grip on a horizontal inner bar and has parallel side arms that follow the forearm, strengthening the blow. A triangular shape blade usually has a central rib that progressively thickens toward the point, reinforcing the blade (which can pierce armor). The better quality katars have koftgari decorations in gold or silver with floral and leaf design. A common variation of the katar has a concealed third blade that is exposed by squeezing the double bar grip. The blade

then opens like scissors, revealing the inner central blade. The double katar is another variation of this weapon. In this case, the inner katar is exposed by pulling on a ring located on the horizontal bar of the inner katar.

A *bhuj* is an Indian axe dagger with single-edged blade mounted on a long metal handle, often concealing a small knife within. Elaborate incised decorations ornate the blade as well as the handle, frequently inlaid in silver, copper, or brass. An incised decoration at the base of the blade is in the shape of an elephant's head.

Indian concealed weapons are very interesting items for collectors. The most common is the *bairogi*, or fakir's crutch, which fit under the armpits and contained a stiletto in the haft; it could even be used as a mace when weighted. Some bairogi have a T handle as the crutch end, with the blade fitted in the shaft of the crutch. Koftgari or gilding frequently decorates the bairogi. The bagh nakh, described earlier, was an effective weapon with which to surprise an opponent. The bagh nakh had three or four curved blades that could be concealed in the clenched fist and another blade extending along the edge of the palm bar. Two rings at the end of the palm bar allowed for insertion of the index and fifth finger. By opening one's hand and extending the fingers, this "tiger claw" would slash through the enemy's face, blinding and temporarily disabling the opponent and thus allowing for use of another dagger concealed in the sleeve or in the hair under the turban. As already described, the bhuj could also conceal a knife in the handle.

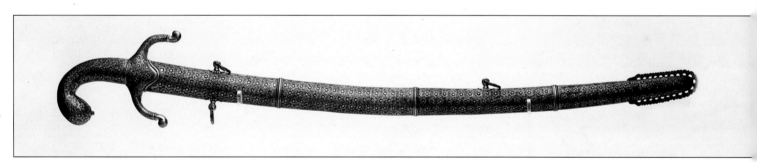

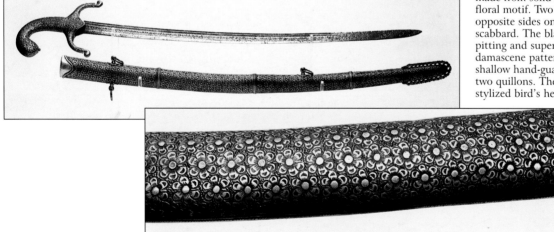

Fig. 4/1. 17th-18th century Indo-Persian shamshir sword. The hilt and the scabbard are made from solid silver chiseled and chased with a floral motif. Two suspension rings are located on opposite sides on proximal and distal part of the scabbard. The blade reveals considerable age with pitting and superficial wear, however the damascene pattern is still visible. Cruciform, shallow hand-guard continuing downward with two quillons. The pommel is in the shape of a stylized bird's head. Blade's length: 33.5" (85 cm.). Sword's length: 42" (106.5 cm.). Estimated value: $15,000.

Fig. 4/2. 19th century silver Moghul khanjar dagger. The entire dagger is made from repoussé decorated silver. A predatory animal that looks like a fox is incised on the hilt. The pommel is made from silver carved in high relief and representing an animal head with a fish in its mouth (probably a sacred crocodile that once inhabited the mother Ganga (Gange) river). Chiseled silver in relief on the scabbard features a lion attacking an unidentified animal that runs after a rabbit. Double-edged, watered blade has an inlaid silver head of a mutton located near the hilt. Blade's length: 10.8" (27 cm.). Khanjar's length: 17" (43 cm.). Estimated value: $5,000.

Fig. 4/3. 19th century Moghul khanjar with hand chiseled silver hilt and scabbard. The hilt features an embracing couple carved in high relief. An antelope is chiseled in the central panel of the silver scabbard, featuring high relief silver decorations with floral motif above and below the main subject. Watered, double-edged blade with intricate damascene pattern. Two inlaid gold circumvolved cartouches are located on the proximal end of the blade, near the hilt, on both sides, with one representing invocation from Koran. Blade's length: 10.8" (27 cm.). Khanjar's length: 17" (43 cm.). Estimated value: $5,000.

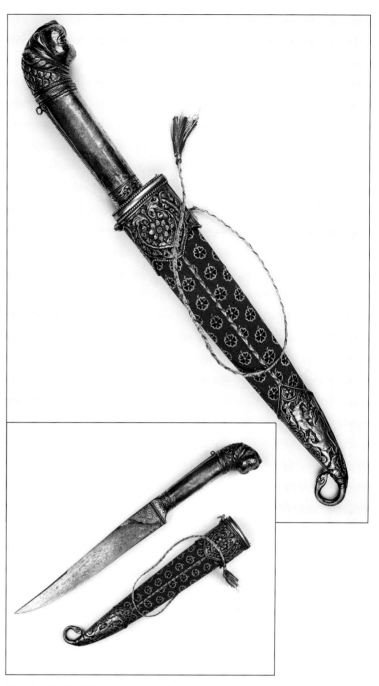

Fig. 4/4. Moghul Empire. 17th-18th century kard dagger, a master-piece of Indo-Persian art. Solid silver hilt with inlaid gold decorations in the distal end featuring a floral design. Very elaborate pommel in the shape of a tiger's head with open mouth. Damascene blade with inlaid gold decorations in the proximal end and the back of the blade. The distal end features a swan's head and neck. This unusual dagger is a hybrid between a kard and a khanjar. The blade is single-edged, but becomes double-edged in the distal third as are most of the Moghul daggers. Gilding is still visible on the high relief hammered and chiseled scabbard and hilt with pierced, open work. The distal part of the scabbard features a tiger attacking a deer, while the proximal end features a floral design. Blade's length: 9" (23 cm.). Dagger's length: 16.2" (41 cm.). Estimated value: $15,000.

Fig. 4/7. Moghul Empire. 18th-19th century khanjar dagger. Hammered solid silver with zoomorphic design constitutes the hilt. A ferocious feline forms the pommel and continues with the hilt, which has an animal on each side—on one side, an animal that resembles an anteater, and on the other side, a feline predator. The scabbard is hammered in fine silver and features several animals, including an elephant, a tiger devouring a gazelle, and others that cannot be identified. Single-edged, watered blade with inlaid gold in a triangular shape featuring a floral design, located near the hilt. The back of the blade also has inlaid gold decorations. Blade's length: 9.9" (25 cm.). Dagger's length: 16.1" (41 cm.). Estimated value: $5,000.

Fig. 4/5. Moghul Empire. 17th-18th century kard dagger typical of Moghul period. The hilt is made from toned ivory with age striations and polychrome carved decorations having very delicate details. The decorations feature birds and flowers on a red background. Single-edged, watered blade tapering toward the point. 20th century replacement scabbard made from red velvet. Blade's length: 9" (23 cm.). Dagger's length: 14" (35.5 cm.). Estimated value: $10,000.

Fig. 4/6. Moghul Empire. 18th-19th century khanjar silver dagger. The hilt is made from solid silver in the shape of an embracing couple dressed in typical Persian outfits of the period. Damascene blade with unusual double-edged serrated edges. Intricate gold koftgari decorations are present on the blade in gold cartouche with Islamic verse from the Koran. Solid silver scabbard has high relief hammered and chiseled decorations with floral design and a central panel with overlapping fans resembling fish scales. One hanger hook for suspension is present on the scabbard. Blade's length: 10.2" (26 cm.). Dagger's length:16.3" (42.5 cm.). Estimated value: $7,500.

Fig. 4/8. Moghul Empire. 18th-19th century khanjar dagger. The pommel is made from solid silver in the shape of a stylized bird. Hammered and chiseled floral decorations adorn the hilt. Cruciform hand-guard has two quillons curved downward and ending in a double floret decoration. Curved, double-edged blade with intricate koftgari decorations in the shape of a mosque with a balance and Islamic inscription within. The inlaid gold decorations involve one third of the blade on the obverse. Damascene blade with intricate pattern. Red velvet scabbard with gold thread ribbon decoration. The red color has faded with age, but the condition is still excellent. An upward connection from the hand-guard forms the hand-knuckles' shield and extends upward to the pommel's bird beak in an elegant curve. Blade's length: 11.5" (29 cm.). Dagger's length: 16.2" (41 cm.). Estimated value: $5,500.

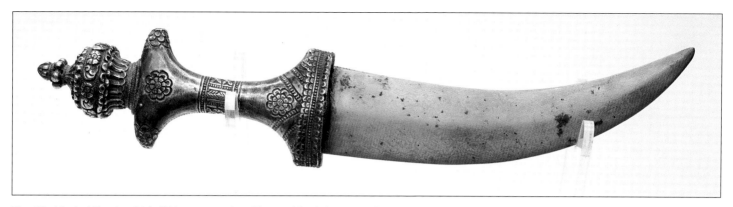

Fig. 4/9. Moghul Empire. 16th-17th century silver khanjar. The hilt is made from high content silver alloy with hammered decorations. Bulbous shape pommel in the shape of a stupa is decorated with floral incised ornaments. Double-edged, curved blade with fine damascene pattern. This early Indo-Persian dagger is very rare! Blade's length: 8.2" (21 cm.). Dagger's length: 15" (38 cm.). Estimated value: $5,000.

Fig. 4/10. 19th century Moghul silver dagger. The hilt is hammered in solid silver and depicts a feline attacking a gazelle. Below, flowers are incised in high relief. The blade has fine damascus and inlaid gold with a flower design in the proximal part near the hilt. The single-edged blade also has inlaid gold decorations on the back of the blade. Hammered silver with floral design constitutes the scabbard. Allegedly, this dagger originates from the personal collection of the Rajasthan's Maharaja. Blade's length: 10" (25.5"). Dagger's length: 17.2" (44 cm.). Estimated value: $5,000.

Fig. 4/11. 18th-19th century Moghul talwar sword. The hilt is made from decorated, incised silver on black bidri background. Round disk pommel with inscription inscribed in relief inlaid silver, which is in Sanskrit, rather than Hindi. Bidri decorates the bulbous portion in the top center of the pommel. Sharply curved single-edged blade. Red velvet scabbard. Blade's length: 24.5" (62 cm.). Sword's length: 28.8" (73 cm.). Estimated value: $5,000.

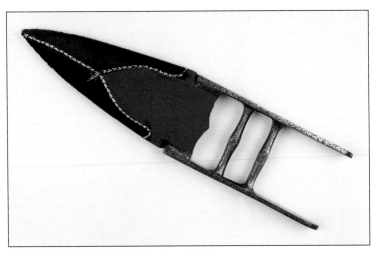

Fig. 4/12. 19th century Moghul folding katar. While the katar is an exclusive Hindu ancient weapon, this katar is decorated with Islamic decorations having inlaid silver and niello decorations with floral design. The interior and exterior of the vertical and horizontal bars are decorated with inlaid silver decorations. Two parallel bars connected by two handles meet a cross bar that is double riveted to the inner blade. Upon applying hand pressure ton the inner bars, the exterior blades open like scissors, revealing the central portion of the inner blade. The scabbard was manufactured in late 19th century and is made from polychrome velvet. Katar's length: 14.8" (37.5 cm.). Estimated value: $4,500.

Fig. 4/13. 19th century Moghul silver khanjar. The hilt and scabbard are decorated with hammered silver ornaments with zoomorphic design. A tiger's head constitutes the pommel. The hilt displays a tiger devouring a goat, with the pattern visible on both sides. A mutton is visible on both sides of the blade, near the hilt. The scabbard has hammered and repoussé decorations featuring a leopard (or tiger) chasing two goats. Blade's length: 6.5" (16.5 cm.). Dagger's length: 11.8" (30 cm.).Estimated value: $3,500.

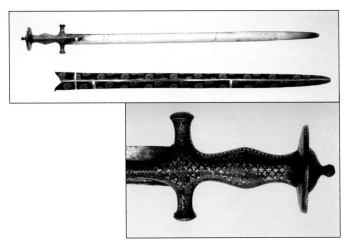

Fig. 4/15. 18th century Moghul talwar sword. The hilt is decorated with inlaid silver and bidri with floral design. Cruciform hand-guard is also decorated with silver and bidri. The blade has two inlaid gold round panels and two depressions that once held inlaid gold. Single-edged blade becomes double-edged in the lower third and ends with a round point. Wooden scabbard covered with colorful fabric. Blade's length: 26.5" (67.2"). Dagger's length: 31.5" (80 cm.). Estimated value: $2,500.

Fig. 4/14. 19th century Moghul silver khanjar. The hilt and the scabbard are covered with hammered and repoussé silver. A mutton's head forms the pommel. Two unidentified animals are displayed on the hilt. A mutton's head made from silver is inlaid on the blade, near the hilt. The scabbard has incised and hammered decorations featuring a tiger chasing two animals. Blade's length: 6.9" (17.5 cm.). Dagger's length: 11.8" (30 cm). Estimated value: $2,500.

Fig. 4/16. 18th-19th century Moghul kard knife. The hilt is made from celadon jade with inlaid rubies in gold. Watered blade with inlaid gold in the proximal part. Inlaid gold and niello are present in the blade's ferrule. Red velvet covers the wooden scabbard. Blade's length: 6.8" (17 cm.). Kard's length: 9" (23 cm.). Estimated value: $2,500.

Fig. 4/17. 19th century Moghul concealed knife. Inlaid gold knife containing a smaller inlaid gold knife in a compartment that opens when a hilt button is depressed. Despite looking real, the large knife is missing a sharp edge. Both knives have watered blades with fine damascus. Blade's length: 5.9" (14.5 cm.). Knife's length: 9.3" (23.7 cm.). Large knife's length: 10.5" (26.7 cm.). Estimated value: $2,500.

Fig. 4/18. 19th century Moghul khanjar dagger with pommel in the shape of a tiger's head. The hilt and the scabbard are decorated with filigree silver and bidri. Islamic inscriptions are present on the scabbard and the hilt formed by filigree silver. Watered blade with scattered isles (bidr and qum) appearance. As an aside, the bidr and qum blade's damascene pattern is much rarer than the linear, parallel damascus pattern named 40 steps (or kirk narduban, also called prophet's ladder). An Islamic inscription is present on an oblong cartouche located on the obverse side. Blade's length: 8.5" (21.5 cm.). Dagger's length: 13.5" (34 cm.). Estimated value: $2,500.

Fig. 4/19. 19th century Moghul dagger decorated with silver koftgari floral decorations on the scabbard. The pommel is in the shape of a horse's head decorated with linear silver koftgari. Hexagonal pieces of carved bone form the hilt. Cruciform hand-guard with short quillons decorated with inlaid silver. Wide, curved, double-edged blade with intricate damascene pattern. A large cartouche with inlaid silver featuring a Koran verset is located on the obverse side. Blade's length: 9" (23 cm.). Dagger's length: 15.5" (39.5 cm.). Estimated value: $3,000.

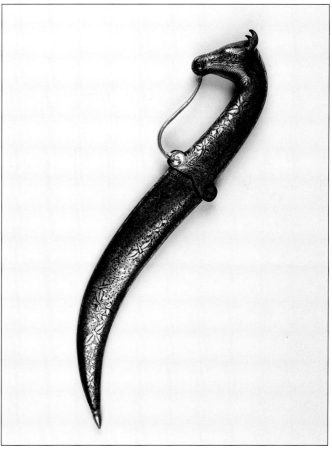

Fig. 4/20. 19th century Moghul silver dagger with chased floral decorations and bidri. The pommel is in the shape of a horse's head and a knuckle-guard links below the horse's mouth. Double-edged, curved blade with intricate damascene pattern. An inscription from the Koran is inlaid in a silver cartouche near the hilt on the obverse side. Blade's length: 8.5" (21.5 cm.). Dagger's length: 14.5" (37 cm.). Estimated value: $1,800.

Fig. 4/21. 19th century Moghul silver khanjar. The hilt and scabbard are decorated with inlaid silver and bidri. The pommel is in the shape of two opposing crocodile heads. The facing crocodile design is seen at the entrance to Hindi temples and represents the sacred protectors of the mother Ganga (Gange) river. Watered blade with inlaid silver cartouche near the hilt and serrated edges. The scabbard chape is formed by a crocodile head with open mouth. Blade's length: 7" (17.8 cm.). Dagger's length: 12.8" (32.5 cm.). Estimated value: $2,500.

Fig. 4/24. 19th century khanjar with chiseled silver decorations in high relief featuring flowers and two birds. A gilded triangular panel with floral design decorates the blade at the proximal part. Single-edged blade with intricate watering. Wooden scabbard with velvet cover. Blade's length: 6.7" (17 cm.). Khanjar's length: 11" (28 cm.). Estimated value: $1,500.

Fig. 4/22. 19th-20th century sterling silver shamshir dagger with pommel in the shape of a goat. The hilt has open work silver with floral design. Red velvet inside the hilt creates an interesting contrast. Cruciform hand-guard with stumpy quillons. Watered, double-edged blade with an inlaid silver cartouche containing Islamic decorations located near the hilt. Wooden scabbard covered with purple velvet. The ends of the scabbard are decorated with inlaid silver and bidri. Blade's length: 8.7" (22 cm.). Dagger's length: 14.5" (36.8 cm.). Estimated value: $1,600.

Fig. 4/25. 20th century silver dagger entirely covered with rubies, peridots, garnets, citrines, and amethyst stones mounted in silver. The blade is made from silver and is single-edged. Blade's length: 7.5" (19 cm.). Dagger's length: 13.4" (34 cm.). Estimated value: $5,000.

Fig. 4/23. 16th-17th century Moghul kard dagger with inlaid gold floral decorations on the blade. The hilt is made from aged, toned ivory. Watered blade, very thick toward the back, curves and tapers toward the point. Blade's length: 8" (20.3 cm.). Dagger's length: 12" (30.5 cm.). Estimated value: $2,000.

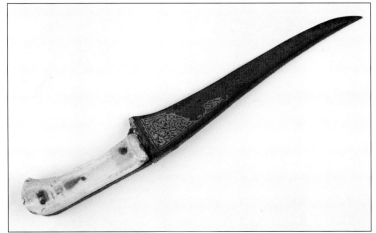

Fig. 4/26. 19th-20th century miniature shamshir. The hilt and the ends of the scabbard are made from steel covered with inlaid gold using the niello technique. A ring in the mid-portion of the scabbard allows for suspension of the knife. The blade has a damascene pattern and on the obverse there is a cartouche with Islamic inscription in inlaid gold. Wooden scabbard covered with purple velvet. Blade's length: 5.8" (14.5 cm.). Knife's length: 9.5" (24 cm.). Estimated value: $1,500.

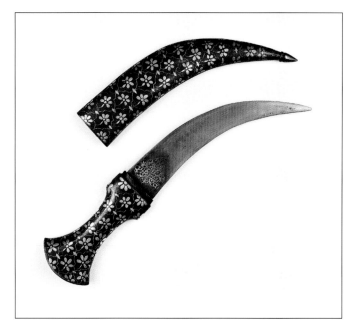

Fig. 4/29. 19th-20th century jambiya dagger. The hilt and scabbard are decorated with inlaid silver on a black bidri background featuring a floral design. Watered blade with inlaid silver cartouche on both sides featuring a floral design. Blade's length: 7" (18 cm.). Dagger's length: 11.8" (30 cm.). Estimated value: $1,400.

Fig. 4/27. 19th-20th century khanjar with chiseled silver decorations in high relief on the hilt and scabbard featuring a floral design. Double-edged blade with damascene design. Blade's length: 5" (12.5 cm.). Khanjar's length: 9" (23 cm.). Estimated value: $1,400.

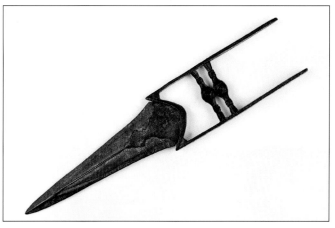

Fig. 4/30. 16th-17th century katar decorated with inlaid gold. Single-edged blade with grooves (fullers) parallel to the edges. The blade thickens toward the point to strengthen and facilitate penetration of the mail armor. Parallel bars with a central knob form the handle. The blade is riveted to a triangular projection from the hilt. Superficial corrosion is present on this dagger. Blade's length: 9" (23 cm.). Katar's length: 15.8" (40 cm.). Estimated value: $2,000.

Fig. 4/28. 20th century khanjar with elephant head pommel. The hilt and the scabbard's ends are decorated with silver and gold koftgari. Watered blade with inlaid silver and gold koftgari having a floral design. Wooden scabbard covered with purple velvet. Blade's length: 11.1" (28 cm.). Dagger's length: 15.1" (46 cm.). Estimated value: $900.

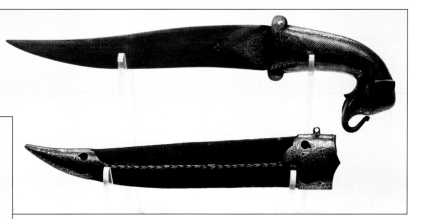

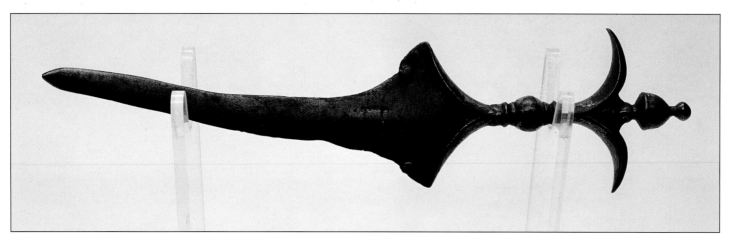

Fig. 4/31. 16th-17th century chilanum dagger with silver plating still retained in parts of the hilt. It was used by Mahratta warriors from southern India battling the Muslim Moghul invasion from the north. Double-edged blade with signs of marked aging. Arcuate proximal part of the hilt continuing with the pommel that is bulb-shaped. Length: 9" (23 cm.). Estimated value: $1,000.

Fig. 4/32. 19th-20th century talwar-shaped dagger. The hilt is decorated with inlaid gold and bidri. Single-edged watered blade with a cartouche located near the hilt containing Islamic calligraphy decorations. The scabbard is made from pink velvet and decorated with inlaid gold on the chape and proximal band, which also has an eyelet for suspension of the dagger. Blade's length: 6.5" (16.5 cm.). Dagger's length: 9.2" (23.5 cm.). Estimated value: $1,400.

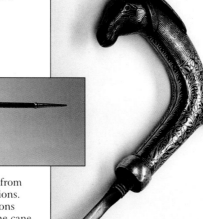

Fig. 4/33. 19th-20th century gupti cane-sword. It is made from silver and bidri with intricate floral and geometric decorations. The handle is in the shape of a mutton's head. Three sections that could be assembled by screwing the ends constitute the cane. Blade's length: 6.5" (16.5 cm.). Cane's length: 37.8" (96 cm.). Estimated value: $1,500.

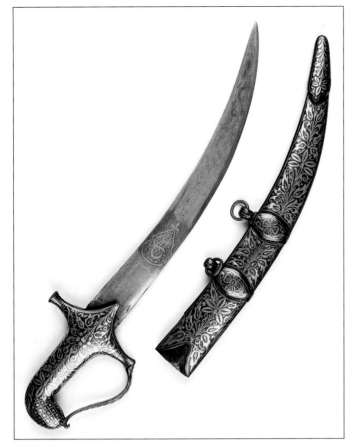

Fig. 4/37. 19th-20th century khanjar dagger that conceals a kard knife and a small knife. The pommel, hilt, and the proximal part of the blades are inlaid with gold and have a floral design. A tiger's head forms the pommel. Watered, single-edged blade. The hilt has a button that, under pressure, releases the pommel to reveal a kard knife with inlaid gold decorations on the hilt and blade, similar to the container dagger. When unscrewed, the pommel of the kard further reveals a small single-edged knife. Khanjar's blade length: 10.6" (27 cm.). Kard's blade length: 9.5" (24 cm.). Dagger's length: 16.2" (42 cm.). Kard's length: 14" (36 cm.). Small knife's length: 4" (10 cm.). Estimated value: $4,500.

Fig. 4/38. 19th-20th century khanjar dagger covered with inlaid gold decorations having a floral motif. The pommel is in the shape of a mutton's head. Watered, double-edged blade with an inlaid gold cartouche with floral design. Blade's length: 11" (28 cm.). Dagger's length: 17" (43 cm.). Estimated value: $3,000.

Fig. 4/34. 19th-20th century miniature shamshir. The hilt and the scabbard are made from steel decorated with inlaid gold and bidri in a floral design. Two rings in the mid-portion of the scabbard allow the suspension of this dagger. The hilt allows only a two finger grip and this leads me believe that it was made for a noble child, or for pure esthetic enjoyment. Watered blade has a cartouche on the obverse side with inlaid gold decorations and Islamic inscription. Blade's length: 7.2" (18.5 cm.). Dagger's length: 9.9" (25 cm.). Estimated value: $1,800.

Fig. 4/39. 19th century khanjar dagger. The hilt and scabbard are made from solid silver and represent a tiger's head and neck. Double-edged blade, well-watered and inlaid with gold having an Islamic representation. Red velvet scabbard of a more recent addition, or replacement. Blade's length: 10.2" (26 cm.). Dagger's length: 17.5" (44.5 cm.). Estimated value; $3,500.

Fig. 4/35. 20th century silver dagger with mounted precious and semi-precious stones, such as rubies, sapphires, peridots, amethysts, aqua-marines, citrines, and garnets. The hand-guard and knuckle-guard are decorated with chased silver. Single-edged silver blade. Blade's length: 12" (30 cm.). Dagger's length: 18" (46 cm.). Estimated value: $6,500.

Fig. 4/36. 19th-20th century khanjar dagger with pommel in the shape of a horse's head. Steel scabbard and hilt covered with bidri and inlaid with gold in a floral pattern. The proximal part of the blade has inlaid gold with floral design on both sides. Blade's length: 5.1" (13 cm.). Dagger's length: 10" (25.5 cm.). Estimated value: $1,500.

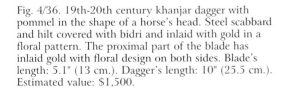

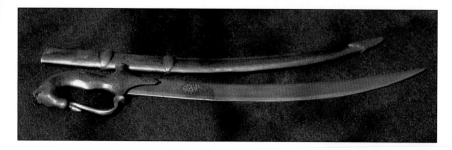

Fig. 4/40. 19th-20th century shamshir sword. The hilt and scabbard are covered with inlaid silver decorations with floral design. Short quillons and a knuckle-guard link to the pommel, which is in the shape of a horse's head. Watered, curved, double-edged blade decorated with inlaid silver having Islamic characters in a cartouche located near the hilt, on the obverse side. The scabbard has two hangers for suspension of the sword. Blade's length: 17.2" (44 cm.). Sword's length: 25.2" (64 cm.). Estimated value: $3,000.

Fig. 4/41. 19th-20th century khanjar. The hilt and pommel are made from agate, with the pommel shaped as a horse's head. The distal part of the hilt, as well as the blade's connection to the hilt, are inlaid with gold having a floral design. Single-edged blade becomes double-edged in the distal third. Watered blade with a central rib in the distal third that strengthens the blade for armor piercing. The scabbard is covered with purple velvet and the ends are inlaid with gold in a floral pattern. Blade's length: 8.2" (21 cm.). Dagger's length: 15.3" (39 cm.). Estimated value: $3,000.

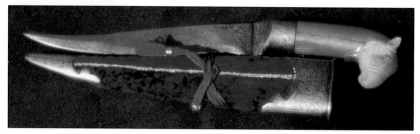

Fig. 4/42. 19th-20th century khanjar dagger. The hilt and pommel are made from rock crystal, with the pommel in the shape of a stylized bird and the hilt decorated with a floral design. Watered, double-edged blade with a central rib in the distal end for reinforcement of the blade. The proximal end of the blade is inlaid with gold having a floral design. Tan color leather covers the wooden scabbard. Blade's length: 11" (28 cm.). Dagger's length: 17.8" (45 cm.). Estimated value: $3,000.

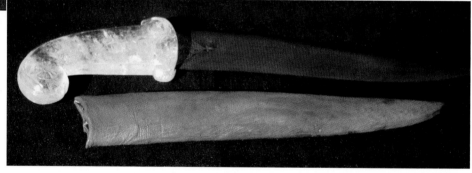

Fig. 4/43. 19th-20th century khanjar. The hilt and pommel are made of yellow jade with a floral design. Double-edged, watered blade with a central rib in the distal third for blade's strengthening. The proximal part of the blade is decorated with inlaid gold in a triangular panel. Red velvet scabbard decorated with inlaid gold at the extremities. Blade's length: 11" (28 cm.). Dagger's length: 17.8" (45 cm.). Estimated value: $3,000.

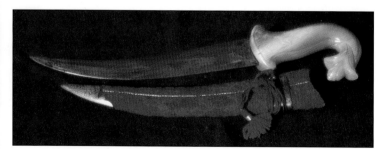

Fig. 4/44. 19th-20th century dagger with hilt made from spinach-green jade inlaid in celadon jade, the design repeating on both sides. The hilt's distal end is decorated with inlaid gold with a bird's design. Double-edged blade of extremely rare form, with alternating serrated and straight edges. The central part of the blade is decorated with an incised leaf pattern design. Inlaid gold in a triangular panel decorates the proximal portion of the blade. In addition, the blade has a wavy pattern. Velvet cover scabbard. Very rare type of dagger, possible unique. Blade's length: 12" (30 cm.). Dagger's length: 19" (48 cm.). Estimated value: $3,000.

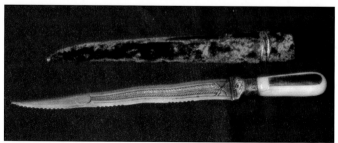

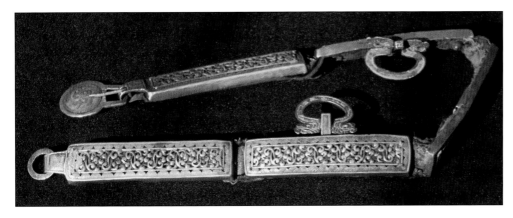

Fig. 4/45. 18th century Moghul silver belt for dagger's wear and attachment. It is made from five silver segments decorated with chiseled silver in high relief and featuring a floral design. Two round hangers provide additional support with bands over the shoulders. Very rare Moghul period artifact! Length: 32.2" (82 cm.). Estimated value: $3,000.

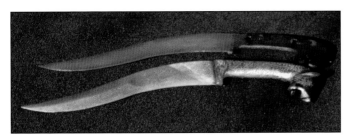

Fig. 4/46. 19th-20th century double khanjar. The dagger is split longitudinally into two daggers. They are attached with two prongs that slide into a T bar that locks the daggers. Watered, curved blades with a peculiar central rib in the distal half that adds strength for armor penetration. The proximal part of the blade has an inlaid gold panel with floral design. Tigers' heads form the pommels. Blade's length: 8.5" (21.5 cm.). Dagger's length: 13" (33 cm.). Estimated value: $2,800.

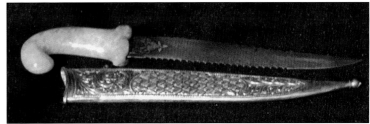

Fig. 4/49. 19th-20th century khanjar dagger. The hilt is made from rose quartz in the shape of a stylized bird. Solid silver scabbard, chiseled in high relief, with floral decorations. Double-edged serrated blade with damascene surface design. Blade's length: 9.2" (23.5 cm.). Dagger's length: 15.8" (40 cm.). Estimated value: $2,500.

Fig. 4/47. 19th-20th century khanjar. The hilt and pommel are made from celadon jade, with the pommel in the shape of a horse's head. Black velvet scabbard. Watered blade measuring 7.5" (19 cm.). Dagger's length: 13.8" (35 cm.). Estimated value: $2,500.

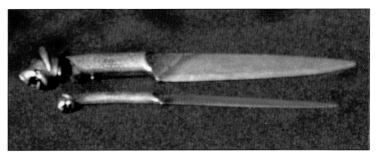

Fig. 4/50. 19th-20th century khanjar dagger with concealed khanjar. The hilt and pommel are decorated with inlaid gold with a floral motif. The pommel of both daggers is in the shape of a tiger's head. The concealed dagger has similar inlaid decorations as the storage dagger. The blades are single-edged, straight and watered, however the storage khanjar's blade is not sharp. Khanjar's length: 13.5" (34 cm.). Inner khanjar's blade: 7.5" (19 cm.). Inner dagger's length: 12" (30 cm.). Estimated value: $2,800.

Fig. 4/48. 18th-19th century silver gupti cane-dagger. The hilt is in the shape of a stylized bird. Panels of inlaid bas-relief silver decorations are scattered along the cane. The cane's handle conceals a small knife screwed on the cane's body. Knife's length: 4" (10 cm.). Cane's length: 22.5" (57 cm.). Estimated value: $2,500.

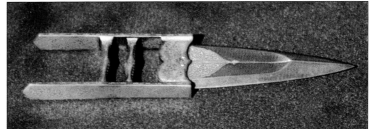

Fig. 4/51. 19th-20th century katar entirely covered with inlaid gold decorations having a floral design. Watered blade with central rib for increased strength. A central inlaid gold decoration in the shape of a mihrab is located on the proximal end of the blade. The third inner blade appears upon pressure on the horizontal hand bar. An inlaid gold cartouche is present on both sides. Blade's length: 7" (18 cm.). Katar's length: 14.1" (36 cm.). Estimated value: $2,500.

Fig. 4/52. 19th-20th century khanjar. The hilt and scabbard are decorated with inlaid gold displaying hunt scenes. Tiger's head shaped pommel. Double-edged serrated blade with damascene surface and inlaid gold panel. Blade's length: 7.2" (18.5 cm.). Dagger's length: 13" (33 cm.). Estimated value: $2,000.

Fig. 4/53. 19th-20th century khanjar. Its entire surface is decorated with inlaid gold displaying a floral design on niello or bidri background. Watered, double-edged, curved blade with inlaid cartouche on the obverse side featuring a floral motif. The pommel is in the shape of a stylized bird. Blade's length: 8.5" (21.5 cm.). Dagger's length: 14.1" (36 cm.). Estimated value: $2,200.

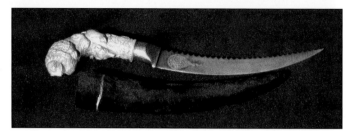

Fig. 4/56. 19th-20th century khanjar dagger. The hilt and pommel are in the shape of a tiger attacking an antelope and are chiseled in solid silver in high relief. The hilt's distal part is inlaid in gold with a floral design. Watered, curved blade with serrated edge on the back and cutting edge on the concave side. A cartouche with Koran invocation is inlaid in gold on the obverse side of the blade. Red velvet scabbard. Blade's length: 9" (23 cm.). Dagger's length: 15.3" (39 cm.). Estimated value: $2,000.

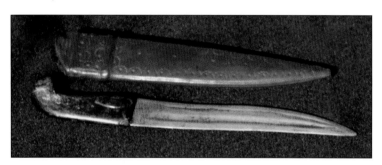

Fig. 4/54. 19th-20th century khanjar dagger with spinach-green jade hilt in the shape of a stylized bird. Watered, double-edged blade with two fullers. On the obverse side of the blade, an Islamic inscription is inlaid in gold on the proximal part of the blade. Embossed leather scabbard. Blade's length: 7.5" (19 cm.). Dagger's length: 13" (33 cm.). Estimated value: $2,000.

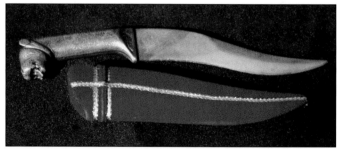

Fig. 4/57. 19th-20th century khanjar dagger with gold and silver koftgari in the hilt, pommel, and proximal part of the blade. The dagger transforms into two daggers by longitudinal sliding. A tiger's head forms the pommel. Watered blades with central rib in the distal half that strengthens the blade for mail piercing. Blade's length: 6.5" (16.5 cm.). Dagger's length: 10.6" (27 cm.). Estimated value: $2,400.

Fig. 4/55. 19th-20th century chilanum dagger with celadon jade hilt and pommel. Double-edged, slightly curved blade with the original and extremely rare pattern of V-shaped watered steel alternating with non-watered steel. Red velvet scabbard. Blade's length: 9" (23 cm.). Dagger's length: 14.5" (37 cm.). Estimated value: $2,000.

Fig. 4/58. 19th century khanjar dagger. The pommel and hilt are made from solid silver. A tiger's head forms the pommel, which is chiseled in high relief and decorated with rubies that form the tiger's eyes. Watered blade with serrated back edge. Velvet covered scabbard with chiseled silver endings. Blade's length: 7.8" (19.5 cm.). Dagger's length: 13.8" (35 cm.). Estimated value: $1,800.

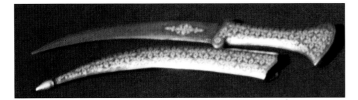

Fig. 4/59. 19th-20th century jambiya dagger. It is entirely covered with inlaid silver and bidri decorations having a floral design. Watered, double-edged blade with inlaid silver cartouche on the obverse side displaying a floral design. Blade's length: 8" (20 cm.). Dagger's length: 14.3" (36.5 cm.). Estimated value: $1,500.

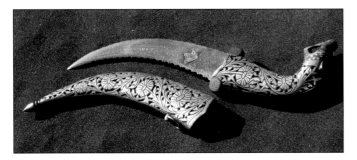

Fig. 4/60. 19th-20th century khanjar dagger covered with inlaid gold decorations featuring a floral design. The pommel is in the shape of a tiger's head. Watered, double-edged serrated blade decorated with an inlaid gold cartouche on the obverse side. Blade's length: 6.8" (17 cm.). Dagger's length: 12" (30.5 cm.). Estimated value: $1,800.

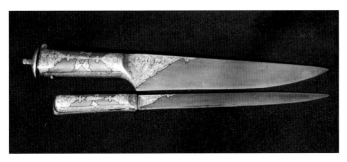

Fig. 4/61. 19th-20th century double dagger with concealed knife within. The storage dagger is in the shape of a straight knife, but the blade is not sharp. The dagger is decorated with inlaid silver featuring a floral design. It contains a kard knife with watered, single-edged blade. The kard has similar inlaid silver decorations as on the container dagger. Dagger's length: 10.8" (27.5 cm.). Kard's blade length: 6" (15.5 cm.). Kard's length: 9.5" (24 cm.). Estimated value: $1,800.

Fig. 4/62. 19th-20th century khanjar dagger covered with inlaid gold and featuring a leaf and flower design. The pommel is in the shape of a horse's head. Double-edged, watered blade, with serrated edges. A circular cartouche with inlaid gold decorates the obverse side of the blade. Blade's length: 7.3" (18.5 cm.). Dagger's length: 13.2" (33.5 cm.). Estimated value: $2,000.

Fig. 4/63. 19th-20th century jambiya dagger decorated on the entire surface with inlaid silver featuring a floral design and niello. Double-edged, watered blade with inlaid silver in a cartouche with the shape of a mihrab. Blade's length: 7.9" (20 cm.). Dagger's length: 14.5" (37 cm.). Estimated value: $1,500.

Fig. 4/64. 19th century gupti cane-dagger. The entire surface is covered with inlaid silver with floral design on a silver background. The pommel is in the shape of an elephant's head. The concealed dagger has a double-edged blade. The distal end of the cane becomes a knife when unscrewed from the cane, and has a peculiar quadrangular blade. Dagger's blade length: 6" (15 cm.). Knife's blade length: 3.1" (8 cm.). Cane's length: 20.9" (53 cm.). Estimated value: $1,800.

Fig. 4/65. 19th-20th century ankus (ancus) axe decorated with inlaid silver displaying a floral and leaf pattern. The axe detaches from the side through a screw mechanism. The ankus (used to train elephants) usually does not have the round axe. Length: 17.3" (44 cm.). Estimated value: $1,500.

Fig. 4/66. 19th-20th century dagger completely covered with inlaid silver featuring a floral design. The pommel is in the shape of a mutton. The dagger has short, chubby quillons and a knuckle-guard linking to the pommel. Double edged, watered blade with inlaid silver in a cartouche on the obverse side of the blade, carrying verse from the Koran. Blade's length: 9" (23 cm.). Dagger's length: 15" (38 cm.). Estimated value: $1,400.

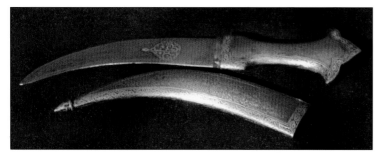

Fig. 4/67. 19th-20th century jambiya dagger made entirely from watered steel. Scabbard and hilt have inlaid gold on the margins. Watered, double-edged blade with inlaid gold in a cartouche displaying a Koran verse. Blade's length: 6" (15.2 cm.). Dagger's length: 11.8" (30 cm.). Estimated value: $1,600.

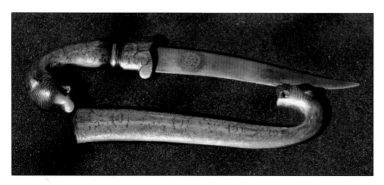

Fig. 4/68. 19th-20th century khanjar dagger of unusual shape. Its entire surface is covered with inlaid silver featuring a floral design. The pommel is in the shape of a tiger's head. Peculiarly, the chape of the scabbard is also in the shape of a tiger's head that curves along the scabbard. Watered, double-edged blade, inlaid with a silver roundel containing religious Islamic script. Blade's length: 8" (20 cm.). Dagger's length: 14" (35.5 cm.). Estimated value: $1,600.

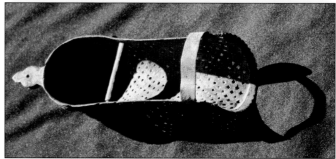

Fig. 4/69. 17th-18th century pata. The pata was a favorite Mahratta warrior weapon that usually has a long, straight blade; it is missing in our specimen. This gauntlet sword covers the forearm up to the elbow and has a horizontal hand bar and an upper band that encircles the forearm. This weapon derives from the katar. The gauntlet is in the shape of a human head and has a double bracket for the blade's attachment. The upper part has open work decorations. Very rare! Pata's length: 11.5" (29 cm.). Estimated value: $2,000.

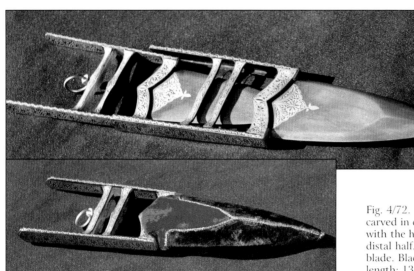

Fig. 4/70. 19th-20th century double katar decorated with inlaid silver featuring a floral design. An inner katar is contained within and is removed by pulling on a ring located on the lower horizontal bar, The blades are watered and decorated with inlaid silver featuring a floral design in a mihrab shape. Green and red velvet covers the wooden scabbard. Blade's length: 6.8" (17 cm.). Katar's length: 12.6" (32 cm.). Inner katar's blade length: 6.2" (16 cm.). Inner katar length: 12.2" (31 cm.). Estimated value: $2,200.

Fig. 4/71. 19th-20th century double katar. The bars, handles, and proximal part of the blades are covered with inlaid silver featuring a floral design. A ring located on the horizontal lower bar allows withdrawal of the second katar. The design is similar for both katars. Katar's length: 13.3" (34 cm.). Katar's blade length: 7" (18 cm.). Inner katar's blade length: 6.5" (16.5 cm.). Inner katar's length: 13" (33 cm.). Green and red velvet scabbard. Estimated value: $2,200.

Fig. 4/72. 19th-20th century khanjar dagger. The pommel is carved in celadon jade in the shape of a horse's head, continuing with the hilt. Double-edged, watered blade, slightly curved in the distal half. Inlaid gold in a triangular cartouche decorates the blade. Black velvet scabbard. Blade's length: 8" (20 cm.). Dagger's length: 13.8" (35 cm.). Estimated value: $2,000.

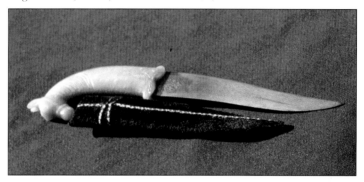

Fig. 4/73. 19th-20th century long dagger with entire surface covered with inlaid silver displaying a floral design. A stylized rooster's head constitutes the pommel. Double-edged, watered blade decorated with an inlaid silver cartouche featuring floral decorations. Blade's length: 10.6" (27 cm.). Dagger's length: 18" (46 cm.). Estimated value: $1,600.

Fig. 4/74. 18th-19th century bank knife with celadon jade handle. The distal part of the hilt is decorated with chiseled silver featuring a floral design. Curved, single-edged blade has the cutting edge on the superior, convex side. This was a typical Mahratta weapon knife for close combat, or defense. Blade's length: 4.3" (11 cm.). Knife's length: 6.2" (16 cm.). Estimated value: $850.

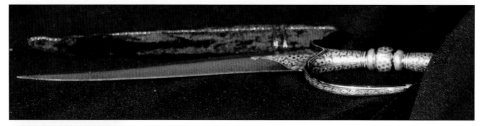

Fig. 4/78. 19th-20th century chilanum dagger. Slightly angled hilt, decorated with inlaid silver with floral design. Small hand-guard with two arched quillons. The knuckle-guard does not reach the pommel, which is arched with upward oriented edges. Double-edged, watered blade with inlaid silver in the proximal end. Green velvet covered scabbard. Blade's length: 8.8" (22 cm.). Dagger's length: 14.1" (36 cm.). Estimated value: $1,500.

Fig. 4/75. 19th-20th century khanjar dagger covered with inlaid silver featuring a floral design. The pommel is in the shape of a mutton. Watered, double-edged blade decorated on the obverse side with a cartouche displaying Islamic symbols. Blade's length: 6.8" (17 cm.). Dagger's length: 13" (33 cm.). Estimated value: $1,500.

Fig. 4/79. 17th-18th century Indo-Persian talwar sword. Iron hilt with a central bulbous protuberance for grip. Two short pointed quillons. Disk type pommel with radial, linear decorations. Curved, single-edged blade, narrowing toward the point. Blade's length: 28.8" (73 cm.). Sword's length: 34.2" (87 cm.). Estimated value: $1,200.

Fig. 4/76. 19th-20th century dagger in the shape of a talwar. The entire dagger is covered with inlaid silver featuring a floral design. Disk-shaped pommel and short quillons. Watered, double-edged blade with inlaid silver featuring a floral deign in a cartouche located on the obverse side. Blade's length: 7.5" (19 cm.). Dagger's length: 14.1" (36 cm.). Estimated value: $1,500.

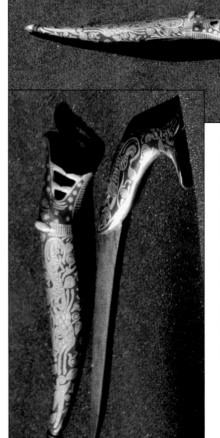

Fig. 4/80. 19th-20th century knife whose entire surface is inlaid with gold on a black niello background and features a tiger hunting a deer. Unusual for Indian knives is the right angle between the hilt and the blade, appearing as a pistol butt. Double-edged, watered blade with inlaid gold decoration on the obverse side. Blade's length: 5" (13 cm.). Knife's length: 10" (25.5 cm.). Estimated value: $1,100.

Fig. 4/77. 19th-20th century khanjar covered with inlaid silver decorations with a floral design. The pommel is in the shape of a horse's head. Watered, double-edged blade with an inlaid silver cartouche featuring Islamic characters on the obverse side. Blade's length: 5.8" (14.5 cm.). Dagger's length: 12.2" (31 cm.). Estimated value: $1,500.

Fig. 4/81. 19th-20th century knife whose entire surface is inlaid in gold on black niello background. The pommel is inlaid with gold displaying Islamic characters and flowers. Double-edged, curved blade decorated with incised ornaments featuring a tiger hunting a deer. Blade's length: 10" (25.5 cm.). Knife's length: 10" (25.5 cm.). Estimated value: $1,100.

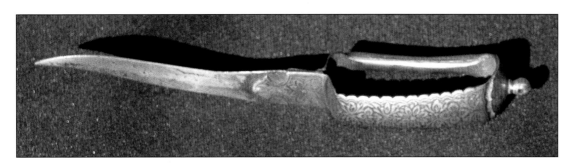

Fig. 4/82. 19th century bichwa knife. The hilt, the knuckle-guard, and the proximal part of the blade are decorated with inlaid gold. Double-edged, curved blade. Blade's length: 5.8" (14.5 cm.). Knife's length: 10.2" (26 cm.). Estimated value: $1,250.

Fig. 4/83. 19th-20th century khanjar knife. The hilt, pommel, and scabbard are made from solid silver. The pommel is in the shape of a horse's head. Chiseled silver in high relief with a floral design adorn the scabbard. Double-edged watered blade with serrated back edge. Blade's length: 4" (10 cm.). Knife's length: 8.6" (22 cm.). Estimated value: $850.

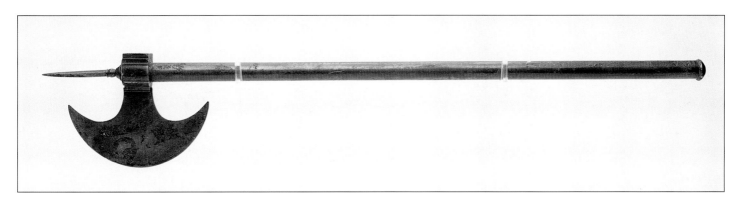

Fig. 4/84. 18th century battle axe with a spear-head end. The hilt is made from steel that continues with the spear. Axe's length: 6.5" (16.5 cm.). Total length: 30.2" (77 cm.). Estimated value: $800.

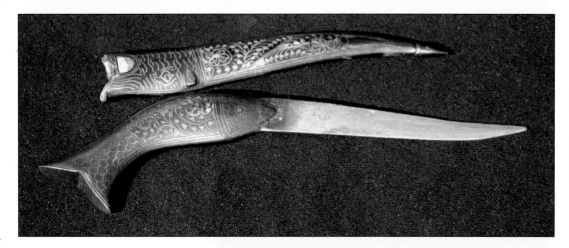

Fig. 4/85. 19th-20th century khanjar dagger decorated on its entire surface with inlaid silver featuring a floral motif. The hilt is in the shape of a fish. Double-edged, watered blade. Blade's length: 5.5" (14 cm.). Dagger's length: 12.5" (32 cm.). Estimated value: $950.

Fig. 4/86. 16th-17th century katar. Triangular shape blade with four converging fullers in the center. The base of the blade has a convoluted decoration made from silver. Open work decorations with a vine-like pattern ornate the side bars. The hand-guard is concave and also has open work decorations. Blade's length: 13.4" (34 cm.). Katar's length: 19.5" (49.5 cm.). Estimated value: $1,000.

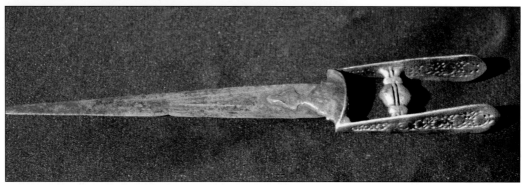

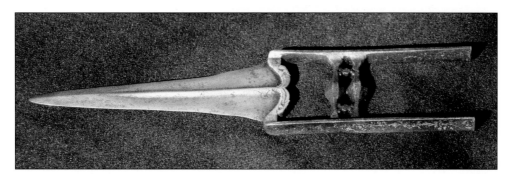

Fig. 4/87. 17th-18th century Moghul katar. The vertical lateral bars are decorated with gold koftgari that is about 80% still visible. The horizontal bars have only traces of gold koftgari, indicating the extensive use of this weapon in the past. Triangular blade with central rib and thickening of the blade toward the point for effective armor piercing. Blade's length: 6.8" (17 cm.). Katar's length: 11.8" (30 cm.). Estimated value: $1,800.

Fig. 4/88. 19th century inlaid silver and niello dagger. The hilt and scabbard are decorated with silver koftgari featuring an abstract floral pattern. A cruciform hand-guard with bulbous ends is also decorated with silver koftgari. Double-edged damascene blade with a cartouche located on the obverse side featuring inlaid silver Islamic inscription. Blade's length: 7" (18 cm.). Dagger's length: 10.6" (27 cm.). Estimated value: $1,000.

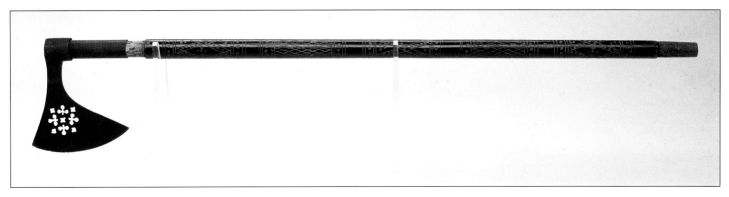

Fig. 4/89. 19th century Moghul axe. The iron axe is decorated with incised roundels, open work trefoil, and rectangles metal work. The wooden handle is decorated with incised ornaments. Axe's size: 5.2" x 4.8" (13 x 12 cm.). Total length: 30.7" (78 cm.). Estimated value: $600.

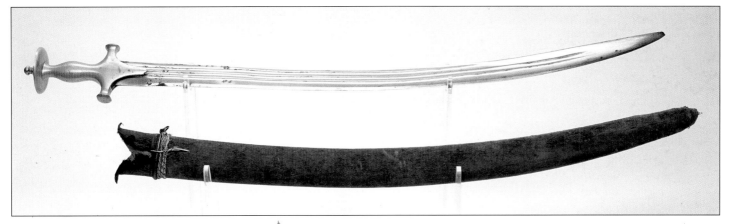

Fig. 4/90. 18th-19th century talwar. The hilt, pommel, and the hand-guard are made from low grade silver. Disk pommel without ornaments. Single-edged blade has three fullers. The scabbard is covered with green velvet that faded with age. Blade's length: 28.8" (73 cm.). Sword's length: 33.5" (85 cm.). Estimated value: $900.

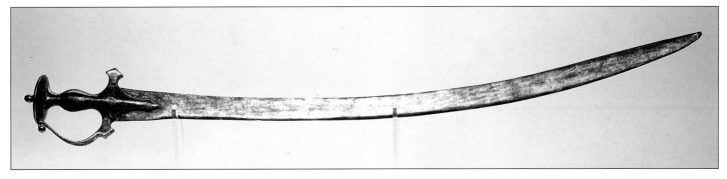

Fig. 4/91. 18th century talwar. Steel hilt with curved hand-guard and short quillons. The pommel is disk-shaped and has simple decorations. Single-edged blade with moderate curve and no fuller. Blade's length: 32.5" (82.5 cm.). Sword's length: 37.5" (95 cm.). Estimated value: $750.

Fig. 4/92. 19th-20th century child's sword. The hilt and hand-guard are made from brass. Brass pommel in the shape of a mutton's head. Single-edged curved blade with engravings in Hindi and decorations, also inscribed, "made in India." Red velvet covers the wooden scabbard. Blade's length: 13.4" (34 cm.). Sword's length: 20.2" (51.5 cm.). Estimated value: $450.

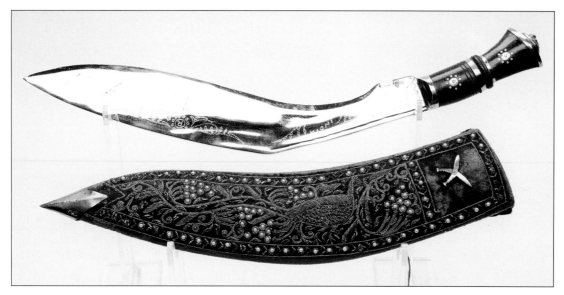

Fig. 4/93. 20th century Gurkha dagger. The hilt is made from black horn decorated with inlaid silver. Single-edged blade, curved and widening in the mid-portion, engraved "India" and having simple decorations. Elaborate scabbard covered with purple velvet is decorated with pearls and gold threads and has a pointed silver chape. The center of the scabbard is decorated with an embroidered peacock with gilt threads. Two crossed silver daggers are centered in a panel located on the blade near the hilt. Blade's length: 16" (41 cm.). Dagger's length: 22" (56 cm.). Estimated value: $850.

Fig. 4/94. 19th century Moghul kard. Very fine damascene blade decorated with inlaid gold on black bidri background, a design that is also present on the back of this single-edged blade. Celadon nephrite jade forms the hilt of the kard. An inlaid gold geometric design decorates the distal part of the hilt. Blade's length: 7.5" (19 cm.). Kard's length: 11.7" (30.4 cm.). Estimated value: $2,000.

Fig. 4/95. 19th-20th century khanjar dagger. The hilt and pommel are made from celadon jade carved in the shape of a horse. A round shaped flower and a pointed pedestal decorate the hilt. Double-edged, watered blade has round inlaid gold decoration with invocation from Koran. Lavender velvet covered scabbard. Blade's length: 7.5" (19 cm.). Dagger's length: 13" (33 cm.). Estimated value: $2,000.

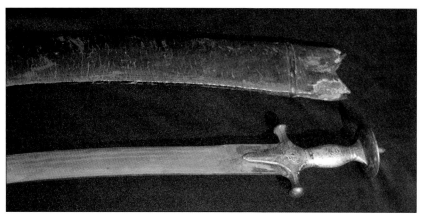

Fig. 4/96. 17th-18th century talwar sword with inlaid silver pommel and hilt. Round disk pommel with traces of the inlaid silver. Curved, single-edged blade with fine watering. Original scabbard is made from wood and covered with black leather. Blade's length: 30.6" (78 cm.). Sword's length: 35.8" (91 cm.). Estimated value: $3,000.

Fig. 4/97. 17th-18th century talwar sword. The hilt is decorated with silver koftgari featuring a floral design. Curved, single-edged blade. The pommel is disk shaped. Red velvet covered scabbard is a 20th century replacement. Blade's length: 31.5" (80 cm.). Sword's length: 38.2" (97 cm.). Estimated value: $1,500.

Fig. 4/98. 17th-18th century talwar sword. The hilt and pommel are decorated with inlaid silver featuring a floral design. Single-edged, curved blade. The scabbard is a 19th century replacement and is made from wood covered with a red floral textile. Blade's length: 29.5" (75 cm.). Sword's length: 35.5" (90 cm.). Estimated value: $2,000.

Turkish Swords and Daggers

Fig. 4/99. Medieval Ottoman kilich sword dating to the 15th-16th century. Ivory hilt with age toning. The scabbard is decorated with copper repoussé bands displaying a zoomorphic design with different animals in five cartouches. The blade is inlaid with silver having a floral design and a verset from the Koran in an oval cartouche. Inlaid gold decorations are on the reverse side of the blade, as well as on the back of the blade that is widening toward the point. Very rare! Estimated value: $12,000.

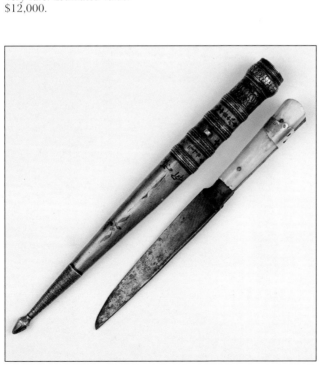

Fig. 4/100. Antique Turkmen dagger with exquisite ornate silver scabbard. The upper part of the scabbard has annular chiseled silver and black enamel using niello and cloisonné techniques. The date and Islamic inscription are located on the reverse side of the scabbard in black enamel. An intricate floral panel is displayed on the obverse side with incised silver decorations and black enamel inlaid in silver cloisons. The chape has a spiral silver wire decoration. Ivory hilt with annular silver retaining wire. Heavy, single-edged blade. Blade's length: 6.5" (16.5 cm.). Dagger's length: 15.8" (40 cm.). Estimated value: $8,500.

Fig. 4/101. 15th-16th century Ottoman yataghan. The blade is curved with pitted corrosion. Intricate inlaid gold and silver decorations ornate the proximal portion of the blade. On the blade's obverse side, an Islamic inscription is contained in a cartouche ending in open floral design. Niello decorations are also present. The hilt is profusely decorated with inlaid gold and silver in an oblong cartouche located at the ends and center of the hilt. The center cartouche on each side has an Islamic inscription. Bi-lobate pommel with inlaid gold and silver decorations. Blade's length: 23" (58.5 cm.). Sword's length: 28.5" (72.5 cm.). Estimated value: $12,000.

Fig. 4/102. 16th-18th century Ottoman silver dagger. The hilt and scabbard are covered with low grade silver decorated with a shallow floral design that became worn out with the age and possible burial in the soil. Double-edged silver blade decorated with Islamic calligraphy on both sides. Obviously, this dagger served for a ceremonial purpose rather than military usage. Blade's length: 9.8" (24.8 cm.). Dagger's length: 17.2" (44 cm). Estimated value: $3,500.

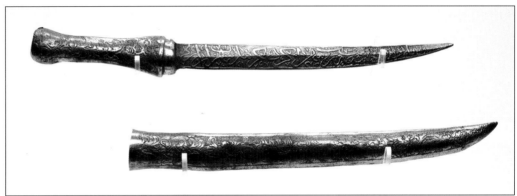

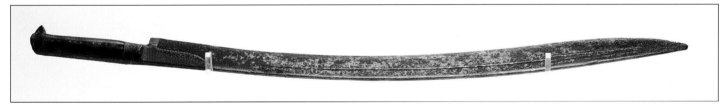

Fig. 4/103. 16th-17th century yataghan sword. Single-edged curved blade, slightly widens toward point. Inlaid silver decorates the blade above a central silver prominent line ending in an arrow style duplication. There is an Islamic inscription on the blade's back. The hilt is made from wood with the end's ears destroyed by age. A decorated rounded metal piece reinforces the blade near the junction with the hilt. Blade's length: 23" (58.5 cm.). Sword's length: 28" (71 cm.). Estimated value: $2,000.

Fig. 4/104. Antique kindjal dagger made from solid silver, chiseled and hammered with Islamic motifs. The hilt has niello and cloisonné decorations contained in a cartouche. An animal head with a silver ball forms the pommel. A bird carrying a cup or a bowl forms the scabbard's chape (could be the holy grail). Steel blade with double fuller has single edge and is slightly curved. Blade's length: 12.5" (32 cm.). Dagger's length: 19" (48.5 cm.). Estimated value: $1,500.

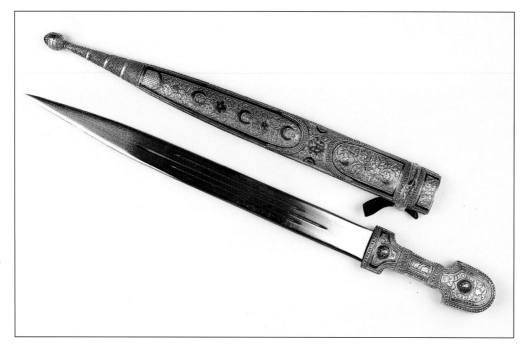

Fig. 4/105. Turkey, Ottoman Empire. Antique silver kindjal dagger decorated with incised and chiseled floral decorations with relief design. Some decorations, such as the panels' borders and some floral designs, are inlaid silver in enamel niello technique. A central decoration has the initial A and a possible Greek sigma. Interestingly, the hilt has a medallion of seated Zeus and the relief head of a bearded man below. The lower part of the scabbard has a raised relief design perceived as a silver wire. Steel blade with three fullers. This kindjal is completely different than the traditional Turkish kindjals with Islamic motifs, as it evidently is Greek in design and imitates the ancient Greek decorations. Most likely, this kindjal was created by a Greek sword-smith in the 19th century. It is very rare and the only kindjal I have ever seen with this design. Blade's length: 14" (35.5 cm.). Dagger's length: 20.5" (52 cm.). Estimated value: $3,500-3,800.

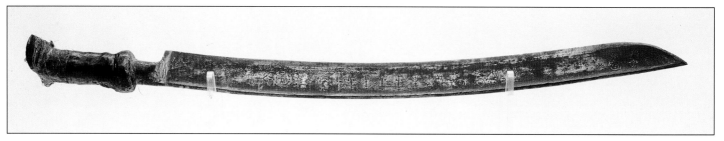

Fig. 4/106. 18th-19th century yataghan sword with waxed cloth covering the wooden hilt. Curved, wide blade with incised decorations and Islamic inscription. Blade's length: 20" (51 cm.). Sword's length: 24.5" (62 cm.). Estimated value: $2,700.

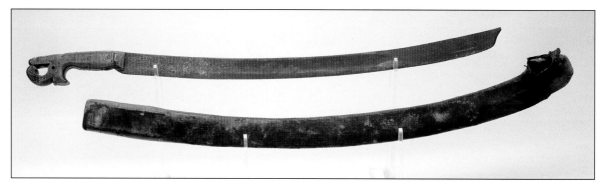

Fig. 4/107. 17th-18th century wide blade saber. The hilt is made from aged ivory that is retained to the tang with many piercing pegs and nails. Unusually shaped pommel with pierced design. Wooden scabbard covered with thick leather. This is a very unusual Turkish sword, probably originating with the silk road caravans from Central Asia. Blade's length: 26" (66.5 cm.). Sword's length: 38" (96.5 cm.). Estimated value: $4,000.

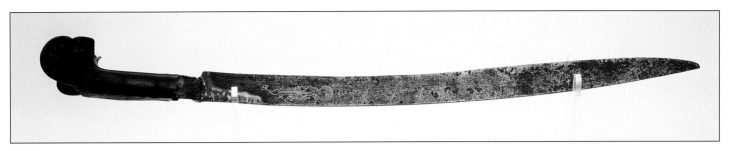

Fig. 4/108. Turkey. Antique yataghan sword. The hilt is made from aged bone with double-lobed bone. Curved, single-edged blade with silver decoration and enforcement on the back. The obverse of the blade has an Islamic inscription and date. The reverse side has floral decorations inlaid with silver. Considerable pitted corrosion is present. Blade's length: 20" (51 cm.). Sword's length: 25" (63.5 cm.) Estimated value: $3,000.

Fig. 4/109. Turkey. 18th-19th century Armenian bichaq. The scabbard is covered with repoussé silver with floral pattern in the central panel. The distal third is decorated with filigree silver, while the proximal third has high relief horizontal lines of ornamental silver. The back has an Armenian inscription. Bone hilt with some age fossilization. This very rare dagger was created in Turkey by an Armenian craft master and is very, very rare! Blade's length: 8.2" (21 cm.). Dagger's length: 14" (36 cm.). Estimated value: $5,000.

Fig. 4/110. 16th-17th century short silver sword with hilt and scabbard decorated in a floral design. Double-edged blade has Islamic inscription on both sides. Slightly curved scabbard follows the blade's curvature. The hammered decorations are worn out due to age. A rectangular hanger is present on the back of the sword for belt threading. Blade's length: 13.8" (35 cm.). Sword's length: 23.6" (60 cm.). Estimated value: $1,750.

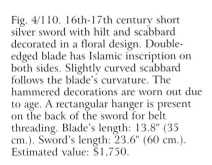

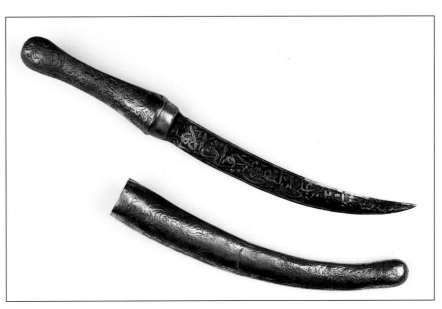

Fig. 4/111. 18th-19th century Ottoman dagger with black horn hilt. The scabbard appears to be a 19th century replacement with low grade silver end ornaments having an incised floral design. Leather covering the wood forms the scabbard. Single-edged, slightly curved blade is definitely older, probably 16th-17th century, and has an Islamic inscription on the obverse side. Blade's length: 11.5" (29.5 cm.). Dagger's length: 17.5" (44.5 cm.). Estimated value: $1,200.

Fig. 4/114. 19th century stiletto knife with hilt and scabbard made from silver and decorated with silver filigree. The double-edged blade has inlaid silver decorations on both sides. Very rare miniature knife. Blade's length: 4.5" (11.3 cm.). Knife's length: 8.5" (21.5 cm.). Estimated value: $750.

Fig. 4/112. 17th-18th century Ottoman dagger. Bone hilt with double ear end. Straight, single-edged blade. Blade's length: 13" (33 cm.). Dagger's length: 19" (48 cm.). $900.

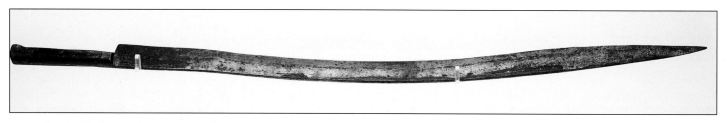

Fig. 4/113. 17th-18th century yataghan sword. Simple wooden hilt reinforced with apical and distal T-shape bars. Three metal pegs hold the hilt to the tang. Single-edged blade with wavy decorations near the hilt. Slightly curved blade has typical widening in the distal third. Blade's length: 32" (81 cm.). Sword's length: 38" (96.5 cm.). Estimated value: $1,000.

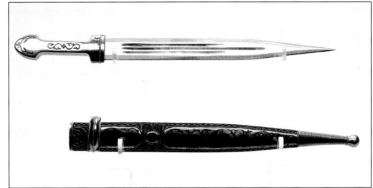

Fig. 4/116. 19th-20th century silver kindjal. The hilt is made from solid silver decorated with niello, filigree silver, and knobs. Straight double-edged blade has an elongated point. Three fullers are present. The scabbard is decorated with filigree silver and niello only on the obverse side. The lower part of the scabbard has coiled heavy silver wire ornament and a terminal knob. Blade's length: 12.2" (31 cm.). Dagger's length: 19.2" (49 cm.). Estimated value: $1,200.

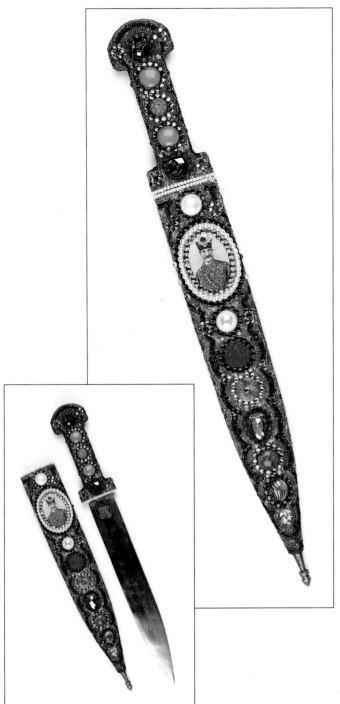

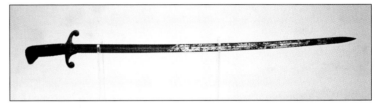

Fig. 4/117. 15th-17th century Ottoman sword resembling medieval European swords. Wooden hilt with hand-guard that has incised decorations and ends in two quillons curling downward, with the ends in spiral form. Single-edged blade with one fuller. This sword was purchased in the Grand Bazaar, Istanbul, in the early 80s. Blade's length: 28" (71 cm.). Sword's length: 32.5" (82.5 cm.). Estimated value: $2,750.

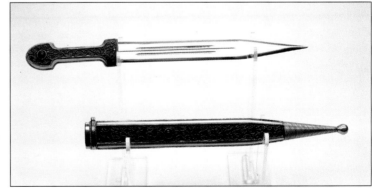

Fig. 4/115. Early 20th century Turkish kindjal entirely covered with colorful glass beads. Obviously, this is a presentation dagger offered to Kemal Atatürk. Atatürk, considered the father of modern day Turkey, introduced the Latin alphabet and brought Turkey up to par with European nations. The scabbard features a hand painted portrait of Atatürk in quasi-military Anatolian dress and plum head-dress. Wide, double-edged blade with incised mark of a lion and Islamic inscription, underneath. Very rare, most likely, unique. Blade's length: 11.8" (30 cm.). Dagger's length: 19.8" (50 cm.). Estimated value: $2,000.

Fig. 4/118. 19th-20th century kindjal entirely covered in decorated silver. The hilt and the scabbard are decorated with filigree silver on a black niello background. Agate stones also decorate the hilt and scabbard. A coiled silver wire ending in a knob forms the chape of the scabbard. Double-edged blade with three fullers. Blade's length: 11" (28 cm.). Dagger's length: 19.5" (49.5 cm.). Estimated value: $1,000.

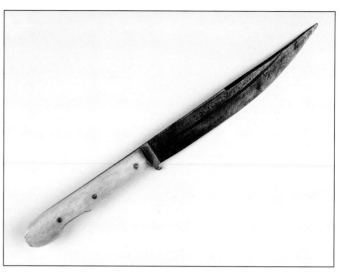

Fig. 4/121. 19th century Ottoman knife. Ivory hilt with split double ear typical pommel. Single-edged blade with one fuller and incised decorations. Blade's length: 6.2" (16 cm.). Knife's length: 10.2" (26 cm.). Estimated value: $700.

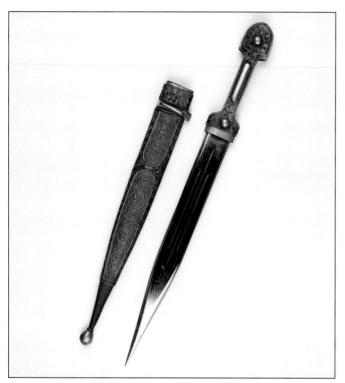

Fig. 4/119. Turkey, Ottoman Empire. Silver kindjal dagger decorated with filigree silver wire. The scabbard has two brass panels decorated with repoussé motifs. Two knob ornaments with rectangular panels form a raised design. Double-edged blade with three fullers. Blade's length: 11.5" (29.2 cm.). Dagger's length: 17.5" (44.5 cm.). Estimated value: $700-800.

Fig. 4/122. 20th century knife. Wooden hilt with two round depressions for better grip. The blade is dated 28.5.1933; it is curved and becomes double-edged in the middle of the blade. The hilt ends in typical double ear form. Blade's length: 5.5" (14 cm.). Knife's length: 9.5" (24 cm.). Estimated value: $400.

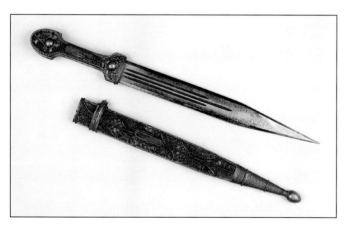

Fig. 4/120. Turkey, Ottoman Empire. Antique kindjal silver dagger decorated with silver filigree wire on the obverse side. Double-edged steel blade with two fullers. Blade's length: 11" (28 cm.). Dagger's length: 17.3" (44 cm.). Estimated value: $700-800.

Fig. 4/123. Ottoman knife with wooden hilt having a double ear pommel and crenellated lower margin for improved grip. Single-edged blade with one fuller. Knife's length: 10" (25.5 cm.). Estimated value: $350.

Other Islamic Swords and Daggers

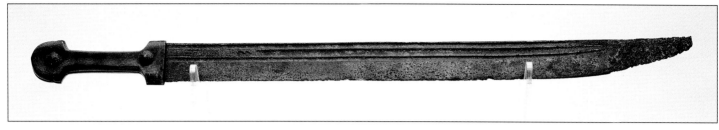

Fig. 4/124. Islamic medieval sword, probably 12th-14th century. It has a rhinoceros hilt and no hand-guard. The blade has three fullers and tapers toward the point. Marked pitted corrosion is present on the blade, especially toward the point. Several notches on this single-edged blade point toward its extensive use in battles. Blade's length: 20.8" (52.8 cm.). Sword's length: 26" (66 cm.). Estimated value: $8,000.

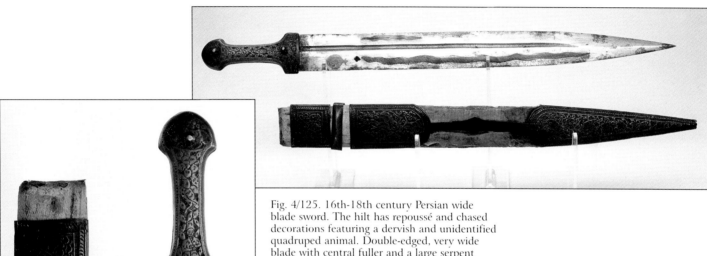

Fig. 4/125. 16th-18th century Persian wide blade sword. The hilt has repoussé and chased decorations featuring a dervish and unidentified quadruped animal. Double-edged, very wide blade with central fuller and a large serpent facing an incised inscription that is present on the other side as well. A smaller serpent is visible on the reverse side. An inlaid silver inscription is seen below the fuller with Koran verse in a cartouche. Wooden scabbard decorated with brass panels featuring birds, flowers, lion, deer, wolf, and rabbit. The original velvet cover of the scabbard disintegrated over the centuries. Blade's length: 24" (61 cm.). Sword's length: 31.8" (80 cm.). Estimated value: $6,000.

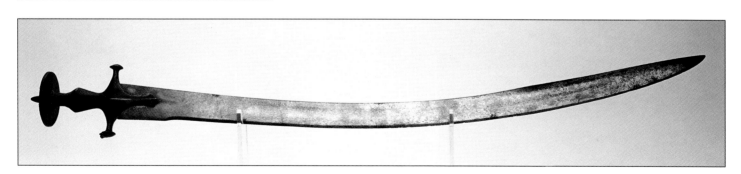

Fig. 4/126. 15th century Moorish shamshir (scimitar) ornamented with gold, silver, and cloisonné decorations. Bronze hilt and pommel. The pommel is disk shaped and has stellar decorations on the disk's top. Short, chubby quillons. Broad, curved, single-edged blade that slightly widens in the distal third. The Moorish shamshirs are extremely rare. Blade's length: 32" (81.5 cm.). Sword's length: 37.3" (95 cm.). Estimated value: $10,000.

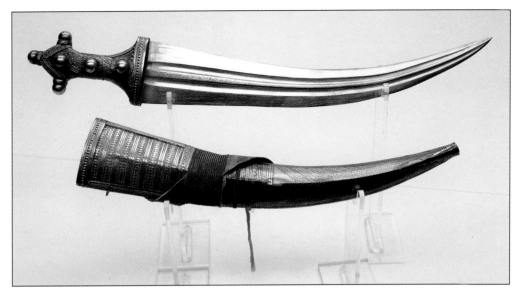

Fig. 4/127. 18th century large Arabian jambiya. The hilt and scabbard are decorated with chiseled silver. Silver knobby decorations and chiseled silver over a wooden grip decorate the hilt. Chiseled silver covers the upper part of the scabbard, while the lower part is covered with gilded brass, or low grade gold in filigree wire and inlaid silver square decorations, as well as incised brass ornaments. Wide, double-edged blade with central rib and two fullers. The back of the scabbard contains a leather pouch for a knife and a leather belt. Blade's length: 11.5" (29 cm.). Dagger's length: 17.5" (44.5 cm.). Estimated value: $3,500.

Fig. 4/128. 17th-18th century Arabian nimcha dagger. Ivory hilt with dark toning. Hand-guard and knuckle-guard that continues with the hand-guard. The blade has longitudinal decorations and tapers toward the point. Repoussé silver decorates the scabbard. Blade's length: 10" (25.5 cm.). Dagger's length: 14" (35.5 cm.). Estimated value: $1,200.

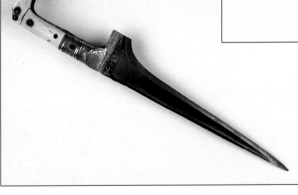

Fig. 4/129. Afghanistan, Khyber Pass, Makhsud tribe. 18th-19th century pesh-kabz dagger. (In Persian, pesh kabz means "fore-grip.") The blade is beveled, straight, very wide near the hilt, and tapers to a very fine point. Due to the thickness of the back of the blade, the blade is actually triangular and able to pierce the mail of an armor. Two ivory plaques riveted to the tang form the hilt. Chased silver decorates the hilt and the exposed part of the tang. Blade's length: 8.5" (21.5 cm.). Dagger's length: 12.7" (32.3 cm.). Estimated value: $1,200.

Fig. 4/130. 18th century Khyber Pass folding knife with two foldings. The hilt is made from bone decorated with circles and concentric bands dyed in red. The mid-section is made from brass decorated with circles and bands. There are two triggers that allow the folding of the knife. One trigger is located on top of the hilt and the second, on the mid-section. The blade is perpendicular to the knife's axe and is sickle-shaped. Very rare and unusual folding knife. Blade's length: 5.2" (13.3 cm.). Open knife's length: 12" (30.5 cm.). Estimated value: $800.

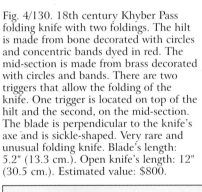

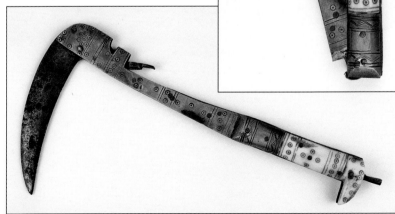

Fig. 4/131. Arabia. 18th-19th century silver jambiya. The hilt is decorated with chiseled and filigree silver. Double-edged blade with three fullers. Silver scabbard decorated with intricate chiseled decorations. The dagger is attached to a decorative 20th century leather belt. Blade's length: 7.8" (19.5 cm.). Dagger's length: 12.5" (32 cm.). Estimated value: $900.

Fig. 4/132. 17th-18th century Islamic jambiya knife. This knife is actually a hybrid between a jambiya and a kindjal. The hilt and scabbard are covered with solid silver chiseled in high relief with floral and animal decorations. Single-edged blade with Islamic inscriptions in gold. Blade's length: 5.1" (13 cm.). Knife's length: 8.2" (21 cm.). Estimated value: $850.

Chapter Five

Southeastern Asia Edged Weapons

Ceylon Edged Weapons

Ceylon, presently known as Sri Lanka, was for a long time under the Dutch East India influence. Two edged Sinhalese weapons from Ceylon are important to describe: kastane and piha khetta. (I have included the Sinhalese edged weapons in the Southeastern Asian chapter as these weapons are not at all related to the Indian or Middle Eastern weapons as far as shape or manufacture.)

The *kastane* is a sword with a curved blade usually bearing the mark of Dutch East India Company. The pommel is in the shape of a dragon's head and carved in wood with exceptional details. Better swords have a hilt made from solid gold or silver. The hand-guard has two stubby quillons with downward elongations and a knuckle guard.

The scabbard is made of carved wood or horn, occasionally covered with embossed silver, gold, or brass. A smaller version of kastane, always bearing the mark of Dutch East India Company, was given to native officials as a mark of office or appreciation.

The typical Sinhalese dagger is the *piha khetta*, a highly ornate dagger with a single-edged, broad blade. Typically, the back of the blade is reinforced with a sheet of silver or brass with intricate incised decorations. The hilt is made from bone carving or ox horn, frequently decorated with ornate bands of silver. Silver or brass with incised decorations matching the blade decorations form the scabbard.

A much rarer Sinhalese dagger is the *sanger*, which is actually used as a processional spearhead with a ribbed haft.

Fig. 5/1. Ceylon (Sri Lanka). 18th century piha khetta (piha kaetta) knife. This is a heavy knife with a rhinoceros hilt that has a crystallized amber appearance due to age. Intricate carving was done on the rhino horn. Hammered repoussé silver decorates the pommel and there are two ornate brass panels that encircle the upper part of the back of the blade. The upper half of the blade has inlaid silver that is adorned with delicate floral decorations. Wooden scabbard decorated with simple adornments. Blade's length: 6" (11.8 cm.). Dagger's length: 11.8" (30 cm.). Estimated value: $3,000-$3,500.

Fig. 5/2. Ceylon. Antique piha khetta knife dating to the 18th century or earlier. The hilt is carved in staghorn antler in the shape of a bird with inlaid brass eyes and eyebrows. Age has produced a vitreous appearance with minute fissures in the staghorn that enhances the beauty of this rare piece. Single-edged blade with inlaid brass having an intricate design on the back of the blade. Typically, the blade widens slightly in the lower third and then curves upward toward the point that is in the back for reinforcement of the blade. Wooden scabbard is carved in the shape of a bird. Blade's length: 6.5" (16.5 cm.). Dagger's length: 12" (30.5 cm.). Estimated value: $1,000-1,500.

Burmese Edged Weapons

Most of the Burmese swords and daggers in collectors' hands date to the 19th century and were used as weapons against the colonial British and Indian troops involved in wars between 1824 and 1886. These single-edged swords and daggers of Burma (presently Myanmar) are called *dha*. Typically, a dha is made from carved wood and has no hand-guard. The scabbard and hilt are frequently covered with a silver sheet displaying repoussé decorations. The pommel might have a bulbous shape and, due to its considerable length, allows a two-hands use. Better quality dhas have intricate wood carvings on the hilt and scabbard with gilding and appliqué of colored glass imitating precious stones. The dha's blade is slightly curved and has incised decorations with figural design. Inlaid silver bands are found on the back of the blade. A slight widening of the blade commonly is found in its terminal third.

To the north of Burma, the Nagas of Assam use a variant of the dha sword named *dao*. The dao sword differs in many ways, but most characteristic for the dao of Assam is a scabbard that resembles the swords of Malaya or Borneo. A typical Naga dao sword has a flattened wooden scabbard whose board sides are bound together with rattan. Highly characteristic for the dao is the presence of two cross-guards. The blade widens in its distal part and has an abrupt convex cut.

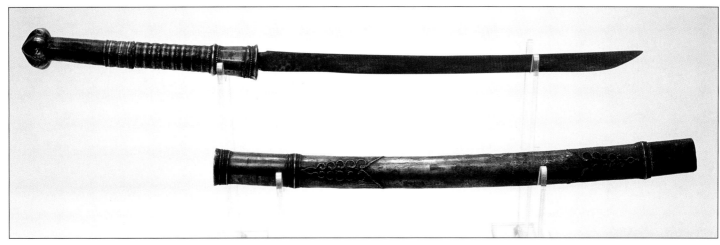

Fig. 5/3. 18th century dha silver sword. The hilt is covered with a silver sheet in the proximal third. The lower two-thirds is covered with bands of filigree silver. A distal solid silver sheet forms the end of the hilt. The length of the hilt allows double-handed holding. Narrow and slightly corroded blade due to high iron content of the alloy. The scabbard is wooden with a heavy silver sheet cover decorated with filigree in a dual spiral design uniting at the top and resembling a stupa. Blade's length: 16" (40.5 cm.). Sword's length: 29" (74 cm.). Estimated value: $2,800.

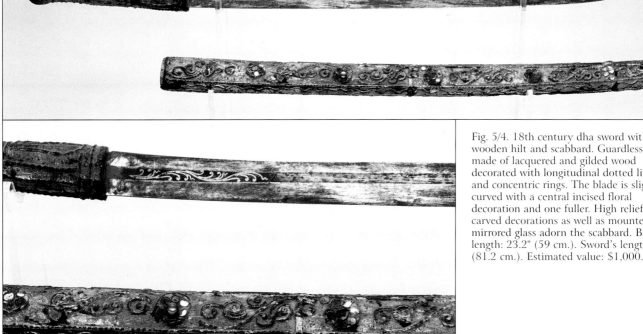

Fig. 5/4. 18th century dha sword with wooden hilt and scabbard. Guardless hilt made of lacquered and gilded wood decorated with longitudinal dotted lines and concentric rings. The blade is slightly curved with a central incised floral decoration and one fuller. High relief floral carved decorations as well as mounted mirrored glass adorn the scabbard. Blade's length: 23.2" (59 cm.). Sword's length: 32" (81.2 cm.). Estimated value: $1,000.

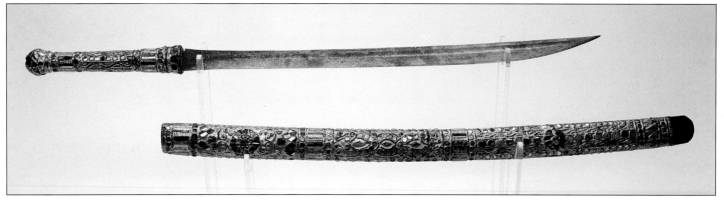

Fig. 5/5. 19th century dha sword. Wooden hilt heavily gilded and decorated with carvings in high relief and adornments consisting of mirrored polychrome beads and mirrors. The length of the hilt allows double handling of this sword. Single-edged blade with one fuller. The blade widens in the distal end. Heavily gilded wooden scabbard is decorated with mirrors and colored glass imitating well the precious and semi-precious stones. Blade's length: 20.5" (52 cm.). Sword's length: 33" (84 cm.). Estimated value: $1,800.

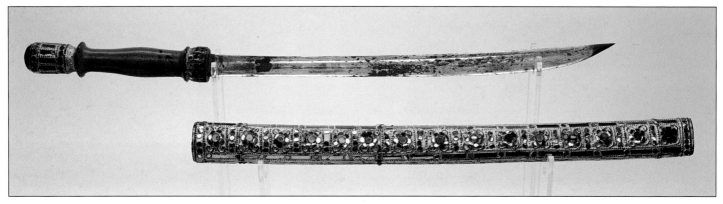

Fig. 5/6. 19th century dha sword. The hilt is made from wood painted in red with gilded ends decorated with mirrors. Single-edged blade once was covered with a heavy layer of silver-nickel that now is peeling off in several places. As is characteristic for the dha, the blade widens toward the point. The scabbard is made from gilded wood with square relief decorations centered by colored glass that imitates precious stone and is surrounded by mirrors. Blade's length: 18.8" (47.5 cm.). Sword's length: 30.5" (78 cm.). Estimated value: $1,800.

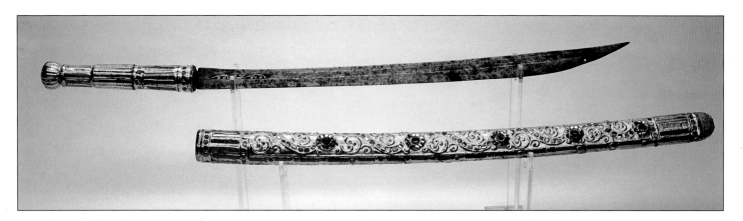

Fig. 5/7. 18th-19th century pair of dha swords (one shown only) with wooden hilt and scabbard heavily gilded and decorated with inlaid mirrors and polychrome glass beads imitating precious and semi-precious stones. Double handed hilt without hand-guard. Knob pommel decorated with vertical striations. Single-edged blade widening in the distal end. A floral inlaid silver decoration is located on the proximal part near the hilt. The wooden scabbard has carved spiral relief decorations and roundels centered by polychrome glass beads. Blade's length: 21.5" (54.5 cm.). Sword's length: 34.5" (87.5 cm.). Estimated value: $5,000 for the pair.

Fig. 5/8. 18th-19th century dha sword. Wooden hilt and scabbard covered with pure gold. Double handed hilt with longitudinal striations that facilitate the grip. Inlaid mirrors decorate the scabbard. Knob pommel with vertical striations. Single-edged blade with one fuller. As is typical for the dha, the blade widens in the lower third before narrowing toward the point. Floral silver decorations are inlaid in the blade close to the hilt. The scabbard has high relief carved decorations in a spiral pattern decorated with mirrors and polychrome glass beads. Blade's length: 23" (58.5 cm.). Sword's length: 34" (86.5 cm.). Estimated value: $1,800.

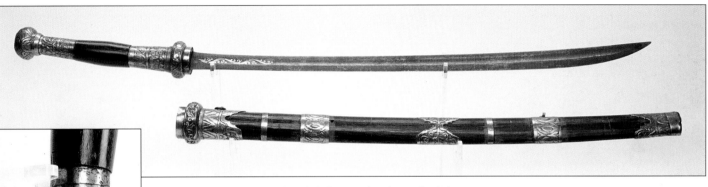

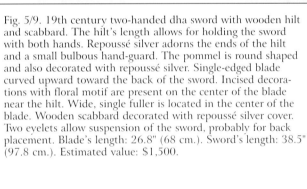

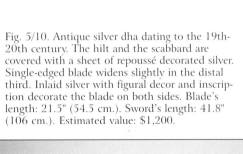

Fig. 5/9. 19th century two-handed dha sword with wooden hilt and scabbard. The hilt's length allows for holding the sword with both hands. Repoussé silver adorns the ends of the hilt and a small bulbous hand-guard. The pommel is round shaped and also decorated with repoussé silver. Single-edged blade curved upward toward the back of the sword. Incised decorations with floral motif are present on the center of the blade near the hilt. Wide, single fuller is located in the center of the blade. Wooden scabbard decorated with repoussé silver cover. Two eyelets allow suspension of the sword, probably for back placement. Blade's length: 26.8" (68 cm.). Sword's length: 38.5" (97.8 cm.). Estimated value: $1,500.

Fig. 5/10. Antique silver dha dating to the 19th-20th century. The hilt and the scabbard are covered with a sheet of repoussé decorated silver. Single-edged blade widens slightly in the distal third. Inlaid silver with figural decor and inscription decorate the blade on both sides. Blade's length: 21.5" (54.5 cm.). Sword's length: 41.8" (106 cm.). Estimated value: $1,200.

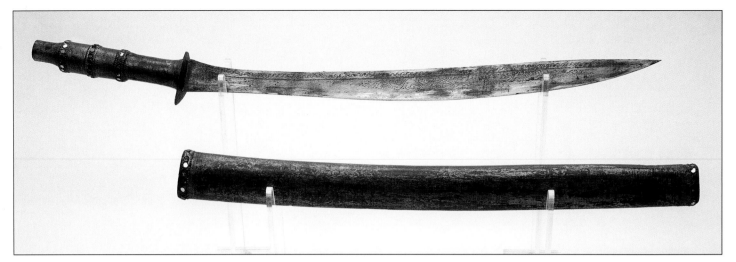

Fig. 5/11. 18th century dha sword with lacquered and gilded wooden hilt and scabbard. Mirrors are mounted as decorations on both hilt and scabbard. Red cinnabar lacquer was used and covered with gold that is still visible. A small hand-guard in an oval shape is present. Chiseled decorations are scattered along the back side of the blade, which characteristically widens in the mid-portion and then tapers toward the point. Blade's length: 19.2" (49.5 cm.). Sword's length: 26.6" (67.5 cm.). Estimated value: $1,500-$2,000.

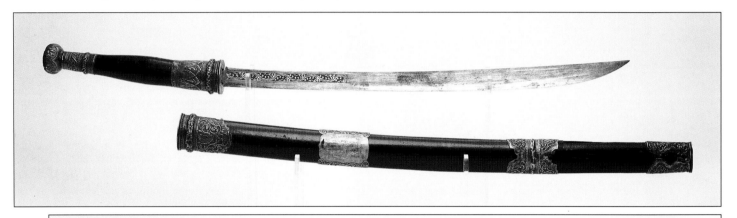

Fig. 5/12. 20th century dha sword made from repoussé silver and ebonized wood. The long hilt allows double-handed handling. Decorations in repoussé silver ornate the proximal and distal part of the hilt. Round pommel with a flat top carrying chased decorations. Wooden scabbard decorated with four annular silver bands with repoussé decorations. The central band has the inscription: "Presented to MG Po Kha of FGI Headman Alaboke Village by the DSP Insein for good work done in 1934." Single-edged blade decorated with inlaid silver with floral scrolls on both sides. Blade's length: 22.6" (57.5 cm.). Sword's length: 37.6" (95.5 cm.). Estimated value: $1,800-$2,000.

Fig. 5/13. 19th-20th century short dha sword. Wooden scabbard and hilt, gilded and decorated with polychrome inlaid glass. Single-edged blade with inlaid figural and floral decorations and Burmese inscription. Blade's length: 11.3" (29 cm.). Sword's length: 20.5" (52 cm.). Estimated value: $1,000.

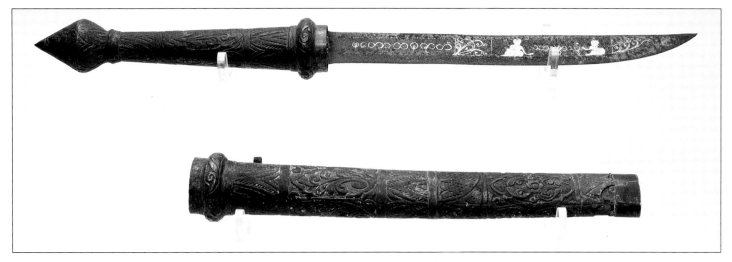

Fig. 5/14. 19th-20th century short dha sword. The hilt and scabbard are covered with gilded silver with intricate repoussé decorations. Stupa shaped pommel. Single-edged blade decorated with inlaid silver with inscription and figural design. Blade's length: 10.6" (27 cm.). Sword's length: 21" (53.5 cm.). Estimated value: $850.

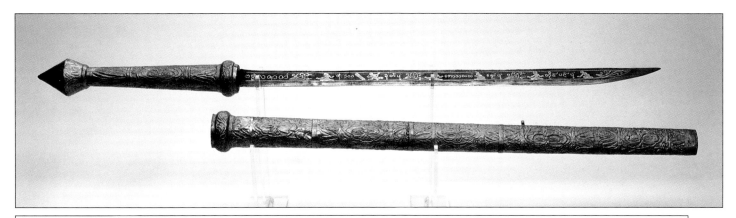

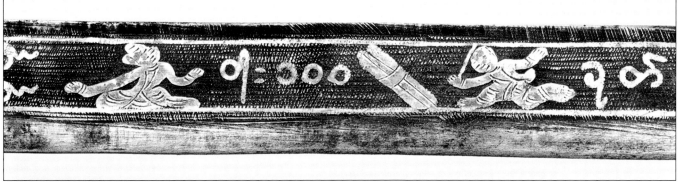

Fig. 5/15. 19th-20th century dha sword. The entire hilt and scabbard are covered with silver (low grade) with repoussé design. Single-edged blade with inlaid silver decorations featuring inscriptions and figural design on both sides on almost the whole length of the blade. Blade's length: 26.3" (67 cm.). Sword's length: 42" (107 cm.). Estimated value: $900.

Fig. 5/16. 20th century silver dha dagger. The scabbard and hilt are decorated with repoussé design. Rather long hilt and bulbous pommel. Single-edged blade is decorated with inlaid silver. Blade's length: 11" (28 cm.). Dagger's length: 18.5" (47 cm.). Estimated value: $700.

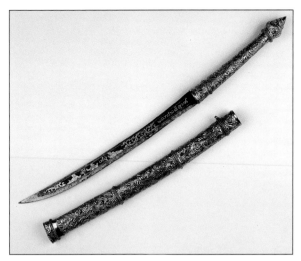

Fig. 5/17. 20th century silver long dagger with repoussé design on hilt and scabbard. Conic shaped pommel with repoussé decorations. Single-edged blade is slightly curved and widens toward the distal third. Inlaid silver decorations on the blade featuring three seated women, scroll and inscription within a frame formed by inlaid copper wire. Blade's length: 11.4" (29 cm.). Dagger's length: 19.2" (49 cm.). Estimated value: $500.

Fig. 5/20. 19th-20th century dagger with wooden hilt and scabbard covered with woven rope and tin bands. Single-edged blade with one fuller. Blade's length: 7.5" (19 cm.). Dagger's length: 14.5" (37 cm.). Estimated value: $375.

Fig. 5/18. 19th century long dha sword. The long hilt allows for two-hand holding. Pommel in the shape of a stupa. Single-edged blade widens in the lower third, has simple floral decorations. Wooden scabbard with rattan bindings. Red rope for suspension. Blade's length: 24.2" (62 cm.). Sword's length: 39.8" (101 cm.). Estimated value: $850.

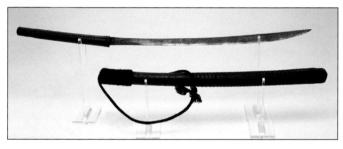

Fig. 5/21. Antique dha sword. Long wooden hilt with rattan wrap. Single-edged blade slightly widening toward the point. Wooden scabbard with rattan decorations and black cord for suspension. Blade's length: 21.5" (55 cm.). Sword's length: 33.5" (85 cm.). Estimated value: $750.

Fig. 5/19. 17th-18th century sickle knife. The handle is made from wood with horizontal ornaments. The pommel is in the shape of a stupa. Curved blade widens in the lower third. It is possible that this type of knife was used to cut rice stalks. Blade's length: 8.2" (21 cm.). Knife's length: 13.2" (33.5 cm.). Estimated value: $300.

Fig. 5/22. 19th century Burmese dha with wooden hilt and scabbard. It is a typical two hands sword with long hilt having concentric carved bands in the lower third that allows a better grip. The pommel is cone-shaped and made from carved wood. The distal end of the hilt has no hand-guard and is made from bronze. Single-edged blade widening in the lower third and then tapering toward the point. Wooden scabbard decorated with rattan bands has a red rope for holding the sword. Blade's length: 25" (63.5 cm.). Sword's length: 39.2" (99.5 cm.). Estimated value: $900.

Fig. 5/23. 19th century short dha. The hilt and scabbard are made from brass that has a dark patina and decorated with incised ornaments. Onion shaped pommel with incised brass decorations. Single-edged blade with inlaid silver featuring Burmese script, floral design, and seated women. Blade's length: 11" (28 cm.). Sword's length: 21" (53.5 cm.). Estimated value: $500.

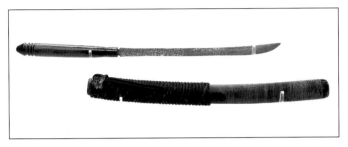

Fig. 5/24. Antique dha sword with wooden scabbard and hilt. The scabbard has woven rattan in the distal end. The proximal part is covered with red cord that serves for the sword's suspension. The long hilt allows double handling despite the light weight of the sword. Single-edged blade slightly widens toward the point. Blade's length: 14.5" (37 cm.). Sword's length: 29.5" (75 cm.). Estimated value: $800.

Fig. 5/27. Antique dha sword with wooden scabbard and hilt. The hilt and the upper part of the scabbard are covered with woven rope. Single-edged blade of uniform width that looks more like a Japanese sword than a Burmese sword. Blade's length: 18.9" (48 cm.). Sword's length: 30.8" (78 cm.). Estimated value: $700.

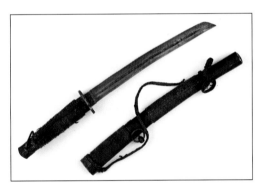

Fig. 5/25. Single-edged blade dha dagger with wooden scabbard and hilt covered with woven cord. The blade has one fuller and is slightly curved. Blade's length: 11" (28 cm.). Dagger's length: 20.2" (51.5 cm.). Estimated value: $500.

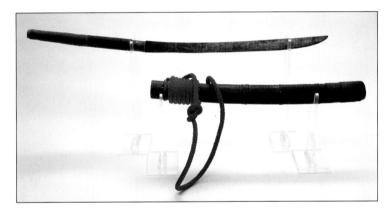

Fig. 5/28. Antique dha sword with wooden scabbard and hilt. The scabbard has a few bands of Manila rope and a red cord for suspension. Long hilt covered with non-slippery cord. Single-edged blade widens toward the point. Blade's length: 15.3" (39 cm.). Sword's length: 27.2" (69 cm.). Estimated value: $750.

Fig. 5/26. Antique dha sword with leather scabbard and carved wood and brass hilt. Single-edged blade widens toward the point, carries a Burmese inscription. Blade's length: 23" (58.5 cm.). Sword's length: 31.8" (81 cm.). Estimated value: $700.

Fig. 5/29. Antique dha sword with wooden scabbard and hilt. The scabbard has a few retaining raffia bands. Red rope is used for holding and suspension. Blade's length: 18" (46 cm.). Sword's length: 32" (81.5 cm.). Estimated value: $1,000.

Fig. 5/30. 19th-20th century short dha. The scabbard is made from wood and bound with raffia bands. Red rope is attached to the scabbard. Long wooden hilt with round decorations. Single-edged blade probably recycled from an old blade, still has the letters KA incised. Simple scroll decorations on the blade. Blade's length: 10.7" (27 cm.). Sword's length: 20" (51 cm.). Estimated value: $550.

Fig. 5/31. 19th century short Burmese sword. The scabbard and hilt are made from a silver and brass alloy plate that is chased in high relief and has repoussé decorations. Onion shaped pommel continuing with the hilt that, due to its length, allows a two hand grip. Single-edged blade decorated with inlaid silver, inscription, and images of two seated women. Sword's length: 21" (53.5 cm.). Blade's length: 10.7" (27 cm.). Estimated value: $600-$700.

Fig. 5/32. Antique knife purchased in Burma, could be of Japanese origin. Single-edged blade with two characters inscription. Iron scabbard with simple brass annular decorations and small ring for suspension. The hilt is partially covered with a brass sheet and has a scabbard lock release. The upper part of the hilt is made from crystal segments plus blue and white segments of what appear to be lacquer. Blade's length: 5.8" (14.5 cm.). Knife's length: 10" (25.5 cm.). Estimated value: $475.

Indonesian Kris Daggers and Knives

The most characteristic edged weapon of Southeast Asia is the *kris*, which was used in a vast geographic area including Indonesia with the Spice Islands, the Philippines, and the Malay peninsula. For local inhabitants of this huge region, the kris was considered to have magical powers and was venerated as a sacred object. In my frequent trips to Indonesia and Malaysia, I have visited small villages where the chieftain had in his house a high corner for ancestors' remembrance and respect. A kris handed down from one generation to the other would rest in this corner, together with a chronicle or history of the village and region written in the Sanskrit language. The owner

will never part with these precious objects, especially the kris to which divine powers were attributed.

Because the kris blade is made from meteoric iron hundreds of years old, it is believed that the blade was made from material that fell from celestial space and has extra-terrestrial powers not understood by common mortals. The hilt as well as the scabbard, being made from wood, would eventually disintegrate with age and require replacement, but the kris blade would remain the way it was created for hundreds of years. Understandably, replacement of the worn-out parts required skilled artisans to create and reconstitute these components of the kris. A large center for manufacturing kris daggers originally existed (and still exists) in Jogjakarta, Indonesia. Many collectors amass antique parts of kris daggers, such as the hilt or the blade itself.

The original manufacturing technique for the kris involved layering steel alternating with meteoric iron after heating and hammering, creating in this manner a very intricate pattern in the blade's metal (called pamor in Bahasa Indonesia, the Indonesian language). The wavy blade required significant labor, as each curve needed to be shaped, heated, and hammered individually. Afterwards, the blade was immersed in a bath containing boiled rice water with sulphur to enhance the pamor appearance. The last steps involved rubbing the blade with lime juice, washing, and then polishing with aromatic oil to preserve the surface. With age, the blade's surface would become gray and dark, but the lamination pattern was always visible.

The layers of lamination (usually seven) are called luk. Kris daggers with as many as eleven layers are known, but are very rare. The kris hilt (ukiran) is made from wood or horn, with the hilts on better krises made from ivory, gold, silver, or bone. Royal hilts were custom made from gold, ivory, or silver, inlaid with precious stones. Demonic figures with the highest quality of carving were created by Indonesian Chinese craftsmen in elephant tusk ivory.

The first kris shown here was made in the 19th century for the King of Bali, who resided in the palace of Klung-Klung. The king was a descendent of the Gelgel dynasty, which ruled Bali starting in the 14th century under the Majapahit empire of Java. Klung-Klung Palace was built by Agung Jambe, a king in the 17th century. Our kris originates from the last king, Dewa Agung, who committed suicide with his entire family in 1908 rather than fall captive to Dutch troops that had invaded Bali. One of the king's sons, Dewa Agung Geg, survived the attempted suicide (puputan) and was exiled to Lombok with his family until 1929. The kris probably belonged to the king and, after his death in 1965, was sold in the late 1960s to a dealer in Denpasar, Bali. I bought this kris in the early 1980s from a Chinese antique dealer in Denpasar, and most probably, originating from the same Royal Bali collection.

The most common carvings on the hilt are in the shape of Garuda, a Hindu bird-shaped deity, carrier of Lord Vishnu. In some cases, the Garuda carvings are extremely stylized and the bird's features are barely recognizable. Some of these hilt carvings are called kingfisher due to the intricacy of the carving. The hilt has a central perforation in the distal part where the tang (paksi), wrapped in a band of cloth, is inserted within. It is easy to understand how a powerful blow could dislodge or turn the blade, as the tang is short and cone-shaped and not permanently attached to the hilt. A ferrule (mendak) connects the hilt to the proximal part of the blade and the tang that is inserted inside. In better made krises, the ferrule is made from gold inlaid with precious stones. The blade can be wavy (dapor lok) or straight (dapor bener), and becomes wide at the proximal end (in Bahasa Indonesia called the ganja). Some krises have a hooked protuberance on the upper part of the ganja in the shape of an elephant's trunk. A central prominent line of the blade (dada) is in the shape of a serpent or dragon and made from inlaid gold, or gilded. The scabbard is usually made of wood, occasionally covered with repoussé sheets of gold or silver (pendak). A horizontal bar (wrangka) is located in the upper part of the scabbard. The wrangka on better quality Balinese krises are elegantly bow-shaped like an orchid and, in very rare specimens, have miniature floral paintings. A few specimens shown in our collection have these magnificent miniature paintings.

In the past, many aristocrats' homes featured a kris stand at the entrance, usually in a figural shape, where the kris was held vertically. Strict etiquette for holding and using the kris was followed, and many manuals were written about this subject. In combat, kris daggers were held in both hands—the left hand carrying the "family kris" used only in an imminent emergency, the right hand carrying the kris used for the actual fight. The Malayan men's vestment was a sarong, a cylindrical shaped garment folded on top. The kris was inserted in the right side of the fold to indicate a peaceful mood. In combat, when only the right hand kris was used, the scabbard would be held firmly while the kris was extricated from it, then the kris would be used vertically, directing the blow downward.

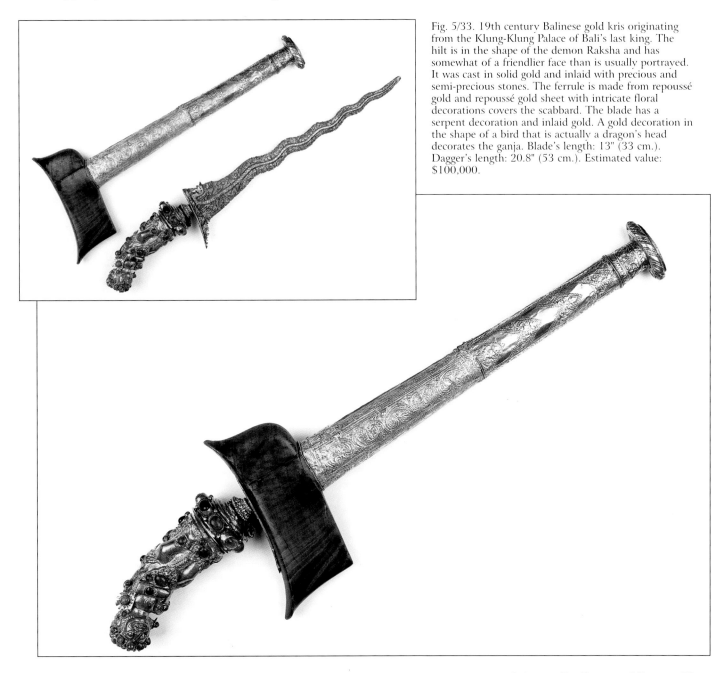

Fig. 5/33. 19th century Balinese gold kris originating from the Klung-Klung Palace of Bali's last king. The hilt is in the shape of the demon Raksha and has somewhat of a friendlier face than is usually portrayed. It was cast in solid gold and inlaid with precious and semi-precious stones. The ferrule is made from repoussé gold and repoussé gold sheet with intricate floral decorations covers the scabbard. The blade has a serpent decoration and inlaid gold. A gold decoration in the shape of a bird that is actually a dragon's head decorates the ganja. Blade's length: 13" (33 cm.). Dagger's length: 20.8" (53 cm.). Estimated value: $100,000.

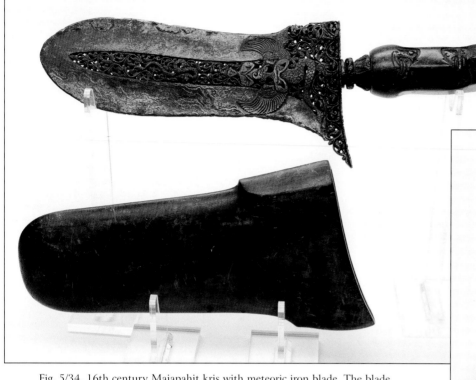

Fig. 5/34. 16th century Majapahit kris with meteoric iron blade. The blade decorations are phantasmagoric with mythological creatures above any description. The ganja has elaborate open work in metal, almost a filigree. A Garuda with open wings and serpent body is in the center of the blade. The center panel of the blade is in open work with a dragon design and serpent body. Elaborate damascene blade with fine pamor. This is an extremely rare dagger used for ceremonial rituals and of unsurpassed beauty for its metal open work. The scabbard and hilt are made from toned aged wood and only the hilt has carved decorations. Blade's length: 11" (28 cm.). Dagger's length: 18" (46 cm.). Estimated value: $15,000.

Fig. 5/35. Royal court ceremonial single-edged sword of very early manufacture, 15th century or earlier, probably a Majapahit sword. A search of world literature on the subject did not reveal any similar sword for comparison purposes. This sword resembles a klewang but does not have the widening toward the point that is typical for klewang. Without doubt, it belonged to a king or ruler. The decorations have no Islamic influence and are stylized, chiseled in high relief on the hilt and bas relief on the scabbard. The main decorations on the scabbard are duplicated above and below the central divination panel that represents a winged figure with open wings, or multi-armed divinity. Slightly curved hilt has a design that appears as a divinity eye continuing downward with what appears to be a clawed bird leg. The blade, which has a high content of meteoric iron, is straight and measures 16.5" (42 cm.). Sword's length: 21.5" (54.5 cm.). Estimated value: $8,000.

Fig. 5/36. Indonesia, Sumatra. Antique golok sword with dark brown toned ivory hilt. Judging by the aged ivory, we date this sword as early as 15th century or earlier. The back of the blade is straight and the cutting edge is convex. It has a wooden scabbard decorated with heavy silver ends. Blade's length: 19.5" (49.5 cm.). Sword's length: 27" (68.5 cm.). Estimated value: $7,000.

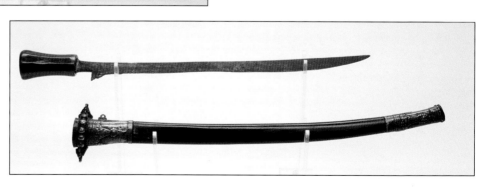

Fig. 5/37. 17th-18th century Javanese kris. Wooden hilt with carved decorations. The blade is much older, probably 13th-14th century with marked age deterioration. Straight edge blade (dapur bener). Silver pendok (scabbard's cover) with intricate repoussé floral decorations, inter-twined snakes and birds. The wrangka is made from kajoe pelet (black spotted brown wood). Blade's length: 12.8" (32.5 cm.). Dagger's length: 18" (46 cm.). Estimated value: $2,000.

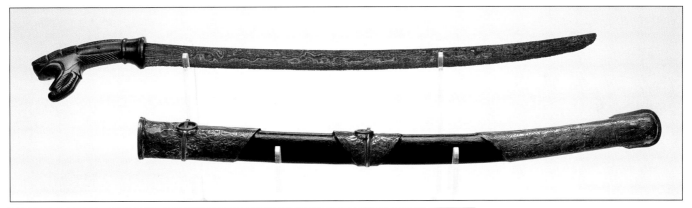

Fig. 5/38. Sumatra. Pedang sword dating to the 17th-18th century. The hilt is made from ivory that is aged with a brown-amber appearance and features the head of an animal with prominent snout. The blade is attached to the hilt through a metal pin and displays a damascene pattern of batulapan kulit pamor. Wooden scabbard with ornate copper at both ends and central portion. The copper ornaments are repoussé with incised hammering as well. Two rings are attached for connection to the belt. Blade's length: 23" (59 cm.). Sword's length: 31" (79 cm.). Estimated value: $5,500.

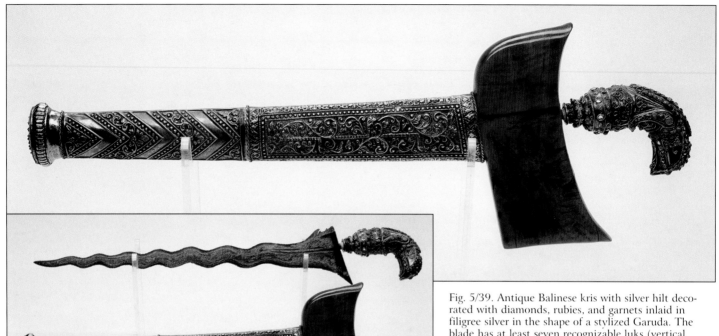

Fig. 5/39. Antique Balinese kris with silver hilt decorated with diamonds, rubies, and garnets inlaid in filigree silver in the shape of a stylized Garuda. The blade has at least seven recognizable luks (vertical striations in the blade) and a high content of pamir (meteoric iron). Highly ornate repoussé and chiseled silver pendak decorates the scabbard (sarong). The blade is wavy (dapur lok). The upper part of the pendak has a floral design, while the lower panel has a geometric pattern. The end of the scabbard is rounded and has filigree silver decorations. The kris dates to the 19th century and probably originates from the Klung-Klung Palace of the king. Blade's length: 15.3" (39 cm.). Dagger's length: 19" (49 cm.). Estimated value: $12,000.

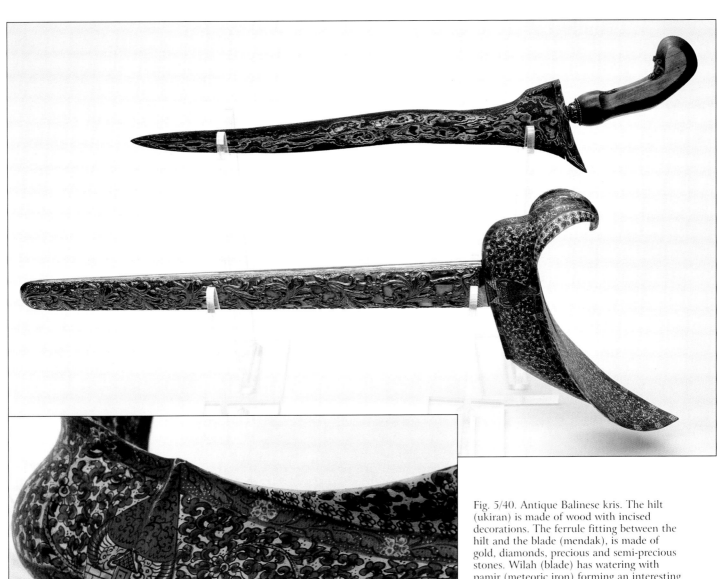

Fig. 5/40. Antique Balinese kris. The hilt (ukiran) is made of wood with incised decorations. The ferrule fitting between the hilt and the blade (mendak), is made of gold, diamonds, precious and semi-precious stones. Wilah (blade) has watering with pamir (meteoric iron) forming an interesting design of pamor. Sarong (scabbard) is covered with pendak yellow metal (gold alloy) decorated with floral ornaments in high relief. Wrangka (the wide top portion of the scabbard) is in the shape of an orchid flower and decorated with miniature hand paintings featuring temples, flowers, and leaves that are masterworks of 19th century Balinese art. Blade's length: 13.5" (34.2 cm.). Dagger's length: 19.8" (50 cm.). Estimated value: $6,000.

Fig. 5/41. 17th-18th century Javanese silver pedang sword. Solid silver hilt in the shape of a human figure holding the abdomen. The figure has very large eyes and a large nose, giving the impression of an owl or a primitive depiction of Garuda. Silver hand-guard is perpendicular to the hilt and repoussé decorated with floral design. Single-edged blade with intricate meteoric iron and nickel pamor. An inlaid silver dragon is located on the proximal end of the blade near the hilt. Corrosion of the edge is due to age and high iron content. Heavy silver sheet covers the scabbard, which is divided in three panels decorated with floral design. I purchased this sword in Jogjakarta in the 1980s and have never located a similar sword or even seen one like it in a museum or private collection. Blade's length: 21.5" (54.5 cm.). Sword's length: 29" (74 cm.). Estimated value: $5,000.

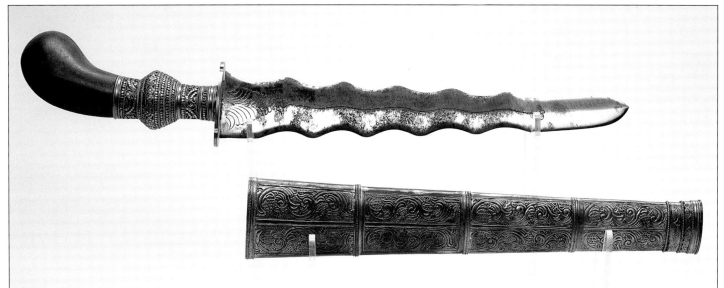

Fig. 5/42. Northern Borneo-Brunei Sultanate. Antique kris with elaborate repoussé and incised scabbard. The hilt is covered with filigree gold decorations. Wide wavy blade (dapur lok) in serpent shape with triangular decorations that start below the hand-guard and continue with a linear decoration along the center of the blade. Note: This sword has been included with the Indonesian swords, despite the fact that technically it would belong in the Malay swords and daggers section. Blade's length: 16" (40.5 cm.). Sword's length: 25" (63.5 cm.). Estimated value: $5,000.

Fig. 5/43. Indonesia-Sumbawa. 15th-16th century kris with toned ivory hilt. The blade is wavy (dapur lok) with five luks (longitudinal waves in the pamor). Blade's length: 11.5" (29 cm.). Dagger's length: 15" (38 cm.). Estimated value: $1,500.

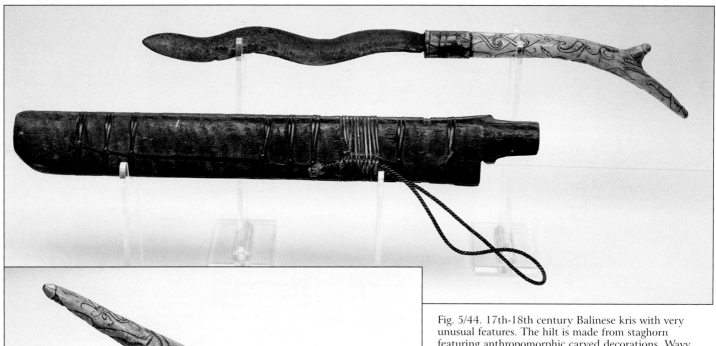

Fig. 5/44. 17th-18th century Balinese kris with very unusual features. The hilt is made from staghorn featuring anthropomorphic carved decorations. Wavy blade (dapur lok) with deep pitting and corrosion. The scabbard appears to be Malay rather than Balinese. It is made from intricate carved wood with several rattan bindings. This sword was purchased in Sanur, Bali in the 1980s. Blade's length: 11" (28 cm.). Sword's length: 30.2" (77 cm.). Estimated value: $2,500.

Fig. 5/45. 18th century executioner kris with toned ivory hilt in the shape of a stylized Garuda. The mendak (metal fitting ferrule between the blade and the hilt) is made of repoussé decorated gold. A straight blade (dapur bener) has watering with elaborate pamor (meteoric iron forging pattern). Wooden sarong (scabbard). Ganja (the upper part of the blade) has an elephant's head decoration. Blade's length: 13.5" (34.2 cm.). Dagger's length: 18" (45.8 cm.). Estimated value: $5,000.

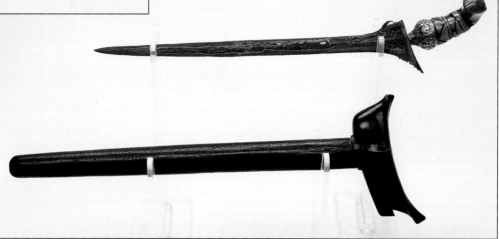

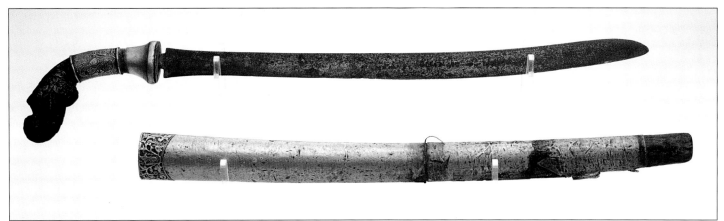

Fig. 5/46. Indonesia-Sumbawa. 18th century silver klewang. The hilt and scabbard are covered with silver. Carved wooden pommel with semi-abstract design features a dragon's head. Single-edged straight blade (dapur bener) appears to be at least two to three centuries older than the sword and the edge dents point toward extensive prior use. Blade's length: 18.2" (46.5 cm.). Sword's length: 29" (73.8 cm.). Estimated value: $2,500.

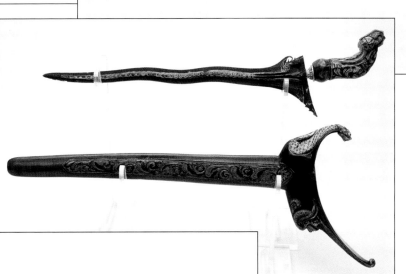

Fig. 5/47. Antique Balinese kris. The ukiran (hilt) is made from polychrome wood in the shape of a naga (serpent)—a very rare rendition of hilt carvings. Mendak (fitting ferrule between the hilt and the blade) is made from gold with diamonds in a circular setting. Wilah (blade) has watering with meteoric iron (pamir) intricate pattern. Sarong (scabbard) is made from wood with polychrome hand paintings. Wrangka has decorations in high relief and polychrome painting and appears as an orchid. The short end of the wrangka is in the shape of a dragon with a cobra's body and head protruding above. The long end is in the shape of a winged mythological creature. Galar (straight part of the scabbard) is decorated with polychrome floral design. Blade's length: 13.5" (34.2 cm.). Dagger's length: 19.2" (49 cm.). Estimated value: $4,500.

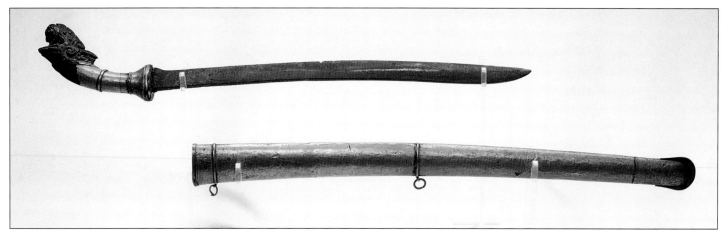

Fig. 5/48. Indonesia-Sumbawa. 18th century silver klewang. The hilt and scabbard are covered with silver. Wooden pommel with semi-abstract design featuring a dragon's head. Single-edged straight blade that displays considerable aging. Blade's length: 18.2" (46.5 cm.). Sword's length: 29" (73.8 cm.). Estimated value: $2,500.

Fig. 5/49. Indonesia-Lombok. Silver covered short sword with repoussé decorations. The hilt is slightly angled and a silver hand-guard with two quillons is soldered to it. One upward oriented quillon has an animal head end, while the downward oriented quillon is flat. The obverse side of the scabbard has a wide cartouche that is blank. The blade is straight and much older than the sword, probably dating to the 14th-15th century; the sword itself dates to the 18th-19th century. Sword's length: 18.5" (47 cm.). Blade's length: 10.1" (27 cm.). Estimated value: $1,500-1,800.

Fig. 5/50. 18th century Balinese kris with ivory hilt carved in the shape of a horse's head and human body. Filigree silver forms the mendak. Wavy blade (dapur lok) with fine pamor. An elephant trunk is visible on the ganja. Sarong covered with repoussé silver with fine, intricate design. The wrangka is in the shape of an orchid or a boat. Blade's length: 12.2" (31 cm.). Dagger's length: 18.5" (47 cm.). Estimated value: $3,500.

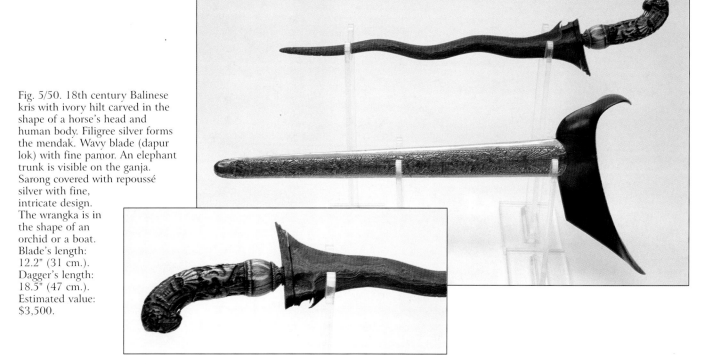

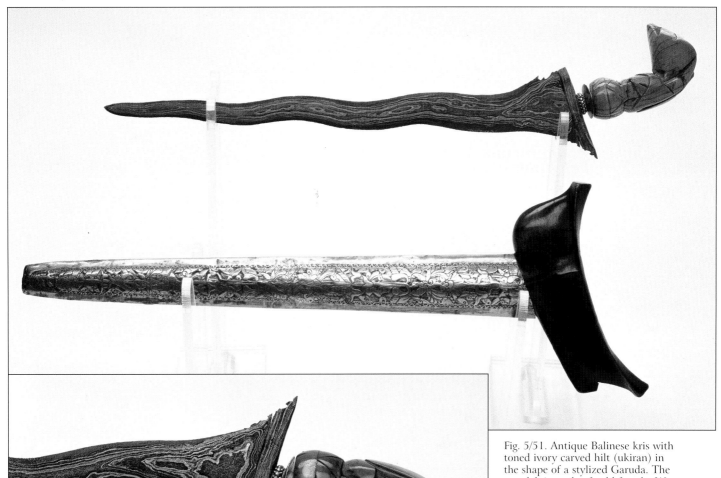

Fig. 5/51. Antique Balinese kris with toned ivory carved hilt (ukiran) in the shape of a stylized Garuda. The mendak is made of gold ferrule. Wavy blade (dapor lok) with fine pamir (meteoric iron). The damascene blade has eight recognizable luks (longitudinal striations resulting from forging the blade). Sarong (scabbard) is covered with repoussé and hammered silver sheet (pendok) forming a floral pattern. Dates to 18th century or earlier. Blade's length: 13" (33 cm.). Dagger's length: 17.5" (44.5 cm.). Estimated value: $2,000.

Fig. 5/52. Antique Javanese kris with typical Javanese carved wood ukiran (hilt) and incised decorations on the inner side. Sarong (scabbard) with hammered silver pendak having an intricate design pattern with elephants, mythological creatures, horse, and floral decorations. Wilah (blade) has fine pamir and straight blade (dapur bener) with damascene pattern. Blade's length: 13.8" (35 cm.). Dagger's length: 20" (51 cm.). Estimated value: $1,400.

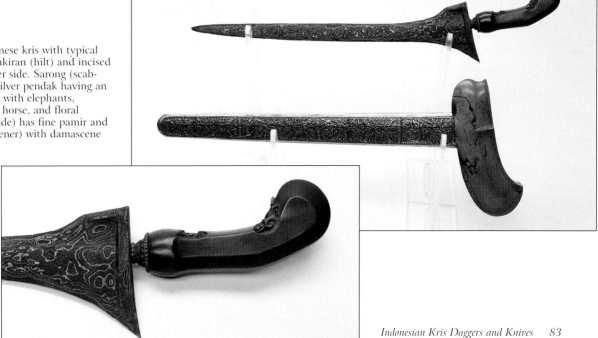

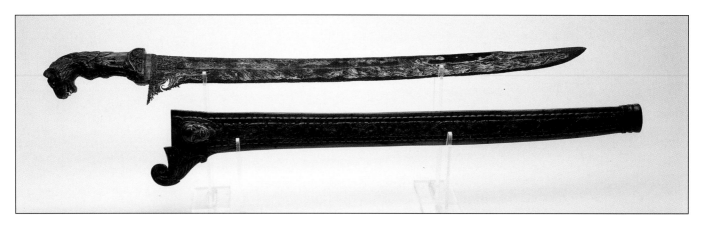

Fig. 5/53. Antique long sword Madura Pedang Larajan. The hilt and scabbard are made from intricately carved wood. A carved wood lion forms the hilt and the lion's head is actually the pommel. Watered blade with meteoric iron (pamor). An elephant's trunk is visible on the ganja (upper part of the blade). One fuller is present on the upper part of the blade's back. Floral decorations and a woman's head decorate the scabbard. Blade's length: 29.1" (74 cm.). Sword's length: 37" (94 cm.). Estimated value: $5,000.

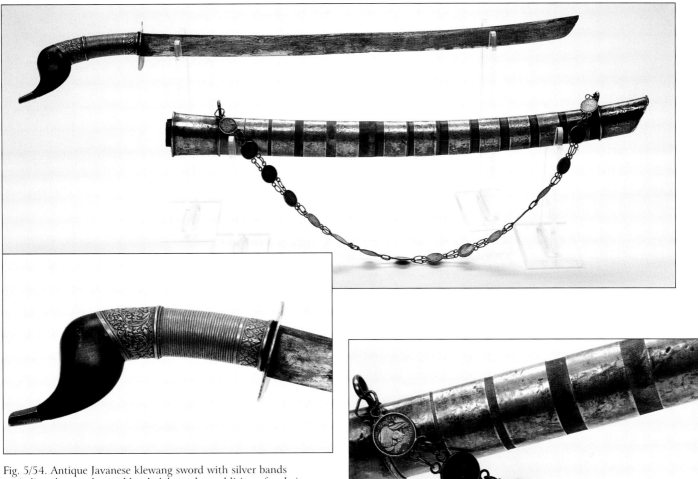

Fig. 5/54. Antique Javanese klewang sword with silver bands encircling the wooden scabbard. A later date addition of a chain made from Indonesian silver coins assists with holding the sword. Silver hilt with intricately chiseled floral decorations. Wooden pommel in the shape of a stylized Garuda. Single-edged blade with a small silver hand-guard. Blade's length: 20.5" (52 cm.). Sword's length: 27.1" (69 cm.). Estimated value: $2,800.

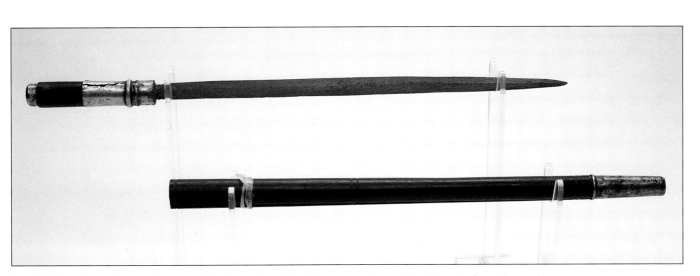

Fig. 5/55. Sumbawa. Antique silver sword dating to the 17th-18th century. The scabbard is made from silver and wood. Straight blade (dapur bener) with watering and fine pamir (meteoric iron). Blade's length: 16.2" (39.5 cm.). Sword's length: 24.2" (61.5 cm.). Estimated value: $1,200.

Fig. 5/56. 18th-19th century Balinese kris with staghorn hilt in the shape of demonic Raksha. Mendak ferrule is made from brass and colored glass beads imitating precious stones. Wilah (blade) is wavy (dapur lok) and displays fine pamor with an elephant trunk visible on the ganja. Sarong (scabbard) is covered with repoussé brass (pendak). Some worm holes are present in the wrangka, pointing toward the old age. Blade's length: 18.2" (46.5 cm.). Sword's length: 26.5" (67.2 cm.). Estimated value: $3,500.

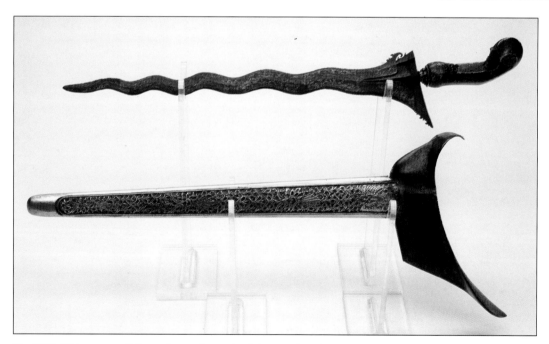

Fig. 5/57. 18th century Balinese kris with wooden hilt carved in the shape of a stylized Garuda. Wilah (blade) is wavy (dapur lok), watered, and has more than twelve visible luks. An elephant trunk is visible on the ganja's top. Sarong (scabbard) is decorated with repoussé silver on the obverse side. Wrangka is elongated and wide in the shape of an orchid petal. Silver and diamonds decorate the mendak. Blade's length: 14.5" (37 cm.). Dagger's length: 20" (51 cm.). Estimated value: $3,500.

Fig. 5/58. Javanese kris with wooden hilt and scabbard. The hilt is carved in the shape of a stylized lion's head. Inlaid gold decorates the blade that is wavy (dapur lok). The central line of the blade ends with a dragon's head on the ganja. Meteoric iron (pamir) is present in the blade that shows extensive watering. The mendak is made from gold and mounted with precious stones. Sarong (scabbard) is made from wood decorated with incised ornaments. Blade's length: 13.5" (34.2 cm.). Dagger's length: 20" (51 cm.). Estimated value: $3,250.

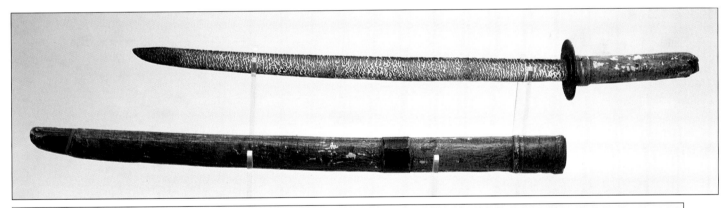

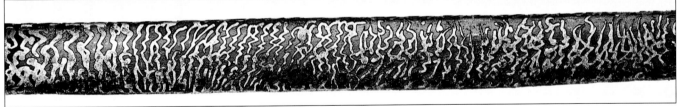

Fig. 5/59. Indonesia-Sumbawa. 15th-16th century sword. The hilt and scabbard are covered with lacquered leather that resisted age deterioration better than the exposed wood of the hilt and scabbard, which show signs of age decomposition. The blade is covered entirely with inlaid silver inscriptions involving even the back edge. The hand-guard is oval in shape with crenellated edges. Blade's length: 21.2" (54 cm.). Sword's length: 31.5" (80 cm.). Estimated value: $4,000.

Fig. 5/60. 18th century Balinese kris with elaborate carved ivory ukiran (hilt) in the shape of a horse. Wavy blade (dapur lok). Intricate meteoric iron pamor pattern in the blade. Silver mendak with diamonds or rock crystal beads. The scabbard (sarong) is covered with repoussé golden metal sheet (gold alloy) decorated with peacocks and floral design. Orchid petal shaped wrangka with incised carvings. Blade's length: 14" (36 cm.). Dagger's length: 18.5" 947 cm.). Estimated value: $2,500.

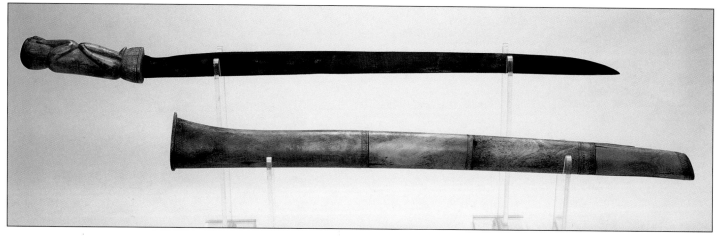

Fig. 5/61. Sumatra. Pedang sword with bone hilt and scabbard. The hilt has elaborate bone carving in the shape of squatting human figure covering the face with both hands. A bone belt hook is attached to the scabbard. The blade is plain and measures 22" (56 cm.). Sword's length: 28.5" (72.5 cm.). Estimated value: $1,500.

Fig. 5/62. 18th-19th century Javanese kris with wooden hilt in the shape of a stylized Garuda. The blade (wilah) is straight (dapur bener) with fine pamor. Repoussé and chiseled silver decorate the scabbard (sarong). Blade's length: 14" (35.5 cm.). Dagger's length: 19" (48.2 cm.). Estimated value: $1,500.

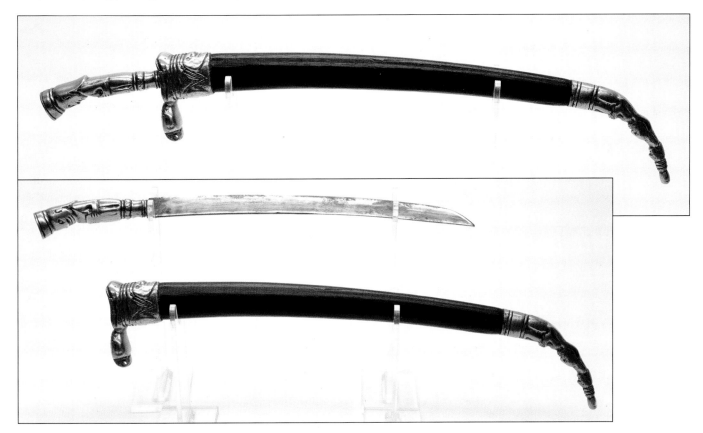

Fig. 5/63. Sumatra. Batak sword with intricate silver decorations. The scabbard is made of wood with heavy silver anthropomorphic ornaments at the ends. The distal part is shaped as a squatting man carrying a cone-head man on his back. The proximal part has human faces displayed, even on the top of the hand-guard. A standing man with a flat hat and holding his abdomen forms the hilt. The blade has the cutting edge on the convex side and was held upright for slashing rather than piercing. Length without scabbard: 19.2" (49 cm.). Sword's length: 25.2" (64 cm.). Estimated value: $2,000.

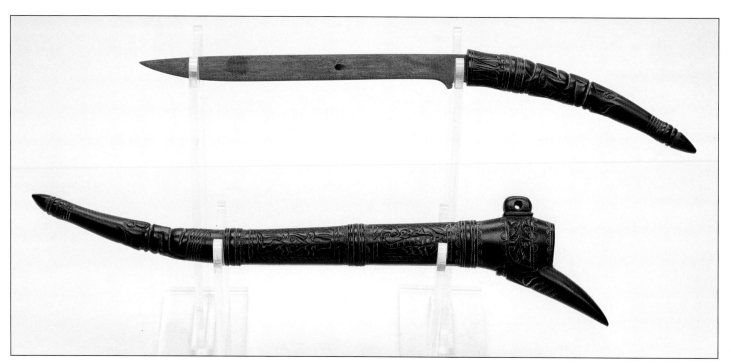

Fig. 5/64. Sumatra. 19th-20th century Batak dagger with intricate wooden carvings on the hilt and scabbard. The hilt has an anthropo-zoomorphic design featuring a man riding an unidentified animal with a mask-like head. The hand-guard has an anthropomorphic carving featuring a cone-head man. The center of the hand-guard has a leaf design carving. A scorpion and a crocodile decorate each side of the scabbard, which ends in the shape of a kneeling cone-head man in a position of prayer. Damascene blade with straight back and slightly concave cutting edge. Size: 8.6" (22 cm). Dagger's length: 20" (51 cm.). Estimated value: $950.

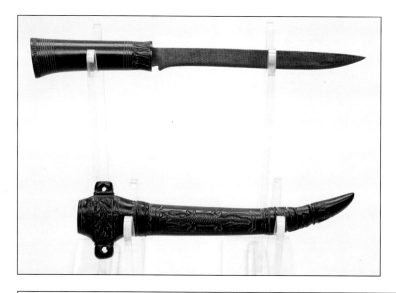

Fig. 5/65. Sumatra. 19th-20th century Batak dagger with intricate high relief carving on the scabbard and the hilt. A scorpion is featured on one side of the scabbard, a carving resembling a crocodile on the other. The distal end of the scabbard is formed by a kneeling human figure with cone-head. High content of iron is present in the blade alloy. While the blade is straight, the cutting edge is slightly concave. Blade's length: 6.4" (16.2 cm.). Dagger's length: 11.5" (29.2 cm.). Estimated value: $700.

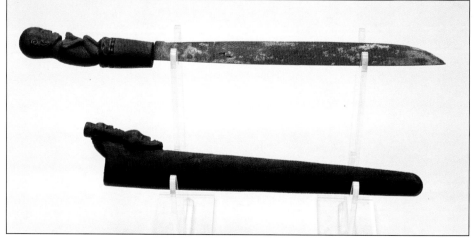

Fig. 5/66. Sumatra. Batak long dagger decorated with anthropomorphic design. It is made from carved wood and the hilt represents a squatting human figure in a position of prayer. The upper part of the scabbard is decorated with two juxta-posed human heads. The upper figure wears a cylindrical hat, but probably has a cone-head. Blade's length: 11.2" (28.5 cm.). Dagger's length: 17.2" (44 cm.). Estimated value: $1,200.

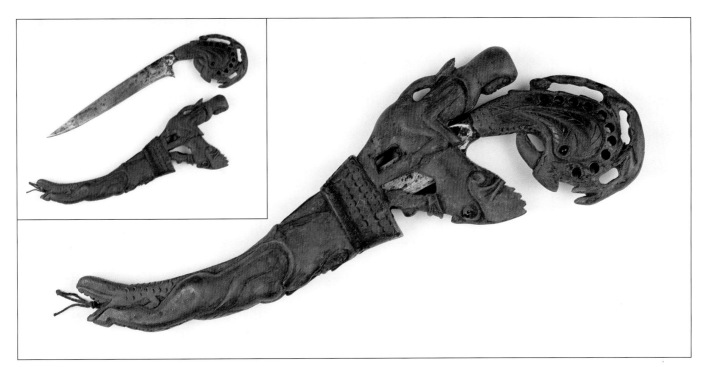

Fig. 5/67. Sumatra. Batak dagger with very elaborate decorative design. The scabbard has a woman riding a mythological animal while the hilt is in the shape of a bird. Scabbard's chape is in the shape of a crocodile. The entire dagger is carved in exotic wood with the proximal part of the scabbard in the shape of a nude woman. Single-edged blade created by an indigenous blacksmith. Blade's length: 6.2" (16 cm). Dagger's length: 11" (28 cm.). Estimated value: $950.

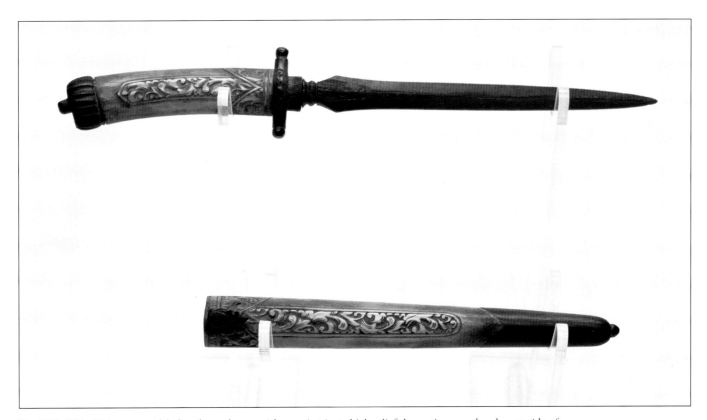

Fig. 5/68. 19th-20th century. Madura bone dagger with very intricate high relief decorations on the obverse side of the scabbard. Islamic influence is present in the carvings, which have a floral or leaf design pattern. The scabbard, pommel, and hand-guard are made of wood. Peculiar diamond shaped blade displaying damascene watering. WP is incised on the tip of the blade, originating probably from the recycled original blade. Size without scabbard: 12.9" (32.7 cm.). Dagger's length: 13.5" (34.2 cm.). Estimated value: $750.

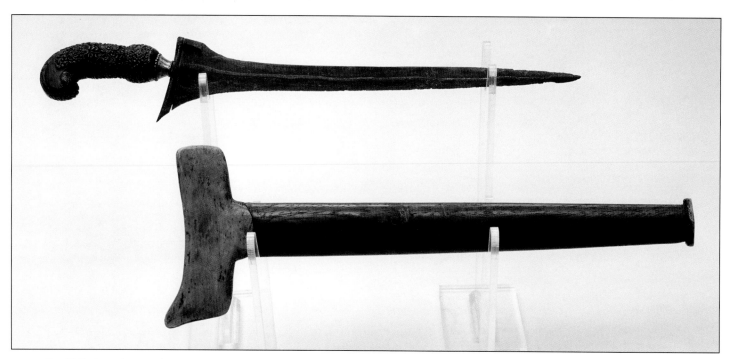

Fig. 5/69. Java. Antique kris sword dating to the 18th-19th century. Wooden hilt carved with minute detailed decorations and in the shape of a stylized Garuda. The blade (wilah) is straight (dapur bener) and displays pamir (meteoric iron) that has undergone age deterioration. Wooden scabbard (sarong) with bone wrangka as well as the chape. Blade's length: 12.2" (31 cm.). Dagger's length: 18.5" (47 cm.). Estimated value: $1,500.

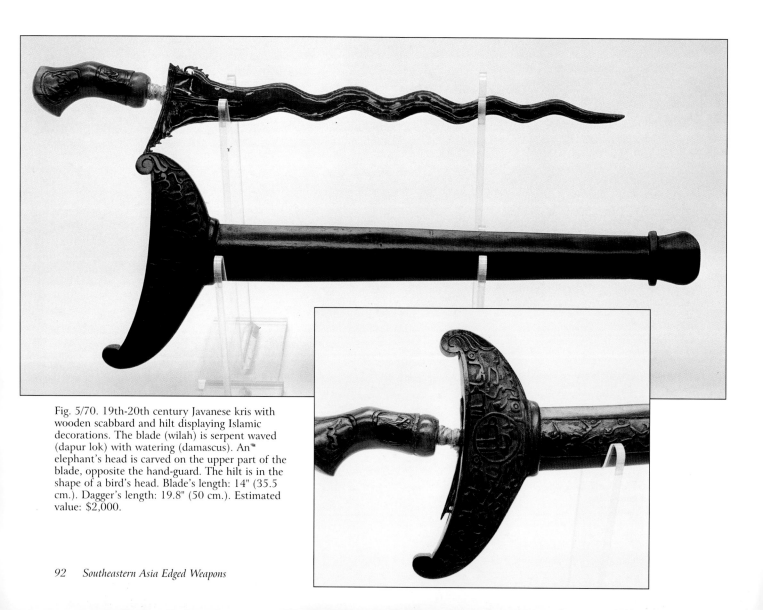

Fig. 5/70. 19th-20th century Javanese kris with wooden scabbard and hilt displaying Islamic decorations. The blade (wilah) is serpent waved (dapur lok) with watering (damascus). An elephant's head is carved on the upper part of the blade, opposite the hand-guard. The hilt is in the shape of a bird's head. Blade's length: 14" (35.5 cm.). Dagger's length: 19.8" (50 cm.). Estimated value: $2,000.

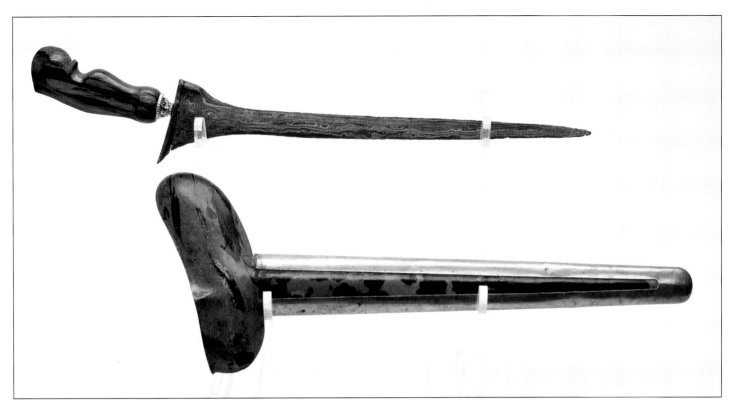

Fig. 5/71. Java. 19th century kris dagger with double-edged straight blade (dapur bener). The scabbard and hilt are made from kajoe pelet (a peculiar tropical wood with burl dark impressions). The high luster gives the wood an appearance similar to tortoise shell. Watered blade with fine pamir and at least nine distinguishable luks. The mendak is made from gold with mounted precious stones. A yellow metal jacket encases the scabbard, but a central portion of kajoe pelet is visible. Blade's length: 11.8" (30 cm.). Dagger's length: 18" (45.6 cm.). Estimated value: $1,500.

Fig. 5/72. Kalimantan. Antique kris with wooden scabbard and hilt. The hilt has elaborate detailed decorations carved in exotic wood with the general appearance of a dragon's head. The blade is decorated with inlaid gold and the ganja that has an inlaid gold dragon. Well watered blade measuring 13.8" (35.5 cm.). Dagger's length: 20" (51 cm.). Estimated value: $3,500.

Fig. 5/73. 19th-20th century kris with silver hilt (ukiran) in the shape of a Garuda with human body and bird's head. Wavy blade (dapur lok) watered with fine meteoric iron (pamir). An elephant's trunk is present on the ganja. The scabbard (sarong) is made of wood and partially covered with chased and repoussé silver with floral design alternating with a grain pattern in the upper and lower part of the scabbard. Blade's length: 13.5" (34.3 cm.). Dagger's length: 19.2" (49 cm.). Estimated value: $1,000.

Fig. 5/74. 19th century kris with hilt in the shape of kingfisher (stylized Garuda with long beak), carved in tropical wood. The blade is wavy (dapur lok) with watering. Blade's length: 13.5" (34 cm.). Dagger's length: 18" (46 cm.). Estimated value: $750.

Fig. 5/75. Sumbawa. 18th century or earlier kris with wavy blade (dapur lok) that appears to be as early as 14th-15th century with visible inlaid gold in the upper portion. An elephant's trunk is identified on the ganja. At least nine luks are identified on the blade, which was probably buried for a prolonged period of time. A stylized figure of Garuda carved in wood forms the hilt. The scabbard (sarong) is made of wood without decoration. Blade's length: 14.8" (37.5 cm.). Dagger's length: 18" (45.7 cm.). Estimated value: $1,600.

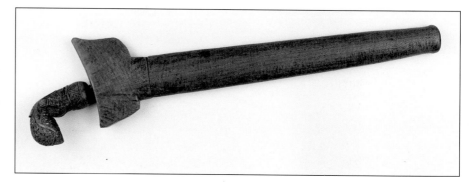

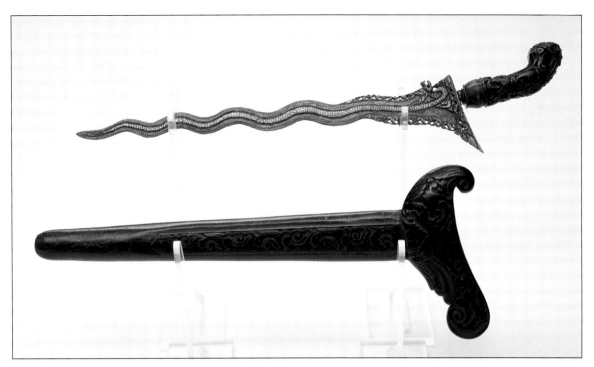

Fig. 5/76. 19th century kris with exquisite wood carving on both the hilt and the scabbard. The hilt is in the shape of a dragon's head. Wavy blade (dapur lok)with gilded dragon in the center. Meteoric iron is present with intricate pamor design. Blade's length: 13.5" (34 cm.). Dagger's length: 18" (45.7 cm.). Estimated value: $2,000.

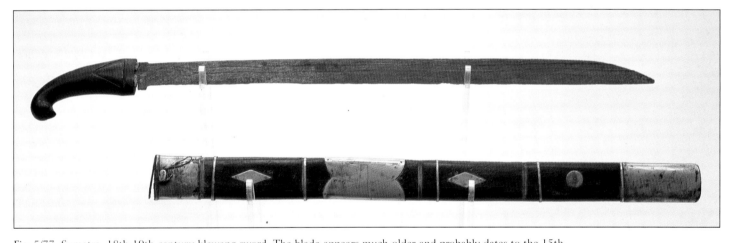

Fig. 5/77. Sumatra. 18th-19th century klewang sword. The blade appears much older and probably dates to the 15th-16th century at least. Single-edged blade with intricate pamor (meteoric iron pattern). The hilt is made from black hardwood in the shape of bird's head. Wooden scabbard decorated with silver bands with etched pattern. Blade's length: 20.9" (53 cm.). Sword's length: 25.5" (65 cm.). Estimated value: $2,000.

Fig. 5/78. Bali. 18th century kris purchased in Sanur in the early 80s. Wooden hilt and scabbard with gold painted decorations that have slightly faded with age. The blade is much older—as is typical with older kris daggers—probably dating to the 13th-14th century and is wavy (dapur lok). Due to the high iron content of the blade, age deterioration has occurred. Blade's length: 13.2" (33.5 cm.). Dagger's length: 19.7" (50 cm.). Estimated value: $1,500.

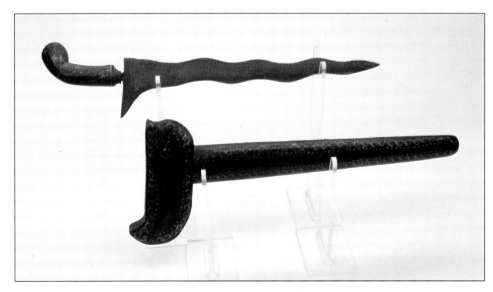

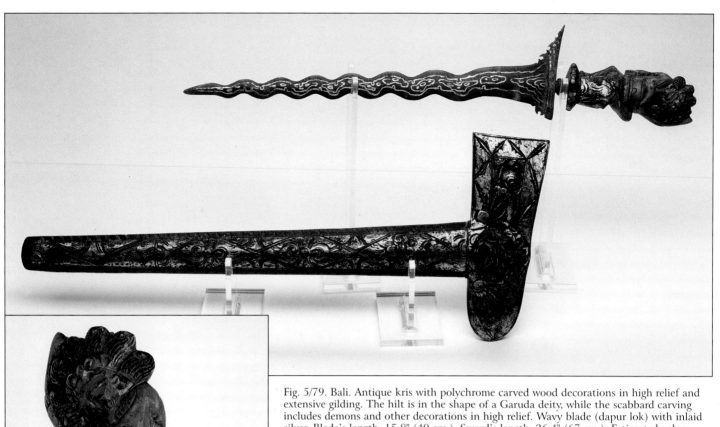

Fig. 5/79. Bali. Antique kris with polychrome carved wood decorations in high relief and extensive gilding. The hilt is in the shape of a Garuda deity, while the scabbard carving includes demons and other decorations in high relief. Wavy blade (dapur lok) with inlaid silver. Blade's length: 15.8" (40 cm.). Sword's length: 26.4" (67 cm.). Estimated value: $1,000.

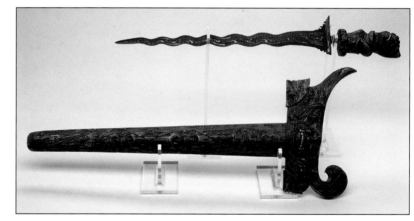

Fig. 5/80. Bali. Antique kris sword with hilt made from carved wood in the shape of a demonic Raksha with polychrome paintings. Gilded ferrule with multi-colored semi-precious stones or glass beads. The scabbard is carved in high relief and covered with polychrome paintings featuring demons and other intricate decorations. Boat shaped wrangka. Wavy blade (dapur lok) with damascene design and meteoric iron. Blade's length: 15.3" (39 cm.). Sword's length: 25.5" (65 cm.). Estimated value: $1,500.

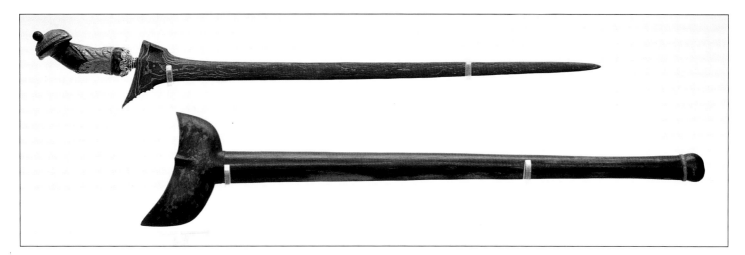

Fig. 5/81. Java. Antique executioner's sword. The hilt (ukiran) is in the shape of a stylized bird (Garuda) and carved in high relief using two colors of tropical wood. The blade (wilah) is long, narrow, and straight with signs of extensive watering of forged meteoric iron. Blade's length: 20.8" (53 cm.). Sword's length: 27.5" (70 cm.). Estimated value: $1,000.

Fig. 5/82. Java. 18th century kris with hilt and scabbard made from kajoe pelet wood. Wavy blade (dapur lok) with complex pamor. The hilt is in the shape of a highly stylized bird. Mendak made from brass and semi-precious stones (possibly high quality colored glass beads). Blade's length: 14.2" (36 cm.). Sword's length: 23.8" (60.5 cm.). Estimated value: $900.

Fig. 5/83. 19th century klewang sword with lacquered wooden hilt and scabbard. The scabbard is bound with rattan bands. The blade has an interesting meteoric iron watering. Blade's length: 20.8" (53 cm.). Estimated value: $800.

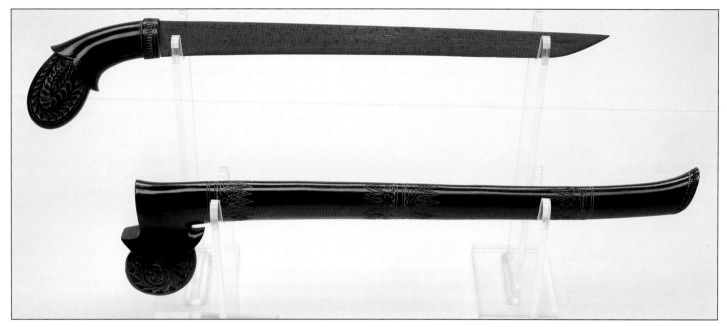

Fig. 5/84. Sumatra. Menangkabau dagger made from mahogany wood with intricate stylized floral decorations on the hilt and scabbard. The upper part of the scabbard has a rounded protuberance giving the appearance of a pistol. Damascene blade with longitudinal pamor bands narrowing toward the point. Blade's length: 13.2" (33.5 cm.). Sword's length: 20" (51 cm.). Estimated value: $700.

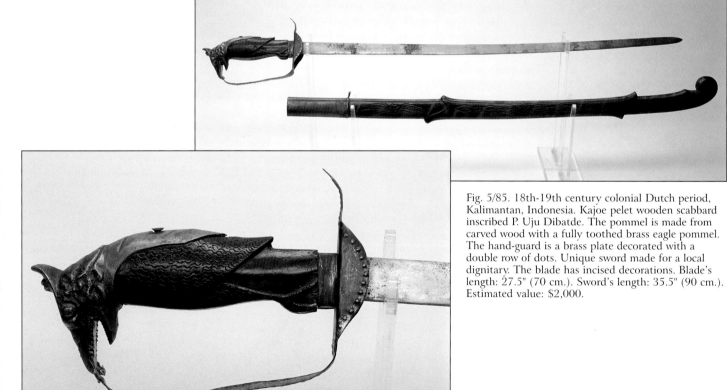

Fig. 5/85. 18th-19th century colonial Dutch period, Kalimantan, Indonesia. Kajoe pelet wooden scabbard inscribed P. Uju Dibatde. The pommel is made from carved wood with a fully toothed brass eagle pommel. The hand-guard is a brass plate decorated with a double row of dots. Unique sword made for a local dignitary. The blade has incised decorations. Blade's length: 27.5" (70 cm.). Sword's length: 35.5" (90 cm.). Estimated value: $2,000.

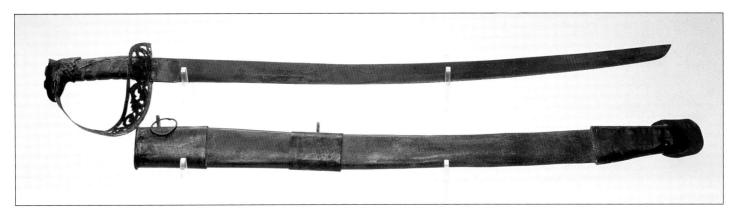

Fig. 5/86. 18th century colonial Dutch period sword dated 1748 and inscribed with the name Agsavercool, Batavia (Java). Basket shield hand-guard. An eagle's head forms the pommel. Blade's length: 28" (71 cm.). Sword's length: 29" (74 cm.). This sword is extremely rare and probably unique! Estimated value: $5,000.

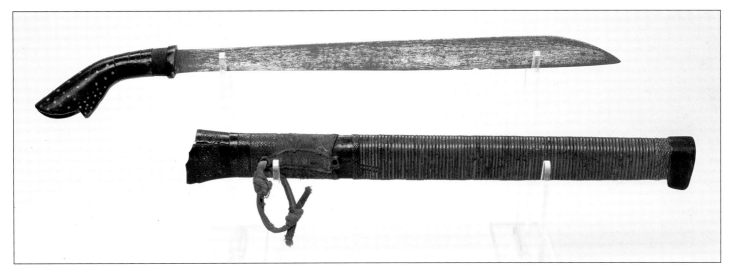

Fig. 5/87. Sumatra. 18th century golok sword. Wooden hilt in the shape of a pistol with inlaid ivory pegs. Single-edged blade with fine damascus. As is typical for this type of sword, the blade widens toward the point, giving strength in cutting or slicing. Wooden scabbard with elaborate proximal end carving. Rattan bands of different dimensions wrap around the scabbard. The chape is made of wood with a central portion made from ivory that is considerably aged. Blade's length: 18.5" (47 cm.). Sword's length: 26" (66 cm.). Estimated value: $2,500.

Fig. 5/88. Central Sumatra. 19th century kris with wooden hilt in the shape of a pistol and representing a stylized bird. The blade is wavy (dapur lok). Fine pamor with gilded dada (central raised line of the blade ending in a dragon's head). The mendak is made of silver and decorated with diamonds. Wooden scabbard without ornaments. Blade's length: 13.5" (34.2 cm.). Sword's length: 21" (53.3 cm.). Estimated value: $2,500.

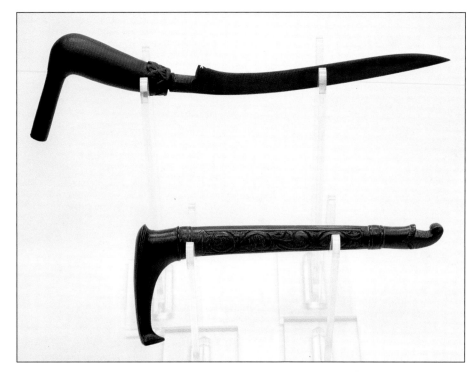

Fig. 5/89. Sumatra. 19th-20th century Rechong Acehnese bade-bade dagger with decorated wooden hilt and scabbard. Black wooden hilt carved in the shape of a stylized bird. The scabbard is decorated with floral and leaf decorations. Slightly curved blade is sharp on the concave edge. Blade's length: 8" (20 cm.). Dagger's length: 14" (36 cm.). Estimated value: $500.

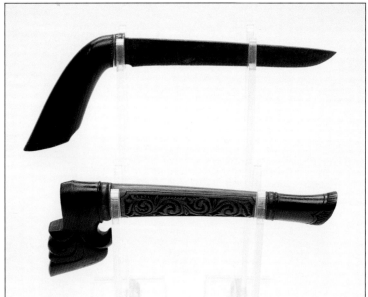

Fig. 5/90. Sumatra. Rechong Acehnese bade-bade dagger made from carved black horn, except for the central portion of the scabbard, which is made from wood carved in high relief. Peculiar for this type of dagger is the pistol shape formed by the scabbard's upper end, which appears as a stylized bird's head. Watered blade with fine damascene pattern. Blade's length: 6.5" (16.5 cm.). Dagger's length: 11.5" (29.2 cm.). Estimated value: $800.

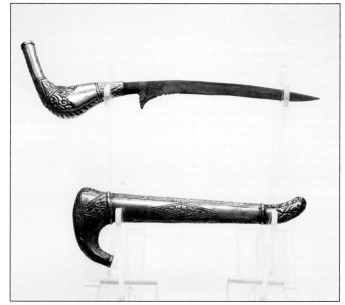

Fig. 5/91. Sumatra. Antique Rechong bade-bade dagger with ornate repoussé and hammered silver scabbard and hilt. Originates from Aceh, Northern Sumatra. The ornaments are typical for the Islamic influence with a floral and leaf design pattern. Single-edged blade, narrow and sharp on the concave edge. Superficial corrosion of the blade is due to the high content of iron in the blade. The hilt is in the shape of a stylized bird. Blade's length: 8" (20 cm.). Dagger's length: 16.8" (42.5 cm.). Estimated value: $1,000.

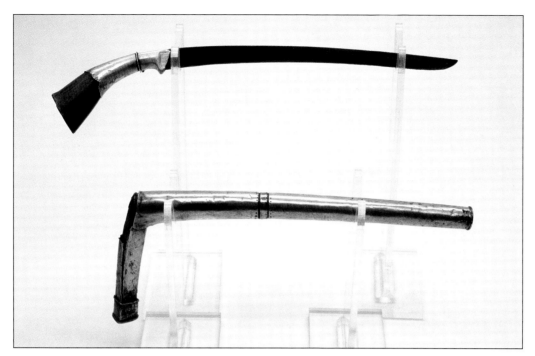

Fig. 5/92. Sumatra. 19th century Rechong Acehnese bade-bade dagger with hilt and scabbard covered with silver. The pommel is made from horn. Typically, the scabbard's upper end forms a right angle to the rest, having the shape of a pistol butt. Watered blade, sharp on the concave edge. Blade's length: 9" (23 cm.). Dagger's length: 13.5" (34.2 cm.). Estimated value: $900.

Fig. 5/93. Sumatra. Rechong bade-bade dagger with ornate repoussé and hammered silver scabbard and hilt. Originates from Aceh, Northern Sumatra. The Islamic influence is seen in the silver decorations that have a floral and leaf design. Narrow blade with concave cutting edge. The hilt is in the shape of a stylized bird's head. Blade's length: 9" (23 cm.). Dagger's length: 14" (36 cm.). Estimated value: $800.

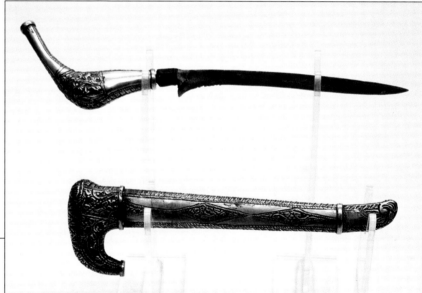

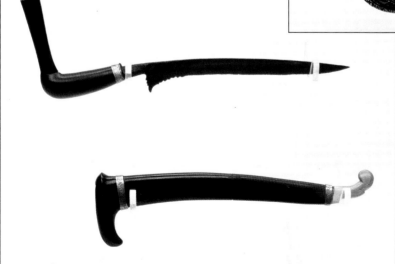

Fig. 5/94. Sumatra. Antique Rechong Acehnese bade-bade dagger with black horn hilt and scabbard. The scabbard's end is formed by a carved ivory piece with yellow-brown tone, attesting to its old age. Two bands of hammered silver decorate the scabbard. The bird shape of the hilt is typical for this type of dagger, which originates from Aceh, Sumatra. Damascene blade containing meteoric iron. The cutting edge of the blade is incurved with concave cutting edge. Blade's length: 8.5" (21.5 cm.). Dagger's length: 15.2" (38.7 cm.). Estimated value: $800.

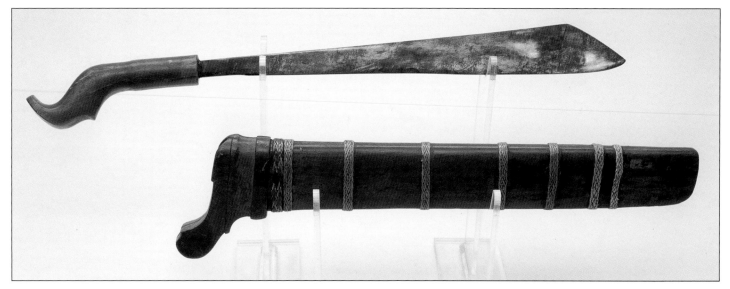

Fig. 5/95. Sumatra. 19th century golok sword. The hilt is made from carved yellow horn. There is a progressive widening of the blade toward the point, giving this sword enhanced power due to a balance point located in the distal third of the blade. Single-edged blade with triangular shaped point. Wooden scabbard decorated with rattan bands that hold the scabbard's sides together. It appears pistol shaped due to angulation of the proximal end of the scabbard and the hilt's pommel. which is angled as well. Blade's length: 15.3" (39 cm.). Sword's length: 22.5" (57 cm.). Estimated value: $700.

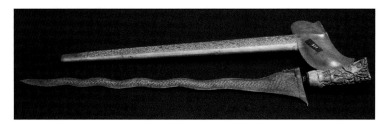

Fig. 5/96. Indonesia-Spice Islands kris dating to the 19th century. The hilt is made from carved bone in the shape of the demon Raksha. Wavy blade (dapur lok), with a carved serpent on both sides of the blade. A repoussé sheet of brass with floral design covers the scabbard. Dagger's length: 19" (48 cm.). Blade's length: 15" (38 cm.). Estimated value: $350-$450.

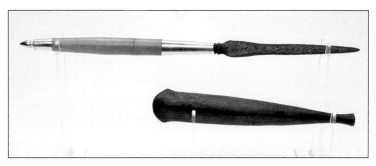

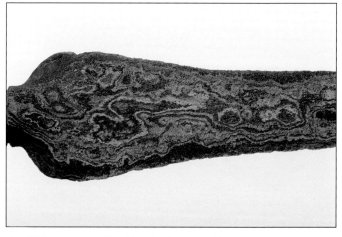

Fig. 5/97. Indonesian spear. Majapahit tombak. Narrow, double-edged watered blade spear with scabbard dating to 15th century. The handle is of more recent manufacture (20th century). Blade's length: 8.2" (21 cm.). Spear's length: 34.5" (87.5 cm.). Estimated value: $800.

Fig. 5/98. Indonesia. Double-edged straight blade spear with fine pamor. The blade is considerably older than the scabbard and the spear's handle, which are of 20th century manufacture. Floral decorations adorn the proximal end of the scabbard. Blade's length: 11" (28 cm.). Spear's length: 37.8" (96 cm.). Estimated value: $750.

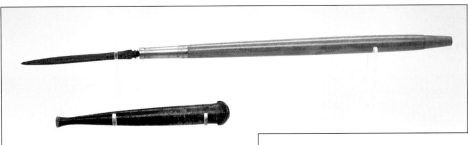

Fig. 5/99. Java tombak spear with 15th century, straight, double-edged blade. Meteoric iron with elaborate pamor pattern is present in the blade. The 20th century handle is made from wood with brass decorations at the ends. The scabbard appears to be 19th century or earlier and is made from unadorned wood. Blade's length: 10" (25.5 cm.). Spear's length: 27" (68.5 cm.). Estimated value: $600.

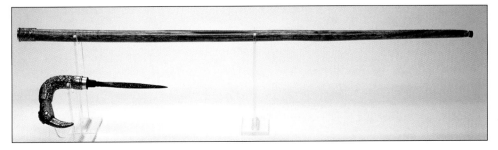

Fig. 5/100. Indonesia. 20th century cane-sword. Silver hilt with repoussé design of a bird's head and floral decor. Fine blade with meteoric iron pamor. Wood cane with silver mount for the hilt. Blade's length: 7" (18 cm.). Estimated value: $450.

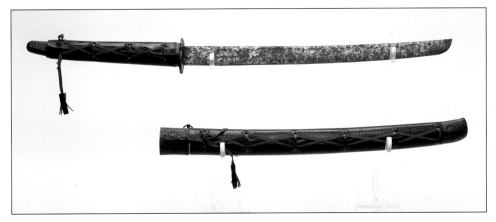

Fig. 5/101. Java. 20th century short sword purchased in Jogjakarta in the 1980s. The scabbard and hilt are covered with black leather tied with red ribbon through eyelets in the leather. Small hand-guard of oval shape. The single-edged blade is rusty, but still sharp. The sword is of Japanese origin, or made to imitate the Japanese wakizashi. Blade's length: 14.5" (37 cm.). Sword's length: 24.5" (62 cm.). Estimated value: $650.

Fig. 5/102. Indonesia. Bali. Collection of batik kris covers with the kris daggers enclosed within.

Malay and Philippine Swords, Daggers, and Knives

The Malayan *golok* is a machete type dagger with a recognizable single-edged straight blade that widens progressively toward the point. Another popular Malayan dagger is the *bade-bade*, a dagger with an angled, pistol-shaped hilt and single-edged narrow blade that is concave on the cutting side. A related type of bade-bade is the *rechong*, which originates from the Aceh region in the northern part of Sumatra. This dagger has a wooden or horn hilt in the shape of a stylized bird's head angled to the blade. (Some of the rechong bade-bade and goloks have already been shown in the previous section on Indonesian weapons.)

A concealed Malay archipelago weapon is the *korambi*, a small knife with a sickle shape blade measuring from 4 to 6 inches in length. A korambi could be concealed in the long hair of Malay men and women and used as the ultimate defense.

The Moro kris is the main type of dagger used in the Philippines. These edged weapons are lacking the meteoric iron and have very wide blades that could be straight or wavy, but are shiny and highly polished. In different parts of the Malay peninsula, these edged weapons are called sundang. The hilt is made from wood, occasionally covered with hammered silver or silver wire. A carved ivory pommel decorates the better quality Moro swords and daggers. The upper part of the blade is frequently decorated with inlaid silver bands. Carved water buffalo horn is the main material used for the hilt and scabbard.

The national weapon of the Moros from Mindanao as well as North Borneo is the *barong*, a long dagger with a characteristic widening in the center of the blade that can reach 3 inches. The blade narrows at both ends, thus giving it an elliptical form. Horn, wood, and ivory are the materials the hilt is made from and the shape is that of a stylized bird's head, formed mostly by the pommel at the apical end of the hilt.

Fig. 5/103. 18th-19th century dagger, most likely unique in design and shape. The blade has inlaid silver Islamic inscriptions on both sides, is double edged and ends with a sharp point. It obviously was used mainly for thrusting. The scabbard is made from crocodile skin and has a reptilian chape. Toned bone hilt with incised terminal decorations. Dagger's length: 22" (56 cm.). Blade's length: 16.5" (34 cm.). Estimated value: $2,000-$2,500.

Fig. 5/104. Malaya-Majapahit kris dating to the 14th-15th century. The hilt is made from dark-amber color ivory that has become translucent with age. It is in the shape of standing human figure with the hands brought to the front. The blade is wavy and has a double circle coiled design in the upper part near the hilt. Missing scabbard and evidence of long time burial. Blade's length: 8.1" (20.5 cm.). Dagger's length: 11.5" (29.1 cm.). Estimated value: $3,000.

Fig. 5/105. Malaya. 17th-18th century silver klewang executioner dagger. This dagger differs from the traditional klewang, as it has a curvature of the back of the blade, not existent in the traditional klewang. It also has a marked widening toward the blade's point. The hilt is decorated with repoussé silver having an intricate design. A related dagger is the panabas, a Moro executioner dagger from the southern Philippines. Blade's length: 12.5" (31.8 cm.). Dagger's length: 17.8" (45 cm.). Estimated value: $1,200.

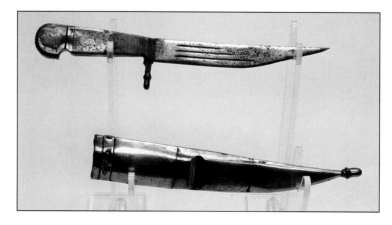

Fig. 5/106. Malaya. 19th century Malay knife with silver plated scabbard and hilt. Superficial round decorations are present on both the scabbard and hilt. The hand-guard is in the shape of a button and threads into the scabbard. The blade is sharp on the curved side and has three fullers. Knife's length: 12" (30.5 cm.) Estimated value: $350.

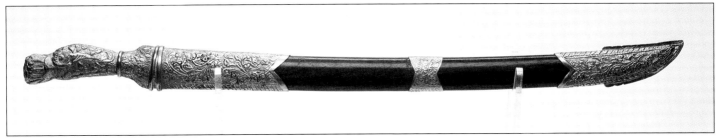

Fig. 5/107. Malaya. 19th century sword with elaborate silver decorations. The hilt is made from solid silver and its shape resembles a stylized animal head. Floral design, repoussé and chiseled silver sheet covers the wooden scabbard. Straight damascene blade with fine pamir. The elaborate decorations lead us believe that this sword belonged to a sultan or a high dignitary. Blade's length: 17" (44 cm.). Sword's length: 23" (58.5 cm.). Estimated value: $6,500.

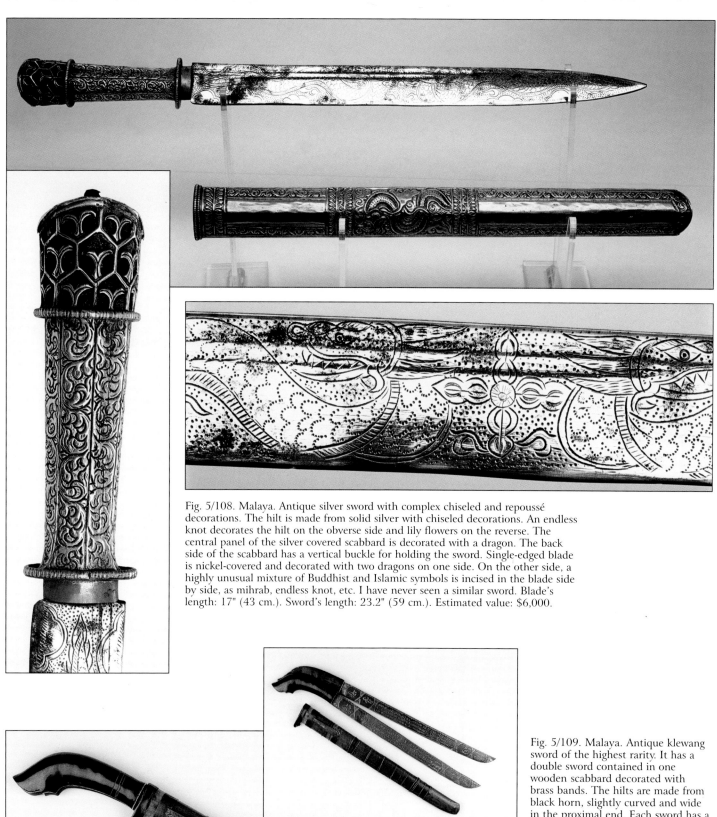

Fig. 5/108. Malaya. Antique silver sword with complex chiseled and repoussé decorations. The hilt is made from solid silver with chiseled decorations. An endless knot decorates the hilt on the obverse side and lily flowers on the reverse. The central panel of the silver covered scabbard is decorated with a dragon. The back side of the scabbard has a vertical buckle for holding the sword. Single-edged blade is nickel-covered and decorated with two dragons on one side. On the other side, a highly unusual mixture of Buddhist and Islamic symbols is incised in the blade side by side, as mihrab, endless knot, etc. I have never seen a similar sword. Blade's length: 17" (43 cm.). Sword's length: 23.2" (59 cm.). Estimated value: $6,000.

Fig. 5/109. Malaya. Antique klewang sword of the highest rarity. It has a double sword contained in one wooden scabbard decorated with brass bands. The hilts are made from black horn, slightly curved and wide in the proximal end. Each sword has a convex blade side and a flat side, which allows the swords to be sheathed side by side. Single-edged blades are engraved on both sides with Islamic calligraphy. While the writing is identical on both swords, a different calligrapher was used for the same text. A leaf shaped buckle on back of the scabbard allows the threading of a belt. Blade's length: 15.3" (31 cm.). Sword's length: 22.4" (57 cm.). Estimated value: $6,000.

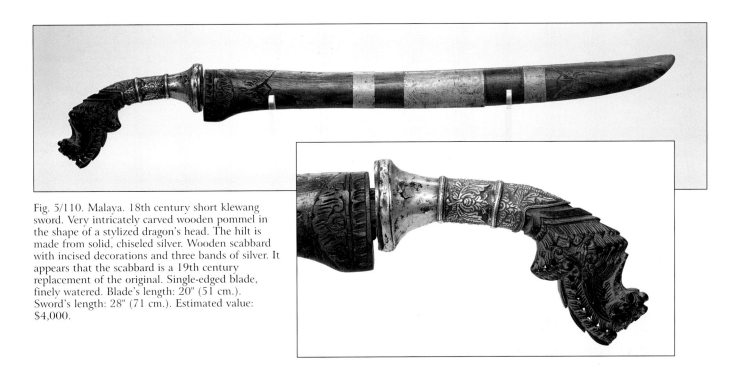

Fig. 5/110. Malaya. 18th century short klewang sword. Very intricately carved wooden pommel in the shape of a stylized dragon's head. The hilt is made from solid, chiseled silver. Wooden scabbard with incised decorations and three bands of silver. It appears that the scabbard is a 19th century replacement of the original. Single-edged blade, finely watered. Blade's length: 20" (51 cm.). Sword's length: 28" (71 cm.). Estimated value: $4,000.

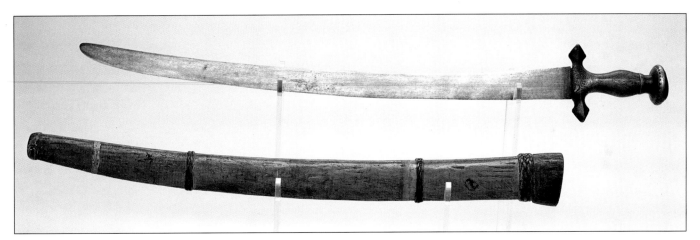

Fig. 5/111. 17th-18th century North Borneo Islamic sword. Bronze hilt and pommel decorated with incised ornaments and having a cruciform hand-guard. Single-edged blade with rounded point. Wooden scabbard with rattan bindings. This very early sword was probably brought to Borneo by pirates. Blade's length: 22" (56 cm.). Sword's length: 26" (68 cm.). Estimated value: $1,500.

Fig. 5/112. 17th-18th century Malay golok. This Islamic sword has a wooden scabbard with worm holes. The lower third is covered with white metal. Oval hand-guard continues upward with a knuckle-guard that ends unattached. The pommel is made from exotic wood with demonic head features. Single-edged blade with marked widening in the lower third typical of the golok swords. Blade's length: 20" (51 cm.). Sword's length: 26" (66 cm.). Estimated value: $2,800.

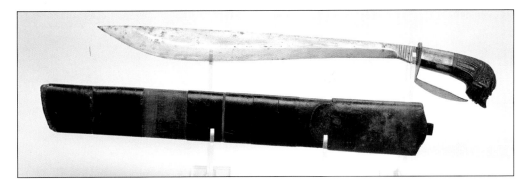

Fig. 5/113. Antique Malay dagger resembling the medieval Majapahit dagger and somewhat close to wedong daggers. The hilt is made from wood adorned with spiral ornaments and ending with a rounded knob pommel. Wide blade, curving toward the point. Line decorations adorn the widest part of the blade near the hilt. The back of the blade is straight for a quarter of the length, then tapers toward the point in a concave fashion. Elaborate decorations adorn the wooden scabbard on the obverse side. The reverse side is plain, except for two conic perforations that serve for the attachment to a shoulder strap. Blade's length: 9.8" (24.8 cm.). Dagger's length: 16.8" (43.5 cm.). Estimated value: $675.

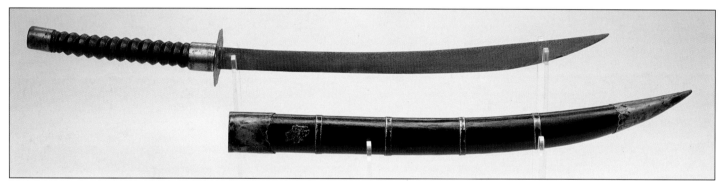

Fig. 5/114. 19th century Malay sword. The hilt is long and allows for two handed holding. Spiral carved wood forms the hilt, ending with brass fittings. Oval shape brass hand-guard with incised decorations. Wooden scabbard with brass endings and annular bands. Single-edged blade widens toward the point and has pitted corrosion due to age. Blade's length: 20.2" (51.5 cm.). Sword's length: 33" (84 cm.). Estimated value: $800.

Fig. 5/115. Malaya. Antique golok dagger with scabbard made from wood with rattan bindings. The hilt is made from toned ivory carved in the shape of several monkeys climbing on jungle vines. Repoussé silver ferrule. The blade is single-edged, curved, widening in the center and tapering progressively in the distal third. Blade's length: 6.1" (15.5 cm.). Dagger's length: 12.1" (30.5 cm.). Estimated value: $1,000.

Fig. 5/116. Malay antique Islamic sword originating from Northern Borneo. Dates to the 16th-18th century. The hilt has elaborate incised decorations in brass. Round pommel with brass incised decorations in open work. Single-edged blade with one fuller and corrosion pitting attesting to the age. Blade's length: 21.6" (55 cm.). Sword's length: 26" (66 cm.). Estimated value: $1,000.

Fig. 5/117. Northern Borneo, Sarawak. Malay kris with silver hilt in the shape of Garuda. The blade is waved (dapur luk) and has fine pamor watering. An elephant trunk is visible on the ganja. Fine repoussé silver decorates the wooden scabbard. This dagger is similar to other Kalimantan kris daggers. Blade's length: 14.5" (37 cm.). Dagger's length: 19.8" (50.1 cm.). Estimated value: $1,200.

Fig. 5/118. Malaya. 19th-20th century pair of swords. This type of sword resembles the Naga dao from Assam, however, it has a hand-guard, while the dao is missing this feature. Chinese folklore obviously influenced the creation of this sword. The hilt is made from carved wood with a figural design. This is a heavy, double-handed sword and probably was used for a ceremonial role, rather than utilitarian. Round disk hand-guard. Steel blade with double-headed dragon design and phoenix birds. The blade is rectangular and single-edged, narrowing toward the center and widening in the lower third. Blade's length: 20" (51 cm.). Sword's length: 31.5" (80 cm.). Estimated value: $1,200 for the pair.

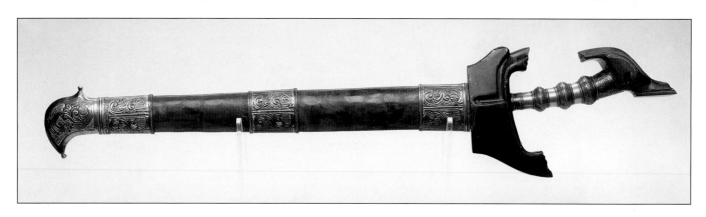

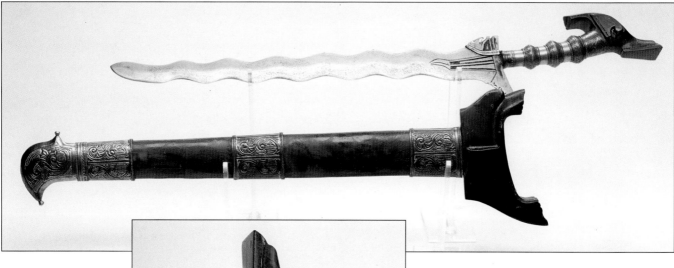

Fig. 5/119. Mindanao. 19th century Moro kris. The hilt is highly decorated with incised copper alternating with brass bands. Large wooden pommel in the shape of a stylized bird. Wavy, watered blade, double-edged and still very sharp. The ganja is in the shape of an elephant's trunk bordered by a silvered copper band. Wooden scabbard decorated with large silvered bands that have elaborate repoussé decoration. The chape of the scabbard is in the shape of a bird. Blade's length: 21" (53.3 cm.). Sword's length: 32.8" (83.2 cm.). Estimated value: $2,500.

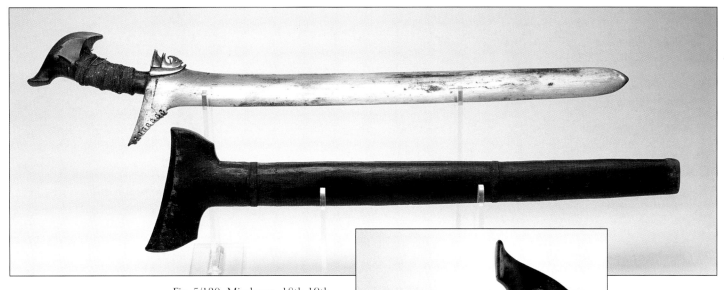

Fig. 5/120. Mindanao. 18th-19th century Moro kris. The pommel is made from carved wood in the shape of a bird. The hilt is made from wood covered with manila rope. Straight, double-edged blade with inlaid silver on ganja that has incised an elephant's trunk. Wooden scabbard with aged wood. Blade's length: 22.3" (57 cm.). Sword's length: 28.8" (73 cm.). Estimated value: $1,500.

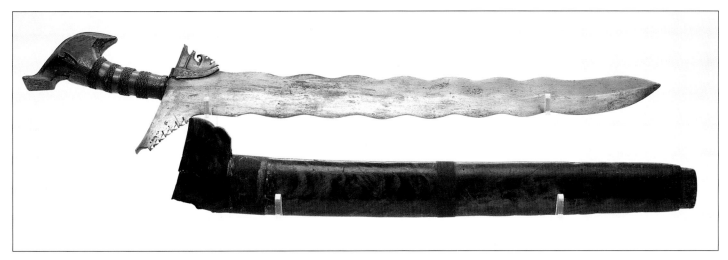

Fig. 5/121. Mindanao. 18th-19th century Moro kris with wooden scabbard and hilt. Incised metal bands and wire decorate the hilt. The pommel is made from carved wood in the shape of a stylized bird. Wide, double-edged blade with undulations along the edges. The ganja is decorated with a human mask and serrations. Blade's length: 22.4" (57 cm.). Sword's length: 28.2" (72 cm.). Estimated value: $1,000.

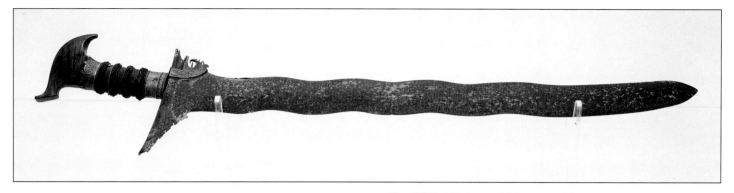

Fig. 5/122. Mindanao. 18th century Moro kris sword with broad wavy blade. The ganja has a vertical silver ornament. Silver hilt with repoussé and filigree decorations. The central portion of the hilt is covered with braided black textile. Wooden pommel in the shape of a stylized bird. Blade's length: 23.6" (60 cm.). Sword's length: 29" (73.6 cm.). Estimated value: $750.

Fig. 5/123. Mindanao. 19th century Moro barong. Typically, this sword has a blade that is wider in the center, single-edged, and curving toward the point and hilt. Watering of the blade is visible with longitudinal striations from the lamination process. The hilt is made from wood with an elaborate carved pommel in the shape of a dog's head. Wooden scabbard carved on the obverse side with a spread wings eagle and below a coat of arms. Above the ornament, a bowed leaf allows the attachment or suspension of the dagger. Blade's length: 13.2" (33.7cm.). Dagger's length: 20.1" (51 cm.). Estimated value: $750.

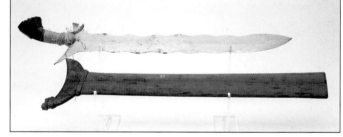

Fig. 5/125. Mindanao. 19th century Moro kris with wooden hilt and scabbard.. The hilt is curved and has incised decorations on the pommel. Wide, wavy blade with sharp double edges. Blade's length: 23.5" (59.5 cm.). Sword's length: 30" (76 cm.). Estimated value: $700.

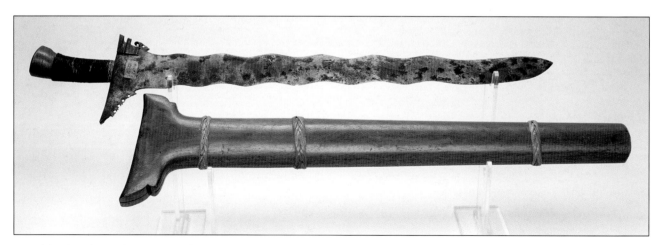

Fig. 5/124. Mindanao. Antique Moro kris. Hilt and wooden scabbard reinforced with raffia bands. Wide, serpent-like blade, typical for Moro swords. The ganja has an incised elephant trunk. Blade's length: 23.2" (59.5 cm.). Sword's length: 29" (74.2 cm.). Estimated value: $900.

Fig. 5/126. Mindanao. Moro barong sword with wooden hilt and scabbard. The hilt is carved in the shape of an animal's head and has a brass grip. Oval shape blade with the widest portion located in the center of the sword. Single-edged blade. Incised decorations are present on the proximal and distal parts of the scabbard. This type of sword is the national weapon of the Moros in Mindanao and Sulu in the Northern part of Borneo. Blade's length: 17.8" (45 cm.). Sword's length: 25.5" (64.8cm.). Estimated value: $500.

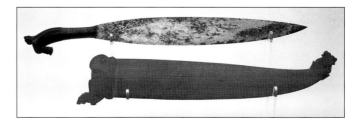

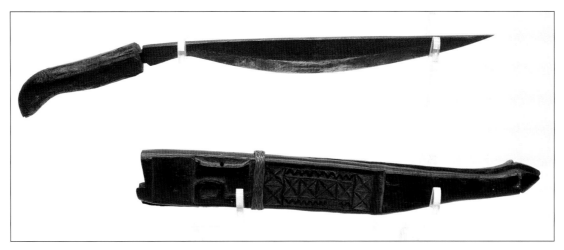

Fig. 5/127. 19th century golok sword. The hilt is in the shape of a snake and carved in wood. Straight back blade with widening in the center and high convex cutting central area. Black wooden scabbard with criss-cross decorations and the initials "PI" (probably Philippines Island). A rattan band holds together the scabbard's sides. Blade's length: 11.5" (29 cm.). Dagger's length: 17" (43 cm.). Estimated value: $500.

Fig. 5/128. 20th century dagger made from water buffalo horn hilt and scabbard. The pommel is carved in the shape of a clenched fist. Floral design decorates the hilt, which is engraved Philippines. A brass eagle forms the hand-guard. Incised floral decorations in horn ornate the scabbard. This dagger is a G.I. souvenir from World War II. Blade's length: 7-9" (20 cm). Dagger's length: 14.1" (36.2 cm.). Estimated value: $400.

Borneo Swords and Daggers

While most collectors' books tangentially mention the headhunters' swords, I have not found any reference book that gives these swords the importance they deserve. The *parang ihlang* (Dyak swords) are specific to the Iban tribe in Northern Borneo, a tribe called Sea Dyaks by the British. Other headhunter tribes in Northern Borneo (which is now part of Malaysia) were the Murut and Kayon tribes; they used the *mandau* (parang ihlang) as well. They believed that the soul resides in the skull and that by collecting the skulls of enemies, the enemies' souls would become protectors of their family. Communal living was practiced (and is still practiced today), and closely related families lived in "longhouses" built near the river, which was the sole means of transportation using long boats. In contrast with the typical Western preference for building houses near the water to admire the water view, these longhouses are oriented with their backs toward the water so the spirits of the river or lake will not bring bad luck. The Ibans were converted to Christianity early in the 20th century by missionaries, but still combine Christianity with animist beliefs in a country that is predominantly Muslim.

Due to the large distances between longhouses, the children of Ibans are educated and actually live in the school, where they are visited by their parents. I have had the privilege and personal satisfaction of visiting longhouses in Sarawak along no-name rivers. The only link to the outside world is via the use of indigent, long, narrow boats able to travel on shallow water. While civilization has brought many changes, the Ibans still live the way their ancestors did: fishing, hunting, and with minimal agricultural soil working. Headhunting on paper ceased early in the 20th century, as it was banned by British colonial rule, however the actual practice continued as late as World War II, during the Japanese occupation of Borneo. While visiting a longhouse in Sarawak, I was shown a collection of old skulls that the elder of the house proudly brought down from the attic. The skulls were given the utmost respect, and liquid food and wine were poured between the jaws. Oddly, an icon of Mary and the Jesus child hung on the wooden wall.

The Ibans were not only fierce warriors, they were also talented craftsmen. Hand woven textiles made using a weaving technique called ikat were dyed with vegetable dyes and woven in back-strapped looms, creating some of the most beautiful and fascinating textiles. Old ikats are very rare today and still manufactured in only isolated places. They require intensive labor and skills, as the patterns were not designed but remembered by heart without drawings. However, this is a different subject, one that I will perhaps have the opportunity at some point in my life to elaborate upon and illustrate.

It is my intent here to familiarize collectors with different types of parang ihlangs used by Ibans and other tribes of Borneo by using the most representative types from my personal collection. The alternative name for this type of edged weapon is mandau. The blade, which was manufactured by local craftsmen using primitive tools, is convex on one side and flat, or even slightly concave, on the other. Several perforations are present on the back of the blade and inlaid with brass dot ornaments. The blade has a single straight edge and occasionally displays marks attesting to its gruesome past use of cutting through the bones of victims. Esthetically, the most attractive section of the sword is its pommel. Staghorn or bone with intricately carved abstract or semi-abstract design patterns are the materials of choice for the pommel, but less elaborate pommels could be made from wood as well. When slightly recognizable, the pommel appears as the head of an animal and occasionally as a bird's head. Tufts of human hair protrude through the pommel's opening. The hilt is made from wood or bone and covered with bands of rattan or a rope type of material. A mandau typically has a scabbard made from two wooden boards bound and decorated with very intricate patterns of rattan weaving. Tufts of human hair, feathers and rope, or rattan balls decorate the scabbard. A rope loop helps to carry the sword around.

An older version of the mandau is the *kampilan* (*campilan*), also used for decapitation of enemies. The difference between the mandau and kampilan is the pommel; on the kampilan, it is made from bone carved in a Y shape. The age of the sword can be measured by the degree of toning seen on the kampilan's bone carved pommel.

Antique parang ihlang are very rare due to an unwillingness of the Iban owners to part with their family venerated swords as well as an inability to export them from Malaysia.

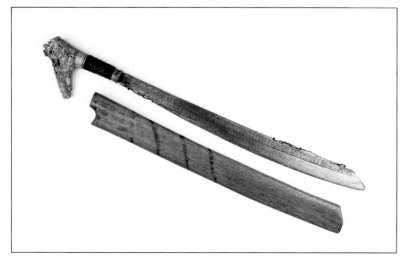

Fig. 5/129. 18th-19th century parang ihlang (mandau). Headhunter Dyak sword with intricately carved staghorn hilt in the shape of an animal's head. The hilt's grip has woven rattan. Elaborate incised decorations ornate the blade, which is single-edged and displays open work on the back side as well as the edge side near the hilt. The scabbard is made from wood and is not decorated. Blade's length: 20.5" (52 cm.). Sword's length: 24.2" (61.5 cm.). Estimated value: $1,800.

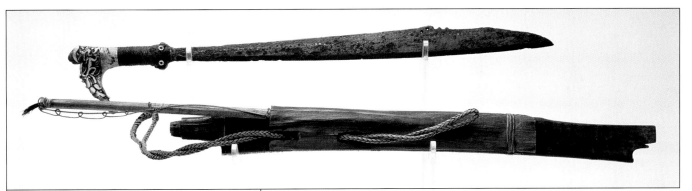

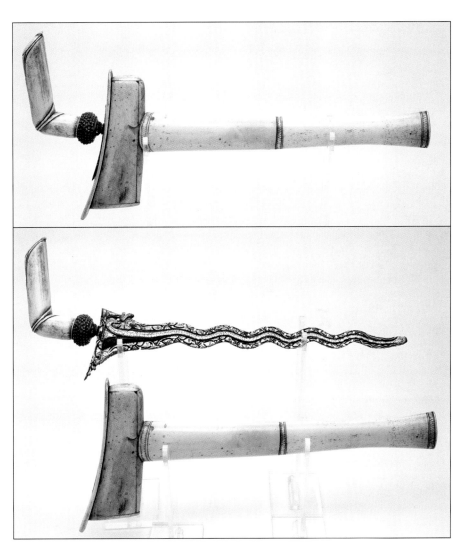

Fig. 5/130. Kohong kalunan sword of Dyaks. This mandau sword is one of the oldest in my collection, dating to the 17th-18th century or earlier. The hilt is made from carved staghorn, showing the highest artistic skill. It is less stylized and allows the view of ferocious animals. The blade is single-edged and has deep age identified through the visible degree of corrosion. Traces of incised decorations and inlaid brass dots are visible on the iron blade. The scabbard is made from wood with intricately carved zoomorphic decorations. Rattan bands also decorate the upper part of the scabbard, which contains a pouch that once stored a small knife. Note: for this sword as well as for several others shown in this section, the reverse side of the scabbard is shown in the photograph. Blade's length: 17.2" (44 cm.). Sword's length: 26" (66 cm.). Estimated value: $6,000.

Fig. 5/131. 19th century kris made entirely from bone. I purchased this sword in the early 1980s in Sarawak, but judging from its appearance, it most likely originates from Sulawesi. While technically this sword belongs in the Indonesian section, I included it here primarily because it was located and bought in Northern Borneo. A stylized figure of Garuda is featured on the hilt. The mendak is made from yellow metal that probably is a gold alloy and has a stellar appearance due to the filigree work. Precious stones are mounted in the mendak. The blade is waved (dapur luk) and has three chased gold lines ending at the ganja. The central line (dada) ends in a figure of a dragon whose tail forms the point of the dagger (putjar). The opposite line ending is in the shape of a mythological animal. Blade's length: 15" (38 cm.). Dagger's length: 18" (45.6 cm.). Estimated value: $4,000.

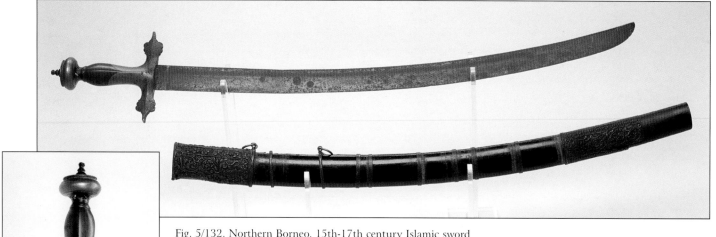

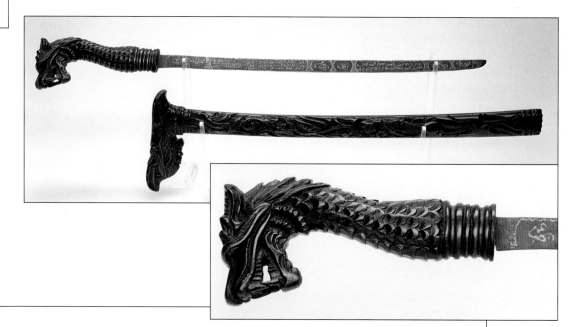

Fig. 5/132. Northern Borneo. 15th-17th century Islamic sword with elaborate silver decorations on the scabbard, which has annular silver retaining rings and still retains most of the original black lacquer on the wood. Bronze hilt with brass decorations on the distal end. Onion shaped pommel with a stupa like ending. Hand-guard with straight quillons. Curved, single-edged blade with one fuller. This sword is typical for late medieval Islamic swords. Blade's length: 23.6" (60 cm.). Sword's length: 29.5" (60 cm.). Estimated value: $5,000.

Fig. 5/133. 19th century pedang sword originating from Northern Borneo. The hilt is in the shape of a threatening lion's head, carved in wood with intricate details. The blade has a straight back and tapers toward the point. Both sides of the blade are engraved with Islamic inscriptions. Deeply incised near the hilt is 4960.0, which probably indicates that this blade was recycled from an older blade. The scabbard is made from wood carved in high relief featuring a roaring lion. A dragon's head is visible on the ganja. Blade's length: 23.8" (60.3 cm.). Sword's length: 34.8" (88.4 cm.). Estimated value: $4,500.

Fig. 5/134. Dyak mandau sword (parang ihlang) with intricate staghorn carving on the hilt (kohong kalunan). The lower part of the hilt has woven rattan in two colors. Corrosion is present on the iron blade, which has no ornaments like most of the earliest Borneo parang ihlang swords. The wooden scabbard has zoomorphic decorations carved in the wood. Three woven rattan bands also decorate the scabbard. The mouth of the scabbard has a rounded carved staghorn. Attached to the back of the scabbard is a pouch made from a palm leaf containing a long handle knife. Blade's length: 18.8" (47.5 cm.). Sword's length: 28" (71 cm.). Estimated value: $3,500.

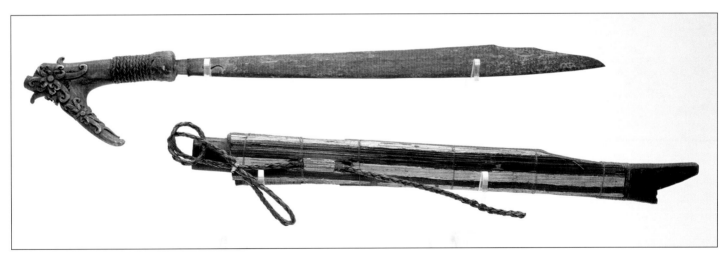

Fig. 5/135. Northern Borneo. 18th century parang ihlang with intricate decorations of the hilt (kohong kalunan) carved in staghorn. The blade is made from forged iron and still very sharp. Woven rattan bands and carved decorations ornate the scabbard. Blade's length: 18" (46 cm.). Sword's length: 26.3" (67 cm.). Estimated value: $3,500.

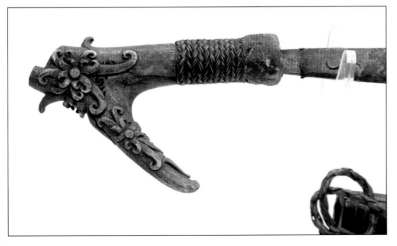

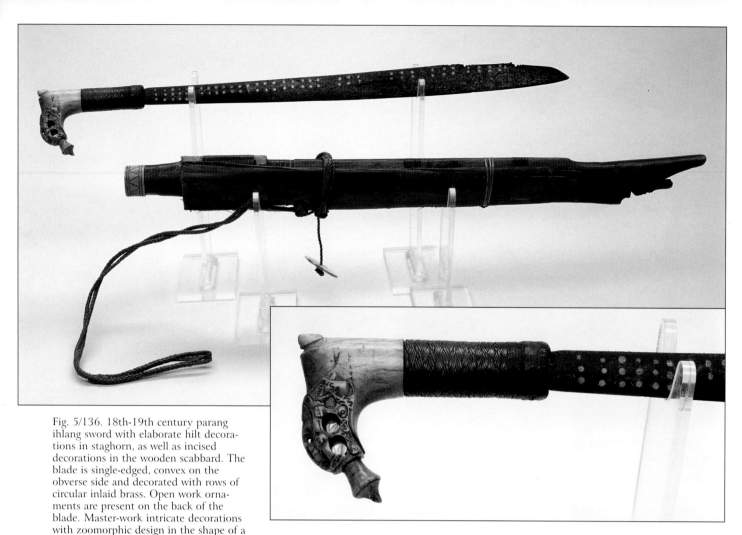

Fig. 5/136. 18th-19th century parang ihlang sword with elaborate hilt decorations in staghorn, as well as incised decorations in the wooden scabbard. The blade is single-edged, convex on the obverse side and decorated with rows of circular inlaid brass. Open work ornaments are present on the back of the blade. Master-work intricate decorations with zoomorphic design in the shape of a billhorn bird's skull are present on the hilt. The scabbard has a staghorn annular proximal attachment and incised zoomorphic design featuring a dragon facing a shamanistic figural ornament. Rattan woven bands and a vegetable ivory toggle disk are also present on the scabbard. A sheet of palm leaf that once contained a small knife is located on the back of the scabbard. Blade's length: 18" (45.7 cm.). Sword's length: 28.2" (71.8 cm.). Estimated value: $3,000.

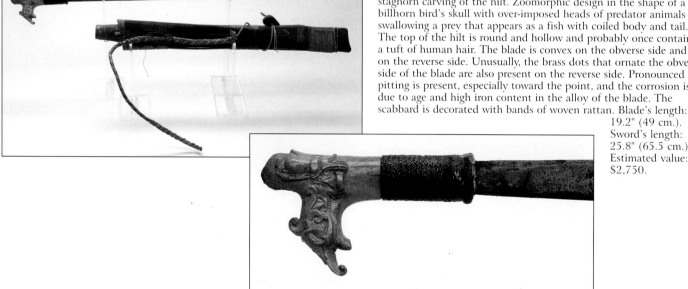

Fig. 5/137. 18th-19th century parang ihlang sword with intricate staghorn carving of the hilt. Zoomorphic design in the shape of a billhorn bird's skull with over-imposed heads of predator animals swallowing a prey that appears as a fish with coiled body and tail. The top of the hilt is round and hollow and probably once contained a tuft of human hair. The blade is convex on the obverse side and flat on the reverse side. Unusually, the brass dots that ornate the obverse side of the blade are also present on the reverse side. Pronounced pitting is present, especially toward the point, and the corrosion is due to age and high iron content in the alloy of the blade. The scabbard is decorated with bands of woven rattan. Blade's length: 19.2" (49 cm.). Sword's length: 25.8" (65.5 cm.). Estimated value: $2,750.

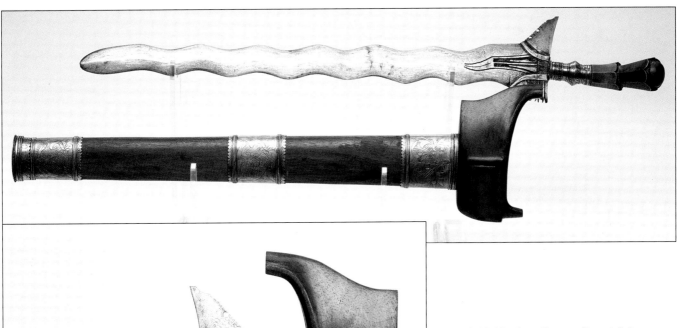

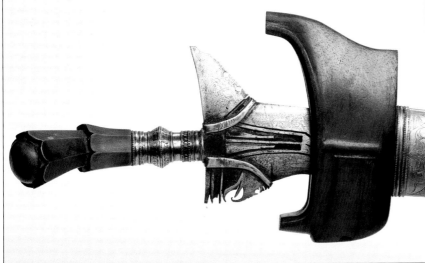

Fig. 5/138. Northern Borneo, Brunei Sultanate. 19th century kris decorated with chiseled silver. Wooden hilt carved in the shape of a lotus bud. Its distal end is made from chased silver. The scabbard is decorated with chiseled silver. Wavy, wide blade with silver decorations on the ganja. Blade's length: 22.3" (57 cm.). Sword's length: 27.5" (70 cm.). Estimated value: $3,000.

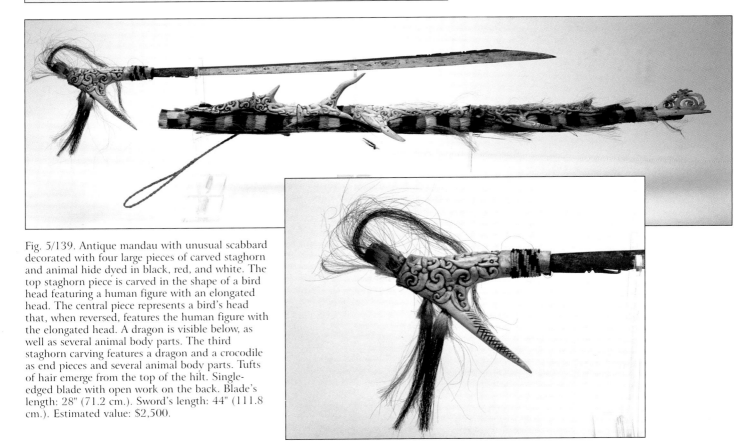

Fig. 5/139. Antique mandau with unusual scabbard decorated with four large pieces of carved staghorn and animal hide dyed in black, red, and white. The top staghorn piece is carved in the shape of a bird head featuring a human figure with an elongated head. The central piece represents a bird's head that, when reversed, features the human figure with the elongated head. A dragon is visible below, as well as several animal body parts. The third staghorn carving features a dragon and a crocodile as end pieces and several animal body parts. Tufts of hair emerge from the top of the hilt. Single-edged blade with open work on the back. Blade's length: 28" (71.2 cm.). Sword's length: 44" (111.8 cm.). Estimated value: $2,500.

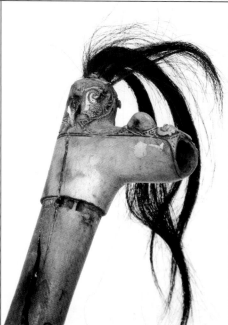

Fig. 5/140. 17th-18th century headhunter mandau sword with staghorn hilt in the shape of an animal. A tuft of human hair emerges from the top of the hilt. The blade is single-edged, widening gradually and reaching maximum width in the distal third. Wooden scabbard with almost fossilized wood and insect boring. Carved wood ornaments are present in the proximal end. Intricate braided rattan bands adorn the scabbard. Blade's length: 18.8" (47.5 cm.). Sword's length: 26" (66 cm.). Estimated value: $2,500.

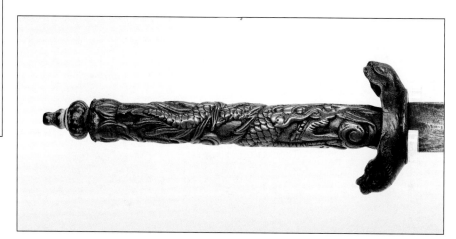

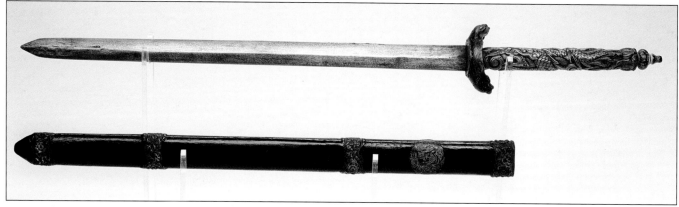

Fig. 5/141. 17th-18th century sword purchased in Northern Borneo in the 1980s that demonstrates the influence of Chinese art in Borneo. The hilt is made from solid brass decorated in high relief with a unicorn and ling zhi. Hand-guard in the shape of opposing mythological beasts. Lacquered wood scabbard decorated with a brass plaque featuring unicorns and a floral design in high relief. Double-edged blade with central raised rib. Pommel in the shape of a stupa. Blade's length: 19.8" (50 cm.). Sword's length: 30" (76 cm.). Estimated value: $2,500.

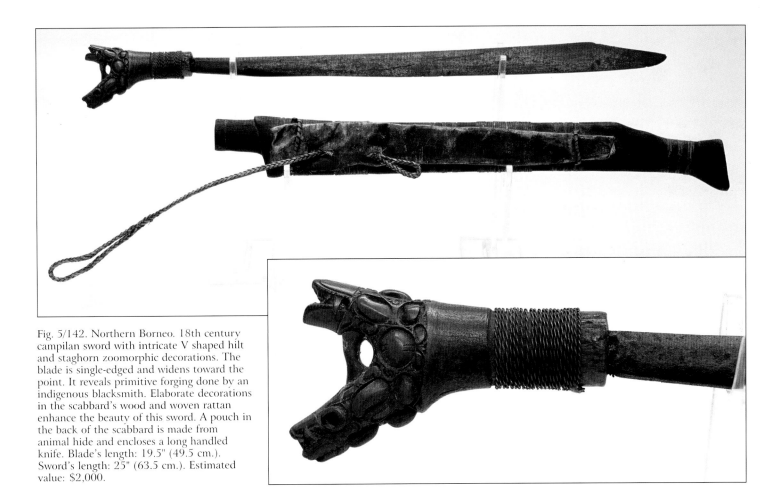

Fig. 5/142. Northern Borneo. 18th century campilan sword with intricate V shaped hilt and staghorn zoomorphic decorations. The blade is single-edged and widens toward the point. It reveals primitive forging done by an indigenous blacksmith. Elaborate decorations in the scabbard's wood and woven rattan enhance the beauty of this sword. A pouch in the back of the scabbard is made from animal hide and encloses a long handled knife. Blade's length: 19.5" (49.5 cm.). Sword's length: 25" (63.5 cm.). Estimated value: $2,000.

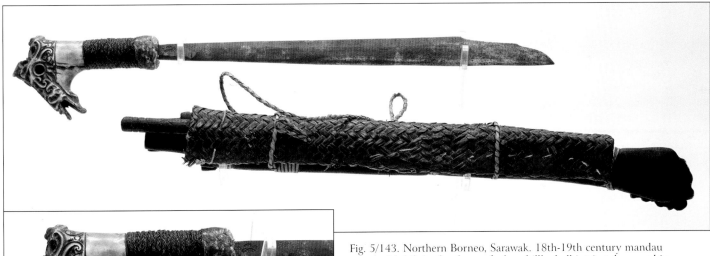

Fig. 5/143. Northern Borneo, Sarawak. 18th-19th century mandau sword with hilt in the shape of a hornbill's skull intricately carved in staghorn with rounded decorations. Bands of woven rattan enforce the grip. A notch on top of the hilt once contained a tuft of human hair. The blade is convex on the obverse side and flat on the reverse. An animal resembling a dragon is incised in the blade near the hilt; this is the first headhunter sword with this type of decoration that I have ever seen. Signs of primitive forging are present on the blade, probably done by an indigenous blacksmith. Elaborate high relief decorations adorn the scabbard. The decorations are highly stylized, but the proximal part of the scabbard near the hilt is decorated with a phantasmagoric, ferocious animal's head. Bands of rattan retain the scabbard's parts. A hand woven rattan sheath on the scabbard's back forms a pouch that contains a knife. Blade's length: 15.2" (38.7 cm.). Sword's length: 26" (66 cm.). Estimated value: $2,000.

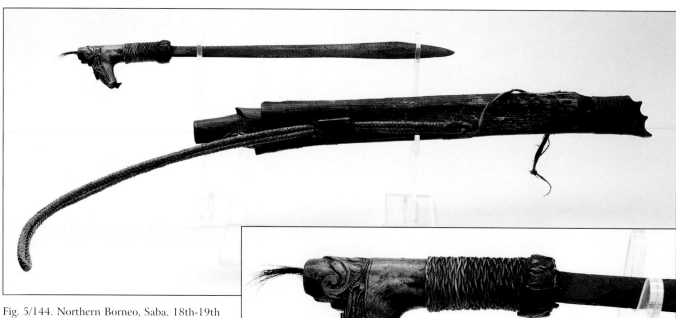

Fig. 5/144. Northern Borneo, Saba. 18th-19th century mandau sword with carved staghorn hilt. The carving is in the shape of a horned animal and tufts of human hair emerge from the top and animal's mouth. The blade is single-edged with convex obverse side and flat reverse. Signs of primitive forging of the blade and pitting of the blade are visible. Wooden scabbard decorated with incised ornaments and bands of woven rattan. A palm leaf forms a pouch on the dorsal aspect of the scabbard and once contained a long handle small knife. Blade's length: 14" (35.5 cm.). Sword's length: 26.2" (66.5 cm.). Estimated value: $2,000.

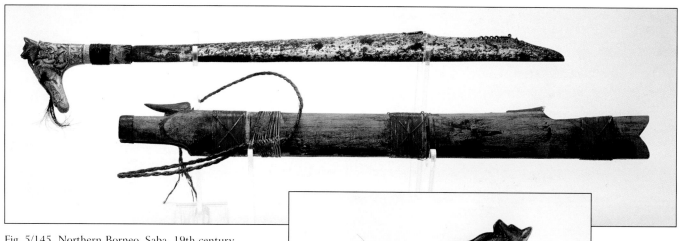

Fig. 5/145. Northern Borneo, Saba. 19th century mandau sword with zoomorphic decorations carved in the hilt's staghorn. A wolf with its tongue sticking out emerges at the top of the hilt and a V-shape is formed at the end by a reptilian swallowing a prey. The scabbard is made from wood decorated with incised ornaments in red and yellow colors. Woven rattan bindings are located toward the ends of the scabbard. Blade's length: 19.2" (49.5 cm.). Sword's length: 27.8" (70.5 cm.). Estimated value: $1,700.

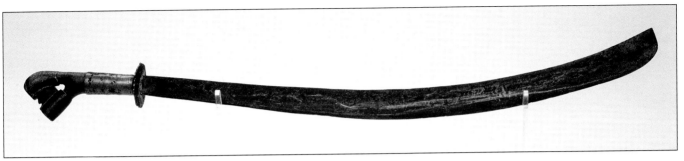

Fig. 5/146. Northern Borneo. Saba. 18th century campilan sword with brass hilt. The blade originates from a European older falchion sword and has the word "canalee" incised. The blade widens in the lower third. Brass hilt continues with an oval incised hand-guard. Wooden pommel with split ends shows considerable aging. Blade's length: 26" (66 cm.). Sword's length: 32" (81 cm.). Estimated value: $1,500.

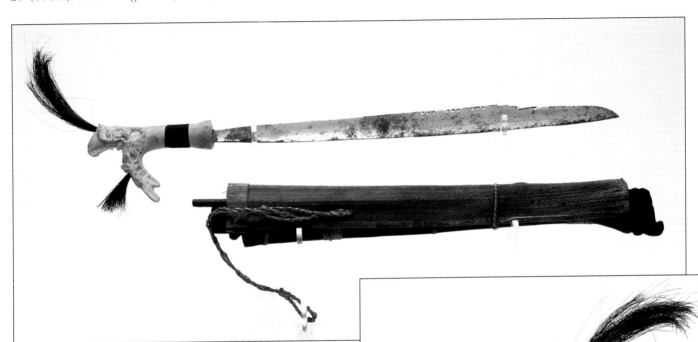

Fig. 5/147. 19th century parang ihlang with staghorn hilt carved with zoomorphic design. Two tufts of hair emerge from the top of the hilt. The blade is single-edged, decorated with four inlaid brass dots and incised ornaments. The back of the blade has open work decorations. Zoomorphic decorations featuring a giant reptile swallowing another reptile ornate the scabbard. On the back of the scabbard, a palm leaf sheet encloses a small knife. Blade's length: 17.9" (45.5 cm.). Sword's length: 24.6" (62.5 cm.). Estimated value: $1,700.

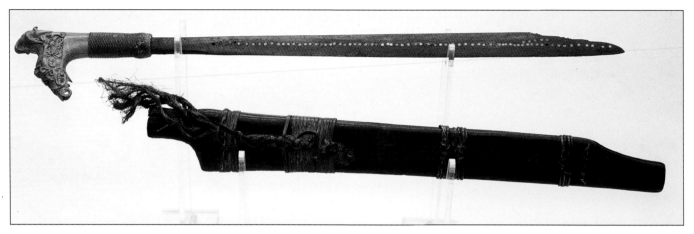

Fig. 5/148. Borneo. Sarawak. 18th century parang ihlang sword with very intricately carved staghorn hilt in the shape of a billhorn's skull. Ferocious animal heads are also seen on the hilt's carvings. The blade was forged using primitive methods and is convex on the obverse and flat on the reverse. The blade widens gradually toward the point. Incised decorations featuring zoomorphic design are present on the scabbard. Rattan bands serve for binding the scabbard, as well as ornaments. A toggle suspended by a cord allows fastening to a hook formed by a proximal cord, thus allowing the sword to be carried on the back, around the shoulder. A back pouch is also present. Blade's length: 20" (51 cm.). Sword's length: 28.2" (71.5 cm.). Estimated value: $1,700.

Fig. 5/149. North Borneo, Saba. 18th century parang ihlang with intricate staghorn carvings in the hilt and scabbard. The scabbard has very intricate staghorn carving with anthropomorphic design and rattan bindings. The hilt has zoomorphic staghorn carving with very intricate design. Two tufts of hair emerge from the hilt, which is in the shape of a bird. The blade has inlaid brass decorations. Blade's length: 20.5" (52 cm.). Sword's length: 29.5" (75 cm.). Estimated value: $2,000.

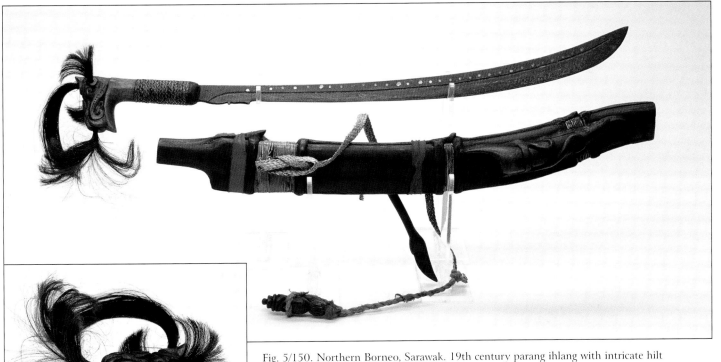

Fig. 5/150. Northern Borneo, Sarawak. 19th century parang ihlang with intricate hilt carving featuring zoomorphic pattern. Tufts of black human hair emerge from the ears and mouth of a mythological animal. The blade widens in the lower third. Inlaid brass dot decorations are located on the back of the blade, above the fuller. The primitive forging points toward manufacture by a native blacksmith. High relief wood carving decorates the scabbard. The high degree of stylization allows for detection of only the serpent coils and possible deer horns in the carving. Bands of rattan encircle the scabbard. The back of the scabbard has a carving of a tailed, headless animal and contains a small pouch. A wooden toggle in the shape of a human being is attached with a rattan cord. Blade's length: 22.2" (51 cm.). Sword's length: 30.2" (77 cm.). Estimated value: $1,600.

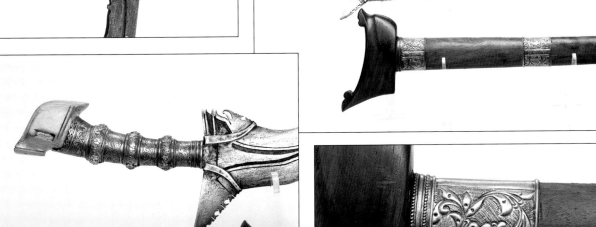

Fig. 5/151. Northern Borneo, Brunei. 18th-19th century Moro kris with ivory pommel and silver and gold decorations. Silver hilt with intricate chiseled decorations and inlaid gold with floral design. Pommel in the shape of a stylized bird. Wooden scabbard with repoussé silver band decorations and inlaid gold. Wavy, wide blade with rounded point. An elephant trunk decoration is present in the ganja along with two silver bands. Blade's length: 22.8" (58 cm.). Sword's length: 29" (74 cm.). Estimated value: $5,500.

Fig. 5/152. Northern Borneo, Sarawak. 18th-19th century parang ihlang sword with black horn hilt having incised facets. Single-edged blade with dragon design in open work on the back of the blade. Both sides of the blade are convex and this is very rare. An incised longitudinal line is present on the obverse. Wooden scabbard with incised decorations in high relief featuring a dragon with bird's head on proximal end and coiled deeply incised design in the center. Bands of woven rattan retain both sides of the scabbard. The scabbard's back contains a small pouch that once contained a knife. Blade's length: 17.5" (44.5 cm.). Sword's length: 28.8" (73 cm.). Estimated value: $1,200.

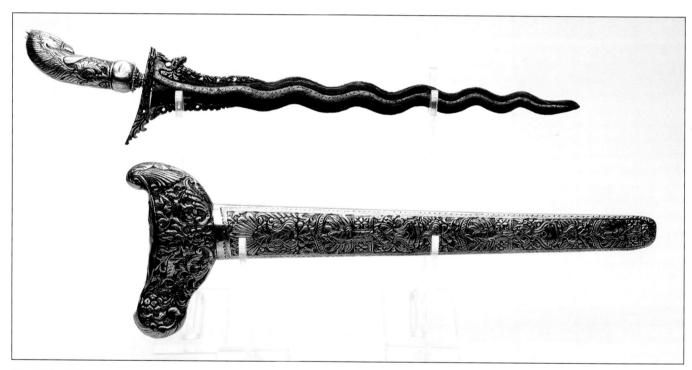

Fig. 5/153. Kalimantan. 19th-20th century kris made entirely from chased and repoussé silver. The hilt is in the shape of a horse with human body and head of a horse. The blade is well watered and inlaid with gold in the center, ending in the shape of a dragon in ganja. The wrangka is decorated in high relief repoussé with two deer surrounded by flowers. Silver scabbard decorated in repoussé high relief on the obverse side. Blade's length: 14.5" (37 cm.). Sword's length: 20.5" (52 cm.). Estimated value: $1,600.

Fig. 5/154. Kalimantan. 19th century parang ihlang with elaborate staghorn carving of the hilt. A tuft of black hair protrudes from the hilt where a mythological animal's mouth is located. Woven rattan allows a better grip of the hilt. The blade is single-edged and made from forged iron. Primitive watering was done by an indigenous blacksmith. The blade is considerably older than the sword, by at least 300 years. Painted decorations and strings with dangling orangutan teeth adorn the scabbard. Blade's length: 17.5" (45 cm.). Sword's length: 27.5" (70 cm.). Estimated value: $1,800.

Fig. 5/155. Northern Borneo, Sarawak. 18th century parang ihlang with elaborate staghorn carving decorations on the hilt. The distal part of the hilt carries braided rattan decorations, while a tuft of human hair emerges from the top. Single-edged blade with incised decorations and eight perforations on the back of the blade. The scabbard, which could be a 19th century replacement, is decorated with relief carvings featuring a scorpion, snake, and insect. Blade's length: 16.5" (42 cm.). Sword's length: 22.5" (57 cm.). Estimated value: $1,400.

Fig. 5/156. 14th-15th century Majapahit short sword. The blade is single-edged and widens progressively toward the point. Very short hilt is represented by the tang only, as the organic material of the hilt disintegrated in the past. A disk protuberance below the hilt is actually a grip enhancer where the thumb and index finger grasp the sword. Blade's length: 16.5" (42 cm.). Sword's length: 19.2" (49 cm.). This is a very rare medieval artifact. Estimated value: $2,500.

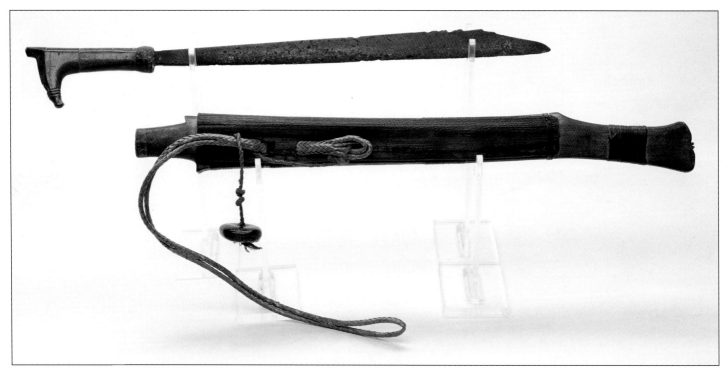

Fig. 5/157. Kalimantan. 18th-19th century parang ihlang with intricately carved decorations of the hilt in the shape of a horse's head. Anthropo-zoomorphic decorations adorn the scabbard. Three ornate rattan bands bind the scabbard's leaves. A round seed ornament is attached to the suspending cord. The back of the scabbard contains a pouch made from rolled raffia that usually contains a small knife. The blade is typically convex on the obverse side and flat on the reverse and has ornaments on the back of the blade. As is common, the blade widens toward the point. Blade's length: 15.8" (40 cm.). Sword's length: 26.3" (67 cm.). Estimated value: $1,500.

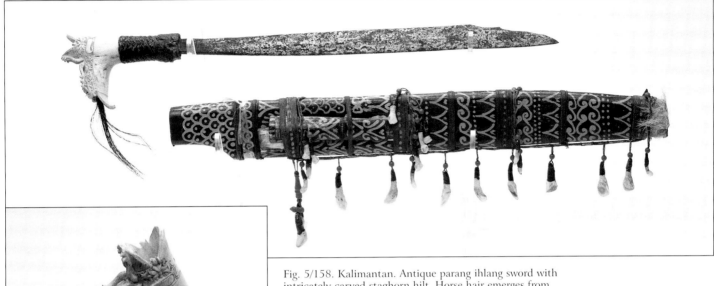

Fig. 5/158. Kalimantan. Antique parang ihlang sword with intricately carved staghorn hilt. Horse hair emerges from the hilt's openings. The hilt's grip is wrapped with woven raffia. The wooden scabbard is painted in red, yellow, and black and decorated with orangutan teeth and vegetable beads dyed in red. A small raffia pouch on the back of the scabbard holds a small knife. The blade widens gradually toward the point and is convex on the obverse side and flat on the other side. Blade's length: 16" (41 cm.). Sword's length: 25" (63.5 cm.). Estimated value: $1,200.

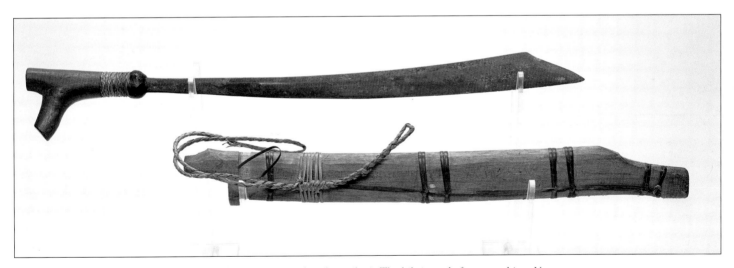

Fig. 5/159. Northern Borneo, Saba. 19th-20th century campilan (kampilan). The hilt is made from wood in a V shape and decorated in the lower part with raffia. The blade widens toward the point and has a convex and a flat side. The scabbard is made from balsa wood and has rattan decorations. Blade's length: 19" (48 cm.). Sword's length: 26" (66 cm.). Estimated value: $800.

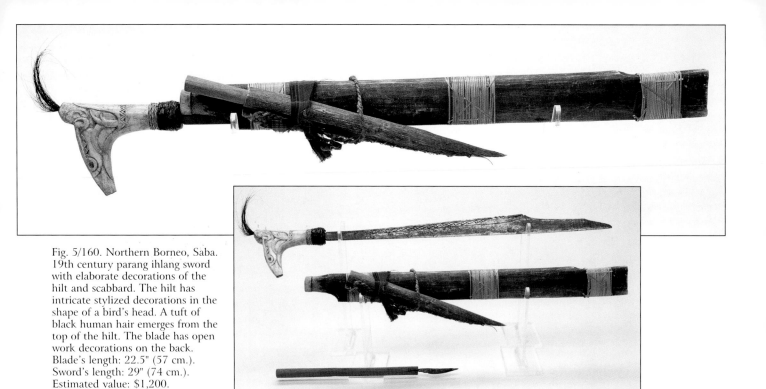

Fig. 5/160. Northern Borneo, Saba. 19th century parang ihlang sword with elaborate decorations of the hilt and scabbard. The hilt has intricate stylized decorations in the shape of a bird's head. A tuft of black human hair emerges from the top of the hilt. The blade has open work decorations on the back. Blade's length: 22.5" (57 cm.). Sword's length: 29" (74 cm.). Estimated value: $1,200.

Fig. 5/161. Northern Borneo, Saba. 18th-19th century Murut headhunter sword. The hilt is made from aged wood with dark patina. Wooden scabbard decorated with rattan bands and incised ornaments. The blade widens toward the point and turns the balance to the distal third where the cutting blow is desired. Old ornaments are still visible on the back of the blade. Blade's length: 18.5" (47 cm.). Sword's length: 24.2" (61.5 cm.). Estimated value: $950.

Fig. 5/162. Northern Borneo, Sarawak. 20th century parang ihlang with carved staghorn hilt. Single-edged blade widens in the lower third and is decorated with incised ornaments on its back. Wooden scabbard decorated with vegetable beads, orangutan teeth, and painted polychrome decorations. A pouch in the back contains a small knife. Blade's length: 17.8" (45 cm.). Sword's length: 28" (71 cm.). Estimated value: $900.

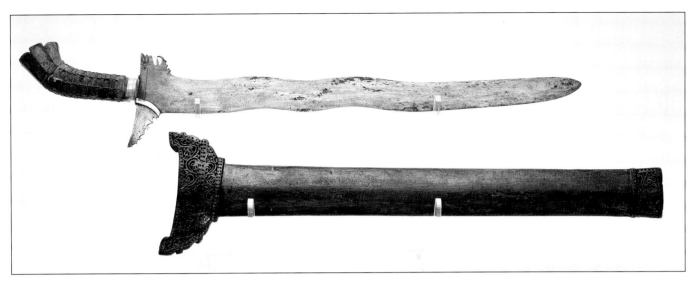

Fig. 5/163. Northern Borneo, Saba. 19th century Moro kris. The scabbard is decorated with intricate wooden carving. Wooden hilt covered with braided textile. The pommel is in the shape of a lotus bud. Wide blade with wavy undulations and silver ornament in ganja. Blade's length: 20" (51 cm.). Sword's length: 26.5" (67.5 cm.). Estimated value: $1,500.

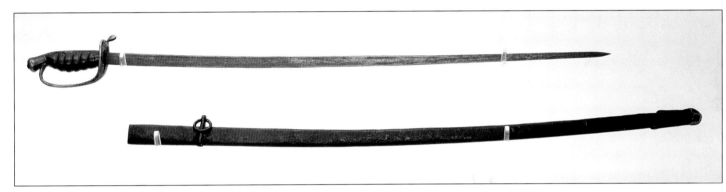

Fig. 5/164. Northern Borneo, Saba. Antique European saber, English or Dutch. Purchased in Borneo in the 1980s. The blade is unmarked, with some oxidation present. Hilt has decorated brass and ray skin and is covered with leather on the grip site. Metal scabbard with one ring for suspension. Blade's length: 29.3" (74.5 cm.). Sword's length: 37" (94 cm.). Estimated value: $850.

Fig. 5/165. Kalimantan. 20th century pair of parang ihlang swords with elaborate staghorn hilts carved in the shape of a billhorn's skull (one shown only). Wooden scabbard with polychrome painting and decorated with vegetable beads and orangutan teeth. The blade is single-edged and decorated with inlaid brass dots and open work on its back. Blade's length: 24.2" (61.5 cm.). Sword's length: 34" (86.5 cm.). Estimated value: $1,200 for the pair.

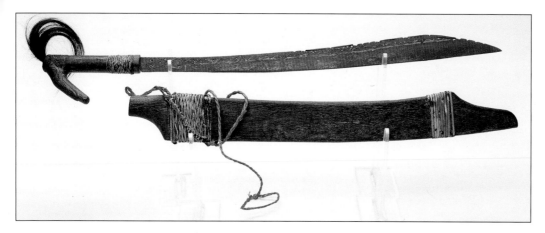

Fig. 5/166. Borneo, Sarawak. 18th century parang ihlang sword with carved hilt in the shape of a horse's head with human hair emerging from the top. Woven rattan forms the hilt's grip. The blade is convex on the obverse and flat on the reverse side. Wooden scabbard with incised decorations on the upper and lower part of the obverse side. Blade's length: 19.2" (49.5 cm.). Sword's length: 25.5" (64.8 cm.). Estimated value: $1,000.

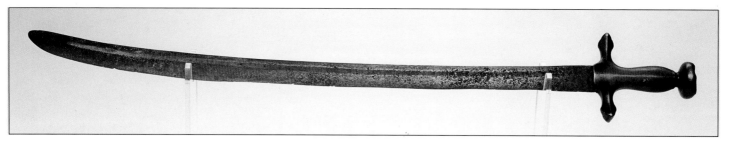

Fig. 5/167. North Borneo, Saba. Antique Islamic sword with bronze hilt and pommel, possibly dating to the 15th-16th century. Cruciform hand-guard. The pommel is round in shape with an open cavity at the end. Single-edged blade widening toward the point has considerable pitting corrosion. A single fuller is present. Blade's length: 25.5" (65 cm.). Sword's length: 29" (74 cm.). Estimated value: $1,250.

Fig. 5/168. Northern Borneo, Saba. Murut tribe parang ihlang with hand painted hilt carved from staghorn. The scabbard is painted and decorated with vegetable beads, animal hide, and orangutan teeth. Single-edged blade with inlaid round brass decorations. Blade's length: 19.7" (50 cm.). Sword's length: 29" (74 cm.). Estimated value: $800.

Fig. 5/169. Northern Borneo, Brunei. 20th century double-edged blade dagger with floral decorations on the blade, which is triangular in shape and widens toward the hilt. The hand-guard and the ferrule are made from silver. Round carved wood forms the pommel. The scabbard is made from wood decorated with silver bands. Blade's length: 8.5" (21.5 cm.). Dagger's length: 14" (35.5 cm.). Estimated value: $550.

Siam and Indochinese Swords and Daggers

Siam Swords, Daggers, and Knives

For the past eight hundred years, Siam was the only country in Southeast Asia that remained independent and free of colonial rule from any Western European colonialist country. The Thai people are independent, prosperous, and an example to the entire world for their benevolence, distaste for violence, and inclination towards a non-aggressive behavior. Thai men are expected to dedicate a few years from their life to be Buddhist monks, learning to be humble, to dissociate from the materialistic way of modern life (what we call "rat races"), to meditate in order to achieve internal peace, to keep personal dignity, and to appreciate a life of compassion and love for other human beings and animals. Buddhism, as well as its root, Hinduism, are not religions by themselves; rather, they are philosophies about life, respect for other human beings, and respect and love for animals.

The population of Siam represents a coalescence of several migratory groups from neighboring countries that settled in Siam over the centuries. The Siamese script, established in the 13th century, is a mixture of Khmen (Khmer) and Mon (Burmese), with the ancient Pali script as its original base. Cambodia remained a vassal state of Siam starting in the 15th century when the Khmer empire collapsed. In 1939, Siam changed its name to Muong Thai (poetic translation for "Land of the free"), and ever since the name Thailand has remained. Thailand is a democratic, constitutional monarchy with its people loving the king, country, and freedom.

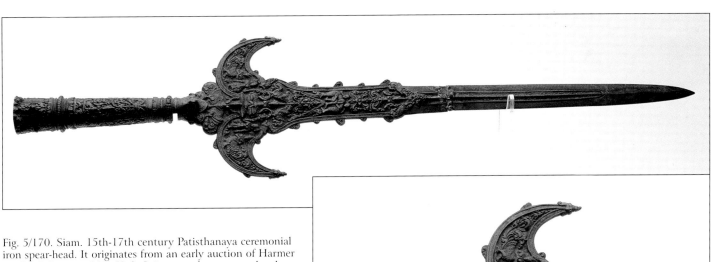

Fig. 5/170. Siam. 15th-17th century Patisthanaya ceremonial iron spear-head. It originates from an early auction of Harmer Rooke Galleries in New York. It is a very heavy spear-head with a long shaft that unfortunately underwent a fracture of the blade, which was soldered rather crudely. The entire sword is made from one piece of cast iron. The shaft is very long, hollow, and decorated on each side with a seated Boddhisattva holding implements in the raised hands. The head is arcuate and has a very intricate design with an enthroned central female figure surrounded by attendants. A fire blowing demon's head is above. The blade is decorated in high relief. In the proximal third of the blade, two wrestlers are competing and above is an enthroned female figure with war implements in the raised hands. The canopy above and the sides are formed by two dragons holding in their mouths a pointed war implement. Double-edged blade with two central fullers. The shaft of the handle is very long and allows for insertion of a wooden pole; this sword could be used for a procession as a standard. The intricate carvings and their multitude lead us to believe that this was a royal standard given by the Sinhalese royalty to the king of Siam. Patisthanaya is a spear described as Sinhalese and originating from Ceylon. However, the Sinhalese speak an Aryan language that is similar to the language spoken in the northern part of India and completely different from that spoken in the southern part of India, which is actually close to Ceylon. Blade's length: 25" (63.5 cm.). Sword's length: 35" (89 cm.). Estimated value: $25,000.

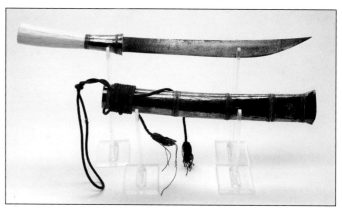

Fig. 5/171. Siam. 18th-19th century silver dagger dha with toned ivory hilt. The scabbard is made from a silver sheet decorated with filigree silver wire with a floral design. Single-edged blade is slightly curved, widens in the lower third. Blade's length: 9.3" (23.5 cm.). Dagger's length: 16" (40.5 cm.). Estimated value: $1,400.

Fig. 5/173. Siam. 18th-19th century sword. The hilt is made from toned ivory and silver and filigree silver in the distal part. Single-edged blade curves upward toward the back. The scabbard is made from silver decorated with filigree silver. A red cord serves for the sword's holding. Blade's length: 14.3" (36.5 cm.). Sword's length: 23" (58.5 cm.). Estimated value: $2,500.

Fig. 5/174. Siam. 18th-19th century silver dagger with toned ivory hilt. The scabbard is covered with silver decorated with filigree silver. Single-edged blade, slightly curved toward its back. Blade's length: 9.3" (23.7 cm.). Dagger's length: 16.5" (42 cm.). Estimated value: $1,400.

Fig. 5/172. Siam. 19th century short silver sword with toned ivory hilt. Wooden scabbard covered with filigree silver decorations on a silver sheet background. Single-edged blade is slightly curved, widens in the lower third. Blade's length: 11.8" (30 cm.). Sword's length: 20.5" (52 cm.). Estimated value: $1,500.

Fig. 5/175. Siam. 19th century silver dagger. The hilt is made from ivory and the distal part is mounted in silver decorated with filigree silver. Lacquered wood scabbard decorated with filigree silver bands. Silver chape also decorated with filigree silver. Single-edged curved blade that widens in the center. Blade's length: 9.5" (24 cm.). Dagger's length: 16.5" (42 cm.). Estimated value: $1,500.

Fig. 5/177. Siam. 18th-19th century silver dagger. The hilt and scabbard are decorated with filigree silver. Long and narrow single-edged blade. The pommel is in the shape of a stupa. Blade's length: 7.2" (18.5 cm.). Dagger's length: 12.5" (32 cm.). Estimated price: $1,000.

Fig. 5/176. Siam. 19th century silver dagger. The hilt and scabbard are made from repoussé silver and filigree silver. The scabbard's chape has a fish incised in the silver. A flower is incised in the pommel. Single-edged blade slightly widens toward the point. Blade's length: 8.5" (21.5 cm.). Dagger's length: 14.1" (36 cm.). Estimated value: $1,200.

Fig. 5/178. Siam. 19th century silver knife. The hilt and scabbard are made from silver and decorated with filigree silver. This is a small knife and was probably used as a concealed weapon. Single-edged blade. Blade's length: 5.8" (14.5 cm.). Knife's length: 10.5" (27 cm.). Estimated value: $700.

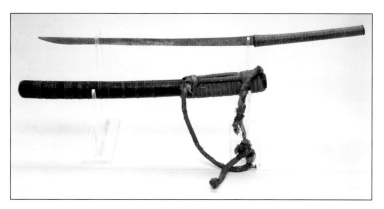

Fig. 5/179. Siam. 18th-19th century dha sword. Wooden hilt covered with woven rattan. The pommel is in the shape of a disk with an inscription. Peculiar for this sword, the blade narrows in the center portion and is single-edged. Wooden scabbard decorated with horizontal bands of rattan. A heavy orange cord allows for suspension of the sword. Blade's length: 18.5" (47 cm.). Sword's length: 30" (76 cm.). Estimated value: $800.

Fig. 5/180. Siam. 18th century knife. The handle is made from wood with a brass ferrule. Single-edged blade widens in the center. Interestingly, the cutting edge and the back of the blade are convex. Wide wooden scabbard in the shape of a box with one large brass band for retention and two wooden pegs. Blade's length: 9.8" (25 cm.). Knife's length: 15" (38 cm.). Estimated value: $375.

Fig. 5/181. Siam. 20th century short dha. The hilt and scabbard are made from teak wood carved in high relief. Single-edged blade widens toward the point. A rope is attached to the scabbard allowing for carrying of the sword. Blade's length: 13.8" (35 cm.). Sword's length: 26.8" (68 cm.). Estimated value: $500.

Vietnamese Swords, Daggers, and Knives

Under French colonial rule, Vietnam, Cambodia, and Laos formed French Indochina. These three countries, despite many similarities in their ways of living, had different historic backgrounds and culture, not to mention multi-ethnic populations. Mountain tribes including the Cham, Meo (called Miao in China), Hmong, and Karen are present in Indochina as well as in the surrounding countries, and are of Austronesian or Austroasiatic group.

The Chams were of Austronesian group origin and had their own language—they used Sanskrit as well as Cham in their stone inscriptions. Very little is known to the Western world about the kingdom of Champa, which existed in the central part of present day South Vietnam (part of the Unified Socialist Republic of Vietnam) from the 2nd century CE until the 19th century. The 15th century actually marked the demise of this highly civilized kingdom, which was Hindu.

Much more is known about another Hindu civilization, the Khmer kingdom that was located in present day Cambodia. While relatively well-preserved vestiges of the Khmer civilization have survived in Angkor Wat, Bayon, and elsewhere in the vicinity, relics from the Champa civilization deteriorated over the centuries and finally disappeared during the 1960s in what the Vietnamese called "American war," through shelling and bombing of the last remaining Cham archeological sites in South Vietnam. Photographs taken in 1942 revealed magnificent Champa buildings in at least three provinces of South Vietnam. Some of these archeological ruins still could be explored, as they are in deep jungle, half or totally buried in areas never explored by French archeologists. Obviously, huge amounts of money are needed for archeological exploration and the donors are still to be found. The socialist republic of Vietnam, which went through a period of famine until ten years ago, doesn't have the financial resources for these plans and the French and American governments are slow if non-existent in these mega projects. So far, UNESCO has not intervened in this issue and UNESCO officials seem content to declare some places as "world treasures" for future preservation.

Fortunately, a museum dedicated to the Cham civilization survived the misfortunes and now houses a collection of 294 carved stone and terracotta pieces of Cham culture. Located in Danang, the museum was looted several times in the 20th century, starting in 1946 during the French colonial protectorate and ending in the late 1980s after the communist reunification of the country. This is the only museum in the world dedicated to the Cham culture. Interestingly, the Indonesian Java culture bore similarity to the Cham culture. In fact, we have in our collection terracotta Majapahit statue heads from the 10th-12th century that are identical to Cham culture terracotta heads of the same period. Conversely, I assume that some of the Majapahit edged weapons were similar to those in the Champa kingdom.

It appears that the Vietnamese people resent the name "Annam," given by the Chinese to their country in the ancient and medieval time, and prefer the name Dai Viet, and Nam Viet. History reveals a continuous fight between the Dai Viet Vietnamese located in the north and the Cham people located in the central and southern areas of Vietnam. In fact, frictions between the Dai Viet, with a Chinese inspired culture, and the Chams' Hindu-influenced culture reflected opposing ethnic and religious beliefs. The Chams also experienced continuous armed struggle with the Khmers, despite the fact that the Khmers also had a Hindu influenced culture and religion.

Our collection of swords from Annam, dating to the 12th-14th century CE, are very interesting in that they are particular to Annam and not seen in other countries. The blades of these swords are thin, single-edged, and made from laminated layers of forged high content iron. Due to their high iron content, the blades are very corroded and almost disintegrate on touch. The hand-guard is in the shape of a disc, most often circular or oval. It is not known if these swords are Cham or Dai Viet, as there is no existing bibliography on this subject and more research is needed. A frieze that I have inspected twice in the past five years extends for a long distance along a wall in Bayon, Cambodia and illustrates a 12th century naval battle in the Tonle Sap lake between the Khmers and Chams. Unfortunately, even though the high relief frieze is well preserved, I could not distinguish clearly the weapons used in that battle. I assume that the swords in this collection are Cham and not Dai Viet, as in all the trips I have taken to North Vietnam, I have never been able to locate any of these elusive swords.

Many antique Chinese edged weapons are found in Vietnam, due to trading and the countries' proximity to each other. The Vietnamese Nguyen imperial rule, which existed under French colonial influence, stimulated the production of magnificent swords. These swords have bronze scabbards and hilts decorated with a plethora of inlaid mother-of-pearl decorations in a multitude of color tones ranging from silver to yellow gold natural hues. These inlaid mother-of-pearl decorations are, in my opinion, the best in the world, even taking into consideration that this handicraft originated in China.

Black lacquer, used not only in decorating the swords and daggers but also in a multitude of handicrafts, represents another superlative artistic expression. The contrast between the inlaid mother-of-pearl and the black lacquer background makes the final product very attractive; the gold hue of the Vietnamese mother-of-pearl is especially appreciated by connoisseurs. Creating this black lacquer is extremely laborious. It involves forming layer upon layer of black lacquer, each layer requiring tedious, prolonged polishing.

Along with the lacquer and inlaid mother-of-pearl, imperial Vietnamese swords have inlaid gold and silver decorations, mostly representing the imperial power symbol, the dragon. Occasionally, a phoenix bird is displayed as well, either together with the dragon or alone. These ornaments obviously originated in Chinese art and reflect the influence of Chinese art in Southeast Asia. Other 19th century Vietnamese swords have scabbards and hilts made from carved wood, brass with inlaid mother-of-pearl ornaments, repoussé silver or brass, etc.

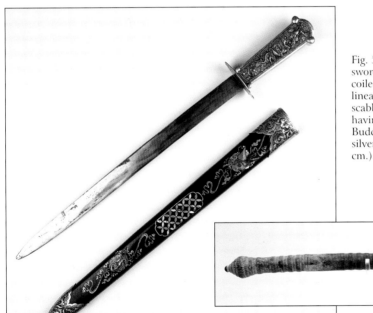

Fig. 5/182. Annam (Vietnam). Nguyen Dynasty, 19th-20th century sword. Silver hilt decorated with chiseled silver in the shape of a coiled dragon. The hand-guard is oval shaped and decorated with a linear design. Double-edged blade with age rust oxidation. Wooden scabbard lacquered in several layers and adorned with mother-of-pearl having gold and silver hues and forming an intricate design with Buddhist symbols. The scabbard's ends are made from hammered silver with highly decorative floral design. Blade's length: 14.5" (37 cm.). Sword's length: 20.7" (52.5 cm.). Estimated value: $3,000.

Fig. 5/183. Annam, Champa Kingdom (South Vietnam). 12th-15th century sword. Double-edged blade with high content iron alloy and severe corrosion. Due to layer welding, or watering, the disintegration of the blade is lamellar. This is a two-handed sword with a long hilt. Concentric metal bands allow a good grip of the handle. The pommel is bulb shaped like a stupa. The hand-guard is round with comma perforations and somewhat resembles the Japanese tsuba. The sword is similar in shape to the Khmer swords and daggers as the Khmer and Cham shared the same Hindu religion and culture. Cham swords and daggers are extremely rare and to the best of my knowledge have not been described in the world literature on edged weapons. Blade's length: 17.2" (44 cm.). Sword's length: 29" (73.5 cm.). Estimated value: $5,500.

Fig. 5/184. Annam, Champa Kingdom (South Vietnam). 12th-13th century Cham sword. This is a double handed sword with long hilt decorated with horizontal metal bands. Iron alloy single-edged blade with considerable corrosion and lamellar disintegration. The scabbard was probably made from an organic material that disintegrated a long time ago. The hilt measures 10" (12.5 cm.) in length. Sword's length: 31.5" (80 cm.). Estimated value: $4,500.

Fig. 5/185. Annam, Champa Kingdom (South Vietnam). 12th-15th century Cham sword with bronze hilt and hand-guard. The pommel has a zoomorphic ornament in the shape of a mythological animal's head. The hand-guard is oval shaped and has incised edges. High iron content alloy blade with lamellar disintegration following the pattern of welding the layers at the time of forging. This sword is extremely rare and to the best of my knowledge no similar specimen was ever exhibited in any museum. Green patina covers the hilt and the hand-guard. Blade's length: 23" (58.5 cm.). Sword's length: 29.8" (75.5 cm.). Estimated value: $5,000.

Fig. 5/186. Annam, Champa Kingdom (South Vietnam). 12th-15th century Cham sword with very long bronze hilt that allows two-hand handling. Concentric bands of iron cover the wooden inner core of the hilt. Peculiar to this sword is an acute angle formed between the hilt and the pommel that now is partially preserved. A round hand-guard with incised edges resembles the Japanese tsuba. Single-edged blade is slightly curved. Due to high iron content, the blade is disintegrating in lamellar pattern following the pattern of watering at the time of forging. This sword apparently was not buried, as the wood core has survived the centuries. Blade's length: 17" (43 cm.). Sword's length: 26.8" (68 cm.). Estimated value: $4,500.

Fig. 5/187. Annam, Champa Kingdom (South Vietnam). 12th-15th century Cham sword with long hilt allowing two-hand handling. Single-edged blade with high iron content now disintegrating in lamellar fashion following the original watering strata forging. Large round hand-guard with four comma like fenestrations. Green patina of the bronze hilt with ring retainers. Blade's length: 23" (58.5 cm.). Sword's length: 33" (84 cm.). Estimated value: $3,500.

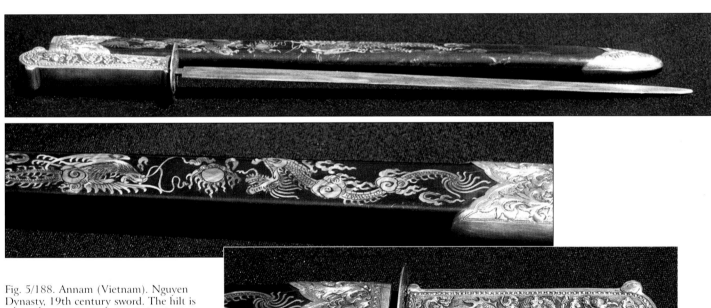

Fig. 5/188. Annam (Vietnam). Nguyen Dynasty, 19th century sword. The hilt is made from solid silver chiseled in high relief and featuring a dragon. An oval shaped hand-guard has an incised decoration. Mahogany wood scabbard with inlaid mother-of-pearl decorations on both sides and featuring a facing dragon, Phoenix bird and ling zhi with gold and silver hues. The proximal and distal part of the scabbard are made from solid silver chiseled in high relief. Double-edged blade with a rounded point. Blade's length: 15" (38 cm.). Sword's length: 22.5" (57 cm.). Estimated value: $4,000.

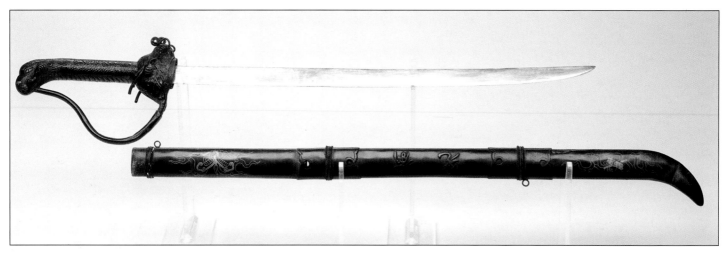

Fig. 5/189. Annam (Vietnam). 19th century sword with black lacquered brass hilt. The hand-guard is in the shape of a mythological horned animal. A knuckle-guard links the hand-guard to the pommel, which is in the shape of a mutton. Single-edged, indigenously made blade. Black lacquered brass scabbard decorated with inlaid silver and copper in the shape of Taoist emblems. Two Chinese characters are carved in high relief on the center of the scabbard on each side. Blade's length: 21.2" (54 cm.). Sword's length: 35.2" (89.5 cm.). Estimated value: $3,000.

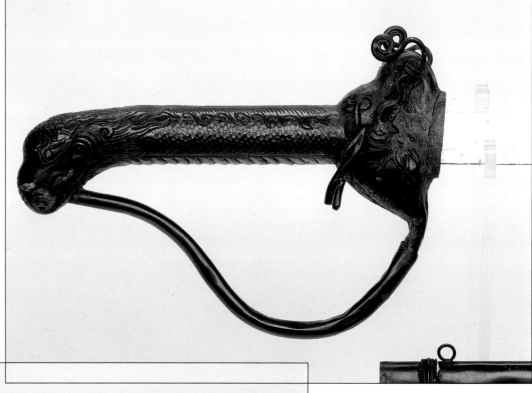

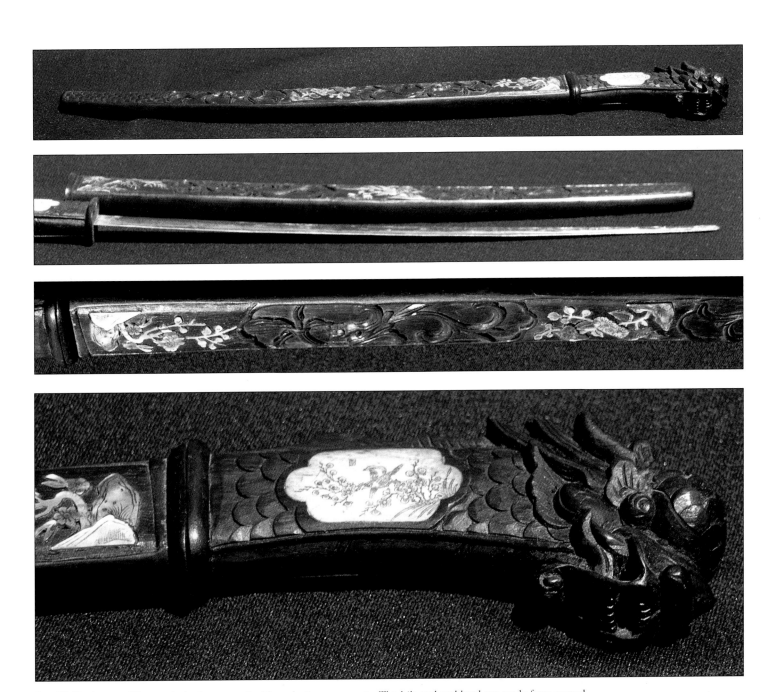

Fig. 5/190. Annam (Vietnam). Antique sword with exclusive ornaments. The hilt and scabbard are made from carved wood. A dragon head forms the pommel. Inlaid bone plaque decorated with polychrome and scrimshaw featuring birds, lotus flowers, etc. The scabbard is decorated with inlaid mother-of-pearl having gold and silver iridescent hues. Carved chape with dragon scales ornaments. Single-edged nickel blade with rounded point. Blade's length: 18.3" (46.5 cm.). Sword's length: 24.3" (62 cm.). Estimated value: $4,000.

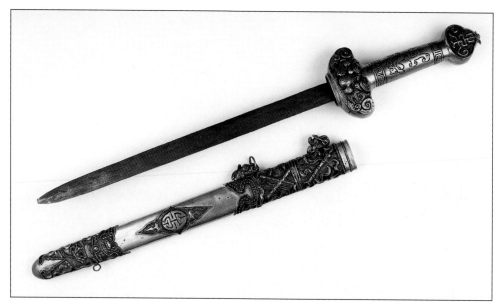

Fig. 5/191. Annam (Vietnam). 19th century silver sword, jian type. The scabbard and hilt are decorated with chased and repoussé silver having a zoomorphic design. Two silver hangers on the scabbard are in the shape of a mythological animal. Another hanger ring is located on top of the pommel. The blade is leaf-shaped, double-edged, and has the number 510 engraved near the hilt (most likely recycled from an old European blade). Blade's length: 14.2" (36.1 cm.). Jian's length: 22.8" (58 cm.). Estimated value: $2,000.

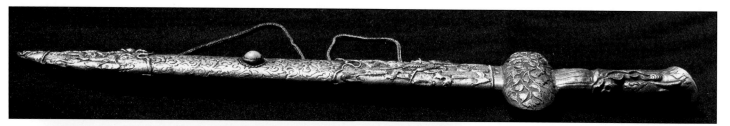

Fig. 5/192. Vietnam. Antique silver short sword decorated with dragons in high relief. The scabbard has two green decorative stones. The obverse of the scabbard features a hydra on the proximal end and lotus buds, flowers, and a bird on the distal end. The reverse side of the scabbard has a phoenix bird on the proximal end and a unicorn on the distal end. The chape is in the shape of a fish. A silver suspension rope is attached to the scabbard. The hilt and hand-guard have high relief decorations with floral design as the main pattern. Silver blade with Chinese inscription on the reverse and a hydra dragon on the obverse side. Blade's length: 13.5" (34.5 cm.). Sword's length: 22.8" (58 cm.). Estimated value: $2,000.

Fig. 5/193. Vietnam. 19th-20th century hand-made silver knife with staghorn pommel. The blade is decorated with incised birds and dragons. Dragon and phoenix bird chased in high relief decorate the hilt. Blade's length: 4.8" (12 cm.). Knife's length: 11.6" (29.5 cm.). Estimated value: $400.

Fig. 5/194. Vietnam. 19th-20th century silver knife with hand decorations on the hilt and blade. The hilt is chiseled in high relief with grapes and squirrels. Hand incised blade with dragons design. Tiger tooth pommel. Blade's length: 4.9" (12 cm.). Knife's length: 8.5" (21.5 cm.). Estimated value: $400.

Fig. 5/195. Vietnam. 19th-20th century silver knife with staghorn pommel. The handle is chased with a phoenix bird and dragon in relief. Single-edged blade. Knife's length: 10.2" (26 cm.). Estimated value: $400.

Fig. 5/196. Vietnam. 19th-20th century silver knife with staghorn pommel. Wide blade with one serrated edge and one sharp edge. Incised dragons decorate the blade on both sides. Grape vines and squirrels are chased in high relief on the hilt. Blade's length: 4.5" (11.5 cm.). Knife's length: 10.6" (27 cm.). Estimated value: $450.

Cambodian Swords, Daggers, and Knives

The Khmer culture flourished in Cambodia during the medieval period. We have in our collection several Khmer spears, axes, and daggers of simple form, well representing this period. Most are made from bronze with a high iron alloy and display green-gray patina and plenty of rust. These weapons were utilitarian and fail to display a degree of esthetic and artistic value.

Fig. 5/199. Cambodia. 13th-14th century Khmer spear. The blade is made from iron and has sustained considerable corrosion as well as a broken point (possibly in battle). The blade becomes wider in the mid-portion, then tapers progressively toward the point. The ferrule is very wide and made from bronze, rather than iron. Multi-faceted decorations with central circle(s) in the center decorate the ferrule. Round iron haft with marked corrosion once contained a wooden pole. Length: 16.5" (42 cm.). Estimated value: $450.

Fig. 5/197. Cambodia. 12th-15th century dagger. Single-edged blade, gradually widens in the distal third. Marked corrosion with pitting is present on the blade. Bronze hilt and hand-guard with elaborate decorations. The hilt is rectangular with pierced openings on each side in the upper, center, and lower third. Round pommel with incised decorations. Wide hand-guard with eight rounded edge indentations. Blade's length: 11.3" (29 cm.). Dagger's length: 17.5" (44.5 cm.). Estimated value: $950.

Fig. 5/198. Cambodia. 12th-13th century Khmer long pole iron spear. Double-edged rhomboid shape blade with a sharp armor piercing point. Round haft accommodates a wooden pole. Length: 17.8" (45 cm.). Estimated value: $500.

Fig. 5/200. Cambodia. 12th-14th century Khmer spear. The blade is markedly corroded. The socket is better preserved with green patina. Blade's length: 5.5" (14 cm.). Spear's length: 11.5" (29.1 cm.). Estimated value: $450.

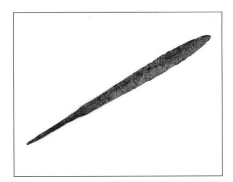

Fig. 5/201. Cambodia. 12th-14th century Khmer spear. Marked corrosion is present on the blade. The shaft tapers to the end. Blade's length: 10.5" (26.7 cm.). Spear's length: 15.5" (39.3 cm.). Estimated value: $450.

Fig. 5/202. Cambodia. 13th-14th century Khmer spear point. It is made from iron and has sustained considerable corrosion. The blade is rhomboid in shape with sharp edges of the distal two sides. The ferrule that connects the spear to the shaft has a multi-faceted diamond shape. The shaft is round and once contained a wooden handle. Length: 16.2" (41 cm.). Estimated value: $450.

Fig. 5/203. Cambodia. 13th-14th century Khmer war axe. It is made from iron and has sustained considerable corrosion. The edge is rounded and sharp. The shaft is round and once contained a wooden handle. Length: 11.4" (29 cm.). Estimated value: $350.

Fig. 5/204. Cambodia. 13th-14th century Khmer spear point. The blade is made from an iron alloy and has considerable surface corrosion and pitting. The blade widens in the center and then tapers toward the point. The shaft is round and hollow to contain a wooden handle. The portion that connects to the blade has geometric decorations. Blade's length: 12.5" (32 cm.). Estimated value: $400.

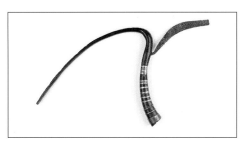

Fig. 5/205. Cambodia. 17th-18th century or earlier sickle dagger. The handle is made from wood covered with concentric bands brass. A sharp V back-turn of the handle contains the blade that is curved, made from iron, and has undergone severe lamellar age disintegration. The dagger was probably used for rice cultivation. Blade's length: 8" (20 cm.). Dagger's length: 27" (69 cm.). Estimated value: $700.

Fig. 5/206. Cambodia. Khmer decorative knife that was used for a ceremonial role, rather than a utilitarian task. The blade is curved and widens toward the center with a promontory, then curves inward toward the point. The most attractive part of this knife is the handle, which is in the shape of a seated monkey holding an offering tray on top of its head. The hand-guard has a rounded shape. Green patina covers the entire knife. Blade's length: 4" (10 cm.). Knife's length: 7" (17 cm.). Estimated value: $800.

Fig. 5/207. Cambodia. 12th-13th century Khmer axe. The shaft is made from hollow bronze that once contained a wood or organic material handle. The shaft is attached to the axe in quite a rudimentary fashion. Round edge axe with superficial corrosion and green patina. Traces of surface ornamentation are present on the side that was up during underground burial. The side that rested on the ground exhibits marked corrosion with surface deterioration. Axe's length: 9" x 6" (23 x 15 cm.). Estimated value: $500.

Chapter Six

Japanese Edged Weapons

Without a doubt, Japanese swords represent the ultimate sword collector's dream. For 1500 years, such swords embodied perfection with respect to the creation of edged weapons. The *samurai* is the typical representative of traditional swordsmanship in Japan, Kendo, or the way of the sword. Before being used, each sword was tested by cutting through human bodies. Many valuable swords manufactured during the Edo period bear an inscription in the tang showing what cutting tests were employed through different parts of the human body, or how many bodies were slashed in one drawing cut. Testing of this kind was done by a specialized person on deceased individuals or criminals sentenced to death. The cut was done in one motion with the sword brought from the high back to a forward motion, while the unfortunate condemned person had the hands tied above his head.

The predominant Buddhist religion of Shinto in Japan attributed three items as divine objects for exclusive use by the royal family: the sword, mirror, and sacred jewel. These divine objects were considered as the earthly presence of gods and named shintai. They were located in Shinto shrines and venerated as gods. Old swords designated as shintai are considered National Treasures and important cultural assets.

Japanese Sword Terminology

My intention in this book is to minimize Japanese terminology; on the other hand, it is important for the sword collector to be familiar with the nomenclature used, without getting drowned in the small details.

The most important part of the Japanese sword is the blade, and in its creation three master craftsmen are involved. First and most important is the smith, second is the polisher, and third is the master embellisher of the blade and sword fittings. The sword-smith creates the blade by enveloping the shingane (the inner core) with the hadagane (outer steel skin layer). The inner core is made of tough steel, which creates the sword's resilience to hard blows encountered in battle and the flexibility to survive bending without breaking. The outer layer has a high degree of carbon in the steel, as its manufacture involves folding on itself several times using carbon ashes and clay each time it is worked, followed by immersion in water. Hadagane, the outer layer, is much harder than the inner steel core, allowing the blade to cut through different body parts with great ease. The tang (nakago) has a hole in its lower third (mekugi ana) for insertion of a wooden peg used in hilt attachment to the tang. The blade's point is called kissaki and the hamachi is the point where the blade ends and the tang continues on.

After the blade is polished by a master craftsman, the hadagane makes visible the welding (watering) of the steel layers with the appearance of a grain pattern called hamon. The hamon has crystallized isles, dark and bright lines with undulations that are specific for each school of sword-smiths and the period of time the manufacture occurred. The hamon turns back toward the point, forming the bashi—which is the most vulnerable part of the blade. A strike of the blade with the bashi on a hard surface may cause kissaki breakage. This is the most likely cause for blade breakage and the only way to repair it is to shorten the sword. Most of the ancient swords and many of the medieval Japanese swords were shortened due to kissaki breakage.

The hamon pattern is of two types: nioi (poetically called visible fragrance) and nie (boiling). Nioi appears as a milky mist while nie appears as frost or milky stars, according to the way the crystals appear. These crystal formations bear poetical descriptions of nature, flowers, mountains, sea waves, water drops, floating sands, tree-tops, etc.

Shinogi is the longitudinal ridge separating the cutting part of the blade from the back, non-cutting portion of the blade. Mune is the back of the blade, which usually is blunt in the Japanese swords. The steel cutting surface (jihada) might have different grain pattern, such as itame hada (wood grain), masame hada (straight parallel lines), mokume hada (irregular circular shapes), or ayasugi hada (parallel wavy lines).

The cutting edge of the blade has a misty-gray appearance and is named ha-tsuya, while the polished area above is called ji-tsuya. Yakiba represents the junction between ha-tsuya and ji-tsuya and is actually the outer limit of the hardened part of the blade. A large variety of pattern yakibas can be obtained by the sword master, changing the shape of the clay outline when the clay cover is placed on the blade prior to heating the blade for hardening. The most common patterns of yakiba are notare (wavy), midare (irregular), sugu (straight), gunome (scalloped), nokogiri (saw-tooth), hyotan (gourd-shape), hitotsuri (irregular clouds), choji (cloves), yahazu (arrow notch), and ashi (rat foot). Frequently, these patterns are combined, as for example: sugu-notare, gunome-midare, etc. Older blades have yakiba parallel to and very close to the edge to grant strength to the blade. In the distal end of the blade and closer to the point, the yakiba line is wider, as the hardness is more important than the strength.

Infrequently, yakiba has two lines and this pattern is called nijiu yakiba.

Sword Ornaments

Carvings in high or low relief on the blade (horimono) are done on both sides of the blade on shinogi-ji (non-cutting edge of the blade). Gilded carvings are common on the blades of Edo and Meiji period swords. High end Japanese swords have hilt fittings as kashira and fuchi made of gold alloys as shakudo (mainly copper and gold) or shibuichi (mainly copper and silver). Animals, flowers, and insects of miniature dimensions made of gold alloy contrasted with the black background for spectacular effect. Kashira represents the cap end of the hilt and fuchi is the distal cap as a rectangular plaque on the hilt with usually shakudo miniatures. Menuki is a decoration under the hilt handle binding, with elaborate shakudo or shibuichi ornaments. Kojiri is a sword ornament representing the chape of the scabbard (distal end). Inlaid gold, silver, low or high relief shakudo, shibuichi decorations may adorn the kojiri.

Tsuba Sword Fittings

Tsuba is the hand-guard, made of metal that could be rectangular, round (maru gata), oval (tatemaru gata), 4 lobes (mokko), octagonal (kaku gata), trapez shape (aori gata), chrysanthemum shape (kiku gata), etc. In my opinion, tsuba is the most important collectible object related to Japanese swords, so it will be discussed in greater detail here.

For the majority of collectors, acquiring an authentic antique Japanese sword represents an almost impossible task, due in part to the high cost of the Japanese swords as well as the relative rarity of these swords. In contrast, the tsuba are more available to the average collector and of course, more affordable. The relative abundance of tsuba on the collectors' market is due to the fact that tsuba were used by samurai as barter for their life necessities and so survived over the centuries.

Earlier tsuba were made from an iron rich alloy and characterized by simple ornaments and the tendency to rust and corrode. The early tsuba of Muromachi (1333-1573) and Momoyama (1573-1603) typically have simple ornaments because the principal role of tsuba was to protect the hand in battle, rather than to provide esthetic appeal of the object. Hoju tsuba of the 6th century CE are characterized by very thin soft metal plates with raised rims in order to increase rigidity to the plate. The Edo period (1603-1867) brought peace and prosperity to Japan after endless fights between the feudal clans that existed during the Muromachi and Momoyama periods. Artistic development reached peaks never attained before, and buyers' wealth and refinement demanded the highest skills of craftsmen. Precious metals were inlaid in iron or bronze, creating realistic images with roots in Japanese mythology and folklore, Buddhist Zen religion, and nature's beauty.

Four plants are commonly represented in the tsuba decorations: orchid, plum blossom, chrysanthemum, and bamboo. Similarly, four auspicious animals are greatly represented in the metal decorations: ryu (dragon), phoenix, unicorn, and tortoise. Ryu symbolizes the imperial power and is also the rain and lightning god. The number of claws on the dragon is significant and points toward the power of the person who owns the dragon ornament. Five claws symbolizes imperial power, while four claws symbolizes only a prince position in the imperial court hierarchy. The three-clawed dragon was reserved for commoners. Ho, or phoenix, is a mythological creature that resembles a combination peacock, pheasant, and bird of paradise. The phoenix is a symbol of immortality and renewal in nature, and also a symbol of imperial authority, especially when represented together with the paulownia flower (kiri). An association of two animals or plants, or a combination of two, may have symbolic significance as a rebus that only a knowledgeable person might identify. For example, the combination of a pine tree with a crane symbolizes longevity.

Taoist philosophy emphasizes the importance of equilibrium between celestial and earthly powers. The earthly principle is symbolically represented by a turtle, while the celestial principle is represented by a crane. In Japanese temples as well as in Chinese Buddhist temples, a large bronze sculpture of a crane riding on a turtle is frequently seen. This is a vivid representation of the universe and also a symbol of immortality. Consequently, either of these two creatures represent longevity. A frequent rebus in Japanese culture is a carp swimming against the water current, symbolizing perseverance and the determination to succeed. Mythological creatures or deities are frequently represented in sword ornaments. Other than the seven immortals, the sennin and raiden figure representations are quite common. The raiden is the deity of thunder and lightning and represented by a man beating drums. The sennins are immortals represented by hermits living in a mountain cave.

The late Edo period tsuba are the most attractive, due to their magnificent high relief shakudo or shibuichi decorations. Gold or gilt; silver; silver alloy containing silver, copper, tin, lead and zinc (shibuichi); copper or copper alloy containing copper, zinc and tin (sentoku); alloy containing gold and copper (shakudo); and copper (ishime) were all used for decorations, most frequently in combinations of two or more kinds of inlaid metals or alloys. Occasionally, the tsuba was made from a sandwich of three layers held together by metal pins through the seppa dai's inner upper and lower edge. (Seppa dai is the area around the tsuba's main opening, the nakago ana). The outer layers of sanmai plate (sandwiched three plates) were made from precious metals as shakudo with a thick inner copper plate (yamagane). To enhance the esthetic appeal, thick gold foil (utori) was applied in the crevices of the shakudo's design.

Kagamishi tsuba was an early tsuba dating to the Kamakura and early Muromachi period and was made from an alloy of bronze and iron. The origin of the name signifies that the master creator was a mirror maker. Mostly, the tsuba master craftsman (tsubako) was a specialist dedicated solely to tsuba creation. Jihada (tsuba's surface) could be plain and smooth, carved, incised, or pierced. Fish roe (nanako) is a technique of using a hollow punch to create round incisions on tsuba's surface imitating the fish roe appearance. Ji sukashi is the technique of open work with pierced design. Open work with the impression of a silhouette is frequently seen in the Edo period tsuba and is called mon sukashi.

Kinko is a tsuba created from softer metals as shakudo, sentoku, shibuichi, copper, silver, gold, etc. The technique of using precious metals or alloys of precious metals applied (inlaid) in a carved or incised area is called iroe. Zogan (inlay) could be superficial and flat to the surface of the tsuba (hira zogan), or a true inlay (hon zogan) that could be raised in relief to the surface of tsuba (taka zogan). Brass inlay (shinchu zogan) was prevalent and specific to the Muromachi and early Edo period. Kyoto's Onin school of tsubakos used small inlaid thin brass in the iron plates Katchushi tsuba. The inlaid brass decorations are of two types: ten zogan and suemon zogan. Ten zogan type of inlay consists of brass dot ornaments and also linear brass inlays called sen zogan, surrounding the seppa dai and ana. Suemon zogan consists of large relief brass inlay with a variety of subjects as decorations.

Metals are not the only type of material found inlaid in the surface of the tsuba. An interesting technique is the insertion of colored enamels in previously incised or carved designs in the tsuba's surface (shippo zogan). Another decoration pattern is called sumi zogan, where the ink is inserted in the chiseled surface of the tsuba and appears as an incuse painting. Still another technique of ornamentation is gomoku zogan, the art of applying brass wire in a previously incised pattern. Nunome zogan refers to the technique of creating incised intersecting hatched lines in the tsuba's surface filled with precious metal inlays, or gold foil applied in the crevices of the lines.

Carved or Incised Surface of Tsuba.

Kebori is a technique of tsuba decoration that uses hair thin incisions of uniform chiseling to create a specific design. Guri bori is a design created by welding layers of shakudo and copper appearing as carved lacquer. Kata kiribori is a complicated technique of chiseling in uneven depth and width and appearing as a brush stroke. A magnificent artistic design is created by carving in relief below the surface of the tsuba (shishi aibori). Sukashi bori is a variant where the ground is chiseled away, leaving a design in high relief. Takabori iroe is the technique of creating a design by using a different metal than tsuba and decorating with inlays of precious metals or alloys. Mokume (wood grain) is a pattern of decoration using alloys and iron that are twisted, carved, and pounded until the surface resembles the "wood grain."

Attributes of Tsuba

The rim (mimi) can be flush to the surface, may have a cover (fukurin), kin fukurin (gold band covering the rim), sukidashi (thick rim), wa mimi (raised edge with rounded surface), etc.

The main opening in the tsuba (nakago ana) is for passing the blade and usually has a triangular shape. The openings for kozuka (kozuka hitsu ana, the small knives described in the next section), commonly have a semicircular and straight line shape. Kogai hitsu ana is provided for the kogai insertion and peculiarly has a rounded surface bearing a rounded protuberance. Occasionally, the opening(s) are plugged with shakudo or other metal plugs. Udenuki ana are two openings in the tsuba representing the sun and the moon; they are usually diagonally opposed. The samurai used udenuki ana for attaching the sword to the wrist during battles, by ingeniously threading a leather belt through the openings. Seppa dai is the area around the nakago ana, frequently used to carry the sword-smith's signature (mei). Sekigane are fillers on the top and bottom of nakago ana. Amid yasuri is a term applied to the lines emerging from seppa dai to mimi.

Reproductions of tsuba have been made since medieval times by casting copies of tsuba using early tsuba as the cast template. Characteristically, the cast copies have rugged areas on the inner edges of the hitsu ana, sukashi, and any openings where the surface was not filled by the forger. Bubble pits are also a sign of casting and a knowledgeable expert eye will detect them promptly. The contemporary fakes are even easier to detect due to lack of patina, fake greenish patina, and unsophisticated workmanship. The contemporary Chinese fakes are very common on the collectors' market and buyers should be alert.

Fig. 6/1. Kamakura period (1185-1392) or earlier, very heavy iron tsuba of cruciform shape. This early medieval Japanese tsuba has a relatively small nakago ana, denoting that a very long blade was threaded through in order to keep balance with the considerable weight of this tsuba. Also peculiar is the kozuka hitsu ana that is rectangular in shape and quite wide. Superficial corrosion and rust is present. Size: 4.5" x 4.2" (11.5 x 11 cm.). Estimated price: $5,000-$5,500.

Fig. 6/2. Muromachi period (1392-1477) very heavy iron tsuba with simple open work form in the shape of a cross and a rhomboid fenestration below. Two opposing head dragons are incised on sides, one double lined and one single lined. The tsuba is a maru gata tetsu sukashi type. Surface rust and superficial erosion are present and typical for this early tsuba. Size: 3.2" (8 cm.). Estimated price: $1,500-$1,800.

Fig. 6/3. Muromachi period (1392-1477) tetsu tate maru gata. This is a very heavy sukashi iron tsuba with pierced decoration in the shape of a partial cross at 12 o'clock and multiple round and other shape decorations. Size: 3.5" x 3.4" (9 x 8.5 cm.). Estimated price: $1,200-$1,800.

Fig. 6/4. Sukashi tetsu tsuba of maru gata design dating to Momoyama period (1477-1603). The edge is serrated and is peculiar in that it has three combined patterns of aoi (malloy leaves), circular and arrow, alternating with a combination of two patterns of combined aoi. Size: 2.8" (7 cm.) in diameter. Very rare shape of tsuba! Estimated price: $1,200-$1,500.

Fig. 6/5. Momoyama period (1477-1603) tetsu maru gata with considerable surface corrosion and rust. This prevents identification of the inlaid gold design, except for a man armed with a lance or harpoon and a large turtle that appear on the obverse side. Raised rim (sukidashi mimi). Size: 3" in diameter (7.5 cm.). Estimated price: $1,500-1,800.

Fig. 6/6. Momoyama period (1477-1603) tetsu mokko gata tsuba. Ji sukashi with incised and pierced decorations in high relief featuring a large coiled dragon around seppa dai. The surface has superficial corrosion and rust. It is quite unusual to find a very early iron tsuba with lavish decorations of this scale. Size: 3.2" x 3" (8.2 x 7.5 cm.). Estimated price: $8,000-$12,000.

Fig. 6/7. Momoyama period (1477-1603) tetsu tate maru gata tsuba with inlaid silver in stylized irregular linear decorations that vary on each side and emerge from the seppa dai toward mimi (amida yasuri). The iron plate is encompassed by a raised brass (shinchu) mimi. There are six pierced open work shapes forming a stylized human head image. Size: 3.1" x 2.9" (8 x 7.5 cm.). Estimated price: $1,500-$1,800.

Fig. 6/8. Early Edo period tetsu tate maru gata tsuba of ji sukashi type with very intricate open work featuring carriage wheels in each of the four corners. This design is also called genji guruma, the name deriving from Heian period, the tale of Genji. Size: 2.5" x 2.3" (6.5 cm. x 6 cm.). Estimated price: $1,000-$1,200.

Fig. 6/9. Early tetsu maru gata tsuba with high relief gilded brass decorations of a roaming horse and flower on the obverse and a similar flower on a tree branch on the reverse. Superficial corrosion and rust is present on the surface. Size: 2.7" in diameter (6.5 cm.). Estimated price: $1,200-$1,500.

Fig. 6/10. 17th century tetsu tsuba of mokko gata shape with raised wide rim decorated with inlaid gold vines and scrolls. Inlaid gold peony flowers and tendrils are featured on both sides of this superlative early tsuba. To some extent, the inlaid filigree gold decorations bear a similarity to Moghul decorations of the same period. Sukidashi mimi also decorated with inlaid gold. Size: 3" x 2.9" (7.5 x 7.2 cm.). Estimated price: $3,500-$4,000.

Fig. 6/11. Early Edo period, 17th century tetsu tate maru tsuba in the shape of a stylized kiku (chrysanthemum flower). Inlaid shibuichi linear, geometric design, decorate this tsuba. Interestingly, the shibuichi decorations continue over the rim to the opposite side. Indentations on the rim could be empty spaces where precious metal was inlaid and disappeared over the centuries. Size: 2.6" x 2.5" (6.5 x 6.2 cm.). Estimated price: $1,000-$1,500.

Fig. 6/12. 17th century tetsu tate maru gata tsuba with intricate sukashi open work in multiple layers. The decorations are carved in shibuichi and gilded. Traces of gilt are also visible on mimi. Two divergent dragons in chase of the luminous pearl are featured. The fine forging and chasing is katakiri. The seppa dai is decorated with multiple incised roundels on the obverse in a double pointed panel—this is very unusual and extremely rare. The kogai hitsu ana and kozuka hitsu ana are surrounded by opposing head gilded dragons. A single gilded dragon is featured at 6 o'clock. Mimi is gilded and the incised rim forms a kiki (chrysanthemum) edge. This exquisite tsuba has chased perforations on multiple levels, profuse shibuichi, and gilded decorations representing very detailed handwork. Size: 2.9" x 2.8" (7.3 x 7 cm.). Estimated price: $2,000-$2,500.

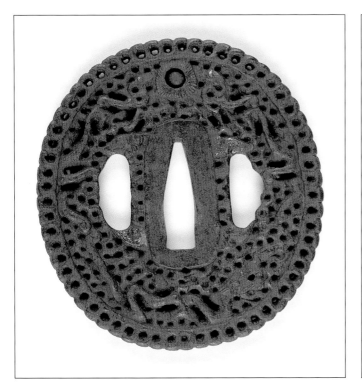

Fig. 6/13. Early Edo period tetsu tate maru gata sukashi with very ornate, chased open work katakiri. The raised rim has central perforations on each rounded segment. This tsuba, decorated with gilded dragons, is a masterwork of the Edo period. At 12 o'clock there are two converging dragons with inlaid gold eyes siding a flaming ball. The adjacent area of seppa dai has four diverging gilded dragon heads. At 6 o'clock there is a large hydra dragon. Size: 3" x 2.8" (7 x 6.5 cm.). Estimated price: $2,000-2,500.

Fig. 6/15. Early Edo period tetsu mokko gata decorated with inlaid gold in the shape of flying birds, grasses, etc. The incised and chased design appears as mountains on the apical portion and on the distal part, as a river with a boat and fisherman plus hanging tree branches (or vines) above. Despite the superficial corrosion and rust, the design is still visible and fresh. Size: 2.8" x 2.5" (7 x 6.5 cm.). Estimated price: $1,200-$1,500.

Fig. 6/14. Early Edo period tetsu mokko gata with relief decorations of inlaid gold, shakudo and shibuichi. The obverse features inlaid gold, shibuichi and copper in the shape of two men resting in a wheelbarrow. Above, there are inlaid gold and shakudo decorations forming leaves, flowers, and tree branches. Strikingly, heavy corrosion affected the tsuba's surface but the inlaid gold and silver ornaments remained practically intact, showing little wear. Kozuka hitsu ana was plugged with shibuichi plug. Size: 3.5" x 3.2" (9 x 8 cm.). Price: $3,500-5,000.

Fig. 6/16. Early Edo period tetsu tate maru gata with shakudo and gold inlaid decorations exhibiting a flying human figure (above) and another human figure offering a gold dish (below). Both the obverse and reverse sides feature an inlaid wavy gold wire decoration. Superficial corrosion and rust do not affect the quality of inlaid decorations. Size: 2.9" x 2.7" (7.3 x 6.8 cm.). Estimated price: $1,500-1,800.

Fig. 6/17. Early Edo period tetsu tanto tsuba of oval shape decorated with shakudo seated sennin and tree sentoku in high relief on the obverse side. The reverse has dotted inlaid gold (hira zogan) decorations. Size: 2" x 1.6" (5 x 4 cm.). Estimated price: $900-$1,300.

Fig. 6/18. Early Edo period shibuichi mokko gata featuring carving in high relief of a flock of birds amongst clouds above and stormy ocean waves below. The pattern continues from one side to the other and one bird is actually carved on the rim. To suggest the water waves effect, the rim also has portions that are raised and folded over. Inlaid gold of unidentified shape and structure is present in the clouds, sky, and on top of the sea waves. Graffiti inscribed as "M849" on seppa dai and "..19.." on the other arm of seppa dai are present and of a date not known. Size: 2.6" x 2.4" (6.5 x 5.5 cm.). Estimated price: $4,000-$5,000.

Fig. 6/19. Early Edo period tanto tetsu tsuba with shakudo bird and gold floral inlaid decorations on the obverse side. The bird is perched on a tree branch made from relief inlaid gold. Inlaid gold leaves are located on a bamboo branch below. The reverse features relief gold decorations in the shape of mushrooms near a water stream. Size: 2.2" x 1.6" (5.5 x 4 cm.). Estimated price: $900-$1,300.

Fig. 6/20. Early Edo period tetsu maru gata gilded bird on a blooming cherry tree, all carved in high relief. Gilded grasses and a blooming cherry branch are identified on the reverse. Size: 2.6" in diameter (6.5 cm.). Estimated price: $900-$1,200.

Fig. 6/21. Early Edo period tetsu tate maru gata with high relief inlaid gold decorations (taka zogan) featuring leaves and buds of kiku flowers and shakudo kiku in full bloom. The reverse side features inlaid gold mushrooms and dots representing stones near a carved country road. Sentoku filler bars were inserted in nakago ana. Size: 2.4" x 2" (6 x 5 cm.). Estimated price: $1,500-$2,000.

Fig. 6/22. Early Edo period tetsu maru gata decorated with inlaid gold featuring a bird in flight and inlaid silver in the shape of crescent moon, as well as a silver bar on the interior straight edge of kozuka hitsu ana. There is superficial corrosion with excellent preservation of inlaid gold and silver. Size: 2.9" in diameter (7.3 cm.). Estimated price: $1,500-2,000.

Fig. 6/23. Early Edo period tetsu mokko gata with inlaid gold in high relief featuring plum blossoms and buds on long stems. Size: 2.8" x 2.5" (7 x 6.4 cm.). Estimated price: $1,000-$1,500.

Fig. 6/25. Early Edo period tetsu mokko gata of quadri-lobate shape. The obverse side is decorated with an inlaid shakudo dog near a house, inlaid sentoku clouds, and inlaid silver bamboo and vegetation. Surface corrosion is present, but the design is intact. Size: 3" x 2.8" (7.5 x 7 cm.). Estimated price: $1,500-$2,000.

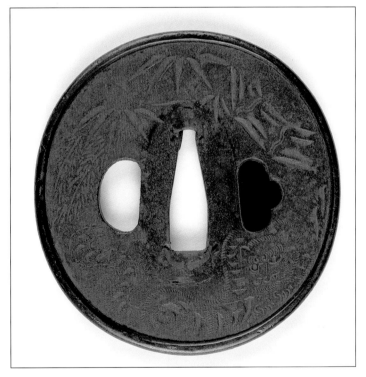

Fig. 6/24. Early middle Edo period tetsu tsuba of maru gata shape. Decorated with incised vegetation and bamboo leaves. It has a raised rounded rim (Wa mimi) and a brass filler on the bottom of nakago ana. A shakudo plug obturates the kogai ana. Superficial corrosion attests to its old age. Size: 2.8" (7 cm.). Estimated price: $1,000-$1,300.

Fig. 6/26. Middle Edo period tetsu tate maru gata of crude metal cutting, not decorated. Signed on seppa dai with three characters. Size: 2.8" x 2.5" (6.3 x 7 cm.). Estimated price: $500-$800.

Fig. 6/27. Middle Edo period tetsu kaku gata with incised decorations featuring grain and rice plant with partially rubbed off gilding. Incuse triangular decorations in the shape of starfish chiseled in high relief below the surface are a particularly rare design for this tsuba (shishi aibori). A silver filler (sekigane) is located in the bottom of nakago ana. Size: 2.7" x 2.4" (6.5 x 6 cm.). Estimated price: $1,000-$1,300.

Fig. 6/28. Middle Edo period tetsu maru gata decorated on the obverse with an inlaid floral design and shibuichi dot probably symbolizing the sun splendor (nikka). The reverse side features three gold inlays probably representing grasses near a water creek. It has an applied shakudo mimi. Size: 2.8" (7cm.). Estimated price: $1,000-$1,500.

Fig. 6/29. Middle Edo period tetsu tate maru gata inlaid with high relief gold (taka zogan) stem and chrysanthemum leaves and flowers. There is an inlaid copper wood stem at the base. Size: 2.5" x 2.3" (6.2 x 5.5 cm.). Estimated price: $1,300-$1,700.

Fig. 6/30. Middle Edo period tetsu tate maru gata decorated with a shakudo noh mask, a few gold linear ornaments, and a raised tree design. The reverse side features grasses on a linear pattern. Size: 2.8" x 2.6" (7 x 6.5 cm.). Estimated price: $800-$1,200.

Fig. 6/31. Middle Edo period tetsu sukashi tate maru gata featuring a heap of rice and two adjacent people's heads. Below, a hatchet is featured in a fenestration of the open work that is visible on the reverse side, while another design is seen from the obverse. Size: 2.5" x 2.4" (6.4 x 6 cm.). Estimated price: $800-$1,200.

Fig. 6/32. Middle Edo period tetsu sukashi maru gata with decorations in high relief featuring trees, vegetation, and pagoda. High relief chased and incised decorations (katakiri) and raised rim (sukidashi mimi). Size: 2.8" (7 cm.). Estimated price: $1,000-$1,200.

Fig. 6/33. Middle Edo period tetsu tate maru gata with inlaid gold decorations on relief iron design. The obverse side features a boy riding a water buffalo. Incised decorations in the shape of tree branches are located above. Inlaid gold decorations are on raised dots. Size: 2.8" x 2.5" (7 x 6.5 cm.). Estimated price: $1,200-$1,400.

Fig. 6/34. Middle Edo period tetsu tate maru gata with inlaid gold, shakudo, shibuichi and copper decorations. It pictures a man riding a horse on a road lined by pine trees. The reverse features inlaid gold grasses. Size: 2.8" x 2.4" 7 x 6.3 cm.). Estimated price: $1,500.

Fig. 6/35. Middle Edo period bronze kaku gata The opposite corners on the obverse side feature an incuse triple diamond pattern with the interior of one depicting a high relief cherry blossom with inlaid gold and the other featuring high relief inlaid kiku shakudo with gold leaves. The reverse side has only one corner with the incuse triple diamond pattern. The incuse design is of rare shishi aibori type. The tsuba's surface has concentric nanako raised impressions. Mimi is a thin raised ring. Size: 2.8" x 2.3" (7 x 6 cm.). Estimated price: $2,500-3,000.

Fig. 6/36. Middle Edo period tetsu tate maru gata decorated with inlaid shibuichi, sentoku, gold taka zogan and ishime. The obverse side features three flying cranes and, above a water stream, bamboo stems and leaves of raised sentoku and shakudo in high relief. A few copper dots representing stones are located near the water stream. Size: 3" x 2.8" (7.5 x 7 cm.). Estimated price: $1,500-$2,000.

Fig. 6/38. Middle Edo period tetsu mokko gata for a tanto, decorated with high relief gold, shibuichi, shakudo and sentoku featuring aquatic vegetation and fish. Size: 2" x 1.5" (5 x 4 cm.). Estimated price: $900-$1,200.

Fig. 6/37. Middle Edo period tetsu tate maru gata decorated with an incised giant kiku bloom and leaves and miniature kiku buds and flowers made from carved and inlaid gold. Most of the carved decorations are in relief, but below the tsuba's surface (shishi aibori). Size: 2.8" x 2.6" (7 x 6 cm.). Estimated price: $1,200-$1,500.

Fig. 6/39. Middle Edo period bronze maru gata decorated with dotted concentric lines on both sides. It also features a shallow rim (mimi). There are traces of possible inlaid attachments that were glued, rather than soldered, and with the passing of time were removed or lost. Size: 3" (7.5 cm.). Estimated price: $800-$1,200.

Fig. 6/40. Middle Edo period tetsu tate maru gata inlaid with gold in relief (taka zogan). The incised decorations feature a smiling man with a golden hat. Vegetation is seen above and below. The reverse side features only incised vegetation. Size: 2.8" x 2.5" (7 x 6.5 cm.) Estimated price: $800-$1,200.

Fig. 6/41. Middle Edo period tetsu mokko gata for a tanto decorated in high relief with inlaid shakudo flowers and gold leaves. The reverse features one leaf each made from relief inlaid gold and silver. Size: 2" x 1.5" (5 x 4 cm.). Estimated price: $800-$1,200.

Fig. 6/42. Middle Edo period tetsu mokko gata for a tanto, decorated with raised shibuichi and kin taka gold zogan in the shape of butterfly, bamboo leaves, and bird. The reverse side has incised decorations as grass and inlaid gold dots. Size: 2" x 1.5" (5 x 4 cm.). Estimated price: $900-$1,200.

Fig. 6/44. Middle Edo period tate maru gata bronze tsuba decorated with nanako (fish roe) incised technique. Size: 2.8" x 2.2" (7 x 5.5 cm.). Estimated price: $600-$800.

Fig. 6/43. Middle Edo period sentoku tate maru gata decorated with three shakudo grape leaves and relief copper tendrils and stems. The reverse side features only one shakudo grape leaf that was partially rubbed off. The tsuba's background is nanako style (fish roe). Size: 2.8" x 2.5" (7 x 6.3cm.). Estimated price: $800-1,200.

Fig. 6/45. Late Edo period tetsu tate maru gata sukashi tsuba carved and chiseled with kiku flowers, buds, and leaves in high relief. Size: 2.8" x 2.7" (7 x 6.5 cm.). Estimated price: $900-$1,500.

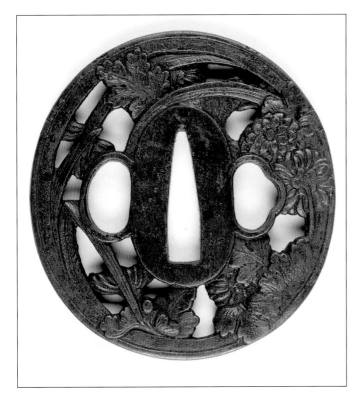

Fig. 6/46. Late Edo period tetsu maru gata sukashi tsuba incised and chiseled in high relief with kiku flowers, buds, and leaves. Size: 2.8" (7 cm.). Estimated price: $900-$1,500.

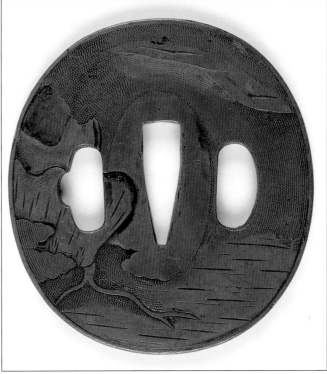

Fig. 6/47. Late Edo period sentoku tate maru gata with incised landscape design on nanako background. Size: 2.8" x 2.5" (7 x 6.3 cm.). Estimated price: $700-$1,000.

Fig. 6/48. Late Edo period bronze aori gata (trapez form) with rounded corners. The obverse features a high relief shakudo rod with a gold dot at the proximal end. The rod is encased in two silver bars in high relief. The rim (mimi) has a crenellated, incised pattern in the shape of a twisted rope—a very rare design and the first we have ever seen. Size: 2.6" x 2.4" (6.5 x 6cm.). Estimated price: $900-$1500.

Fig. 6/50. Late Edo period sanmati maru gata with outer layers made from shakudo and inner layer of bronze. This tsuba is thin, about half the thickness that is common. It is decorated with incised ornaments in the shape of grasses and a spider web on the obverse side and grasses on the reverse. Size: 2.6" x 2.4" (6.5 x 5.5 cm.). Estimated price: $800-$1,000.

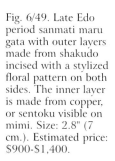

Fig. 6/49. Late Edo period sanmati maru gata with outer layers made from shakudo incised with a stylized floral pattern on both sides. The inner layer is made from copper, or sentoku visible on mimi. Size: 2.8" (7 cm.). Estimated price: $900-$1,400.

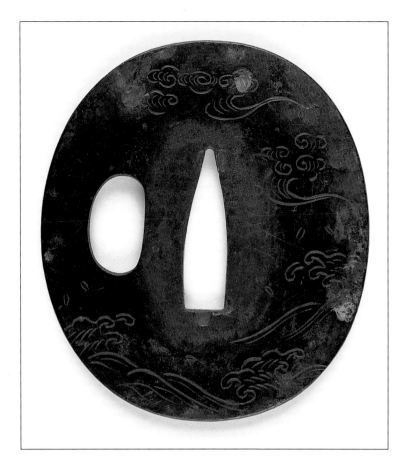

Fig. 6/51. Late Edo period bronze tate maru gata decorated with an incised stylized ocean waves design. Size: 2.8" x 2.3" (7 x 6 cm.). Estimated price: $600-$800.

Fig. 6/52. Late Edo period bronze kaku gata with rounded edges. The obverse is decorated with an incised design featuring a boy playing a flute, a crane and kiku. The reverse is decorated with kiku, drum, hoe, and a raking tool. Size: 2.3" x 2" (6 x 5 cm.). Estimated price: $700-$900.

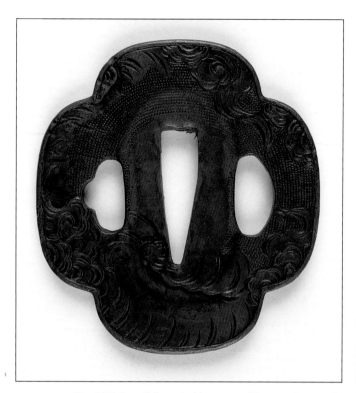

Fig. 6/53. Late Edo period bronze mokko gata decorated with incised clouds, fungus of immortality, and sea waves. The background is in the shape of nanako oriented in concentric lines. Size: 2.4" x 2.2" (6 x 5.5 cm.). Estimated price: $800-$1,200.

Fig. 6/54. Late Edo period sukashi shibuichi tate maru gata carved and incised in high relief tsuba made for a tanto. It features a bird perched on a tree branch, fungus, and flowers. Facing the bird is a stylized dragon. Size: 2.2" x 1.8" (5.5 x 4.5 cm.). Estimated price: $900-$1,300.

Fig. 6/55. Late Edo period bronze tate maru gata decorated with dotted decorations in concentric lines. Size: 2.8" x 2.5" (7 x 6.3 cm.). Estimated price: $500-$800.

Fig. 6/56. Late Edo period sentoku mokko gata decorated with incised oblique lines. It has a sharp edge rim (mimi). Size: 1.8" x 1.1" (4.5 x 3 cm.). Estimated price: $200-400.

Fig. 6/57. Late Edo period brass sukashi tate maru gata with open work in the shape of four bats. Three shibuichi inlaid pyramid shape decorations are together on the obverse; on the reverse, one inlaid pyramid is exiting the tsuba from the opposite diagonal poles. In my opinion, this tsuba of simple form is a funerary tsuba that, together with the sword, was probably buried with the owner some time in the past. The obverse side with the three pyramids together represents life, while the reverse depicting one of the pyramids diverging represents the departing soul. The rebus of death is symbolized by the four bats that are on each side. This rebus originates from Chinese mythology. Estimated value: $2,000.

Fig. 6/58. Late Edo period sentoku tate maru gata of simple design and convex surfaces. Size: 2.8" x 2.6" (7 x 6.5 cm.). Estimated price: $600-$900.

Fig. 6/60. Late Edo period sukashi sentoku tsuba with intricate open work featuring an eagle perched on a tree branch, grass vegetation, and a small bird featured below. Relief inlaid gold decorations (taka zogan) are represented by grasses and the bird. Size: 2.2" x 2" (5.5 x 5 cm.). Estimated price: $1,000-1,500.

Fig. 6/59. Late Edo period bronze mokko gata with simple, undecorated surfaces. Size: 2.6" x 2.3" (6.5 x 6 cm.). Estimated price: $500-$800.

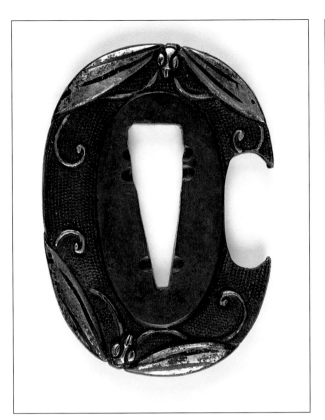

Fig. 6/61. Late Edo period oval shape shakudo tsuba having a bronze seppa dai. Decorations on this tsuba are inlaid high relief gold ornaments in the shape of two butterflies on the obverse side. The reverse side has inlaid floral and leaf decorations that are a direct continuation of the butterflies from the obverse; the design is carried on the rim. A nanako pattern in concentric lines is seen on both sides. Size: 2" x 1.3" (5 x 3.5 cm.). Estimated price: $1,500.

Fig. 6/62. Late Edo period sentoku tate maru gata tsuba with a plain surface. Size: 2.8" x 2.6" (7 x 6.5 cm.) Estimated price: $400-$800.

Fig. 6/63. Late Edo period brass mokko gata decorated on the obverse with eight incised characters. Size: 3" x 2.5" (7.5 x 6.3 cm.). Estimated price: $700-$1,000.

Kogai and Kozuka, Japanese Knives

Kogai is a cylindrical, blunt-edged knife resembling a skewer and fitted into a pocket of the scabbard near the hilt. Elaborate relief decorations with shakudo or shibuichi are usually present on the handle of the kogai. Its use as a hair ponytail knot thread or opener is unlikely; most probably, it was used as a lock for the sword that would not fall out of the scabbard while the sword was being carried. Another possible use was for piercing the enemy's ankle artery. Occasionally, the kogai is divided into two parts that serve as chop sticks (hashi). *Koi-guchi* is a ring shaped sword fitting located at the opening of the scabbard that has decorations in silver or gold alloys on better swords and daggers.

The most important sword fitting following the tsuba is *kozuka*, a small knife that is inserted in the scabbard. The blade of kozuka is straight and tapering toward the point. It is made of kataha plates that are constructed by welding a plate of iron to a plate of steel. The iron plate is rough and carries the decorations, while the steel plate is highly polished but left undecorated and always inward oriented when sheathed in the scabbard. The most elaborate decorations are located on the handle—inlaid, low or high relief with shibuichi and shakudo. Occasionally, the decoration of the master sword-smith is on a plate (ji-ita) that is inserted by an apprentice into the handle of kozuka. The decorations on the back are usually incised or en-graved and a short poem might be incised for the enjoyment of the owner. Rarely, the kozukas are made from carved wood, bone, ivory, or staghorn. Being a highly decorative object, kozukas are adorned with a combination of inlaying, engraving, chiseling, carving, and enameling for the ultimate artistic expression. Two examples of kozuka are included in the next section, as are as a few examples of trousse sets composed of knife(s) and chopsticks.

***

Japanese swordmanship was governed by rigid rules of behavior and combat protocols. Kendo schools of swordmanship taught discipline, devotion to master, and enlightment of the spirit. The medieval schools of Kendo developed in Shinto temples and emperor's sons became samurai monks. A noble samurai was above the laws of the commoners and responsible only to the emperor for his actions. Before battle, the long hair was washed and the ponytail attached to the top of the head that was shaven. Inside the helmet, a sachet of fragrance was enclosed in the event of death and possible decapitation. After battle, the head of the opponent was cut with *koshigatana*, a smaller sword attached to the belt. *Seoi tachi* or *no tachi* is a sword attached to the back and used for fast development. A final word for Japanese sword collectors involves the Japanese nomenclature—the pronunciation is not English, but Latin.

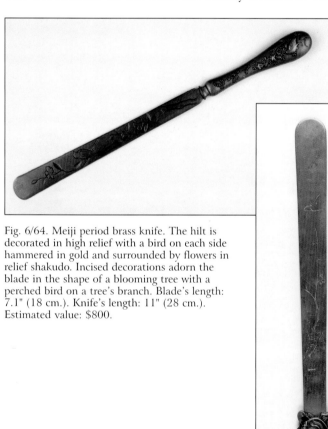

Fig. 6/64. Meiji period brass knife. The hilt is decorated in high relief with a bird on each side hammered in gold and surrounded by flowers in relief shakudo. Incised decorations adorn the blade in the shape of a blooming tree with a perched bird on a tree's branch. Blade's length: 7.1" (18 cm.). Knife's length: 11" (28 cm.). Estimated value: $800.

Fig. 6/65. 19th-20th century, Meiji period knife. The hilt is a masterpiece of craftsmanship with high relief decorations in gold featuring two birds, flowers, grapes, and vines. Above is a solitary copper bird. Brass blade, rounded at the point and decorated with incised ornaments. Blade's length: 9" (23 cm.). Knife's length: 30 cm.). Estimated value: $900.

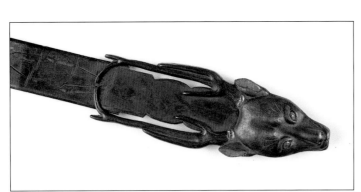

Fig. 6/66. 19th-20th century, Meiji period knife. The hilt is in the shape of a deer head and made from shakudo. The deer's eyes, ears, and other highlights of the head are gilded. Brass blade with rounded point and incised decorations. Blade's length: 7.5" (19 cm.). Knife's length: 9.5" (24 cm.). Estimated value: $1,000.

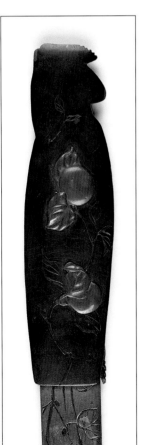

Fig. 6/68. 19th-20th century, Meiji period knife. The hilt is decorated in high relief with gilded ornaments in the shape of longevity God. The blade has a triangular shape at the point and is decorated with incised ornaments. Blade's length: 7.5" (19 cm.). Knife's length: 9.5" (24 cm.). Estimated value: $900.

Fig. 6/67. 19th-20th century, Meiji period knife. The hilt is made from shakudo and decorated in high relief with peaches. Brass blade decorated with incised ornaments. Blade's length: 6" (15 cm.). Knife's length: 8" (20 cm.). Estimated value: $900.

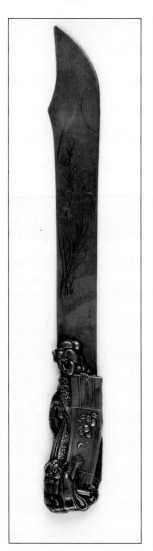

Fig. 6/69. 19th-20th century, Meiji period knife. The hilt is decorated with high relief ornaments in the shape of a Geisha holding a big plaque and child below. The brass blade is in the shape of a falchion and decorated with incised ornaments. Estimated value: $800.

Fig. 6/70. 19th-20th century Meiji period highly ornamental knife. The hilt features high relief decorations inlaid in gold showing cranes surrounded by lotus. The blade is decorated with incised blooming flowers and a flying bird, a design that is present on both sides. Blade's length: 10" (25.5 cm.). Dagger's length: 14.2" (36 cm.). Estimated value: $1,400.

Fig. 6/71. 19th century, Meiji period kozuka knife. The hilt is made from shakudo with inlaid gold decorations in high relief (taka zogan) and represents an oni suspended by a long rope. A man below is pulling the rope and apparently trying to catch the oni. The reverse side features an identical scene. The blade carries an inscription close to the hilt. Blade's length: 4.2" (11 cm.). Knife's length: 8.2" (21 cm.). Estimated value: $1000.

Fig. 6/72. 19th century, Meiji period kozuka knife. The handle (hilt) is made from shakudo with high relief inlaid gold decorations (taka zogan) and represents three tortoises swimming amidst sea waves. The design is represented on both sides. The blade carries an inscription on an area close to the hilt. Blade's length: 4.2" (11 cm.). Knife's length: 8.1" (20.5 cm.). Estimated value: $1,000.

History and Development of Japanese Swords, Daggers, and Knives

Kofun and Nora Period (300-794 CE)

The early Kofun swords bear a strong resemblance to Sassanian Persian swords, not only in shape and size, but also in their decorations and mountings. The warriors of Kofun originated from China and Korea and were represented by nomadic horsemen wielding long swords (*chokuto*) as well as shorter swords and daggers named *warabiti-tachi* (young fern). The name warabiti-tachi derives from the appearance of the hilt, which is curled toward the end and resembles a young fern. Examples of the earliest swords from this period have been excavated from burial mounds. Later on, Nora period chokuto and warabiti-tachi were preserved in Shinto temple collections over the centuries. These swords were straight, as the first curved swords appeared during the Heian period. At the beginning, they had only a curved hilt and straight blade. A transitional sword called *kenuki gata tachi* (tweezer shaped sword) had a central split in the tang, probably for fastening of the hilt and very much resembling tweezers.

Heian Period (794-1185)

This period is characterized by the appearance of the samurai class, formed by the armed aristocrats from provinces and military officers. Heian swords were of shinogi zukuri type. with a curvature accentuated toward the hilt and a broadening of the blade toward the tang. These swords are considered the best Japanese swords, as the metallurgical skills of the sword-smiths reached the peak. The different schools of sword-smiths from this period are identified by the patterns of visible hada (the outer steel layer of the blade), as well as by the hamon pattern or jihada (cutting edge surface of the blade) pattern.

Kamakura Period (1185-1392)

Early in this period, the samurai class revolted against the central government in Kyoto and the first shogun of Kamakura, Yoritomo of Minamoto clan. Also during this period, the Mongol emperor Kublai Khan, the first emperor of Yuan dynasty of China, tried unsuccessfully to conquer Japan. The Mongols' invasion brought some changes to sword manufacture and for the first time, the sword became the principal weapon, rather than the bow and arrow. Longer blades and spears were produced in greater quantities and became the standard weapons. Different schools of sword-smiths flourished during the Kamakura period and their respective work is recognizable in the blade's hamon and yakiba (the junction between ha-tsuya and ji-tsuya).

Yoshino or Namboku Cho Period (1333-1393)

This period is characterized by sixty years of continuous warfare between northern and southern emperors fighting for exclusive authority. Different schools of sword-smiths proliferated during this period. Many of the long swords of the previous period were shortened, mostly be- cause of the damage incurred in battles. In this process, part of the blade's tang that contained the original signature of the sword-smith was discarded and a new inscription with the name of the smith's school founder was added.

Muromachi Period (1392-1477)

The Muromachi period was also called the age of wars, due to continuous warfare between clans of samurai aided by conscripted ruler, the ashigaru. Mass production of swords appeared, driven by an increased demand for sword manufacture and the consequent effect on lower standards of blade quality. In addition, hundreds of thousands of swords were produced for export to China. On the positive side, the arts reached a new zenith. The noh theatre, flower arrangement, tea ceremony, and gardening landscape art became universally popular in Japan. Cultural exchange with the fine arts of the Ming dynasty in China brought new ideas and an influx of Chinese master craftsmen. Zen Buddhism became the spiritual power of the Japanese aristocratic class. Samurai class etiquette required the use of two swords, *katana* (long sword), which was only for outdoor use, and *wakizashi* (short sword), which could be used outdoors or indoors. As a matter of fact, a samurai will never be unarmed and without a sword in close vicinity, even when sleeping on the mat.

Momoyama Period (1477-1603)

The shogun Nobunaga, who brought Japan under full control, made Kyoto the capital of the country in 1568. During this period, the use of matchlock guns brought deep changes in the use of weapons and the supremacy of the swords.

Edo Period (1603-1867)

After the end of the Nobunaga and Hideyoshi shogunates, Tokugawa Ieyasu became shogun and moved the capital to Edo (Tokyo). This period marks an era of prosperity and peace that lasted for 250 years. While the new class of bourgeoisie merchants became increasingly richer, the samurai feudal class became unemployed and with no means of living in a society where warfare had ended. Many became vagrants and were called ronin (wave men), others gave up the sword and became employed in different professions. A few of the samurai opened schools for teaching Kendo, or became militant monks named yamabushi (mountain warriors). Yamabushi were dressed partly in military dress and partly as Zen monks. Instead of helmets, they wore polygonal caps and carried with them a rosary, conch shell trumpet, basket, and of course, the sword. The yamabushi sect had been destroyed but not annihilated by the shogun Nobunaga in the 16th century due to the threat they posed to the central power. The ronin became a threat to the shogun government by instituting secret societies and engaging in violent games such as tsuji-giri—games where innocent victims were killed at cross roads in ambush type. Finally, the kabukimono brotherhood and the tsuji-giri games were outlawed by the shogun government.

Starting in the 17th century, several decrees were issued to prevent the possession of swords by commoners and to limit the length of swords worn by merchants and samurai attendants. Later on, Kendo schools initiated the development of a shorter sword with a curved blade, narrowing progressively toward the point. This sword was named kambun shinto, after the Kambun era (1661-1673). The Edo period's swords were named shinto, or new swords, in contrast to the old swords, koto. The long, high quality Edo period swords are very rare, due to the impoverishment of the samurai class that could not afford to commission swords from renowned sword-smiths. On the positive side for collectors, a large number of tsuba have survived, mostly because the samurai used the sword's tsuba for bartering when constrained by harsh life conditions. Another positive fact is that wealthy merchants could afford to pay substantial amounts of money for elaborately decorated wakizashi; this explains the relative abundance of short swords and daggers from the Edo period.

A revival of the sword-smiths' artistry occurred in the 18th century and early 19th century, when swords were created in the style of koto and also good imitations of the Kamakura and Yoshino periods. Due to their high quality of workmanship, some of these old reproductions were mistakenly believed to be famous medieval swords; because of their extreme rarity and lack of availability, they are owned primarily by museums or Zen shrines.

Meiji Period (1867-1912)

This period marked the end of the samurai and swordsmanship romantic era. The exhibiting or wearing of swords and daggers in public became forbidden by official decrees. As sword-smiths became unemployed, they had to look toward other professions where their skills could be used. These master embellishers of swords became very successful in such areas as metal sculpture, gold and silver alloy ornaments, and netsuke carving.

Taisho Period (1912-1926)

This period was unremarkable with regard to production of swords.

Showa Period (1926-1989)

High demand for collecting old swords created an increase in the production of swords with significant artistic ornamentation, mostly sword fittings, with less interest in the quality of the blade produced by laborious forging of the metal. High quality imitations of Edo period swords originate from this era; unfortunately, since many of them had engraved or chiseled signatures of master craftsmen from the Edo period, they are subject to being labeled fakes.

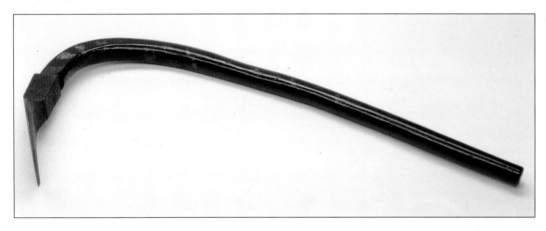

Fig. 6/73. 16th century, Momoyama period Fuetsu axe, probably a sacrificial axe. The power by vertical exertion is much higher than for axes mounted on a pole (ono), or for masa kari, where the blade is mounted on frontal plane. While the axe appears as a hoe, the cutting edge is very sharp. The wooden handle is black lacquered and decorated with gold (makie). This axe is the earliest makie decorated Japanese objet d'art that I have ever seen! Axe dimensions: 6" x 4" (15 x 10 cm.). Handle length: 26.5" (67 cm.). Estimated value: $4,000.

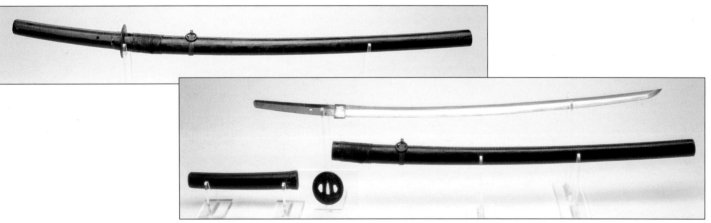

Fig. 6/74. Edo period katana sword. Black lacquered wooden hilt and scabbard. Bronze tsuba with incised decorations and inlaid gold. Single-edged blade with un-inscribed tang. Blade's length: 28.2" (72 cm.). Sword's length: 40.5" (103 cm.). Estimated value: $4,500.

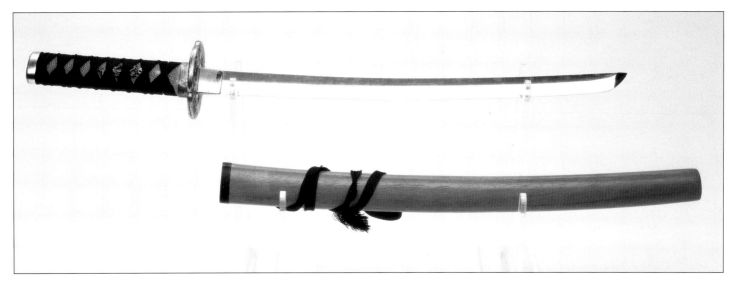

Fig. 6/75. 20th century wakizashi sword. Ray skin hilt decorated with silver menukis in the shape of dragons. Silver tsuba decorated with senin riding a tiger. Kashira and fuchi are made from silver decorated in bas relief with senin riding tiger. Wooden scabbard without ornaments. The blade has fine hamon of kobushi gata choji and appears to be made by a master sword-smith during the Showa period (1926-1989). Blade's length: 17.5" (45 cm.). Sword's length: 26.3" (67 cm.). Estimated value: $3,500.

Fig. 6/76. 19th-20th century bone wakizashi sword. The scabbard has on each side three panels decorated in polychrome scrimshaw with very intricate landscape, figural, and birds design on toned bone. The scabbard's ends are made from repoussé decorated copper. Scrimshaw decorations are present on the hilt with landscape and figural design. Single-edged nickel blade, slightly curved and with a rounded point. This is a very unusual Japanese sword, probably made for the western market, but with a highly artistic execution, well above that of tourist souvenir objects. Blade's length: 15.3" (39 cm.). Sword's length: 21.6" (55 cm.). Estimated value: $3,500.

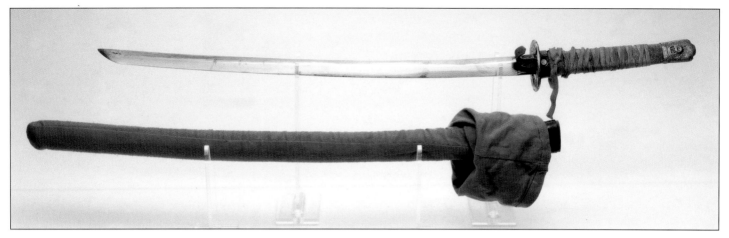

Fig. 6/77. 19th-20th century katana sword. The hilt is elongated and allows for two handed holding. Textile and green ray skin cover the wooden hilt. Brass tsuba with frog and marine vegetation design. Wooden scabbard covered with leather and textile hood. The tang has no inscription-signature. Single-edged blade, sharp. Blade's length: 24.8" (63 cm.). Sword's length: 38" (97 cm.). Estimated value: $2,000.

Fig. 6/78. 19th-20th century katana sword. The hilt is covered with braided leather. Single-edged blade carries an inscription on the obverse side. The scabbard is covered with leather and has annular brass attachments. Blade's length: 27" (68.5 cm.). Sword's length: 37" (94 cm.). Estimated value: $1,800.

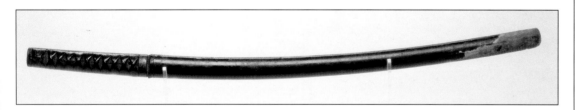

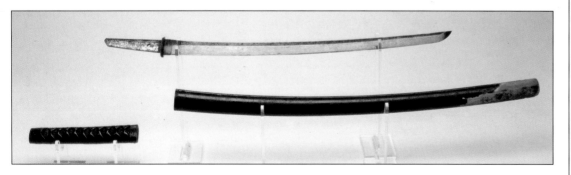

Fig. 6/79. 20th century katana sword. It was purchased in Java, Indonesia, in the 1980s and probably represents a World War II trophy. The hilt is covered with ray skin and on top of menuki, braided leather covers the grip. Single-edged blade, slightly curved toward the back of the point. The scabbard is made from black lacquered wood. Blade's length: 21.8" (55 cm.). Sword's length: 35" (89 cm.). Estimated value: $1,500.

Fig. 6/80. 19th century, Edo period tanto dagger. It is made from carved staghorn and has high relief decorations on the hilt and scabbard. Two figures are carved in a central panel. Brass blade decorated with incised floral design. Blade's length: 6" (15 cm.). Dagger's length: 10" (25.5 cm.). Estimated value: $2,000.

Fig. 6/81. 19th century, Meiji period ivory trousse set. The knife has a wooden handle and ivory pommel. Elaborate scrimshaw decorates the case. Pair of ivory chopsticks without decorations. Trousse's length: 13.2" (34 cm). Estimated value: $700.

Fig. 6/82. 18th-19th century, Edo period. Trousse set of knife and two chopsticks. The case is made from lacquered wood inlaid with micro-mosaic of ivory and mother-of-pearl with very intricate floral design. The knife's wooden handle is decorated with a silver flower at the proximal end. Trousse's length: 13.2" (34 cm.). Estimated value: $750.

Fig. 6/83. 19th century, Meiji period bone tanto with intricate figural designs on the hilt and scabbard. Single-edged blade. Blade's length: 6" (15 cm.). Knife's length: 12.5" (32 cm.). Estimated value: $550.

Fig. 6/84. 19th century, Meiji period carved bone tanto with intricate figural design in high relief. The blade is single-edged and chrome plated from European sources, in the European style, and made for European export. Blade's length: 8.6" (22 cm.). Dagger's length: 15" (38 cm.). Estimated value $600-$800.

Fig. 6/85. 19th century Edo period wakizashi sword. At first sight, the sword appears as a hybrid Chinese sword, however the features are typical Japanese. The hilt and scabbard are covered with a metal sheet made from an alloy of gold and brass. The obverse side of the hilt and the scabbard feature a ho bird, symbol of imperial power, especially as is associated with the paulownia tree. The scabbard has one suspension ring on the obverse side. Double-edged blade tapering toward the point. Short, small tsuba. Blade's length: 13.8" (35 cm.). Sword's length: 22" (56 cm.). Estimated value: $1,000-$1,500.

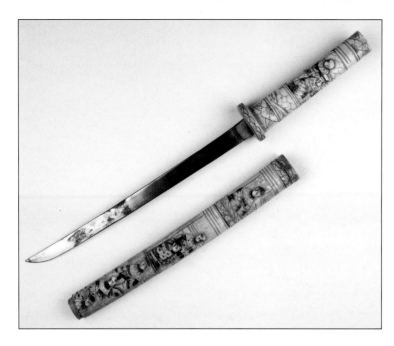

Fig. 6/86. 19th-20th century carved bone wakizashi sword. The hilt and scabbard are decorated with a figural design pattern. Single-edged blade. Blade's length: 13" (33 cm.). Sword's length: 20" (51 cm.). Estimated value: $750.

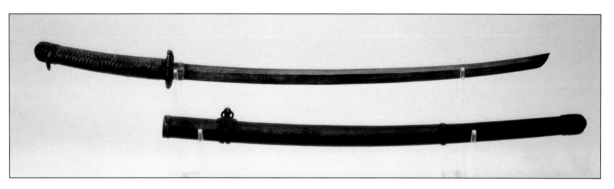

Fig. 6/88. 20th century wakizashi sword. The hilt and scabbard are covered with leather. The pommel and the hilt's distal end are made from brass with incised decorations. Brass tsuba with obliterated decorations. Single-edged blade with an inscription in the proximal part. The scabbard has two annular incised brass plaques, one of them with attached ring for the sword's suspension. Blade's length: 19.5" (50 cm.). Sword's length: 28" (71 cm.). Estimated value: $800.

Fig. 6/87. 19th-20th century Meiji period tanto dagger. The hilt is in the shape of a dragon, whose head forms the pommel. Bone scabbard carved in high relief features a dragon and a facing tiger. This design is present on both sides. Single-edged blade. Blade's length: 7.5" (19 cm.). Dagger's length: 15.6" (39.5 cm.). Estimated value: $750.

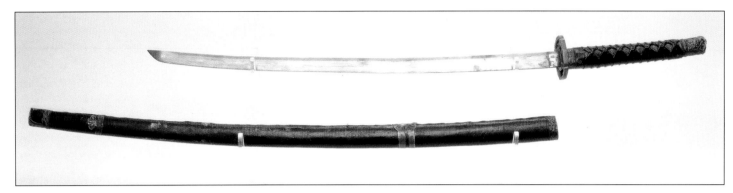

Fig. 6/89. 20th century katana sword purchased in Jogjakarta, Indonesia in the 1980s. The scabbard and hilt are covered with black leather. Oval, pierced tsuba, with open work design. Single-edged blade. Ornate brass chape. Blade's length: 24.8" (63 cm.). Sword's length: 39.5" (100 cm.). Estimated value: $850.

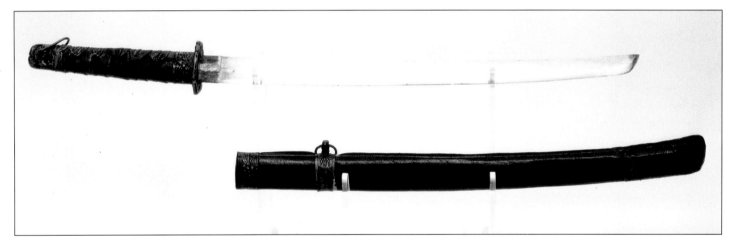

Fig. 6/90. 20th century wakizashi. The hilt and scabbard are covered with leather. Single-edged blade with an inscription on the obverse. It was purchased in Bali in the early 1980s and probably represents a World War II trophy. Blade's length: 19.8" (50 cm.). Sword's length: $650.

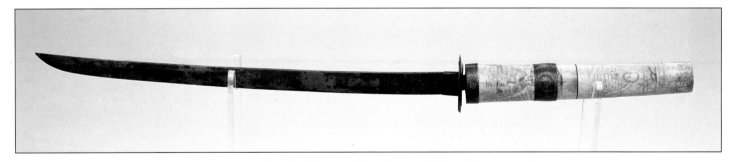

Fig. 6/91. 20th century wakizashi sword. The hilt and scabbard are made from bone with figural decorations. Brass annular scabbard's bands are decorated with three Aoi (mallow leaves). Simple brass tsuba and single-edged blade. Blade's length: 16" (40.5 cm.). Sword's length: 24.8" (63 cm.). Estimated value: $450.

Fig. 6/92. 20th century bone wakizashi sword. The hilt and scabbard are made from carved bone with intricate figural design. Single-edged blade. Blade's length: 12.5" (32 cm.). Sword's length: 22.5" (57 cm.). Estimated value: $500.

Fig. 6/93. 20th century bone tanto. The hilt and scabbard are carved in bone and decorated with a figural design. Single-edged blade. Blade's length: 7.7" (19.5 cm.). Dagger's length: 16" (41 cm.). Estimated value: $500.

Japanese Swords Manufactured in China

The invasion of Manchuria by Japanese troops in the 19th century created a new industry of mass produced swords by Chinese smiths for use by Japanese imperial troops. Initially, the new swords were created to replace those that were damaged and worn and were destined to be used only by non-commissioned officers of the Imperial Nippon army. Nevertheless, the quality of the newly produced blades was not comparable to the original blades produced in Japan, mostly due to a lack of the extensive time necessary to forge high quality blades and the poor skills of the labor-forced Chinese workers. A second wave of Japanese swords being mass produced in Manchuria occurred before World War II, during a subsequent Japanese invasion of Manchuria. Again, the swords produced were of poor quality and used for replacement of non-commissioned officers' swords. Many of these swords apparently remained in Chinese arsenals until they were released by the Chinese government for sale through private channels. These swords flooded the collectors' market in the early 1990s, available at very reasonable prices.

Characteristic of these old swords is the mon or imperial mark of a chrysanthemum on the scabbard's hangers. If concealed wooden parts (such as the scabbard's interior) are viewed, the wood shows signs of aging that cannot be faked. Due to the success of selling old Japanese swords made in China prior to World War II, entrepreneurs started to produce imitations of the old arsenal weapons that had accumulated dust for decades. This resulted in the contemporary mass production of Japanese sword fakes. In such cases, a reproduction is made to resemble an old sword, the metal parts are artificially aged with fake green patina, inscriptions on the aged tang are added, artificial etching of the blade resembling an antique hamon is created, etc. In contrast, the genuinely old Chinese arsenal swords usually display severe oxidation and rust and the blades have not been finished, sharpened, or polished.

The newly mass produced Japanese swords made in China are labeled "ancient Japanese swords" and are sold by unscrupulous dealers on the Internet. In this way, thousands have been sold to collectors in the past few years. Consequently, the market for antique Japanese swords has suffered tremendously. A lack of confidence on the part of buyers has resulted in decreased sales of Japanese swords and sword fittings and a tremendous drop in the prices of antique Japanese swords on the collectors market. It is estimated that the majority of Japanese swords and sword fittings on the collectors' market at the present time are 20th century reproductions. Since the greatest interest of sword collectors is in the antique Japanese swords, it is easy to understand how the plethora of reproductions sold as originals has created a downward trend in the market.

Chapter Seven

Chinese, Tibetan, and Nepali Edged Weapons

Chinese Edged Weapons

While the literature in this field is quite scarce, there is a wealth of Chinese edged weapons starting from prehistoric times to the modern era. Neolithic jade swords, daggers, or knives attest to the ceremonial use of edged weapons in the pre-dynastic era.

The first metal sword was made during the legendary Xia period and was a single-edged short sword, a dao. However, there is no archeological or documentary evidence proving the existence of this type of sword other than its legendary fame. If ever this Xia period dao existed, without doubt it would be attributed to a more recent historical era.

The first recognized bronze daggers were made during the Shang period. These daggers were single-edged, slightly curved, and decorated with animal heads or tao tieh masks on the pommel. Another edged weapon, the *ge,* was a halberd in axe form and actually used in battle. Prototypes of these axes were made in jade and featured marvelous carved decorations. These jade versions were apparently used for ceremonial purposes only, however, rather than in battle.

The Shang, or first dynastic, swords were rather long daggers with a blade length of only 14 inches. This type of *jian* was a double-edged, straight sword with a disk pommel and a tang that was cylindrical or tubular in shape. Zhou dynasty swords were of similar type, but in addition had a small hand-guard. Gold inlaid ornaments and incised tao tieh masks appeared during the Eastern Zhou period. Archeological digging at Xian revealed long bronze swords (33 inches) of jian type with the blade alone measuring 26 inches in length. These swords had rectangular pommels and narrow hand-guards that were cast separately.

The first iron daggers and swords were made during the Western Han period. A Han period jian sword with ornate lacquered scabbard is on exhibit at the British Museum. The abundance of jade sword fittings dating to the Han period attest to the large number of swords that existed at that time. Since iron corrodes very easily, it appears that the metal part of these swords unfortunately disintegrated over time, while the jade fittings survived.

The predominant type of sword used during the Wei period was a single-edged dao sword with a ring pommel. During the Sui and Tang periods, single-edged dao weapons were mainly used in military operations. Ring pommels with elaborate gilding and decorations were present in many of these straight dao weapons.

Following the Tang dynasty, the Song dynasty was established in southern China. The northern part of China during this period was dominated by nomadic Mongolian tribes who established the Liao dynasty, which lasted from 916 until 1125. The Khitans that formed the Liao dynasty had cavalry troops equipped with bows and arrows, halberds, and maces, but only the high ranking officers had swords—this is reflected in the scarcity of swords in archeological diggings and surviving specimens.

The Mongols, originating from Manchuria, conquered the Liao territory and formed a new dynasty, Zhin. Eventually the Mongols were unified by their great leader, Genghis Khan, who annexed the Zhin territory to the Mongol Empire of Central Asia. The grandson of Genghis Khan, Kublai Khan, subsequently conquered China and established the Yuan dynasty. The Mongol swords of the Uighurs, Khitans, and Ruzhen tribes were similar and consisted of dao type single-edged blades, typically curved in contrast to the former straight jians.

The Yuan period carried on the tradition of these curved single-edged dao swords and daggers. During the Ming dynasty that followed Yuan, the single-edged curved dao sword was named *chang dao* and the single-edged curved dagger was called *duan dao.* Other cutting edge weapons that existed during the Ming period included a halberd called zhi dao and a long pole single edge, called *gu dao.* Straight edge jian swords coexisted with the curved dao, but mostly represented vestiges of the much earlier period of Tang.

The Manchurian dynasty, Qing, was founded in 1644 and lasted until 1912, representing a period of burgeoning arts, prosperity, and advancement of the sciences. Most of the Chinese swords and daggers surviving to the present time were actually manufactured during the Qing period. The great majority of these weapons were mass produced however, and are of poor quality. Brass hilts and scabbard ornaments decorate these swords. The scabbard was usually made from wood and covered with green ray or shark skin.

An innovation in Qing sword manufacture was the shuang jian, a double blade contained in one scabbard. In order to fit in the scabbard, the facing swords were flat and convex on the opposite facets. Much rarer are the pairs of curved, double-edged dao swords and daggers called shuang dao. These paired swords and daggers are much sought after by sword collectors as well as by martial arts practitioners.

Broad blades of the falchion type were present in both the Ming and Qing periods and properly called "executioner swords" because of their infamous use for decapitating the condemned in public executions. In this collection, we have a large representation of these executioners' swords. The two-handed and "hand and a half" swords of jian type are rare, and most belonged to the emperor or high ranking officers. Usually these swords have ivory hilts, are decorated with inlaid solid gold or silver, and are at premium due to their rarity. A tri-lobate (trefoil) pommel is typical for Qing dynasty swords and late Ming swords The hand-guard usually is of a bulbous type with short quillons oriented upward. Dragon ornaments are present both in the pommel and hand-guards, with hammered gold or gilded silver used in the imperial swords or imperial court high ranking officers' swords.

Fig. 7/1. Shang period, circa 14th century BCE. Green jade ceremonial axe decorated with tao tieh masks on both sides. The handle has criss-cross decorations on a geometric pattern design. Size: 11.8" x 6.8" (30 cm. x 17 cm.). Estimated value: $1,500.

Fig. 7/2. Shang period, circa 14th century BCE. Jade spear decorated with tao tieh masks on both sides. Bronze shaft with two eyelets and incised decorations. Green patina and corrosion are present on the bronze shaft. Length: 9.2" (23.5 cm.). Width: 3.1" (8 cm.). Estimated value: $1,200.

Fig. 7/3. Western Zhou period. Bronze dagger with celadon jade hand-guard, pommel, and hilt. The hand-guard is oval-shaped and decorated with tao tieh mask framed by vertical incisions. Round pommel, decorated with C and reverse S scrolls. Double-edged, serrated blade with archaic inscriptions on both sides. Estimated value: $2,000.

Fig. 7/4. Shang period, circa 14th century BCE. Jade rectangular axe with bas-relief S-shaped decorations. The axe has an attached bronze handle decorated with incised ornaments including a tao tieh mask. The handle's end has a longitudinal wide split for the attachment of a wooden pole. Length: 8" (20 cm.). Estimated value: $1,600.

Fig. 7/5. Shang period, circa 14th century BCE. Bronze hand spear with jade handle. Sharp, triangular shaped spear with longitudinal decorations. Yellowish-brown jade handle with horizontal grooves and onion-shaped pommel. Blade's length: 4" (10 cm.). Spear's length: 11" (28 cm.). Estimated value: $1,800.

Fig. 7/6. Shang period, circa 14th century BCE. Bronze spear point with cone-shaped shaft decorated with incised ornaments in high relief. The bronze shaft once contained a wooden pole. Length: 8" (20 cm.). Estimated value: $750.

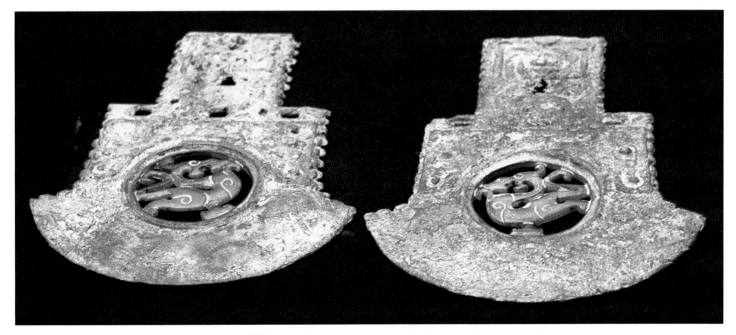

Fig. 7/7. Mid-Zhou period, circa 7th-6th century BCE. Pair of bronze axes decorated with a jade dragon located in the center's round opening. Highly artistic axe, obviously used for ceremonial rituals. The rounded edge of the axe is sharp. Incised decorations ornate the surface. Size: 7" x 6" (18 cm x 15 cm.). Estimated value: $2,000-$2,500 for pair.

Fig. 7/8. Han period, circa 100 BCE. Iron halberd with single convex edge. The vertical arm has a horizontal split for attachment to a wooden pole. Greenish-gray patina covers the entire surface. Size: 10.5" x 4" (27 cm x 10 cm.). Estimated value: $900.

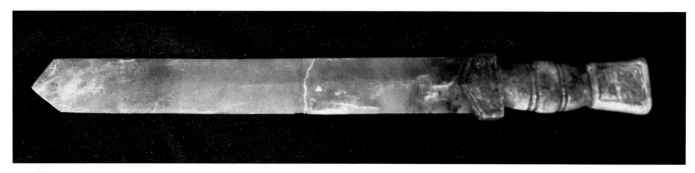

Fig. 7/9. Shang period, circa 13th century BCE. Yellow-green jade dagger with double-edged blade and triangular point. The hilt has horizontal striations to facilitate the grip. The pommel and the distal end of the hilt are decorated with tao tieh masks. Blade's length: 11.8" (30 cm.). Dagger's length: 17.5" (44.5 cm.). Estimated value: $1,700.

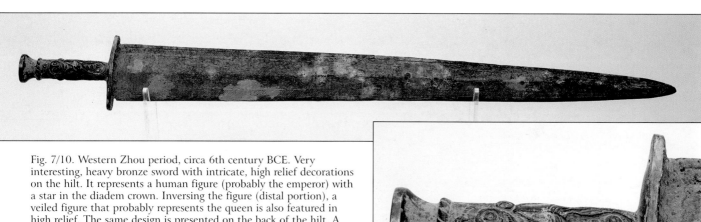

Fig. 7/10. Western Zhou period, circa 6th century BCE. Very interesting, heavy bronze sword with intricate, high relief decorations on the hilt. It represents a human figure (probably the emperor) with a star in the diadem crown. Inversing the figure (distal portion), a veiled figure that probably represents the queen is also featured in high relief. The same design is presented on the back of the hilt. A repeat pattern of spiral, hollowed sphere design forms the pommel. A multitude of mingling linear and spiral decorations ornate the pommel. In some areas, the spiral design is almost rectangular and forms the so-called "Greek key" pattern. Triangular shape blade with figural design of the seated emperor on 7 repeat design. The figure holds both arms up with an outward palms posture, described several hundreds years later as Buddha in "no more wars" posture. The edge of the figural design is formed by a continuous row of oblique lines. Greenish-gray patina covers the surface of this monumental bronze sword. Sword's length: 35.2" (89 cm.). Estimated value: $8,000.

Fig. 7/11. Shang period, circa 13th century BCE. Bronze sword covered with green patina. The hilt has two annular bands for retention of the organic part of the hilt that has already disintegrated. A round flat disk forms the pommel. The proximal part of the blade is decorated with tao tieh mask. Traces of archaic inscriptions and raised borders decorated with S scrolls ornate the blade. Blade's length: 23" (58.5 cm.). Sword's length: 27" (68.5 cm.). Estimated value: $1,800.

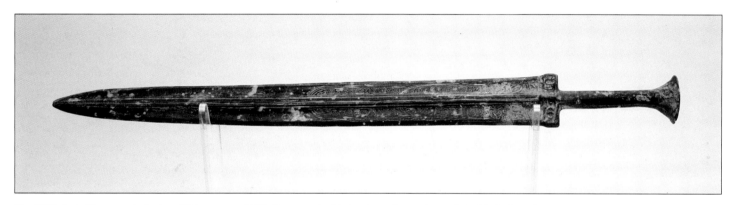

Fig. 7/12. Late Shang period, circa 12th century BCE. Jian sword with intricate decorations of the blade featuring a "Greek key" pattern and longitudinal scrolls divided in the center by a grooved, raised central line. In addition, a tao tieh design decorates the apical part of the blade. The hilt is cylindrical, ending with a round hollow pommel. Blade's length: 17.8" (45 cm.). Sword's length: 21.8" (55.2 cm.). Estimated value: $1,800.

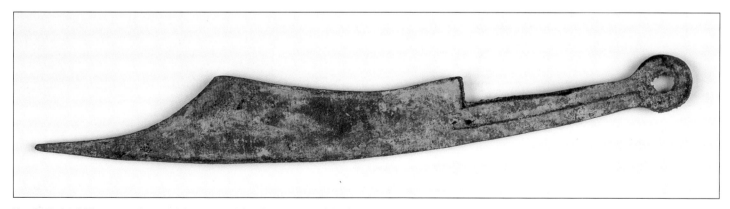

Fig. 7/13. Mid-Zhou period, circa 6th century BCE. Bronze curved knife covered on its entirety with green patina. Called "knife money," as it was used as legal tender coinage. Round pommel with central perforation. The hilt has longitudinal incised decorations. Pointed falchion-style blade with one inscribed archaic character on the obverse side. Length: 6.5" (16.5 cm.). Estimated value: $700.

Fig. 7/14. Mid-Zhou period, circa 5th century BCE. Knife money in the shape of a curved knife with green patina on its entire surface. Round pommel with central perforation. The hilt has longitudinal striations. Falchion-style blade with one inscribed archaic character. on the obverse side. It was used as legal tender coinage. Length: 5.5" (14 cm.). Estimated value: $650.

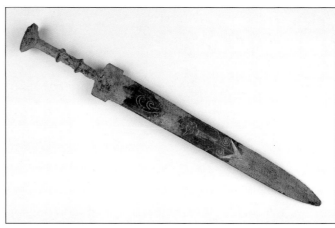

Fig. 7/16. Eastern Zhou period bronze dagger. The blade is decorated with inlaid silver and gold, forming a geometric design with a dragon in the center. The hilt has crenellation for the wood retention, or ivory that once formed the grip of the hilt. A round disk forms the pommel. Blade's length: 12.5" (31.8 cm.). Dagger's length: 16.8" (42.5 cm.). Estimated value: $1,300.

Fig. 7/15. Mid-Zhou period, circa 4th century BCE. Spade money in the shape of a stylized spade that resembles a standing human being. It is the type with square feet and has a central perforation on the handle that is obliterated. On the obverse side are two archaic characters separated by a midline. The reverse side has only a longitudinal line linking the central occluded perforation with the area between the feet. Length: 2.2" (5.8 cm.). Estimated value: $400.

Fig. 7/17. Western Han period, circa 1st century BCE, green jade halberd decorated in relief with a dragon head. The halberd is double-edged with a central rib. The handle is rectangular and has a round central perforation for attachment to an elongated wooden pole. The side has three rectangular perforations used for attachment to the handle. Size: 7.5" x 3.8" (19 x 9.5 cm.). Estimated value: $1,500.

Fig. 7/18. Western Han period, circa 1st century BCE. Iron halberd with double-edged blade. The shaft has a slide with three openings and the horizontal arm has only one central opening for attachment to a wooden pole. Archaic inscriptions and incised decorations are present on the horizontal arm. Green patina and some corrosion is present. Size: 7.9" x 5" (20 cm. x 13 cm.). Estimated value: $800.

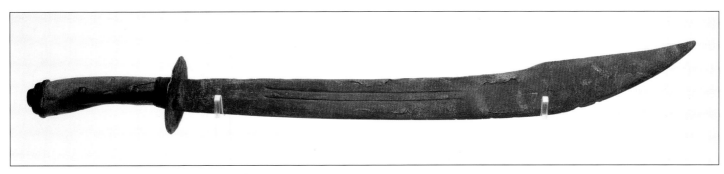

Fig. 7/19. Ming period executioner sword falchion chang dao. Wooden hilt with iron pommel of tri-lobate form. Thin, oval shape hand-guard. The blade widens in the lower third and curves slightly upward. Two fullers are present only on the obverse side of the blade. Blade's length: 21" (53.5 cm.). Sword's length: 27.1" (69 cm.). Estimated value: $1500.

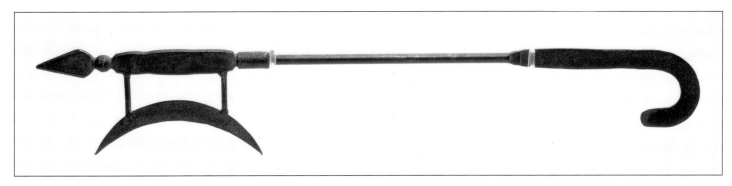

Fig. 7/20. Ming period combination spear and axe head weapon. In contrast to related European weapons, this spear-axe is not mounted on a wooden pole; rather, its metal pole is held with one hand in the center while the other hand holds the curved end that resembles a cane. The axe's blade is concave, unlike other medieval weapons where the blade is convex. The end is in the shape of a spear that is part of the metal pole. Blade's length: 8" (20 cm.). Total length: 31.5" (80 cm.). Estimated value: $2,000.

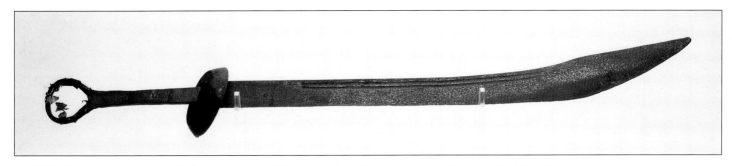

Fig. 7/21. Ming period ring pommel chang dao sword. This type is also called an executioner's sword. The hilt is long and allows for two handed holding of the sword. The grip of the hilt was made from an organic material and disintegrated. Single-edged, heavy blade, curved upward toward the back of the blade where the blade is wide and becomes double-edged. An inscription of four characters is on the obverse side of the blade, on the ricasso. Two fullers are present in the center of the blade. Pitted corrosion is present on the blade. Blade's length: 28" (71 cm.). Sword's length: 35" (89 cm.). Estimated value: $2,500.

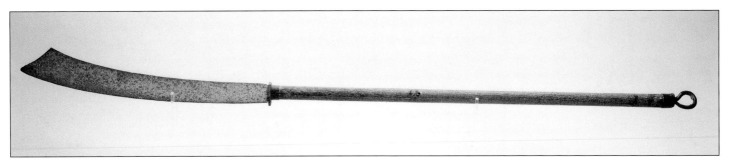

Fig. 7/22. Ming period pole axe gu dao. The handle is made from wood and shows the ravages of age, with partial fossilization of the hard wood. Falchion type of blade, widening toward the point. Most likely used as an executioner's weapon. The blade has superficial corrosion and superficial pitting. One hole is located near the point and probably served for suspension. Blade's length: 22" (56 cm.). Total length: 59.5" (151 cm.). Estimated value: $1,800.

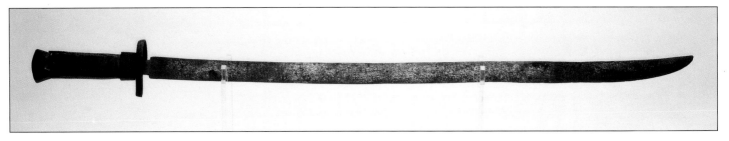

Fig. 7/23. Ming period falchion executioner sword chang dao. Wooden hilt was at one time lacquered and this probably helped to preserve the wood. The blade typically curves upward toward the back, while widening. Incised decoration is present on the ricasso. The sword bears signs of intensive use. Blade's length: 27" (68.5 cm.). Sword's length: 33" (84 cm.). Estimated value: $2,000.

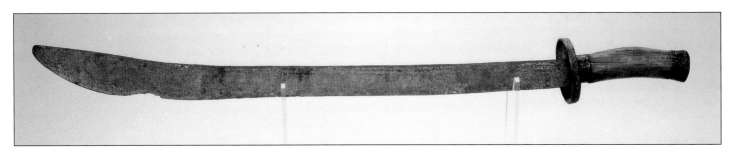

Fig. 7/24. Ming period large falchion executioner's sword chang dao. Long, wooden hilt allows two handed handling. Round, large hand-guard. Broad, single-edged blade, widens toward the point and carries considerable weight with the balance in the lower third where the cutting strength is needed. The indentations on the lower third of the blade point toward intensive past use of this sword. Blade's length: 29.5" (75 cm.). Sword's length: 36.2" (92 cm.). Estimated value: $2,000.

Fig. 7/25. 17th century short sword duan dao. The hilt and scabbard are covered with cloisonné decorations featuring a floral design. Watered, single-edged blade. This rare sword was purchased during one of my trips to Nepal, but undoubtedly was manufactured in China. Blade's length: 13.5" (34 cm.). Sword's length: 21.6" (55 cm.). Estimated value: $5,000.

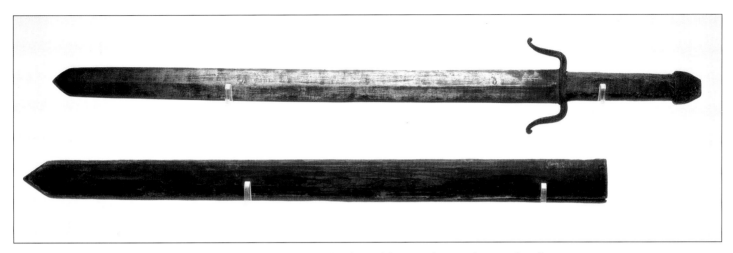

Fig. 7/26. 17th century jian sword. Wooden scabbard and hilt. No hand-guard, but two downward oriented quillons are present. Double-edged blade with seven inlaid brass dots. Undecorated iron pommel. Blade's length: 23.5" (60 cm.). Sword's length: 32.5" (82.5 cm.). Estimated value: $1,000.

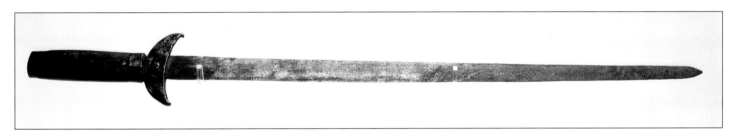

Fig. 7/27. 17th-18th century jian sword. Wooden hilt with metal cupped endings. The hand-guard is semi-circular and oriented downward. Double-edged blade decorated with incised ornaments in the shape of a stylized dragon. Blade's length: 27" (69 cm.). Sword's length: 34.2" (87 cm.). Estimated value; $1,000.

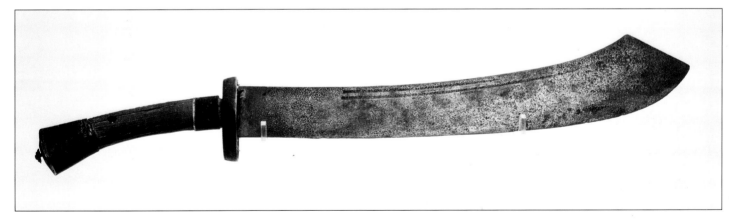

Fig. 7/28. 17th-18th century wide blade falchion chang dao sword, also called executioner's sword. Wooden hilt with brass endings decorated with incised floral design. The hand-guard is made from brass, oval shaped and also decorated with incised floral motif. Broad blade widens in the distal third, with obtuse cut end. It has two fullers in the center. This sword is heavy and allows double handed holding. Pitted corrosion is present on the blade. Blade's length: 21.8" (55 cm.). Sword's length: 31.1" (79 cm.). Estimated value: $1,800.

Fig. 7/29. 18th century shuang jian double sword. The entire sword including the blade is convex on one side and flat on the reverse, allowing for threading within one scabbard. The hilt is made from aged bone decorated with scrimshaw figural design of a mandarin on the obverse side and noble standing woman on the reverse. The pommel and hand-guard are made from incised decorative brass. India ink inscriptions are visible on the reverse side. Double-edged blade with inlaid gilded decorations featuring a dragon and women on the obverse and archaic inscriptions on the reverse. Blade's length: 29" (74 cm.). Sword's length: 37" (94 cm.). Estimated value: $4,500.

Fig. 7/30. Qing period. Mandarin dagger shou dao (hand sword). The hilt is covered with red velvet and repoussé gold decorations. Metal scabbard decorated with repoussé gold ornaments. The chape has an inscription. Double-edged blade with central fuller and inscription on both sides. Blade's length: 10" (25.5 cm.). Dagger's length: 15" (28 cm.). Estimated value: $7,500.

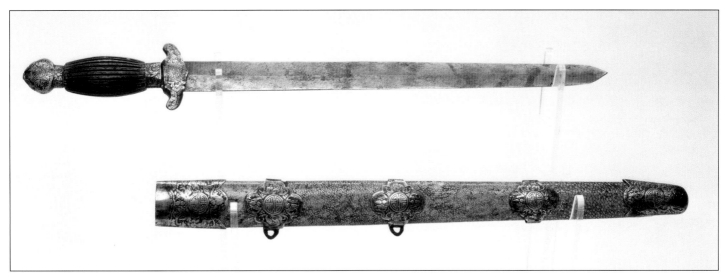

Fig. 7/31. 18th century Mandarin sword yao dao (waist sword). Wooden hilt with vertical striations. The pommel and hand-guard are decorated with incised ornaments in gold. Double-edged blade with triangular point. The scabbard is covered with ray skin and decorated with bands of incised ornaments. Blade's length: 15.5" (39.5 cm.). Sword's length: 23" (58.5 cm.). Estimated value: $5,000.

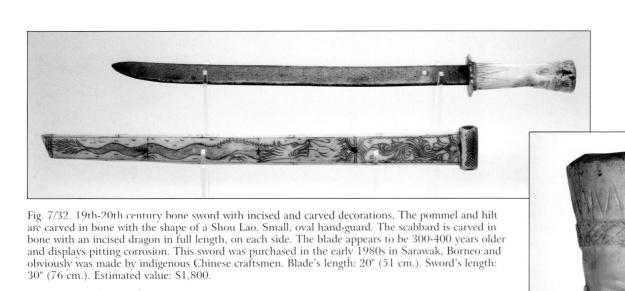

Fig. 7/32. 19th-20th century bone sword with incised and carved decorations, The pommel and hilt are carved in bone with the shape of a Shou Lao. Small, oval hand-guard. The scabbard is carved in bone with an incised dragon in full length, on each side. The blade appears to be 300-400 years older and displays pitting corrosion. This sword was purchased in the early 1980s in Sarawak, Borneo and obviously was made by indigenous Chinese craftsmen. Blade's length: 20" (51 cm.). Sword's length: 30" (76 cm.). Estimated value: $1,800.

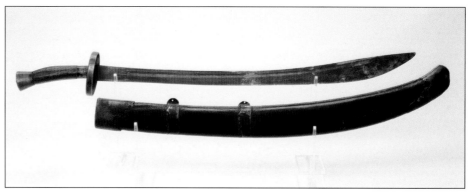

Fig. 7/33. 18th-19th century (or earlier) trident weapon. The head is made from bronze with high relief decorations in the shape of opposing dragons. A wooden pole is attached to the trident. Greenish-brown patina is present in the crevices. Length: 20.5" (52 cm.). Estimated value: $850.

Fig. 7/35. 18th-19th century double-handed sword da dao. Wooden hilt with brass pommel connected to the hand-guard that is oval and cup-shaped. The blade is curved and widens toward the point. A fuller is present toward the back of the blade. Wooden scabbard with brass end protectors. Two brass annular bands have perforated hangers for suspension of the sword. Blade's length: 31.5" (80 cm.). Sword's length: 39.8" (101 cm.). Estimated value: $1,500.

Fig. 7/34. 18th-19th century jian sword. The hilt and scabbard are covered with yellow ray skin. Double-edged serrated blade. Brass pommel and hilt distal end are decorated with repoussé ornaments. Blade's length: 34" (86.5 cm.). Sword's length: 40" (101.5 cm.). Estimated value: $1,500.

Fig. 7/36. Qing period. Stiletto knife designed to be concealed in clothing. The scabbard is covered with green ray skin and has brass endings. Wooden hilt with small brass hand-guard. Double-edged blade with slightly rounded point. Blade's length: 5.5" (14 cm.). Knife's length: 9" (23 cm.). Estimated value: $500.

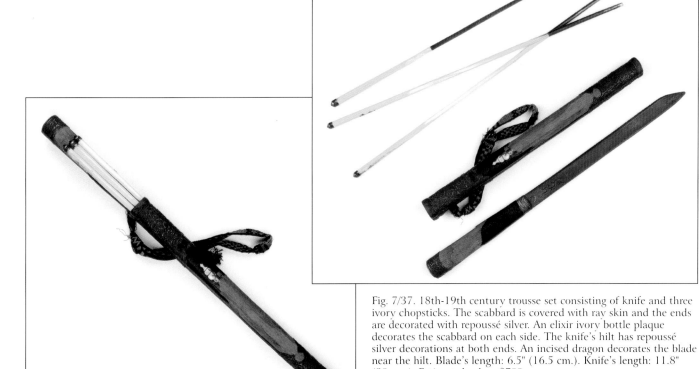

Fig. 7/37. 18th-19th century trousse set consisting of knife and three ivory chopsticks. The scabbard is covered with ray skin and the ends are decorated with repoussé silver. An elixir ivory bottle plaque decorates the scabbard on each side. The knife's hilt has repoussé silver decorations at both ends. An incised dragon decorates the blade near the hilt. Blade's length: 6.5" (16.5 cm.). Knife's length: 11.8" (30 cm.). Estimated value: $700.

Fig. 7/38. 18th-19th century trousse. Unlike other Chinese trousse sets, this one contains two knives, rather than one knife and two chopsticks. The scabbard is made from yellow ray skin and has brass appendices. The larger knife has brass endings and the small knife has an ivory pommel. Estimated value: $600.

Fig. 7/39. 19th century trousse set with knife and two chopsticks. The scabbard is covered with green ray skin and the end is carved in ivory. Wooden hilt and single-edged blade. Estimated value: $450.

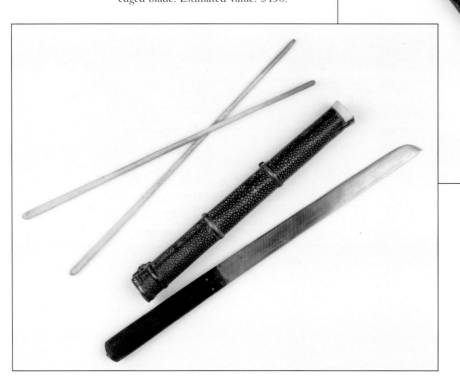

Fig. 7/40. 19th century dagger with double-edged blade decorated with seven inlaid brass dots. Wooden hilt with brass hand-guard. The hand-guard and pommel feature brass engraved decorations. Green ray skin covers the scabbard, which has annular brass decorations. Blade's length: 8" (20.3 cm.). Dagger's length: 14" (35.5 cm.). Estimated value: $400.

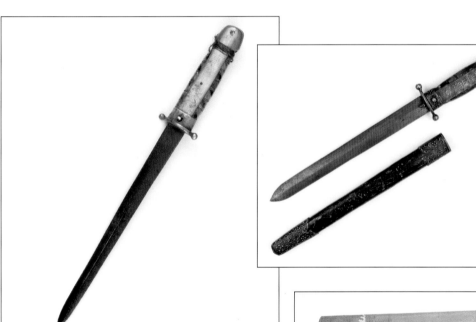

Fig. 7/41. 19th century dagger. The hilt is made from brass plates over a reptilian skin cover bound with brass wires. Double-edged blade with central fuller. Blade's length: 9.2" (23.5 cm.). Dagger's length: 14" (35.5 cm.). Estimated value: $450.

Fig. 7/42. Shou dao (hand sword) dagger dated 1926. The hilt, covered with lacquered leather and brass, bears a Chinese inscription on both sides plus the date, 1926. Two knobby quillons are located at the ends of the hand-guard. Double-edged undecorated blade. Black lacquered scabbard with terminal ornaments. Blade's length: 9.8" (24.7 cm.). Dagger's length: 15.8" (40 cm.). Estimated value: $500.

Fig. 7/43. Late Ming-early Qing period. Three rectangular wooden containers for sword storage. The wood is covered with toned, aged ray skin. Container sizes vary from 39" x 5" (99 cm. x 12.5 cm.) to 48" x 5" (122 cm. x 12.5 cm.). Estimated value for each container: $500-$800.

Tibetan Swords and Daggers

High-end Tibetan swords are quite ornamental. They were manufactured in Tibet with blades originating occasionally from China. The hilts and scabbards of these swords are made from solid gold or silver. Less expensive swords have heavy gilding and silver wire ornaments. Tibetan swords and daggers typically have profuse decorations with carved turquoise and coral inlaid in the scabbard and pommel, occasionally in the hilt itself. Many of these magnificent Tibetan swords and daggers have intricate incised silver decorations on the hilt, hand-guard, and the scabbard, and even more frequently, a filigree silver wire hilt that facilitates a good grip.

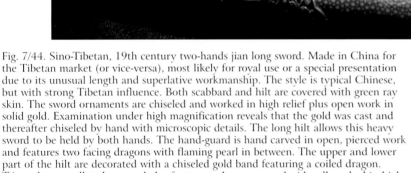

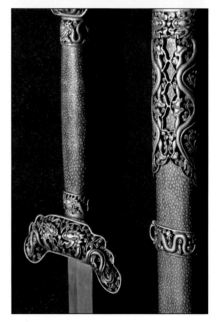

Fig. 7/44. Sino-Tibetan, 19th century two-hands jian long sword. Made in China for the Tibetan market (or vice-versa), most likely for royal use or a special presentation due to its unusual length and superlative workmanship. The style is typical Chinese, but with strong Tibetan influence. Both scabbard and hilt are covered with green ray skin. The sword ornaments are chiseled and worked in high relief plus open work in solid gold. Examination under high magnification reveals that the gold was cast and thereafter chiseled by hand with microscopic details. The long hilt allows this heavy sword to be held by both hands. The hand-guard is hand carved in open, pierced work and features two facing dragons with flaming pearl in between. The upper and lower part of the hilt are decorated with a chiseled gold band featuring a coiled dragon. Triangular, crenellated pommel also features a dragon on each side, all worked in high relief. The scabbard has proximal and distal decorations in gold worked in high relief, plus a pierced design featuring two facing dragons with the flaming pearl in between. Peculiarly, the obverse side of the chape has facing dragons with heads at both extremities. Three annular gold plaques with a dragon in relief decorate the mid-portion of the scabbard. Sharp, double-edged blade with damascene design visible pattern. Blade's length: 31.8" (81 cm.). Sword's length: 43" (109 cm.). Estimated value: $100,000-150,000.

Fig. 7/45. Tibet. 18th century silver sword decorated with turquoise, coral, and yellow chalcedony. Both the scabbard and hilt have repoussé silver decorations and applications of copper and brass with different representations, such as two brass seated deer, copper mirror, copper horse and water buffalo, etc. The hilt has two metal applications, a copper vajra (thunderbolt) and a brass conch. On the reverse side, there are shallow, incised decorations in the silver sheet. The proximal and distal ends of the scabbard have gilded, repoussé silver decorations. Indigenously produced, wide, single-edged blade with two fullers, appears rudimentary, but hand manufactured. Incised decorations in the shape of flowers decorate the blade. In addition, a large vajra and two Tibetan characters are incised and gilded on the blade, close to the hilt. The blade is very heavy and wide and the long hilt allows for two handed holding. This sword may have been used for executions, although this is only speculation without any solid proof of such. Blade's length: 24.8" (63 cm.). Sword's length: 31.8" (81 cm.). Estimated value: $12,000-15,000.

Fig. 7/46. 19th-20th century sword. The scabbard is covered with silver chiseled in high relief featuring different animals and Buddhist symbols. Two facing dragons are on the obverse side of the scabbard, chiseled in gold with high relief features. In the center of the scabbard, two turquoise and one coral carving are mounted in silver; however, more turquoise and coral carvings are found on the scabbard's extremities. Primitively laminated, double-edged blade with central rib. The pommel and the oval hand-guard are chiseled in high relief in high grade silver. The hilt is covered with black leather of a more recent addition. Reverse side of the scabbard is chiseled in silver and gold alloy in low relief and has two hangers for attachment to the belt. Blade's length: 14.5" (37 cm.). Sword's length: 21.2" (54 cm.). Estimated value: $5,000.

Fig. 7/47. 18th century silver sword. The scabbard has two central silver longitudinal plaques held by an encompassing U shaped metal edger. The obverse side of the scabbard is chiseled in high relief silver and features two dragons facing two turquoise and 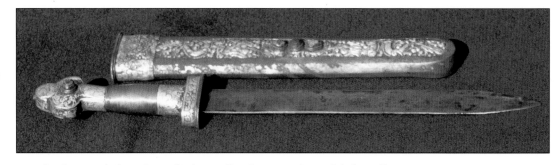 one coral carving. On the reverse side, the central silver plaque displays endless knot, two facing fish, lotus flowers, etc. The scabbard's proximal end is in the shape of a mythological figure. Chiseled silver hilt with silver wire as a grip. Trefoil shape pommel with turquoise on the obverse side. Single-edged, straight blade created by an indigenous blacksmith displays primitive forged lamination. Blade's length: 11" (28 cm.). Dagger's length: 17.2" (44 cm.). Estimated value: $4,000.

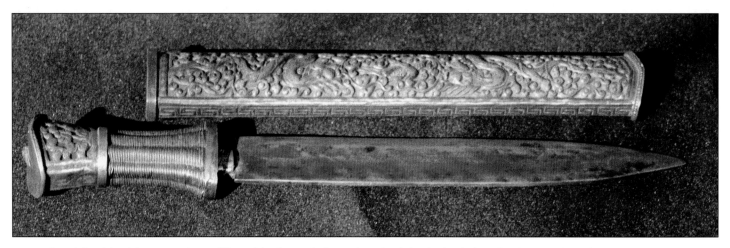

Fig. 7/48. 18th-19th century dagger. The scabbard is made from silver chiseled in high relief on the obverse side and features two dragons facing a phoenix bird located in the center. The reverse side has bas relief decorations. Silver hilt with silver wire grip. The pommel is chiseled in high relief with open work. Single-edged blade made by a local blacksmith displays primitive forge lamination. Blade's length: 10.8" (27 cm.). Dagger's length: 16.5" (42 cm.). Estimated value: $1,800.

Fig. 7/49. Tibetan-Nepali silver knife dating to the 19th century. The hilt as well as the scabbard are covered with a heavy silver cover decorated in high relief. In addition, the scabbard has coral and turquoise stones imbedded in the silver. One coral decoration is present in the hilt. Single-edged blade with one wide fuller. Blade's length: 3.3" (8.5 cm.). Knife's length: 8.2" (21 cm.). Estimated value: $500-$600.

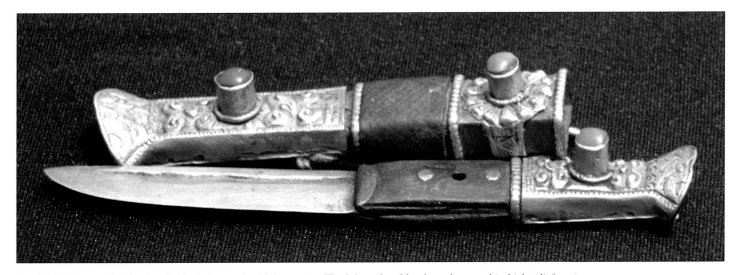

Fig. 7/50. Tibetan-Nepali silver knife dating to the 19th century. The hilt and scabbard are decorated in high relief on the obverse in silver. In addition, the scabbard features a coral and turquoise stone affixed to the silver. The hilt has a single coral decoration imbedded in the silver. The reverse side has an incised decorated brass plate. Blade's length: 3" (7.5 cm.). Knife's length: 7.8" (19.5 cm.). Estimated value: $450-$550.

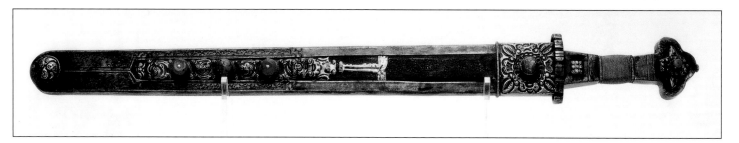

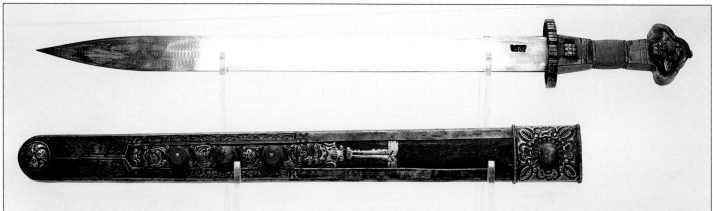

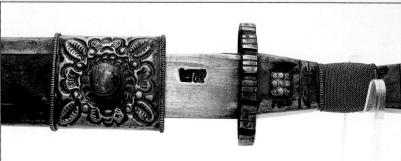

Fig. 7/51. 18th-19th century sword with repoussé silver sheet on the proximal end of the scabbard, which is made from wood covered with yak skin and decorated with coral and turquoise. Single-edged, straight blade has a Tibetan inscription on the ricasso. Steel hilt with silver wire grip displays silver repoussé decorations on the distal end with one coral decoration. Oval-shaped hand-guard with crenellated edges. Blade's length: 21" (53.5 cm.). Sword's length: 27.8" (70.5 cm.). Estimated value: $10,000.

Fig. 7/52. 18th century sword with high relief gilded silver decorations on the scabbard, featuring two facing dragons, lion, chimera, and unicorn. The reverse side of the scabbard has low relief decorations on silver. Single-edged blade with forge lamination. Wooden hilt with brass ends that are chased and hammered and have open work decorations. Blade's length: 20.9" (53 cm.). Sword's length: 26.8" (68 cm.). Estimated value: $8,000.

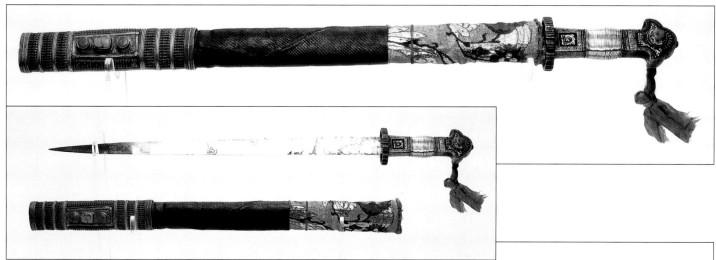

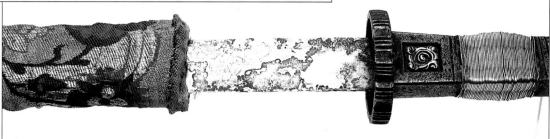

Fig. 7/53. 18th century sword with scabbard covered in yak skin and decorated with repoussé silver and copper, mounted in silver, turquoise, and coral carvings. Triangular, single-edged, straight blade is well watered. Steel hilt with silver wire grip and chiseled silver with silver-mounted coral. Oval-shaped hand-guard. Blade's length: 20" (51 cm.). Sword's length: 26.5" (67.5 cm.). Estimated value: $5,000.

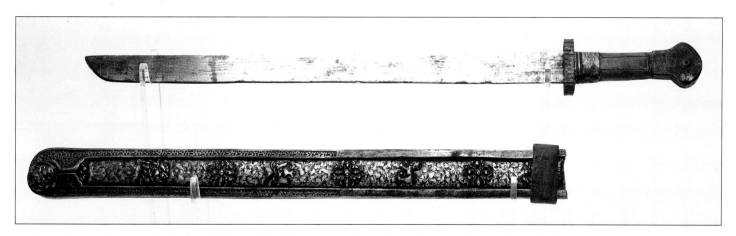

Fig. 7/54. 18th century sword with chased silver scabbard featuring a unicorn, lion, chimera, and vajra. Single-edged primitively watered blade. Wooden hilt without decorations. Small, rectangular hand-guard. Blade's length: 19.1" (48.5 cm.). Sword's length: 26" (66 cm.). Estimated value: $4,000.

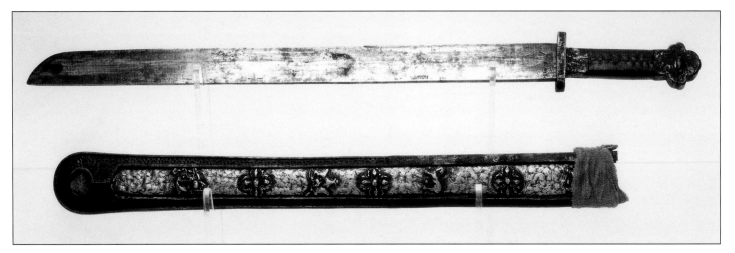

Fig. 7/55. 18th century sword. The hilt is covered with black leather and decorated with chiseled silver at the ends. Silver, crenellated hand-guard. Steel scabbard's frame in the shape of a U is decorated with intricate open work. The scabbard is made from high content silver alloy decorated in high relief with unicorns, bat, octopus, and floral bosses. The reverse side has incised floral decorations. Single-edged straight blade forged by an indigenous blacksmith. Blade's length: 20" (51 cm.). Sword's length: 25.5" (65 cm.). Estimated value: $4,000.

Fig. 7/56. 18th century short sword. The scabbard is made from steel bars in the shape of a U displaying elaborate open work and encircling a yak leather sheet. The obverse side has a silver central plaque decorated with dragons in high relief. All silver decorations are gilded, with most of the gilt still retained. Metal hilt with silver wire grip. The pommel is lobate and has a turquoise carving mounted in silver. Small, crenellated hand-guard. Single-edged, straight blade with signs of primitive forging. Blade's length: 15" (38 cm.). Sword's length: 22" (56 cm.). Estimated value: $3,500.

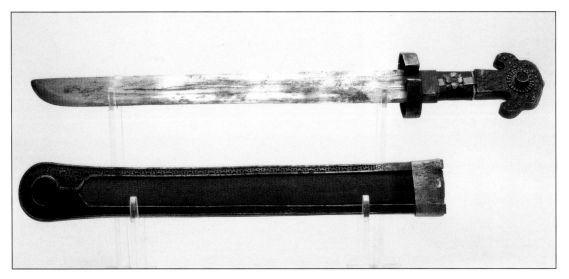

Fig. 7/57. 18th century sword. The hilt is made from iron and yak skin and decorated with a silver boss ornament. Crenellated iron pommel decorated with repoussé and chased silver. Wide, straight, and single-edged blade displaying primitive, but elaborate forging manufacture. Oval-shaped hand-guard with two large openings. The scabbard has a typical U frame made of steel, featuring elaborate open work and encircling a wooden base covered with green velvet that has faded with age. Blade's length: 16" (40.5 cm.). Sword's length: 22" (56 cm.). Estimated value: $2,500.

Fig. 7/58. 18th century trousse set consisting of a knife, two ivory chopsticks, silver flint-match box, jade toggle, and silver belt attachments. The case is made from wood with annular silver ornaments. The ivory chopsticks have incised silver proximal ends. Single-edged blade with one central fuller. Natural annular wood polychrome bands form the hilt. A flint purse decorated with incised silver is attached through a mutton fat jade toggle carved in the shape of a chrysanthemum. Two incised silver ornaments are attached with leather bands. Very rare! Trousse's length: 13.2" (33.5 cm.). Blade's length: 6.5" (16.5 cm.). Knife's length: 11.5" (29 cm.). Estimated value: $2,700.

Fig. 7/59. 19th century silver dagger. Brass and steel scabbard decorated with annular, incised heavy bands of silver. A leather belt with end opening for arm insertion has seven embossed silver roundels with chiseled decorations. Single-edged straight blade with one fuller and two crossed arrow decorations. The scabbard is made from horn with brass, copper and inlaid silver decorations. Blade's length: 6" (15 cm.). Dagger's length: 11.5" (29 cm.). Estimated value: $2,000.

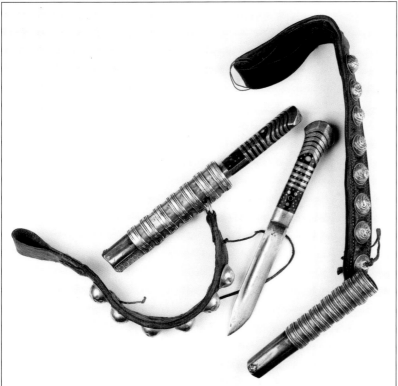

Fig. 7/60. 18th century sword. Wooden hilt with incised silver decorations on the distal third. Round steel pommel with central indentation. Wooden scabbard covered with yak skin. The scabbard displays a gold alloy boss with incised decorations that are worn due to considerable age. Long brass chape. Single-edged straight blade with indigenous manufacture shown in the primitive watering. Small, irregular shaped hand-guard. Blade's length: 25.2" (64 cm.). Sword's length: 32" (81.5 cm.). Estimated value: $2,000.

Fig. 7/61. 19th century silver dagger with intricate chiseled and gilded silver hilt and scabbard. The main ornamental pattern consists of dragons. The gilded silver hand-guard is in the shape of a unicorn and vaguely resembles a Japanese tsuba. Incised dragons decorate the single-edged blade that is slightly curved upward. Blade's length: 9.5" (24 cm.). Dagger's length: 15" (38 cm.). Estimated value: $1,100.

Fig. 7/62. 19th century silver dagger. The hilt has low relief decorations while the pommel displays high relief ornaments featuring a gilded dragon on the obverse side. The blade has one blood line and dotted decorations near the point. High relief decorations of chiseled silver decorate the scabbard, featuring a deer on the apical part. The distal end displays a panel with incised decorations featuring a gilded serpent dragon surrounded by floral decorations. The reverse side of the dagger has low relief ornaments and a rectangular hanger. Blade's length: 5.2" (13.4 cm.). Dagger's length: 9.5" (24 cm.). Estimated value: $800.

Fig. 7/63. 18th-19th century silver dagger. The hilt has a silver wire hand grip and a repoussé decorated pommel. High relief incised decorations adorn the scabbard on the obverse side. The reverse side has shallow, incised decorations and a square hanger. The blade appears of a more recent manufacture and displays a decorative incised pattern on both sides. Single-edged blade, very sharp. Blade's length: 7.9" (20 cm.). Dagger's length: 11.8" (30 cm.). Estimated value: $750.

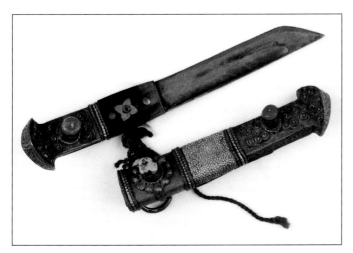

Fig. 7/64. 19th-20th century dagger in the shape of a boat. The hilt is decorated with ornate silver and coral. Brass sheet covers the back of the scabbard and hilt. The blade has signs of primitive watering. Ornate scabbard, decorated with silver and mounted turquoise and coral. The central part of the scabbard is covered with ray skin and bordered with silver and copper bands. Blade's length: 5.3" (13.5 cm.). Dagger's length: 10.5" (26.6 cm.). Estimated value: $800.

Fig. 7/65. 20th century silver dagger decorated with semi-precious stones. Chased low grade silver with zoomorphic decorations in the shape of a dragon. A dragon forms the two ring hanger, an incised dragon decorates the hilt. The blade tapers toward the point. Blade's length: 7.2" (18.5 cm.). Dagger's length: 14" (35.5 cm.). Estimated value: $450.

Fig. 7/66. 19th-20th century silver knife, also called Bhutanese knife. The hilt is covered with silver wire for the handle's grip. Hammered repoussé silver pommel. Single-edged blade with one fuller. The scabbard is decorated with repoussé silver in the shape of a dragon on the obverse side, while the reverse has only incised decorations. Blade's length: 5.5" (14 cm.). Estimated value: $500.

Nepali Edged Weapons

Traditional Nepalese weapons are *kukuri* daggers (for unknown reasons, this is mispronounced by westerners as kukri, or khukri) and *kora* swords. The kora sword has a heavy blade that typically widens in the lower third and curves upward. Occasionally, the kora has a forked end. Much more intensively used and popular is the curved, sheathed dagger, kukuri, the favorite weapon of the warriors of Nepal, Gurkhas.

The collection shown here also includes significant representation of ceremonial Nepali-Tibetan ritual knives called *phurbas* (or *phurbus*), allegedly used by lamas for exorcising the evil spirits. The phurbas illustrated reach the peak of esthetic pleasure induced when intricate workmanship is used to create an art object of supreme visual and tactile satisfaction. Antique phurbas made from precious metals have vanished from the collectors' market and only modern reproductions are available for sale. It is easy to distinguish a new phurba from an antique one by looking at the iron blade; on an antique, the blade will always display patina and metal corrosion. Although phurbas are usually included with Tibetan weapons, we have included them in this Nepali section out of respect for Tibetan religious freedom that the Tibetan refugees got in Nepal, and for their leader Dalai Lama, who prefers to live as a refugee in India, rather than under Chinese communist occupation of Tibet.

Due to the current political instability in Nepal, it is likely that Nepali antiques will become more scarce and therefore escalate in value.

Fig. 7/67. 19th century phurba. Large ceremonial solid silver dagger decorated with mounted turquoise and coral carvings. The hilt has three crowned human heads with diabolic expressions. Above them is a horse's head and neck (prototype seen frequently in the Indian daggers). A vajra (thunderbolt) decorated with filigree silver, turquoise, and coral is located in the center portion. Below the vajra, a very intricate chiseled dragon holds in its mouth the dagger blade, which is triangular in shape, made from patinated iron, and decorated with appliqué silver decorations. The phurba dagger is used by lamas for exorcising evil spirits and is also referred to by Westerners as "ghost dagger" or "exorcising knife." This is the largest phurba I have ever encountered, chiseled in solid silver and with the most sophisticated decorations. Dagger's length: 17" (43.7 cm.). Estimated value: $10,000.

Fig. 7/68. 19th century phurba dagger. The pommel is in the shape of vajra (thunderbolt), formed by three ferocious looking human heads carved in ivory. Above their heads is a crown decorated with turquoise carvings. High above in the center, a silver horse's head forms the pommel. The hilt is highly decorated with turquoise, lapis lazuli, and coral carvings mounted in silver. The blade is a triangular shape with inlaid silver decorations and inscription. A dragon head engulfs the blade. The dragon's snout is in a bird shape with turquoise decorations and eyes formed by coral mounted in filigree silver. Blade's length: 3.5" (9 cm.). Dagger's length: 10.2" (26 cm.). Estimated value: $5,000.

Fig. 7/69. 19th century silver phurba decorated with mounted coral and turquoise carvings. The hilt is in the shape of vajra (thunderbolt), decorated with filigree silver, coral, and turquoise. A dragon's head is located at the distal end. The dagger's blade is in the shape of a stylized bird. Iron blade with rusty patina. A government red seal of antiquity is attached to the dagger. Dagger's length: 10" (25.5 cm.). Estimated value: $3,500.

Fig. 7/70. 19th century silver phurba decorated with mounted turquoise, coral, and lapis lazuli carvings. The hilt is in the shape of vajra (thunderbolt). Below, a dragon with elaborate chiseled silver decorations and semi-precious stones is holding an axe in the shape of a bird's head. The axe is made from white metal and bears an inscription on both sides. A bird emerges from the dragon's snout. A government red seal of antiquity is attached to the phurba. Dagger's length: 9" (22.8 cm.). Estimated value: $2,500.

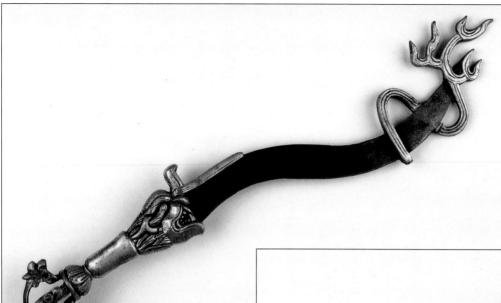

Fig. 7/71. 19th century silver phurba. The hilt is in the shape of vajra (thunderbolt). The distal end of the hilt features a dragon with open mouth where a wavy iron blade emerges. The end of the blade is adorned with silver in the shape of fire. Length: 15" (38 cm.). Estimated value: $1,500.

Fig. 7/72. 18th-19th century bronze phurba with zoomorphic design. Three crowned elephant heads form the hilt. Above them, a horse's head and upper part of the body emerges from the convex end. A dragon's head is located on the distal end, holding in its mouth the blade that is in the shape of an axe. This is the only phurba I have seen with elephant head decoration. This bronze phurba is very heavy! Dagger's length: 12.2" (31 cm.). Estimated value: $950.

Fig. 7/73. 18th-19th century sword. The hilt is made from carved staghorn in the shape of an animal's head. The hand-guard is disk-shaped and also made from staghorn. Single-edged blade, slightly widening toward the point and having two fullers. The scabbard is made from yak hide and is strong and thick. Blade's length: 21" (53 cm.). Sword's length: 27" (68.5 cm.). Estimated value: $1,800.

Fig. 7/74. 19th century knife with the hilt and pommel made from solid silver. The pommel is in the shape of a stylized bird with five silver protuberances on its top. Leather scabbard decorated with chiseled silver. Blade's length: 4.8" (12 cm.). Knife's length: 11" (28 cm.). Estimated value: $900.

Fig. 7/75. 18th-19th century bronze chopper. Bronze hilt with vajra (thunderbolt) design in the apical part. The lower part of the hilt has a stylized zoomorphic design. Rounded blade with incised Tibetan script on one side and feathery design on the reverse. Some pitted corrosion is present on the blade due to its high iron content. Size: 7" x 6.8" (18 x 16.5 cm.). Estimated value: $900.

Fig. 7/76. 18th century kukuri dagger. Wooden hilt with incised, simple design. The blade has signs of primitive manufacture by local blacksmiths. Some rust and corrosion as well as notched depression from manufacture are present. Leather scabbard, well weathered, decorated with circles forming a design pattern on the obverse side. The reverse side has two pouches for storage of knives. Blade's length: 11" (28 cm.). Dagger's length: 17" (43 cm.). Estimated value: $700.

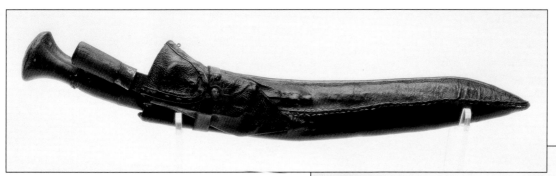

Fig. 7/77. 18th-19th century kukuri dagger. Wooden hilt with simple carved ornaments. The blade is curved, widens in the mid-portion, and tapers toward the point. Incised decorations are present on the upper part of the blade, near the back. Leather scabbard with two small miniature kukuri inserted in the back pouch. Blade's length: 12.2" (31 cm.). Dagger's length: 19.2" (49 cm.). Estimated value: $500.

Fig. 7/78. 18th-19th century kukuri. The scabbard is made from wood covered with heavy leather. Wooden hilt with simple decorations. Single-edged blade, widens in the center of the blade and gradually tapers toward the point. Blade's length: 10.6" (27 cm.). Dagger's length: 18.5" (47 cm.). Estimated value: $450

Fig. 7/80. Antique knife with tiger tooth pommel. The hilt is covered with brass sheet and silver bands. Dates to 19th century, or earlier. Knife's length: 7.9" (20 cm.). Estimated value: $450.

Fig. 7/79. Antique bronze phurba. The pommel is in the shape of three friendly and smiling human faces, crowned with human skulls. Three mythological animals with bird's beaks are located in the distal end. The dagger's triangular shape blade emerges just below the zoomorphic trio. Raised decorations ornate the blade. Very rare type of phurba with tantric design. Dagger's length: 10" (25.5 cm.). Estimated value: $500.

Fig. 7/81. 18th-19th century kukuri. Wooden hilt and scabbard with some worm holes. Simple decorations adorn the wooden hilt. Single-edged blade widens in the mid-portion where it curves downward. The scabbard has two tin rings and a tin distal end (chape). Blade's length: 9.5" (24 cm.). Dagger's length: 15.2" (38.8cm.). Estimated value: $400.

Chapter Eight
African Edged Weapons

One of the least known and understood fields of sword collecting is, without doubt, that of African swords. Africa never went through a bronze age (except in the northern Mediterranean coastal area) and iron age workmanship began in the 3rd to 2nd century BCE in Northern Nigeria, Sudan, and Northwest Tanzania. Most likely, blacksmith skills were imported from the vicinity of the North African coast and Egypt, rather than spontaneously developing in the inner African continent. It appears that the arts represented in wood carving, textile manufacturing, metal working in general, and sword production in particular, started and developed on the west coast of Africa between the river basins of Congo and Niger.

Until the early 20th century, there were no writings about edged weapons of Africa. For antique collectors, African art in general and swords in particular are still virgin territory, explored mostly by sophisticated art collectors or modern era artists strongly influenced by primitive art that is reflected in their own creations. African antiques prior to the 18th century are virtually unseen, even in major museums exhibiting African art. African art from the 19th century, including edged weapons, is very rarely seen, and when available, prices are stratospheric. The African climate, with its extreme humidity, heat, or extreme dryness, created an unfavorable habitat for antiques, which were virtually destroyed through exposure to nature's elements. Iron is very durable, however it will rust and corrode rapidly when exposed to humidity.

The most attractive and skillfully created metalwork of considerable interest to antique collectors was and still remains the Benin bronze sculptures and famous Benin ceremonial swords. Although there are no written annals, it is believed that the unified kingdom of Benin rose to power in the 14th century CE in southern Nigeria by consolidation of power and government related to different tribes and clans. While artistic traditions were certainly present prior to the 14th century CE, the royal power of Benin allowed for rapid progress in the social, political, cultural, and military arenas of the Benin kingdom.

The first dynasty of Benin, the Ogiso kingdom, had a supreme ruler named Egiso (ruler of the sky), having absolute power over Benin inhabitants. Regalia associated with the absolute ruler included the *ada*, a ceremonial sword with a ritual symbolic role of "divine kingship." The unlimited power of Ogiso brought discontent to the Benin people, who ultimately revolted and overthrew the king. The following dynasty had a foreign supreme ruler, who was actually sought by the people of Benin to become their leader. The Oba (king) originated from the neighboring Yoruba kingdom of Nigeria. The friendship between those two kingdoms allowed for prosperity and peace, both essential to development of the arts and culture. The ada sword became the symbol of Oba, representing royal power and unification. Another ceremonial sword was the *eben*, a sword with a peculiar broad blade in the shape of a fan, with several openings and open work plus inlays of brass and copper—a magnificent art object! This ceremonial sword was used on special occasions as a dance sword in honor of the ruler's ancestor father. At these ceremonial functions, the king himself danced with the eben, twirling and tossing it high in the air.

The Ashante kingdom developed in the area of present day Ghana, reaching its peak of artistic perfection in the mid-18th century. The king was considered to have divine powers and was called Asantehene in the Akan language. The *afena* sword was a symbol of his supreme power. The afena had an interesting shape, featuring a flat bilobate blade decorated with pierced open art work. Another ceremonial Ashante (also known as Asante) sword is the *mponponsuo*, which served as an instrument of allegiance for the tribal chieftains in the Ashante confederation. Mponponsuo was a wide blade sword decorated with open work metalware and with leopard skin covering the scabbard and hilt. Heavy gold cast ornaments, named abosodee, decorated the scabbard and hilt. Perhaps the most important sword of the Asantehene was the *bosommuru*, the sword used by the king to swear allegiance to the nation. On very special occasions, the bosommuru was used in ritual dances by the Asantehene himself, similar to how the eben was used by the Benin king. Yet another type of ceremonial sword was the *asomfofena*, a sword carried by the king's representative (governor) when advising local chieftains. The power of Asantehene was recognized by seeing asomfofena, the symbol of royal authority, with the abosodee's decorations having special meaning to the local governing authority. In addition, two ceremonial swords were used exclusively by the Akan king. On his right side, he would wear *akrofena*, a sword representing the spiritual and religious power of Asantehene. On his left side, Asantehene would wear the *bosomfena* sword. representing the political authority of the king, the supreme ruler of the Akan confederation.

The Kuba kingdom existed in the area that at present is Zaire. Local blacksmiths created ceremonial swords along with utilitarian knives. The most representative Kuba dagger is the *ikul*, a dagger having a leaf shaped, double-edged blade and a short hilt. The royal ceremonial dagger was *mbombaam*, a pointed leaf shaped blade knife decorated with longitudinal incisions and a long hilt inlaid with copper. This dagger-knife was usually used as a spear, as the hilt was affixed to a long wooden stick and bound in several places with multi-colored beads or bands. More commonly used in Kuba were the throwing knives (*shongo*), which unfortunately became extinct due to an edict of King Shyiam forbidding use of these deadly weapons.

African Throwing Knives

This type of edged weapon was widely used in central Africa. Some were in the shape of an F or E and others were circular. These legendary throwing knives were known to pivot around when hitting a solid target such as a regular shield and kill the warrior behind it (who considered his shield to be a protective piece of equipment, rather than an adjuvant to his demise).

One type of throwing knife was *Momfu*, used in northern Zaire. The Momfu blade was circular with a bulbous contour. In the same geographic area, the Mongbetu tribe produced one of the most attractive throwing knives. The knives of the Momfu and Mongbetu tribes in northern Zaire are very much prized by collectors for their hilts, which were carved in ivory with incised decorations.

Blacksmiths from the Ingassana tribe of Sudan also created throwing knives of considerable aesthetic appeal. These knives are called *mudar* and the blades have incised zoomorphic decorations in the shape of a scorpion. A similar throwing knife, *sap*, has a blade in the shape of a coiled snake. More frequently, ornaments decorating the blades of these throwing knives contain a mixture of zoomorphic and anthropomorphic designs. It is believed that the blade represents a human head, with the spur below the curvature of the blade symbolizing a woman's breasts and the handle believed to represent human legs. The stylization of the ornaments and the symbolic integration of man and fauna attest to a high degree of sophistication for people living in the most primitive conditions.

A final word for collectors: the abundance of African "tourist souvenirs" has made many collectors avoid this collecting field. The reality is that antique, high quality African art objects—including swords, daggers and knives—are very, very rare! Be aware that many "African antiques" are deceptively made to look old, but are in reality brand new.

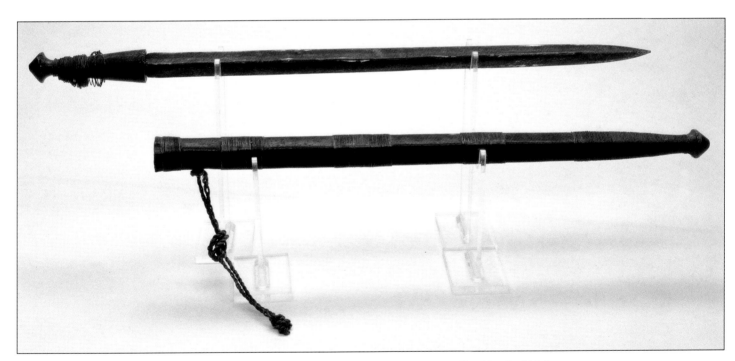

Fig. 8/1. Northern Nigeria. 19th century sword. Wooden hilt covered with coiled copper wire. Double-edged blade with a central rib. The scabbard is made from wood in a rectangular shape and decorated with bands of coiled brass wire. Blade's length: 23" (58.5 cm.). Sword's length: 29.5" (75 cm.). Estimated value: $3,000.

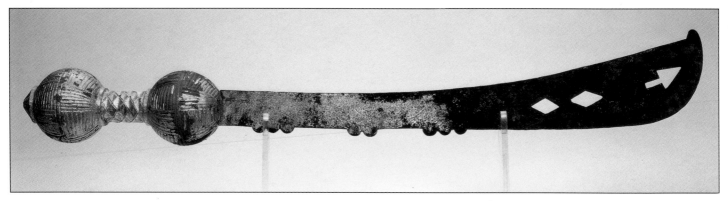

Fig. 8/2. 19th century, or earlier Asante Kingdom (present day Ghana). Mponponsuo sword, the most important of the state swords, used by tribal chiefs in swearing allegiance to the Asantehene (supreme ruler). The hilt is gilded on a reddish wood base. Curved blade, decorated in open work with an arrow and two rhombs. Blade's length: 18.5" (47 cm.). Sword's length: 27.5" (70 cm.). Estimated value: $2,500.

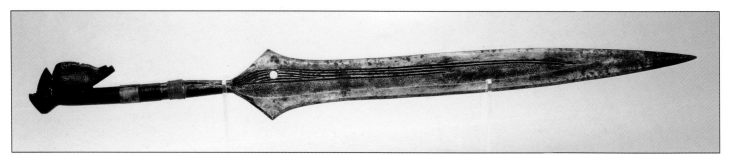

Fig. 8/3. Zaire, Kuba. Antique large chieftain sword with very long hilt and elongated pommel serving as a royal scepter. The wooden pommel is in the shape of a human head. The length of the wooden hilt allows two handed holding of this sword. Copper wire and a tin band ornate the hilt. Double-edged blade tapers toward the point and has four fullers that are reduced to two fullers in the lower third. It was made by an indigenous blacksmith with great skills using primitive tools. Blade's length: 27" (69 cm.). Sword's length: 39.5" (100 cm.). Estimated value: $2,000.

Fig. 8/5. Congo (Zaire). 18th-19th century royal ceremonial short sword named ngodip. Typical for this type of sword is the wavy blade with three undulations that create successive narrowing and widening of the blade. Ebony wood hilt with brass round pins decorating the pommel. Leather scabbard decorated with animal fur and skins. Blade's length: 17.2" (44 cm.). Sword's length: 23.5" (59.5 cm.). Estimated value: $3,000.

Fig. 8/4. Zaire, Kuba. 18th-19th century. Royal Bakuba court sword named ngodip. Wooden hilt with prominent carved bands. The scabbard is made from wood and covered with leather and leopard skin. The blade has several convolutions, making it narrower or wider along its length. A braided fiber band allows for suspension. Provenance: Ex-Don Selchow collection, a prominent American artist and world traveler. Blade's length: 19" (48 cm.). Sword's length: 25" (63.5 cm.). Estimated value: $3,500.

Fig. 8/6. Congo (Zaire). 19th century ceremonial dagger. Wooden hilt decorated with vertical striations. Anthropomorphic wood carving of the scabbard resembles a human figure holding two large bowls. Two equal size bowls emerge from the top of his head. Circular and rhomboid decorations are also present. The double-edged blade appears hundreds of years older and displays pitting corrosion on its surface. Blade's length: 6" (15.5 cm.). Dagger's length: 14.5" (36.8 cm.). Estimated value: $2,000.

Fig. 8/7. Congo (Zaire). 19th century Mangbetu sickle dagger, also called "executioner dagger." The blade is curved in right angle, double-edged on upper part. The lower part of the blade has two large round perforations. Two cylindrical prongs are located on the back of the blade. Wooden hilt with simple decorations. Blade's length: 10" x 9.5" (25 x 24 cm.). Dagger's length: 16.2" (41.3 cm.). Estimated value: $1,200.

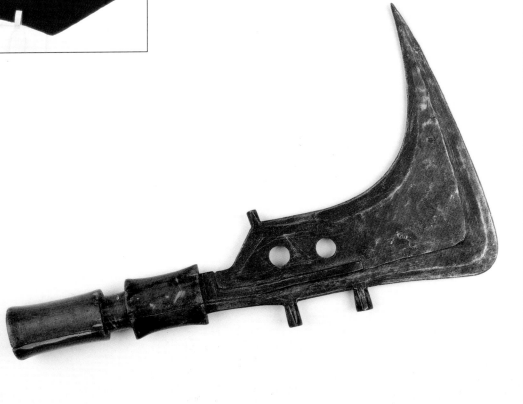

Fig. 8/8. Congo (Zaire), Kuba. 18th-19th century ceremonial dagger. The blade is decorated with a lion on one side and a long neck bird on the reverse side. One fuller is surrounded by incised decorations. The hilt is decorated with concentric bands of ivory and horn. Blade's length: 9" (23 cm.). Dagger's length: 13.3" (34 cm.). Estimated value: $950.

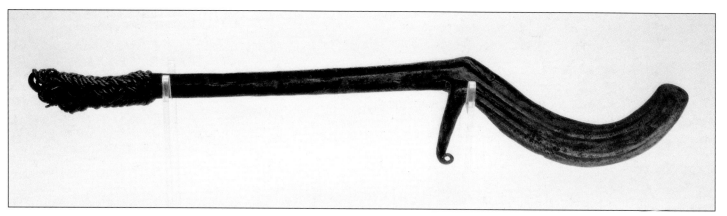

Fig. 8/9. Congo (Zaire). 18th-19th century royal court sword. Copper hilt covered with horizontal bands of brass. Large wooden pommel covered with round brass head pins. Very wide double-edged blade with an oval shape and tapering toward the point. Blade's length: 17.2" (44 cm.). Sword's length: 22.4" (57 cm.). Estimated value: $2,000.

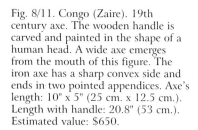

Fig. 8/10. Congo (Zaire). 19th century throwing knife weapon. This is a very rare type of "throwing knife" and, due to the large dimensions, could be called a "throwing sword." It has a braided leather hilt. The blade is curved, sickle shaped, and double-edged with three fullers. According to the history of this weapon, it was collected early in the 20th century by Warren Buck. Length: 23.6" (60 cm.). Estimated value: $950.

Fig. 8/11. Congo (Zaire). 19th century axe. The wooden handle is carved and painted in the shape of a human head. A wide axe emerges from the mouth of this figure. The iron axe has a sharp convex side and ends in two pointed appendices. Axe's length: 10" x 5" (25 cm. x 12.5 cm.). Length with handle: 20.8" (53 cm.). Estimated value: $650.

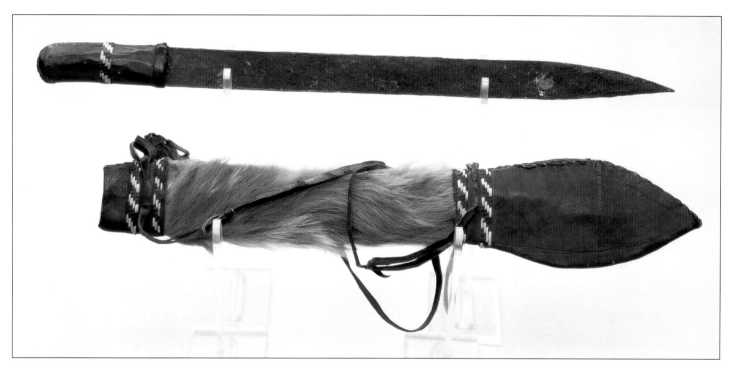

Fig. 8/12. Nigeria. Short sword with leather hilt and scabbard decorated with elaborate stitching. The blade appears much older, probably 18th-19th century, and was crudely manufactured by an indigenous blacksmith. Two large leather balls are suspended with leather strings attached to the scabbard. Blade's length: 16.5" (42 cm.). Sword's length: 22.5" (57 cm.). Estimated value: $600.

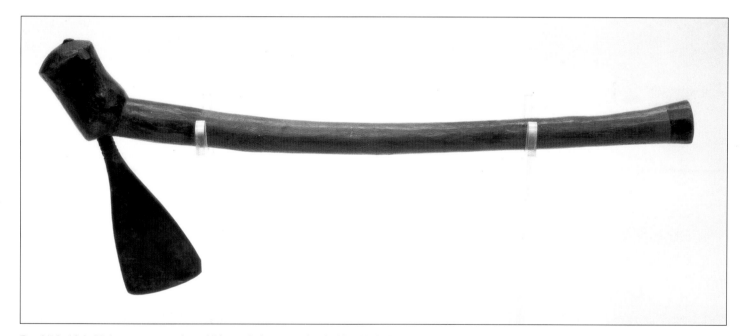

Fig. 8/13. 19th-20th century axe shaped like an Indian tomahawk. The blade has a triangular shape and is sharp. Signs of aging are displayed by the wooden handle. Axe's size: 7" x 2.2" (18 cm. x 5.5 cm.). Handle's length: 16.5" (42 cm.). Estimated value: $675.

Fig. 8/14. East African dagger made from cowhide and steel, decorated with black and red strips of leather. Obviously, this dagger was used for ceremonial rituals. It has five strips of woven leather used for the dagger's suspension. The blade was indigenously made and has a central rib on each side that reinforces its strength. Dagger's length: 13" (33 cm.). Blade's length: 7.2" (18.5 cm.). Estimated value: $450-$550.

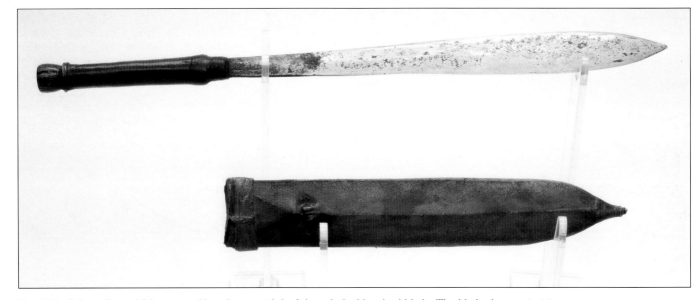

Fig. 8/15. Gabon, Seme. 19th century Kota dagger with leaf shaped, double-edged blade. The blade shows primitive watering and age corrosion pitting. Original leather sheet covers the hilt. Heavy leather forms the scabbard, which has a perforation in the back for attachment. Blade's length: 13" (33 cm.). Dagger's length: 19.9" (50 cm.). Estimated value: $600.

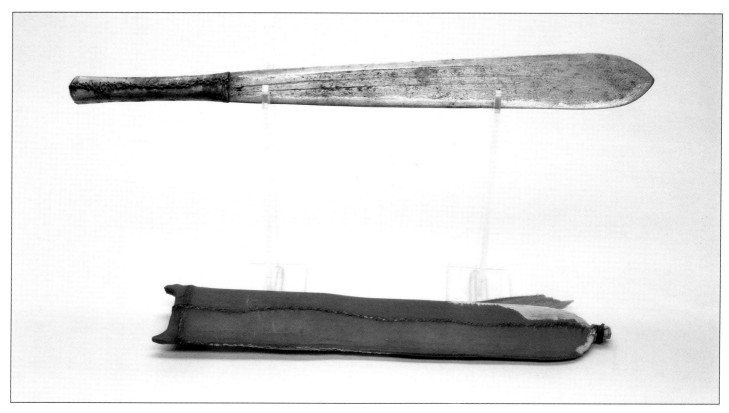

Fig. 8/16. Ghana. 19th century short sword, machete-type with leather hilt and red leather scabbard. Double-edged blade that widens toward the point is lance-shaped. Estimated value: $500.

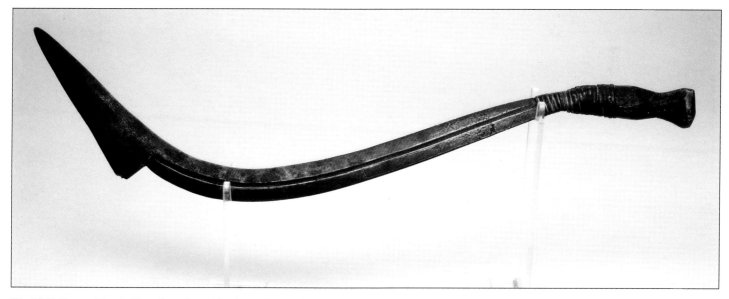

Fig. 8/17. Congo (Zaire). Ngombe tribe in Northeast Congo. Sickle shaped sword with bird's head end. It is a single edged, semi-circular sword allegedly used as an executioner's sword. These type of weapons are also called throwing knives or swords. The blade has simple incised decorations. Wooden hilt with raffia bindings. Blade's length: 24" (61 cm.). Sword's length: 30" (76 cm.). Estimated value: $850.

Fig. 8/18. Belgian Congo. Set of three 18th century iron spear points used as money for the exchange of goods. Pitted corrosion is present on the surface of these spear points, which were created by indigenous blacksmiths. Length varies between 5.1" (13 cm.) and 5.5" (14 cm.). Very rare primitive money! Estimated value: $600.

Fig. 8/19. Congo (Zaire). Ikul Kuba dagger with leaf-shaped triangular blade having a central, longitudinal incised decoration. The hilt and scabbard are made from wood with intricate, carved decorations. A knobbed perforation on the back of the scabbard allows for portability. Blade's length: 8.4" (21.3cm.). Dagger's length: 15.5" (39.3cm.). Estimated value: $500.

Fig. 8/20. Ivory Coast. 19th-20th century spear. Double-convoluted spear body with long needle-like point. Spear's length: 8" (20 cm.). Pole's length: 5' (152.5 cm.). Estimated value: $550.

Fig. 8/21. Congo (Zaire). Northeast Zaire Momfu tribe, wide blade sickle-shaped sword. Named also as a throwing sword, despite the fact that this practice is disputed by the scholars in the field, mostly because the metal weapons were very precious and warriors could not afford to lose them. Long wooden hilt covered with hide stripes. Blade's length: 11.8" (30 cm.). Sword's length: 24" (61 cm.). Estimated value: $800.

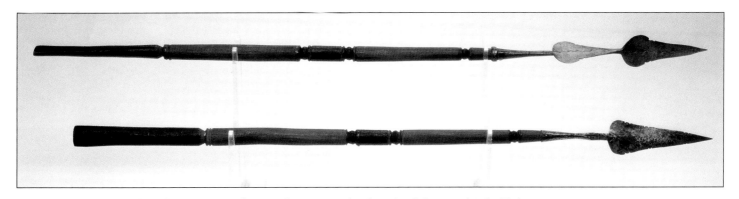

Fig. 8/22. Masai tribe. 19th-20th century pair of spears. One is triangular shaped and the second is double-heart shaped. Made from one piece of metal and facing different directions. Piercing with this spear makes withdrawal almost impossible. Allegedly used for hunting elephants. Wooden handle with simple decorations and painting. Lengths: 57" (145 cm.) and 54" (137 cm.). Estimated value: $1,000 for pair.

Fig. 8/23. Northern Nigeria. 19th-20th century dagger. Wooden hilt with linear decorations. Leather scabbard with fringed distal end. The blade is the work of a primitive indigenous blacksmith and has rough watering. Blade's length: 7.5" (19 cm.). Dagger's length: 12" (30.5 cm.). Estimated value: $400.

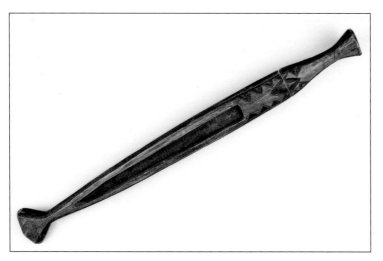

Fig. 8/24. Gabon. 19th-20th century dagger with wooden hilt and scabbard. Simple decorations adorn the obverse side of the scabbard and hilt. An opening in the scabbard allows the blade on the obverse side to be viewed. The scabbard's reverse side has a wooden knob for the dagger's suspension. The blade appears older than the dagger itself and bears signs of a primitive blacksmith's work. Blade's length: 12.5" (31.7 cm.). Dagger's length: 17.5" (44.5 cm.). Estimated value: $400.

Fig. 8/25. Gabon. 19th-20th century dagger. The wooden hilt and scabbard have linear decorations. The obverse side of the scabbard has an opening for viewing the blade. A wooden knob with leather string is located on the reverse side of the scabbard. Double-edged, sharp blade. Blade's length: 8" (20.5 cm.). Dagger's length: 14" (35.5 cm.). Estimated value: $400.

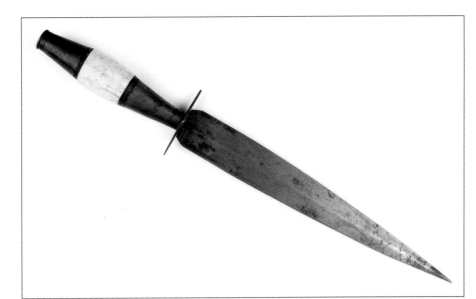

Fig. 8/26. Northern Nigeria. 19th-20th century Hausaland dagger. Bone and brass hilt with a bi-conic shape. The blade is double-edged and very sharp. Blade's length: 8" (20.5 cm.). Dagger's length: 11.8" (30 cm.). Estimated value: $300.

Fig. 8/27. Gabon. Tribe of Kota people, fang knife. Double-edged, sharp pointed blade with a criss-cross of ornamental lines in the center. The hilt and pommel are made from wood decorated with linear decorations. Blade's length: 8" (20.5 cm.). Knife's length: 12.6" (32 cm.). Estimated value: $300.

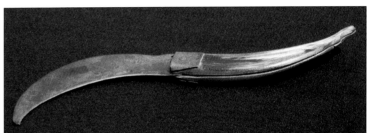

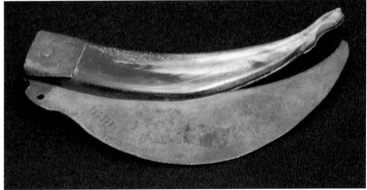

Fig. 8/28. Congo. 19th-20th century Kuba folding knife with carved horn hilt. The blade is made from imported European steel and marked "IROCIOL". Single-edged blade, sickle-shaped and sharp. Blade's length: 6.5" (16.5 cm.). Knife's length: 13.5" (34 cm.). Estimated value: $400.

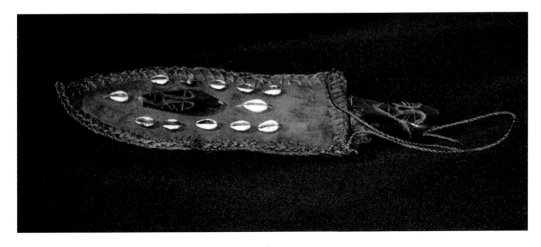

Fig. 8/29. West Africa-Ivory Coast. 19th-20th century dagger with carved ivory hilt in the shape of a human figure. The blade is double-edged with two curves and shows surface pitted corrosion. The scabbard is made from animal hide decorated with cowries shells. Its edges are of woven raffia, which also forms a cord for easy carrying. A toned ivory carving in the shape of a human figure is attached to the center of the scabbard. Blade's length: 8.6" (22 cm.). Dagger's length: 12.8" (32.5 cm.). Estimated value: $600.

Moroccan Edged Weapons

Moroccan edged weapons have been separated here from other African edged weapons due to their superior workmanship and different style. One could argue that the logical classification of Moroccan edged weapons would be to include them with Islamic edged weapons. Nevertheless, due to significant exchange between the Western and Islamic worlds in Morocco, it appears to us that the country's geographic location should be considered the prime factor in determining classification.

Most reference materials on edged weapons have tangential information—or no information at all—about Moroccan edged weapons. Most likely the massive importation of cheap, "tourist" type Moroccan koummiyas led to a false impression of low quality, bulk production of Moroccan jambiyas. The reality is completely different. High quality edged weapons have indeed been manu-factured in Morocco by highly skilled craftsmen. In the 18th, 19th, and beginning of the 20th century, high quality koummiyas and nimchas were manufactured by Jewish sword-smiths, trained by family traditions with skills communicated from father to son. Tedious chiseling of silver, gold, and inlaying of precious metals was done by artists interested in manufacturing the best art object, regardless of the time required to produce a single item. Of course, a premium price is demanded for these rare pieces.

Koummiya is the most common Moroccan dagger and is actually a jambiya. Skilled Moroccan artisans also manufactured nimcha swords with magnificent chiseled silver hilts. There is ample representation here of koummiyas and one museum-quality nimcha. Saharan Tuareg takuba (takouba) swords are also represented here, both high-end examples chiseled in silver and decorated with semi-precious stones, plus more modest ones made from leather and having little or no silver decorations.

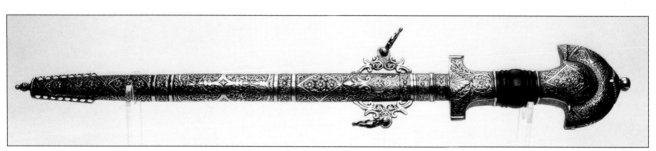

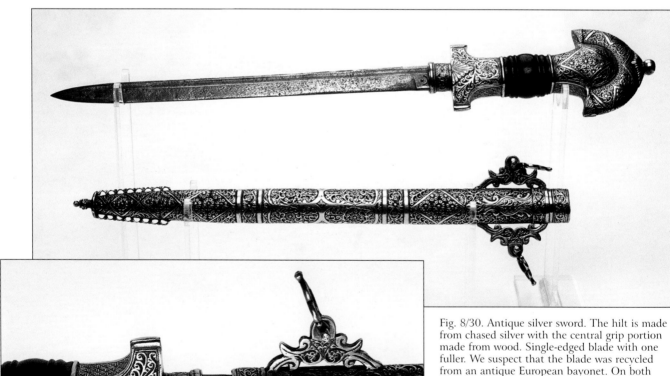

Fig. 8/30. Antique silver sword. The hilt is made from chased silver with the central grip portion made from wood. Single-edged blade with one fuller. We suspect that the blade was recycled from an antique European bayonet. On both sides of the ricasso there is a mark of a star and wheeled semicircle. The scabbard is made from solid silver chiseled in relief with an intricate Islamic motif. Blade's length: 14.5" (37 cm.). Sword's length: 26.8" (68 cm.). Estimated value: $8,000-$10,000.

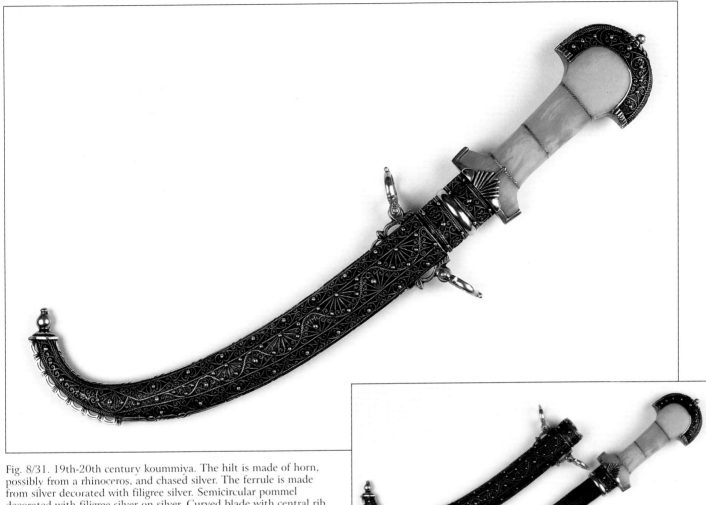

Fig. 8/31. 19th-20th century koummiya. The hilt is made of horn,
possibly from a rhinoceros, and chased silver. The ferrule is made
from silver decorated with filigree silver. Semicircular pommel
decorated with filigree silver on silver. Curved blade with central rib,
becomes double-edged in the distal half. Silver scabbard decorated
with intricate silver filigree design. Two silver rings for suspension are
located on the proximal part of the scabbard. A heavy cord baldric
(not shown) serves to suspend the dagger over the right shoulder.
Blade's length: 9.5" (24 cm.). Dagger's length: 17.2" (44 cm.).
Estimated value: $10,000.

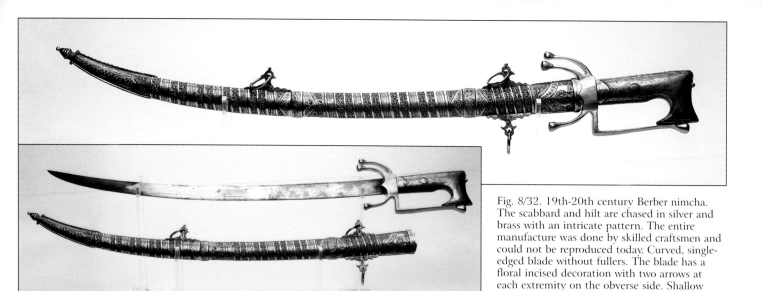

Fig. 8/32. 19th-20th century Berber nimcha. The scabbard and hilt are chased in silver and brass with an intricate pattern. The entire manufacture was done by skilled craftsmen and could not be reproduced today. Curved, single-edged blade without fullers. The blade has a floral incised decoration with two arrows at each extremity on the obverse side. Shallow hand-guard with two quillons on one side and a single quillon on the opposite side, continuing upward to form a straight line knuckle-guard linked to the pommel. Blade's length: 24.2" (61.5 cm.). Sword's length: 33.5" (85 cm.). Estimated value: $10,000.

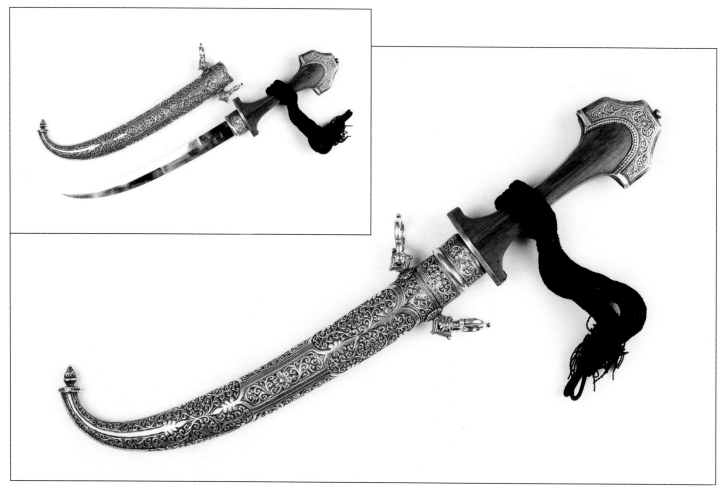

Fig. 8/33. 19th century silver koummiya. The dagger has King Hassan's mark inscribed. Wooden hilt with silver fitting ferrule for the blade. The pommel is pentagonal in shape, decorated with incised silver with floral and tendrils design. King Hassan mark consisting of a goat with coiled horn is located on the edge of the pommel. Heavy, chrome-plated blade with inscribed coat of arms located near the hilt on both sides. The blade also has a representation of three lilies below the royal crown. Blade's length: 9.2" (23.5 cm.). Dagger's length: 16.2" (42 cm.). Estimated value: $8,500-$9,000.

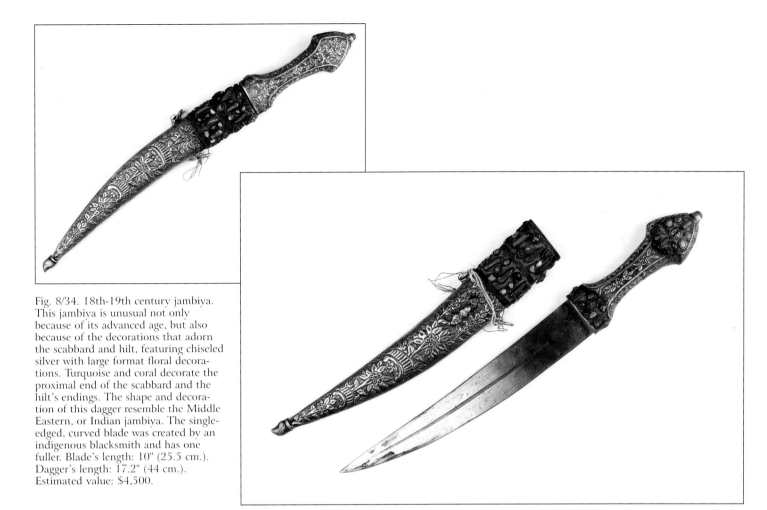

Fig. 8/34. 18th-19th century jambiya. This jambiya is unusual not only because of its advanced age, but also because of the decorations that adorn the scabbard and hilt, featuring chiseled silver with large format floral decorations. Turquoise and coral decorate the proximal end of the scabbard and the hilt's endings. The shape and decoration of this dagger resemble the Middle Eastern, or Indian jambiya. The single-edged, curved blade was created by an indigenous blacksmith and has one fuller. Blade's length: 10" (25.5 cm.). Dagger's length: 17.2" (44 cm.). Estimated value: $4,500.

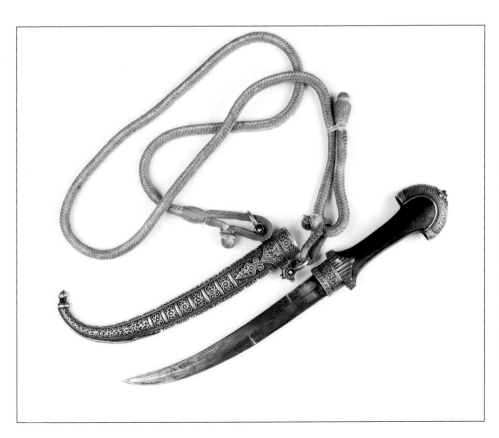

Fig. 8/35. Antique koummiya dagger. The scabbard is made from chiseled silver with a repeating floral pattern. On the reverse side there is an Islamic inscription and a date in Arabic numerals that appears as 1350. Two lateral silver rings hold a suspending baldric cord. Single-edged, curved blade becomes double-edged in the lower third. An older European blade was used in creating this dagger and carries partially visible letters reading Meso and above, capital MC. Wooden hilt with silver decorations in the distal end. Round-shaped silver pommel. Blade's length: 9" (23 cm.). Dagger's length: 16" (40.5 cm.). Estimated value: $3,500.

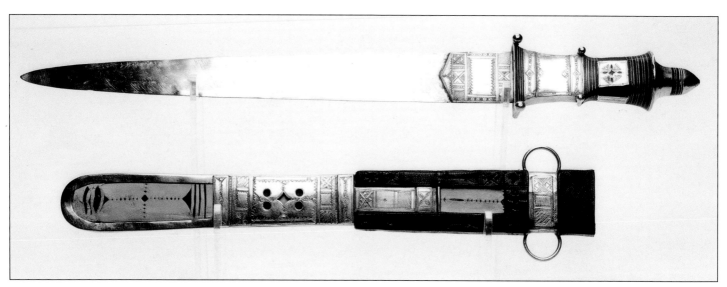

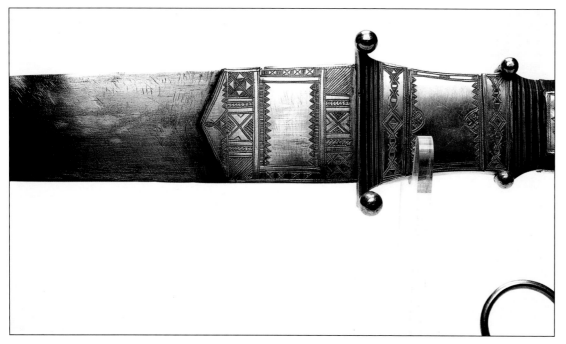

Fig. 8/36. 19th-20th century Tuareg sword, takuba. The hilt and scabbard are decorated with chased silver and the silver pommel is decorated with incised ornaments. Embossed green and brown leather cover the scabbard, many areas having a typical cruciform pattern. Double-edged, wide blade with silver ricasso decorated with incised geometric decorations. The blade displays a crude manufacture typical of those that are indigenously created. Two silver eyelets located on the upper part of the scabbard serve for the sword's suspension. This type of sword is carried on the right shoulder using a leather and string baldric. Blade's length: 17.2" (44 cm.). Sword's length: 24.8" (63 cm.).Estimated value: $4,000.

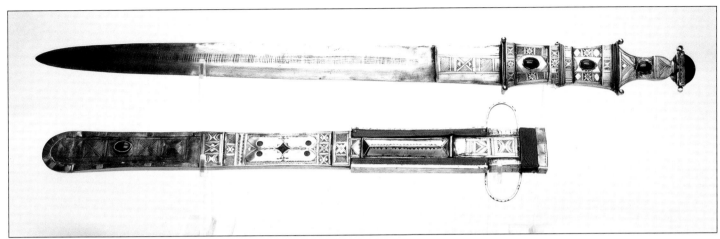

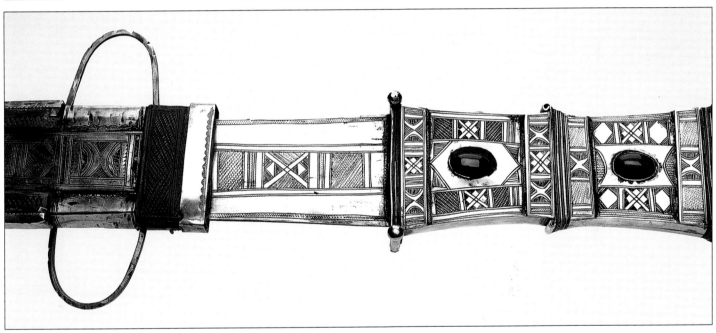

Fig. 8/37. 19th-20th century Sahara Tuareg silver sword, takuba. The hilt is made from chased silver with a geometric design and two large mounted carnelian carvings. Large silver pommel with chased silver decorations and mounted semicircular agate on top. Double-edged, wide blade, indigenously manufactured. A large silver plaque is attached to the ricasso and decorated with geometric design. Silver scabbard with chased geometric decorations and embossed brown leather. One carnelian stone decorates the chape. Blade's length: 31.5" (80 cm.). Sword's length: 32.5" (82.5 cm.). Estimated value: $4,000.

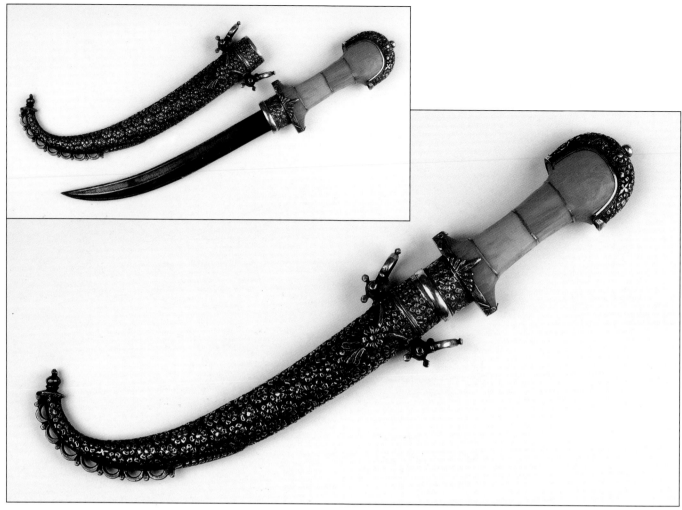

Fig. 8/38. Antique koummiya dagger. The scabbard is made from chiseled silver with a floral design. The obverse side has an un-inscribed silver panel. The hilt is most likely made from rhinoceros horn segments linked with silver bands. The distal part is made from chiseled silver. Silver pommel, oval shaped. The blade has a central rib for reinforcement. In the distal end, the blade becomes double edged. Blade's length: 9.5" (24 cm.). Dagger's length: 17.2" (44 cm.). Estimated value: $10,000.

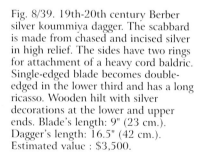

Fig. 8/39. 19th-20th century Berber silver koummiya dagger. The scabbard is made from chased and incised silver in high relief. The sides have two rings for attachment of a heavy cord baldric. Single-edged blade becomes double-edged in the lower third and has a long ricasso. Wooden hilt with silver decorations at the lower and upper ends. Blade's length: 9" (23 cm.). Dagger's length: 16.5" (42 cm.). Estimated value : $3,500.

Fig. 8/40. Antique koummiya silver dagger. The scabbard is covered with chiseled silver displaying typical Islamic hammered decorations in high relief. An Islamic inscription and date are enclosed in a cartouche. The hilt is made from horn and the distal end has a chiseled silver decoration. Crenellate, hammered decorations in silver decorate the pommel. The blade is curved and becomes double-edged in the lower third. A round inscribed mark with a lion is barely visible on the blade's ricasso. Blade's length: 9.1" (23 cm.). Dagger's length: 16.2" (41 cm.). Estimated value: $3,500.

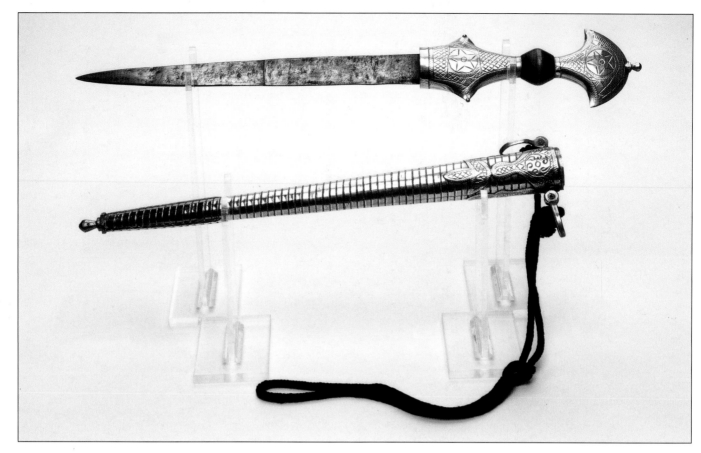

Fig. 8/41. Antique Moroccan silver sword. The hilt has a wooden grip and is made from chiseled silver, as is the scabbard. The blade was recycled from an antique sword blade. Blade's length: 12.2" (31 cm.). Sword's length: 23.5" (59.5cm.). Estimated value: $3,500.

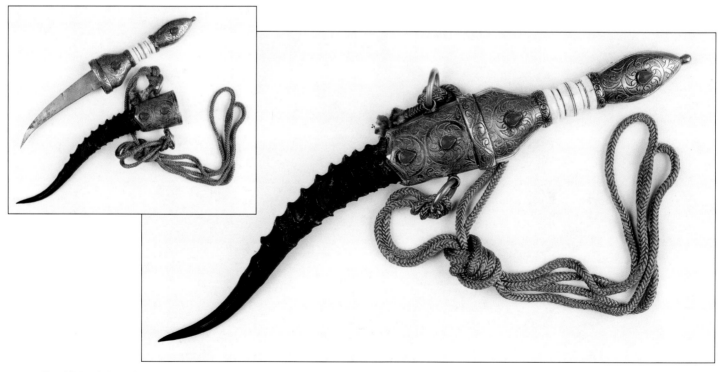

Fig. 8/42. 19th-20th century tribal Berber koummiya. The scabbard is made from chiseled silver in the proximal part and mountain goat horn in the distal portion. The hilt is made from chiseled silver, decorative red ornaments, and carved ivory in the center. Typically, the blade is double-edged in the distal part. Blade's length: 6.2" (16 cm.). Dagger's length: 17.2" (44 cm.). Estimated value: $3,000.

Fig. 8/43. 19th-20th century silver koummiya. The scabbard is decorated with chiseled and hammered silver in relief. Silver pommel envelops the upper part of the wooden hilt. Single-edged blade becomes double-edged in the distal third. Blade's length: 8.2" (21 cm.). Dagger's length: 15" (38 cm.). Estimated value: $3,000.

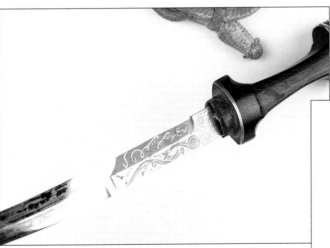

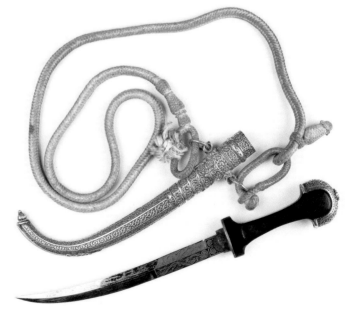

Fig. 8/44. Antique silver koummiya. The scabbard is covered with solid silver hammered and chiseled with intricate decorations and Islamic motif. Wooden hilt with silver pommel. Heavy nickel-plated blade of European origin with etched silver decorations featuring an Islamic inscription. As with the majority of koummiyas, the single-edged blade becomes double-edged in the distal third. Blade's length: 9" (23 cm.). Dagger's length: 15.3" (39 cm.). Estimated value: $3,000.

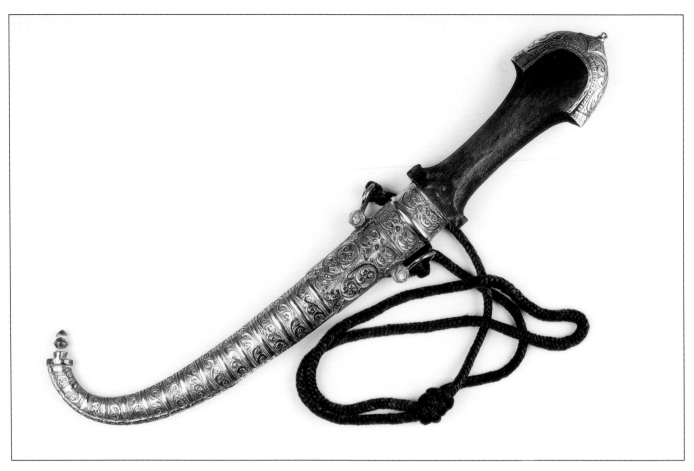

Fig. 8/45. Antique silver koummiya. The scabbard is made from chiseled silver in relief and has horizontal panels featuring tendrils and vines. Two rings hold a heavy cord baldric for carrying the dagger on the right shoulder. Wooden hilt with silver terminals and silver decorated pommel. The blade becomes double-edged in the distal third. Blade's length: 8.5" (21.5 cm.). Dagger's length: 16" (40.5 cm.). Estimated value: $3,000.

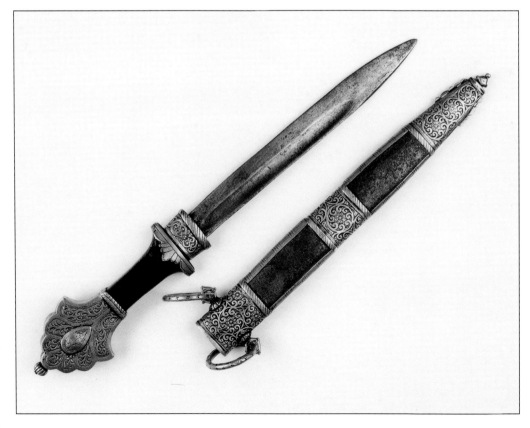

Fig. 8/46. 19th century koummiya dagger. Wooden hilt with chiseled silver in the proximal end. Silver pommel in the shape of a cock's comb. Unusual blade for a koummiya, with one fuller and single edge. It was probably made from a European sword end or a bayonet. Iron scabbard decorated with chased silver on the central part and extremities. The sides are made from chased brass. Two large rings serve for attachment of the baldric cord. Blade's length: 9" (23 cm.). Dagger's length: 18.2" (46.3 cm.). Estimated value: $2,000.

Fig. 8/47. Antique silver koummiya with hammered and chased silver scabbard. Wooden hilt with decorated silver distal end and silver pommel. Curved, double-edged blade in the distal third. Blade's length: 9" (23 cm.). Dagger's length: 16.5" (42 cm.). Estimated value: $2,500.

Fig. 8/48. 19th-20th century koummiya long dagger. Wooden hilt decorated with chased silver on the distal end. Semicircular chiseled silver pommel. Chiseled silver scabbard with Islamic motif decorations. Two rings are located on the upper part of the scabbard for attachment of the baldric. Curved blade with incised coiled serpent decoration. The blade becomes double-edged in the distal half. Blade's length: 11.2" (28.5 cm.). Dagger's length: 19.5" (49.5 cm.). Estimated value: $2,500.

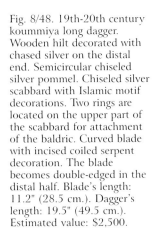
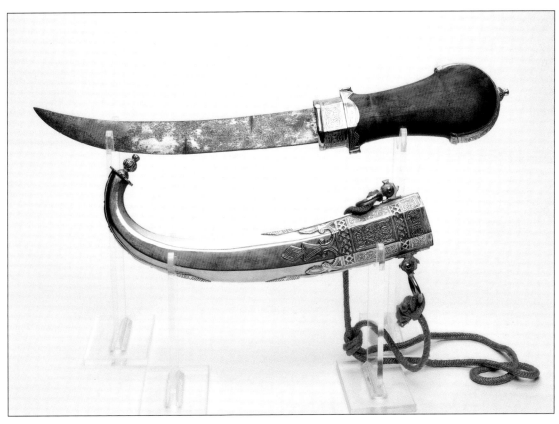

Fig. 8/49. 19th-20th century silver koummiya. The scabbard has chiseled silver decorations with Islamic motif. Wooden hilt with chased silver at the distal end and silver pommel that covers the apex of the hilt. The blade is an old Spanish recycled, nickel plated sword blade. Near the hilt, the blade has the inscription "Agadero" and a coat of arms with the letter Z. Gilded decorations, apparently of Spanish origin, decorate the back of the blade. As is customary, the blade becomes double-edged in the lower part. Blade's length: 8.8" (22 cm.). Dagger's length: 16.5" (42 cm.). Estimated value: $2,500.

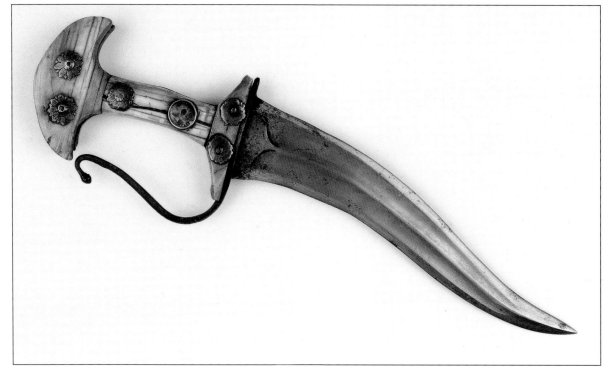

Fig. 8/50. 18th-19th century jambiya. Ivory hilt and pommel decorated with floral design silver bosses. Two bosses were apparently replaced with silver coins of Queen Victoria. The slim knuckle-guard does not reach the pommel. Double-edged blade with central rib. Blade's length: 8.2" (21 cm.). Dagger's length: 13" (33 cm.). Estimated value: $1,000.

Fig. 8/51. 19th-20th century Sahara Tuareg takuba sword. Double-edged, wide blade made from indigenously manufactured steel. The proximal part of the blade has four central fullers. A double mark resembling turtles is present on both sides of the blade. The blade's point is rounded. Cruciform hand-guard is covered with leather and ends in two chased brass quillons. Black leather covers the cylindrical hilt. Disk-shaped pommel with a chased, pyramid shaped terminal. The scabbard is made from embossed leather with two large leather baldric suspenders. The chape is decorated with green leather and incised brass. Blade's length: 33.5" (85 cm.). Sword's length: 40.5" (103 cm.). Estimated value: $1,000.

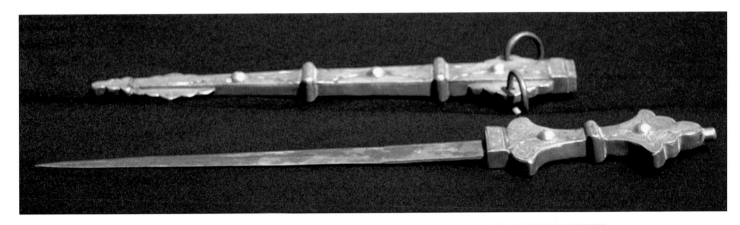

Fig. 8/52. 19th-20th century Tuareg short sword. The hilt and scabbard are covered with silver on the obverse side and decorated brass on the reverse side. Double-edged blade with sharp point. Blade's length: 13" (33 cm.). Sword's length: 21.2" (54 cm.). Estimated value: $2,000.

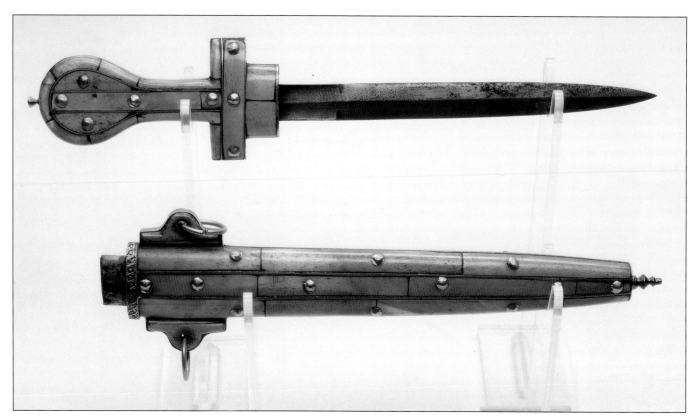

Fig. 8/53. 19th-20th century dagger with hilt and scabbard made from camel bone. Silver decorations are inlaid in the bone. The blade is straight and double-edged. Blade's length: 9.5" (24 cm.). Dagger's length: 19.2" (49 cm.). Estimated value: $900.

Fig. 8/54. 19th century silver koummiya. The scabbard has intricate, chiseled silver decorations with Islamic motif. Wooden hilt with chiseled silver pommel encircling the proximal end of the hilt. Typical koummiya blade with single edge in the proximal part and double edge in the distal portion. Blade's length: 8.8" (22 cm.). Dagger's length: 16.5" (42 cm.). Estimated value: $1,800.

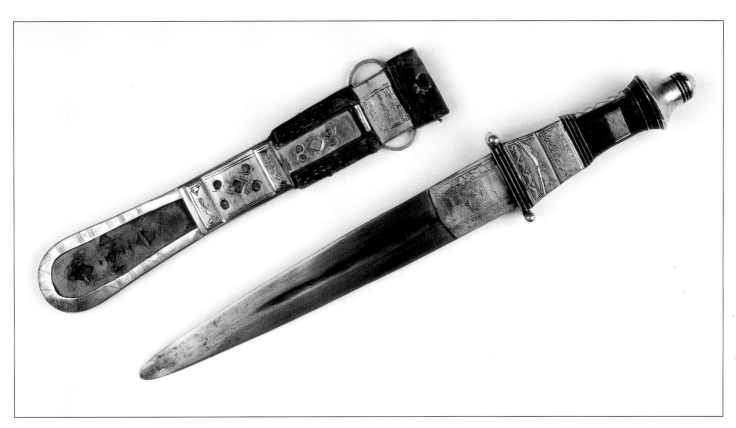

Fig. 8/55. 20th century Tuareg dagger. Wooden hilt and scabbard covered with silver and embossed leather ornaments. Double-edged blade with central rib. Silver ricasso with incised decorations. Blade's length: 5.5" (14cm.). Dagger's length: 8.5" (21.5 cm.). Estimated value: $400.

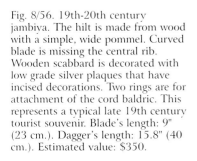

Fig. 8/56. 19th-20th century jambiya. The hilt is made from wood with a simple, wide pommel. Curved blade is missing the central rib. Wooden scabbard is decorated with low grade silver plaques that have incised decorations. Two rings are for attachment of the cord baldric. This represents a typical late 19th century tourist souvenir. Blade's length: 9" (23 cm.). Dagger's length: 15.8" (40 cm.). Estimated value: $350.

Fig. 8/57. 19th-20th century koummiya. Double-edged blade, still sharp. The hilt is made from wood with simple decorations on the pommel. Incised decorations are present on the scabbard, which is made from brass. Two rings on the scabbard serve for the baldric's attachment. This is a typical koummiya tourist souvenir from the late 19th century. Blade's length: 8.5" (21.5 cm.). Dagger's length: 16.1" (41 cm.). Estimated value: $350.

Fig. 8/58. 20th century Sahara Tuareg dagger. The hilt and scabbard are made from brass with incised silver decorations. Embossed leather in brown and green decorates the scabbard. Double-edged blade with central rib. Blade's length: 7.8" (19.5 cm.). Dagger's length: 12.5" (32 cm.). Estimated value: $400.

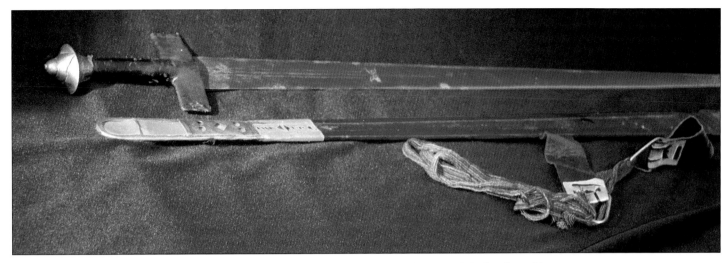

Fig. 8/59. 19th-20th century Sahara Tuareg takouba sword. The hilt is covered with leather and the hand-guard has a cruciform shape, also covered with red leather. Oval shape brass pommel. The scabbard is covered with embossed red leather in the upper part and green leather decorated with brass in the lower third. Two leather straps hold the sword and form the baldric for the right shoulder. Wide, double-edged blade with three fullers is decorated with a semi-circle and a wavy line and ends with a round point. Blade's length: 32.2" (82 cm.). Sword's length: 29" (99 cm.). Estimated value: $900.

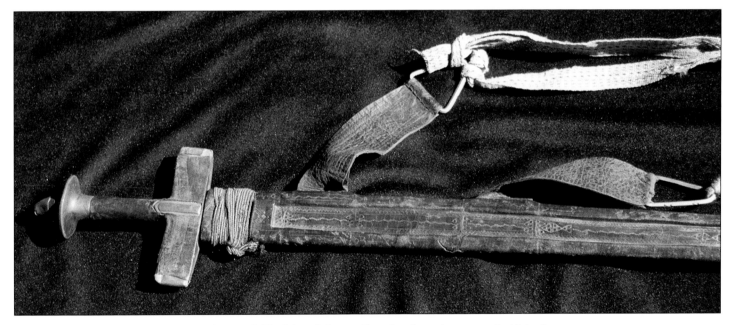

Fig. 8/60. 19th-20th century Tuareg takouba sword. The hilt and the cruciform hand-guard are covered with leather. The pommel has a pyramid shape and is decorated with bands of brass and copper. Embossed leather scabbard with brass and tin decorated chape. Two leather straps form the baldric. Double-edged blade with three fullers and round point. Blade's length: 28" (71 cm.). Sword's length: 34.6" (88 cm.). Estimated value: $900.

Chapter Nine

Pre-Columbian and Pre-Conquest America Edged Weapons; New Guinea and Oceanic Edged Weapons

Sharpened hard stones, obsidian and jade, were used extensively during the Neolithic period. Metallurgy was known in South America since 1500 BCE, as a late bronze age. Bronze, copper, silver, and gold were mined, smelted, and cast for centuries. Interestingly, bronze and copper were not used for producing war implements, but rather for sacrificial and ceremonial purposes. The Andean civilization that developed in present day Bolivia and Peru produced a large variety of sacrificial knives made from copper or bronze and used for decapitation, a method widely employed for obtaining head trophies of enemies killed or captured in battles. The Moche (Mochica) civilization, which lasted from the first century CE to 600 CE, produced copper axes tied to the waist through two perforations; they were also used primarily for decapitation of enemies' heads. The last indigenous Peruvian civilization, the Inca, used a bronze knife shaped as an axe with a rounded blade, called *tumi*. The tumi's handle had elaborate decorations. In battle, the Incas used an axe type of halberd made from hardstone, occasionally reinforced with a metal edge slotted into the stone. The most common decoration was that of a standing priest or king with elaborate open work headdress. Occasionally, turquoise or jade mosaic ornaments were inlaid in the metal.

Meso-America, including southern Mexico and Central America, did not use metallic weapons in battle or for ceremonial practices. The most effective weapon used by the Aztecs and the Mayas was a double-edged wooden sword with slots along the edges where obsidian blades were inserted and glued. Spanish chronicles of the period attest to the formidable effectiveness of this *macuahuitl* sword, which could cut an enemy as well as or better than a metallic sword. Unfortunately, there are no survivors of the macuahuitl and the only way we know about this feared weapon is through Spanish illustrations of that period. An Aztec sacrificial knife with elaborate mosaic decorations in the shape of an eagle on the handle was given to Cortes as a present by Motecuhzoma II, an Aztec king. According to Michael D. Coe, this golden obsidian knife was presented to Emperor Charles V and presently is in the collection of the Museum of Mankind in London. A surviving Mayan sacrificial knife was retrieved at Chichen Itza in Yucatan, in the sacred well Cenote. Amazingly, the wooden handle of this ceremonial knife was well preserved in the well and displays entwined serpents. The blade is made from obsidian with silver iridescence. The knife is housed in the Peabody Museum of Archeology and Ethnology at Harvard University.

North American Indians did not use bronze or copper edged weapons. The Old Copper Complex culture appeared about 2000 BCE in Wisconsin and Ontario and lasted until 500 BCE. The rudimentary knives produced in Wisconsin of Tlingit culture were used for hunting and fishing and originated from indigenous found copper that was cut, hammered, or annealed for shape forming. Northwest coast natives created highly artistic daggers, despite their lack of knowledge about metal smelting. Forging was very primitive and drift metal objects that came from floating barrels and storm related shipwrecks were used to create knives and other utilitarian metal objects. The daggers had ornate hilts with animal heads and inlaid fragments of abalone shell. The hilt handle was wrapped with caribou skin that provided a comfortable grip.

An advanced metallurgic culture called Dene existed in Alaska and northwestern Canada. It is still unexplained to the present day how the Dene people learned and developed such advanced methods of forging copper or even steel. Dene daggers had a characteristic hilt in the shape of a contorted and flattened metal spiral. Caribou skin or plant fibers tied with twine covered these hilts. More available to collectors are 19th and 20th century Eskimo knives from the Northern territories, and Alaskan knives with hilts made from walrus tusk ivory. The latter feature detailed scrimshaw scenes illustrating everyday life of the indigenous population plus scrimshaw inscriptions in Russian, English, or the rarest, both Russian and English, most frequently with poor orthography. We have in our collection examples of these rare historical Alaskan knives, from prior to or immediately following the USA's purchase of Alaska from Russia.

Fig. 9/1. 19th century walrus tusk carving in the shape of a single-edged blade that becomes double-edged near the point. This walrus tusk knife was made prior to the purchase of Alaska from Russia. A misspelled inscription using the Russian alphabet (Alayaska, rather than Alaska), appears on the obverse side of the blade. In continuation, it is displayed Katyaka: Alaska (apparently the name of the Inuit artist in Alaska). The reverse side of the blade illustrates an Eskimo hunting an animal. All the decorations are done using scrimshaw. Slightly curved hilt with three walruses on one side and an Eskimo house with water pontoon on the other side. On the side of the hilt is inscribed in scrimshaw, Kodiak-Alaska, this time using the Latin alphabet. This is a very rare historic relic of Alaska prior to its becoming part of the USA. Blade's length: 4'2" (11 cm.). Knife's length: 7.5" (19 cm.). Estimated value: $5,500.

Fig. 9/2. Mexico, Toltec civilization, edged axe-chisels. Right: Pre-Columbian bronze chisel-knife that resembles the Inca tumi. It is made from a bronze-rich alloy and is in the shape of an axe with a sharp edge. It measures 6" x 6" (15 x 15 cm.). Left: The second Toltec axe-chisel is made from an iron-rich alloy and has a peculiar shape as a spatula with a marked widening of the central portion. It has a rounded cutting edge that is still sharp. The tapering shank was probably attached to a wooden handle for increased leverage and control. Dimensions: 14.5" x 4.5" (37 cm. x 11.5 cm.). Both axe-chisels are very rare and I was unable to view any similar items in a Pre-Columbian civilization museum. Estimated value: $5,000 for both.

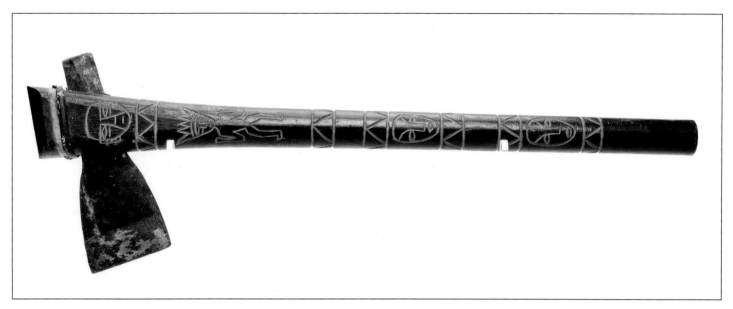

Fig. 9/3. Polynesia. Antique axe with wide iron blade. The wooden handle is carved with a representation of a crowned standing figure, probably the royalty. Above is a carved human head that I attribute to a deity representation. On the lower end are two carved human heads that might be human sacrificed heads. Very rare! Axe's length: 7.5" (19 cm.). Length including the handle: 23" (58.5 cm.). Estimated value: $800-$1,500.

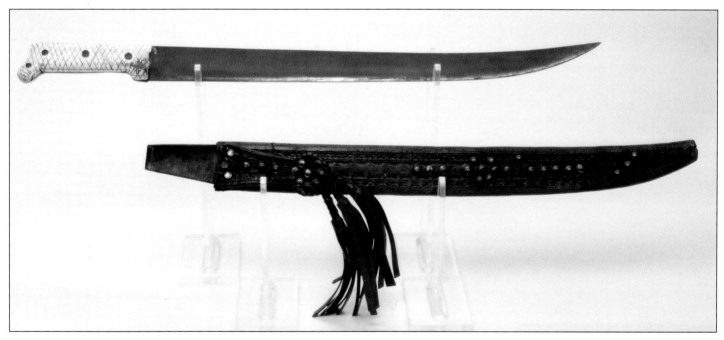

Fig. 9/4. Guatemala. 19th-20th century short sword, or machete. Bone hilt with criss-cross decorations. Single-edged blade, slightly curved in the distal third and with a convex edge. The scabbard is adorned with round metal tacks and three fringed leather appendices. The top of the scabbard has a band that allows a belt to be threaded through. Blade's length: 18.8" (47.5 cm.). Machete's length: 24.5" (62.2 cm.). Estimated value: $450.

Fig. 9/5. Guatemala. 19th-20th century sword-machete. The hilt is made from bi-color horn (black with a white-yellow horn in the center). The hand-guard is made from brass with a straight quillon. On the opposite side of the hand-guard is a ring that permits insertion of the index finger. Brass pommel with an ornament representing a Mayan chieftain. Single-edged blade with convex edge widening toward the center. The scabbard is decorated with elaborate leather embossing representing Mayan priests, one with a serpent headdress and the other with a bird headdress, leather fringes, and metal rings. Blade's length: 17.1" (43.5 cm.). Sword's length: 25.8" (654.5 cm. Estimated value: $700.

Fig. 9/6. Peru. 19th-20th century machete. The hilt is made from greenish oxhorn. The blade was manufactured in the USA and is marked Collins & Co., Hartford, acero puro, calidad garantizada. It widens gradually toward the point. Blade's length: 18"(46 cm). Machete's length: 23" (58.5 cm.). Estimated value: $450.

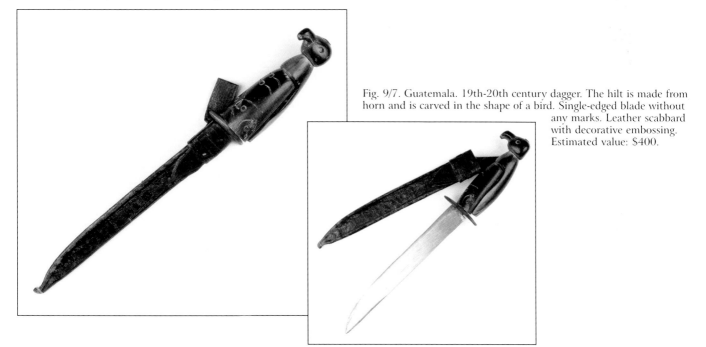

Fig. 9/7. Guatemala. 19th-20th century dagger. The hilt is made from horn and is carved in the shape of a bird. Single-edged blade without any marks. Leather scabbard with decorative embossing. Estimated value: $400.

Fig. 9/8. Mexico, Aztec culture. Aztec axe. Made from an alloy of tin and iron, it has rounded edges and thin body. The axe was used as money (also called Aztec hoe money). Very rare! Size: 7.5" x 2.8" (19 cm. x 7 cm.). Estimated value: $875 -$1,500.

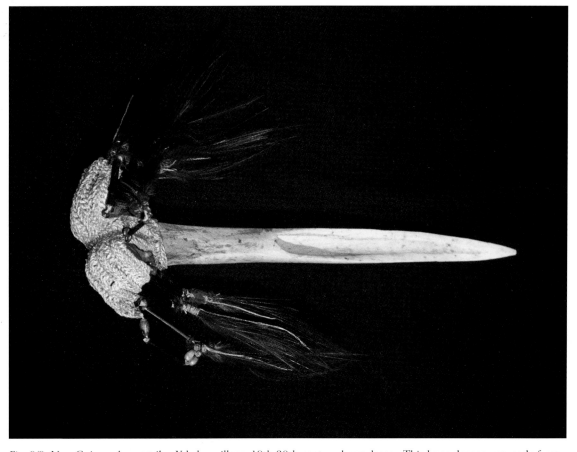

Fig. 9/9. New Guinea. Asmat tribe, Yakakor village. 19th-20th century bone dagger. This bone dagger was made from cassowary bird tibia bone and has a braided hilt decorated with beads, shells, and hair tassels. As it is very sharp, it was used for utilitarian tasks as well as ceremonials. Rare! Estimated value: $800-$1,500.

Chapter Ten

Decorative Swords, Daggers, and Knives

This chapter includes edged weapons used for esthetic or decorative purposes, rather than for utilitarian tasks. Oriental edged weapons are the only ones included, as a penchant for beauty of objects per se is prevalent to the Oriental arts. As swords and daggers became obsolete weapons in modern times, some were retained primarily for the pleasure they brought their owners as true art objects. As such, no limits were imposed on skilled artisans to create highly artistic objects in response to art collectors' demand. Of course, utilitarian tasks were occasionally assigned to these decorative objects as well, with some serving as letter openers or desk ornaments.

Fig. 10/1. China. 20th century ivory sword. The hilt is decorated with a human face design and flowers in scrimshaw. A dragon's head with open mouth decorates the pommel. Single-edged blade with scrimshaw decorations on the back side. Decorative carving of the scabbard in high relief features dragons and fish in the central panel. The entire surface has a polychrome incised design in scrimshaw. Very fine, intricate carving decorates the scabbard's end. The entire sword was carved on whole elephant ivory tusk. Sword's length: 24" (61 cm.). Estimated value: $8,000.

Fig. 10/2. 18th-19th century falchion dagger with ivory blade that widens toward the point. The hilt and pommel are made from solid silver chased in high relief. A coat of arms and a cross are located on the center of the hilt. Blade's length: 13" (33 cm.). Sword's length: 19.5" (49.5 cm.). Estimated value: $3,500.

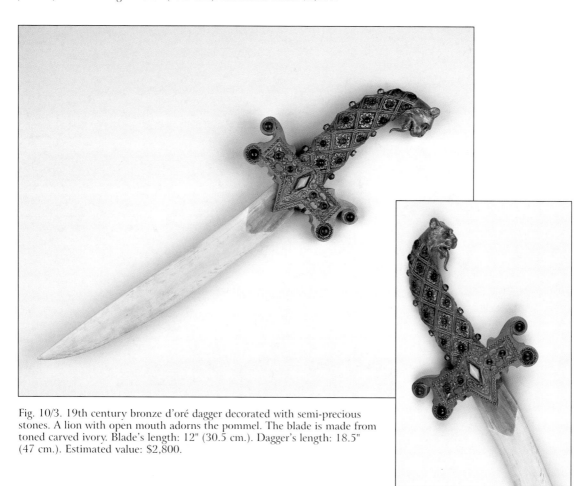

Fig. 10/3. 19th century bronze d'oré dagger decorated with semi-precious stones. A lion with open mouth adorns the pommel. The blade is made from toned carved ivory. Blade's length: 12" (30.5 cm.). Dagger's length: 18.5" (47 cm.). Estimated value: $2,800.

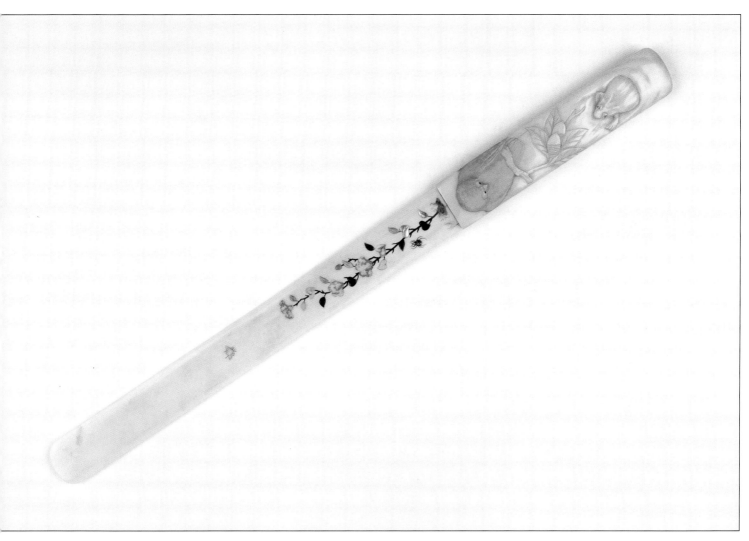

Fig. 10/4. Japan. 19th century shibayama knife made from ivory and decorated with mother-of-pearl featuring gold hues, carnelian, and agate. The handle has incised decorations in the shape of an owl perched on a tree branch and watching a mouse. Miniature decorations on the blade feature a long blooming plant with miniature flowers made from silver and gold and a spider and butterfly to complement the floral decor. The reverse side has a design made from miniature decorations featuring a tree branch. Dagger's length: 14" (35.5 cm.). Estimated value: $1,500.

Fig. 10/5. Japan. 19th century mother-of-pearl knife decorated with a pair of birds, flowers, and scrolls. The background for the incised decorations is a silver hued mother-of-pearl shell. A central portion fissure was repaired in the 19th century using a silver stabilizing plaque. Length: 9.5" (24 cm.). Estimated value: $750.

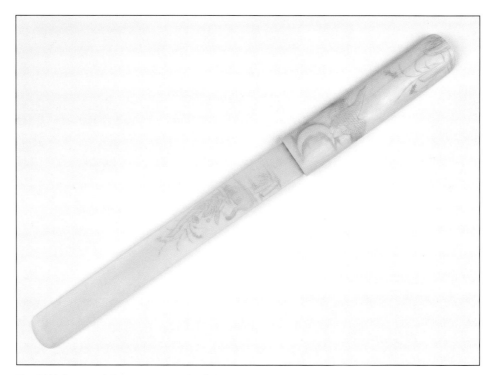

Fig. 10/6. Japan. 19th century ivory knife decorated on the obverse side with relief carvings featuring a pond, aquatic vegetation, and ducks. The reverse side has two inscriptions in red (one with two characters represents the artist's signature) and blooming lotus flowers. Length: 9" (23 cm.). Estimated value: $700.

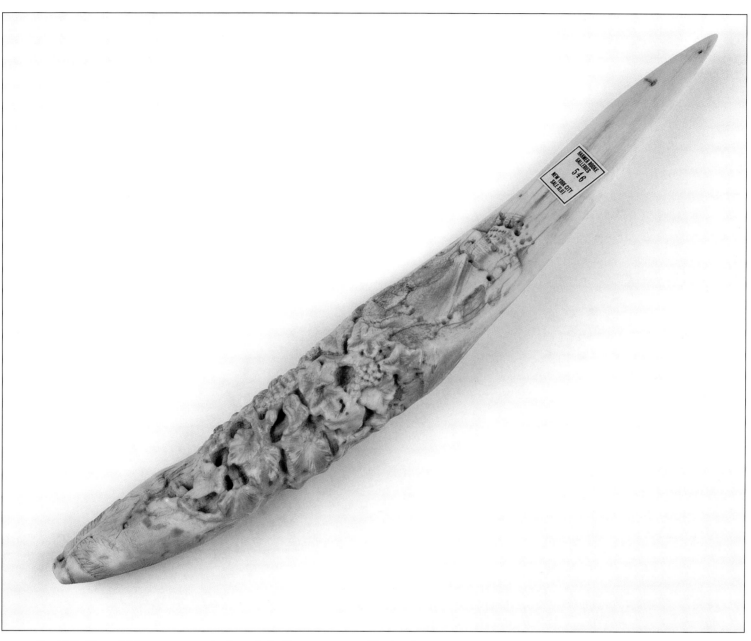

Fig. 10/7. China. 18th century ivory knife made for European export. The handle is carved with intricate grapes, leaves, and tendrils. Double-edged blade decorated with a crown above a royal coat of arms. Golden-brown toning is present on the ivory carved from full elephant tusk. Provenance: Harmer Rooke Galleries, NYC. Length: 12.6" (32 cm.). Estimated value: $2,000.

Fig. 10/8. China. Bone carved sword decorated with dragons. The hilt has criss-cross ribbon-like decorations. Round hand-guard with incised decorations. The scabbard is decorated with a dragon and ling zhi, as well as the blade. Blade's length: 13.5" (34 cm.). Sword's length: 27.5" (70 cm.). Estimated value: $1,000.

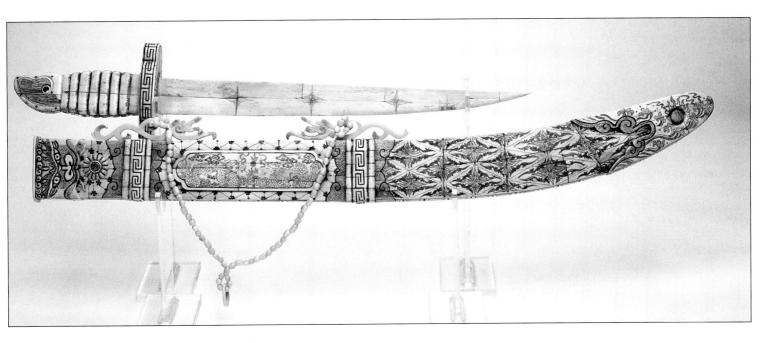

Fig. 10/9. China. Bone sword with ample decorations: incised, polychrome scrimshaw, and appliqués. Tao tieh masks adorn the proximal portion of the scabbard. The scabbard's central panel features a high relief carved cartouche with two dragons and the flaming pearl in between. Suspension of the sword is achieved through a chain made from bone beads anchored to two dragons attached to the scabbard. Blade's length: 17" (43 cm.). Sword's length: 36.5" (93 cm.). Estimated value: $1,000.

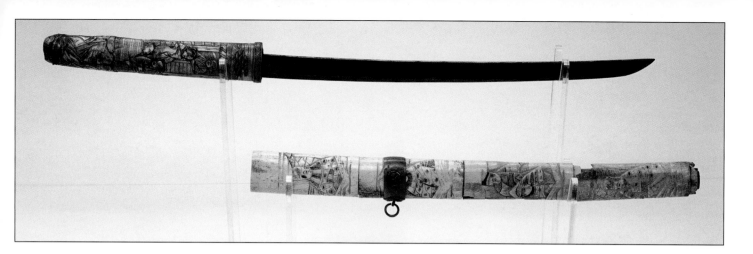

Fig. 10/10. Japan. 19th century bone hilt wakizashi sword decorated with figural design. Bone scabbard also features a figural design. One brass ring with mon encompasses the scabbard. Blade's length: 15" (38 cm.). Sword's length: 24.8" (63 cm.). Estimated value: $850.

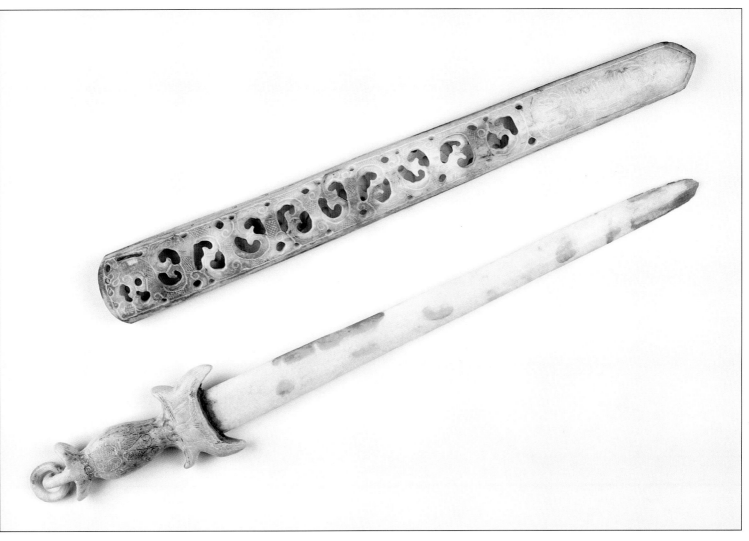

Fig. 10/11. China. Eastern Zhou period white jade dagger with open work, high relief decorations of the scabbard. The pommel has an open ring decoration. Double-edged jade blade with triangular point. Blade's length: 13" (33 cm.). Dagger's length: 18" (46 cm.). Estimated value: $2,000.

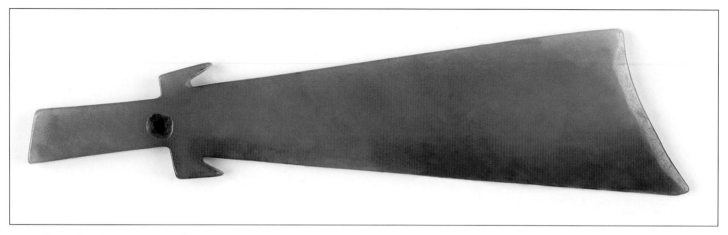

Fig. 10/12. China. Han period, circa 1st century BCE. Celadon-green jade falchion. It has a central perforation on the hilt for suspension purposes. Knife's length: 7.2" (18.5 cm.). Estimated value: $550.

Fig. 10/13. China. Ming period. Green jade falchion made from spinach-green jade. Single-edged blade, widens toward the point. Oval hand-guard and cylindrical hilt. Blade's length: 16.5" (42 cm.). Sword's length: 22" (56 cm.). Estimated value: $1,000.

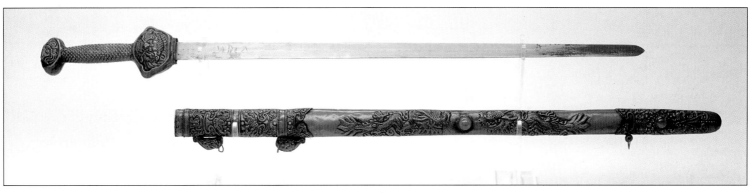

Fig. 10/14. China. 20th century copper covered hilt and scabbard sword. Inlaid turquoise and agate ornaments decorate the scabbard. Two facing dragons are separated by the agate carving that represents the luminous pearl. The scabbard and hilt are entirely done in high relief repoussé. The lower part of the hilt is in the shape of a mask and the handle has repoussé dragon's scales. Seven inlaid stars and an inscription are present on the blade. This sword was probably used in Chinese opera. Blade's length: 27" (70 cm.). Sword's length: 38.5" (98 cm.). Estimated value: $650.

Fig. 10/15. China. 20th century bone falchion. The blade is made from bone with scrimshaw decorations featuring a landscape and figural design. Oval, crenellated bone hand-guard with floral design. Wooden hilt with inlaid bone plaques featuring scrimshaw decorations. Estimated value: $450.

Fig. 10/16. China. Early 20th century bone sword decorated in high relief with a dragon featured in a series of fourteen panels bordered by brass frames. The blade has longitudinal forging striations. Blade's length: 24.5" (62 cm.). Sword's length: 36" (92 cm.). Estimated value: $1,200.

Chapter Eleven

Fantasy and Imitation Swords, Daggers, and Knives

This chapter includes some controversial antique edged weapons whose proof of being original is, or could be, disputed. Several are imitations of weapons from a previous dynastic period, but are of more recent manufacture. My way of demonstrating the antiquity of these weapons is to take a look inside the scabbard. The scabbard itself or the wood lining inside will reveal the true age of the weapon. If it is antique, the wood will show age deterioration in the form of rotting, dark color with cracks, signs of intensive threading of the blade through, worms drilling through the wood, or fragmentation. These wood changes can't be imitated or faked. (In contrast, metal is not a reliable material for determining age, as fake patina, rust, and even corrosion can be artificially produced.)

Several of the fantasy swords are therefore antiques, as proven by the scabbard's inner wood aging and the tremendous skill used to manufacture them using heavy lacquer inlaid with mother-of-pearl, inlaid decorations, etc.

The cost of producing similar items today at low cost appears to me impossible. The wages and the standard of living in China are much higher today then several years ago and the manufacturing of high quality reproductions at a low cost seems highly improbable. On the other hand, the collectors' market is flooded with cheap reproductions of Japanese or Chinese edged weapons that can clearly be recognized as new. Of greater concern is the flooding of the market with new reproductions labeled as antiques on Internet web sites and considered to be of high quality by many collectors who can't purchase the antiques. As long as the reproductions are not labeled antiques, the selling of these copies is ethical. In an earlier chapter, I mentioned the release of stored Chinese weapons manufactured for the Japanese army in Manchuria starting as early as the end of 19th century. Swords and daggers of this type demonstrate clearly the aged wood of the inner scabbard as the sole criterion for identification.

Chinese Fantasy Edged Weapons

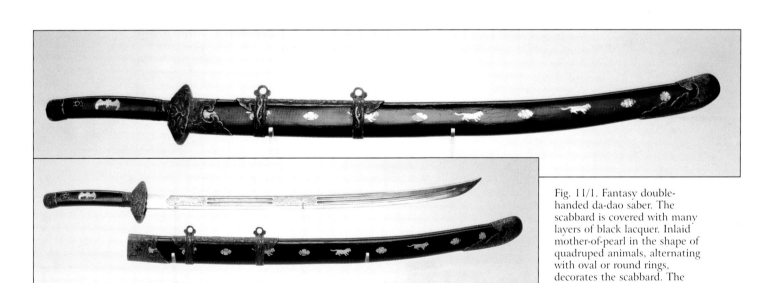

Fig. 11/1. Fantasy double-handed da-dao saber. The scabbard is covered with many layers of black lacquer. Inlaid mother-of-pearl in the shape of quadruped animals, alternating with oval or round rings, decorates the scabbard. The ends of the scabbard are decorated with chiseled bronze pieces and there are two bands that serve as suspension rings, linked with a chiseled bronze plaque. The inner wood lining of the scabbard reveals considerable aging. Single-edged blade with incised decorations featuring a tiger hunting a gazelle on one side of the blade and an inscription with incised roundels of a rabbit and a horse on the other side. Two fullers are present. The hilt is covered with heavy black lacquer decorated with inlaid mother-of-pearl bat (the character for bat and luck is the same: foo). Incised bronze decorations are present on the pommel, hilt, and handguard. Blade's length: 29.5" (75 cm.). Sword's length: 41" (104 cm.). Estimated value: $3,000.

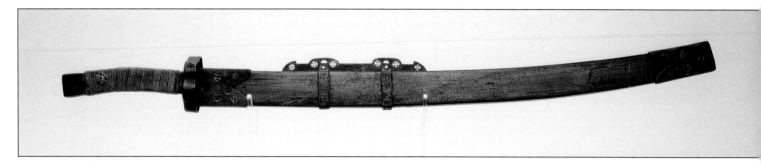

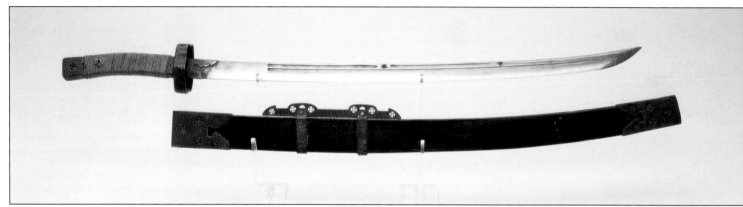

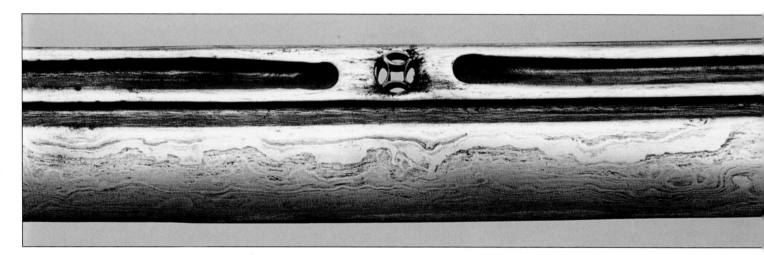

Fig. 11/2. Fantasy da-dao (double-handed) sword. The single-edged blade has fine damascus and has engraved a clenched knuckles fist. Two copper wheels are inserted on the back of the blade. An archaic characters seal inscription is present on the blade near the hilt. The blade curves upward toward the back and the point. Reddish-brown reptilian skin covers the scabbard, which is rectangular in shape. The ends of the scabbard are made from rectangular bronze pieces, decorated with five copper wheels on each side. Two annular bands and the suspender are made from bronze and are decorated with perforated wheels. The wood lining of the scabbard demonstrates that the sword is antique. A textile material covers the hilt. The pommel and the distal part of the hilt are decorated with copper wheels. Perforated wheels decorate the bronze hand-guard. Blade's length: 30.8" (78 cm.). Sword's length: 40.1" (102 cm.). Estimated value: $3,500.

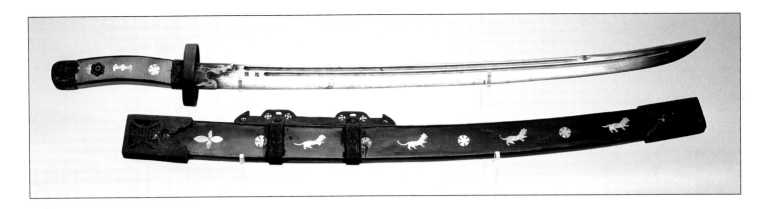

Fig. 11/3. Fantasy double-handed da-dao sword with heavy black lacquer hilt and scabbard. Long hilt allows for two hand holding and is decorated with inlaid mother-of-pearl in the shape of a bat surrounded by two wheels. Chiseled iron roundels adorn the pommel and the hand-guard. Watered blade with fine damascene design. Copper wheels decorate the blade, which has two fullers. Single-edged blade curves upward toward the back. Inlaid mother-of-pearl lion ornaments alternating with mother-of-pearl wheels decorate the lacquered scabbard. The ends of the scabbard are formed by rectangular, incised iron ornaments displaying heavy oxidation and superficial corrosion. Suspension of the sword is achieved by an iron plaque decorated with wheels and held by two iron bands. The aged wood of the scabbard's inner lining and the iron corrosion attest to the antiquity of the sword. Blade's length: 30.5" (77.5 cm.). Sword's length: 40.5" (103 cm.). Estimated value: $3,500.

Fig. 11/4. Fantasy, two-handed jian sword. Single-edged, damascene blade with engraving of two horned animals near the hilt. The hilt and scabbard are rectangular in shape and covered with reptilian skin. Incised bronze ornaments with floral design decorate the pommel and the ends of the scabbard. There is no hand-guard, but the end of the hilt and the scabbard's proximal end match the design of an unidentified animal. Blade's length: 27.3" (69.5 cm.). Sword's length: 40.5" (103 cm.). Estimated value: $2,500.

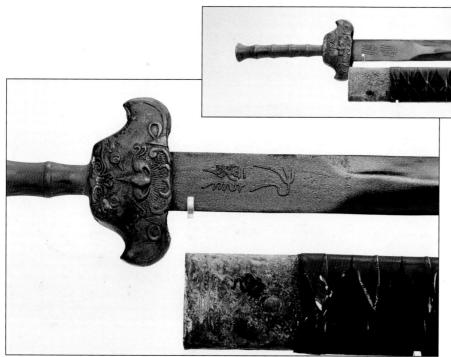

Fig. 11/5. Fantasy jian sword of medieval appearance. Faux bamboo bronze hilt with simple linear decorations. The hand-guard is wide and decorated in relief with double tao tieh design on both sides. Double-edged blade ending in a triangular point. A different inscription with archaic characters is present on each side of the proximal part of the blade. The scabbard is made from wood covered with embossed tin metal sheet with a very intricate design. A more recent leather cover was added in the 20th century. The interior of the scabbard shows marked aging of the wood lining, attesting to the antique labeling. This is a very heavy double-handed sword, most likely used for ceremonial purposes. Blade's length: 30.5" (77.5 cm.). Sword's length: 41.8" (106 cm.). Estimated value: $3,000.

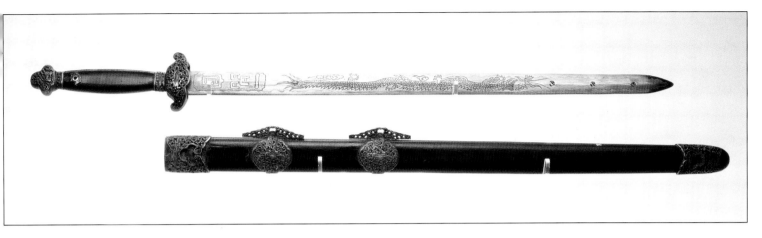

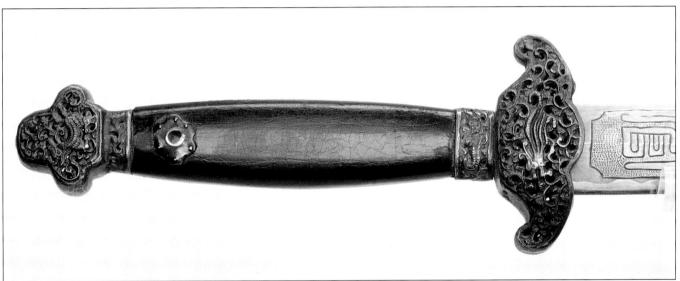

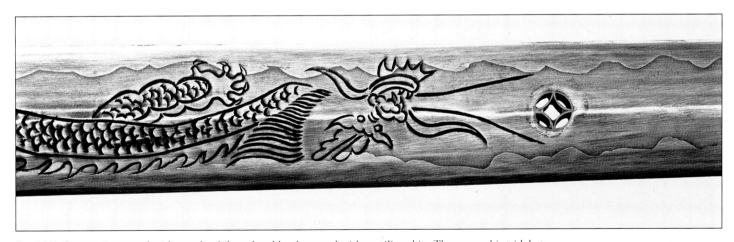

Fig. 11/6. Fantasy jian sword with wooden hilt and scabbard covered with reptilian skin. The pommel is tri-lobate with relief design of a horned dragon in bronze. The same design decorates the hand-guard. Double-edged blade with fine damascene design. A dragon is incised on the length of the blade with inscription visible on both sides. Three perforated copper wheels are inserted in the blade near the point. The scabbard is decorated with incised bronze terminal pieces as well as two annular bronze oval plaques decorated with lizards, which hold the suspension hangers. Blade's length: 28.6" (72.5 cm.). Sword's length: 40.3" (102.5 cm.). Estimated value: $2,750.

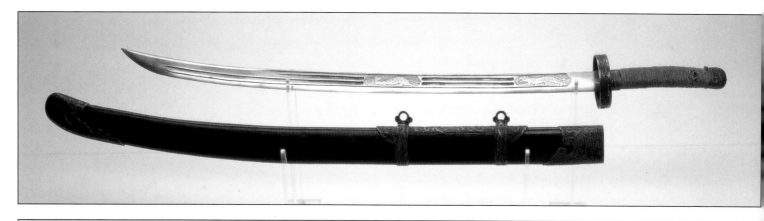

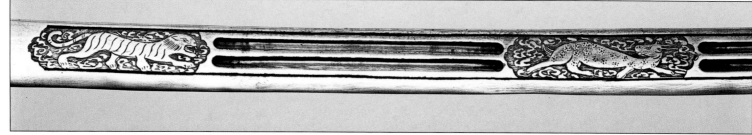

Fig. 11/7. Fantasy two-handed da-dao sword. Fine, watered blade with incised feline separated by the fullers from another vignette featuring a running goat. The blade's reverse side features a running horse in the central panel and a hare in a roundel with an inscription near the hilt. Round hand-guard with incised decorations in brass. A textile material wraps the hilt. The pommel has intricate incised decorations in brass. Wooden scabbard with incised decorations in brass featuring mythological animals. The inner wood lining of the scabbard reveals very old wood and the metal parts show age patina attesting to the antiquity of the sword. Blade's length: 30.8" (78 cm.). Sword's length: 41.5" (105.5 cm.). Estimated value: $2,500.

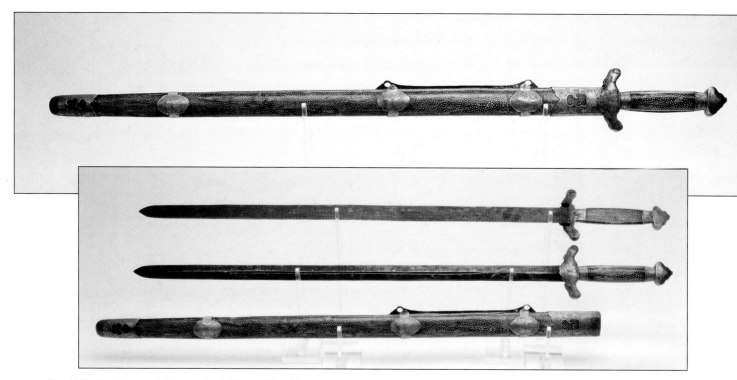

Fig. 11/8. Double sword (shuang jian). The scabbard has two partitions that allow the blades to be contained side by side. Ray skin and incised brass decorate the scabbard. Two annular brass pieces hold two eyelets that act as suspenders. The triangular shaped pommel is decorated with incised brass. The shuang jian allows for double threading due to the fact that the hilts and the blades are convex on one side and flat on the other side. One fuller is present on the blades, which have seven inlaid round brass decorations. An image of an archaic ting vessel is seen near the hilt. The hand-guard is made from brass decorated with incised lines. Blade's length: 26.8" (68 cm.). Sword's length: 37.2" (94.5 cm.). Estimated value: $850.

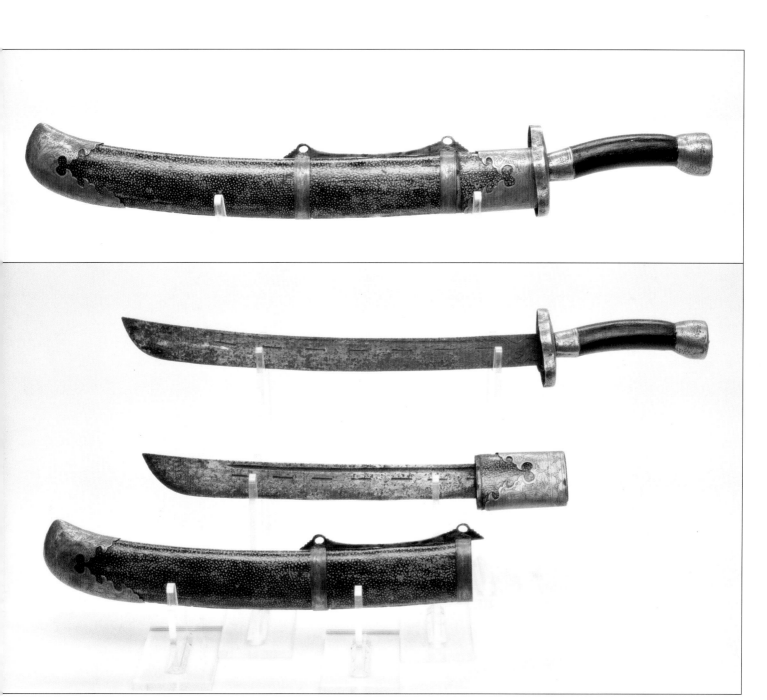

Fig. 11/9. Double sword (shuang dao), a pair of swords contained in the same scabbard. The shuang dao sabers are much rarer than their counterpart shuang jian. The main dao is longer and has a lacquered wood hilt. Incised brass decorates the knob-shaped pommel and the hand-guard. The blade is single-edged and curved, with one fuller and interrupted longitudinal lines separated by three dots. A dragon chasing the flaming pearl is incised near the hilt on both sides. The main sword threads into the auxiliary sword, whose hilt is an elongation of the scabbard. Green ray skin covers the scabbard and is decorated with incised brass bands. Blades' lengths: 19.7" (50 cm.) and 16" (40.5 cm.). Sword's length: 27.5" (70 cm.). Estimated value: $850.

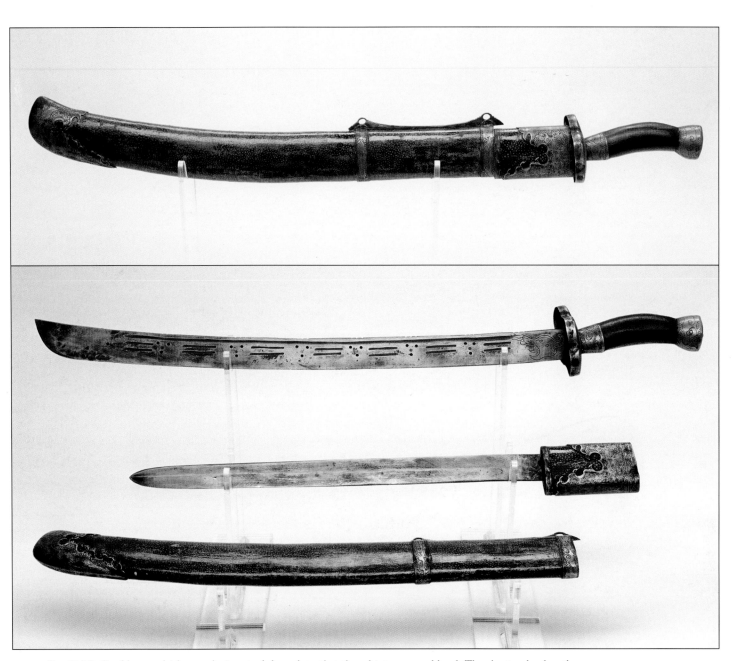

Fig. 11/10. Double sword (shuang dao), paired dao sabers that thread into one scabbard. The shorter dao has the proximal part of the scabbard used as a hilt. The scabbard is covered with ray skin and decorated with a brass chape with dragons. Two annular brass bands suspend the swords. The hand-guard is made from oval brass incised with the design of a dragon and phoenix bird. The main blade has a fuller and, underneath, interrupted parallel lines separated by four incised dots. Blades' lengths: 19.9" (50.5 cm.), and 16.3" (41.5 cm.). Sword's length: 27.5" (70 cm.). Estimated value: $850.

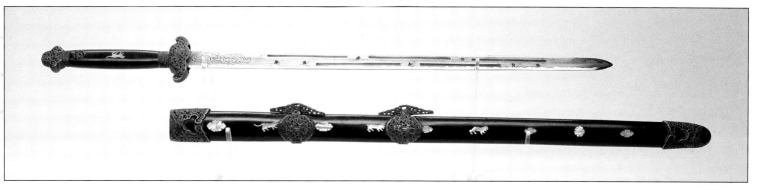

Fig. 11/11. Fantasy jian sword, two-hands holding. The blade is double-edged and decorated with seven copper wheels. A dragon is incised on both sides, near the hand-guard. Wooden hilt with heavy black lacquer cover is adorned with a mother-of-pearl lion on both sides. The pommel and hand-guard are hand-chiseled with the design of a mythological animal in the shape of a reptile. Wooden scabbard covered with many coats of black lacquer and decorated with mother-of-pearl lions alternating with oval shape wheels. The ends of the scabbard as well as the annular brass suspension bands are hand chiseled in brass and decorated with a reptilian mythological animal. Age patina is present on the brass ornaments. The inner wood lining of the scabbard reveals marked aging through decaying wood. All these features point toward the authenticity of the sword as an antique object. Blade's length: 28.2" (71.5 cm.). Sword's length: 43.5" (110.5 cm.). Estimated value: $2,000.

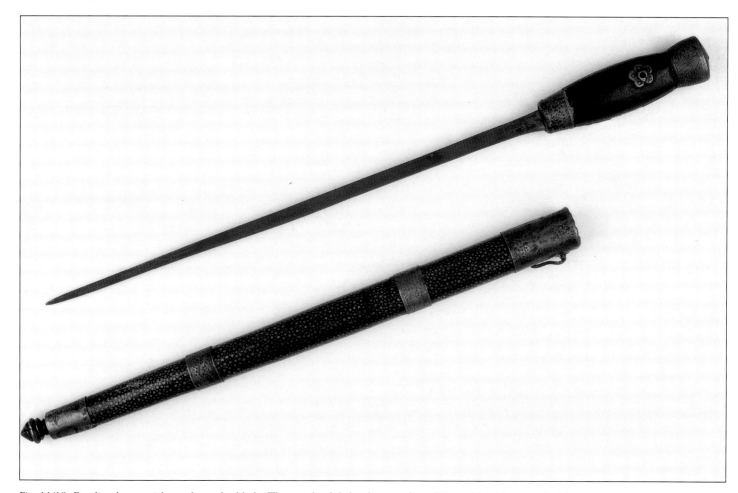

Fig. 11/12. Peculiar dagger with quadrangular blade. The wooden hilt has brass endings. The scabbard is covered with ray skin and also has brass endings. Blade's length: 11" (28 cm.). Dagger's length: 15" (38 cm.). Estimated value: $800.

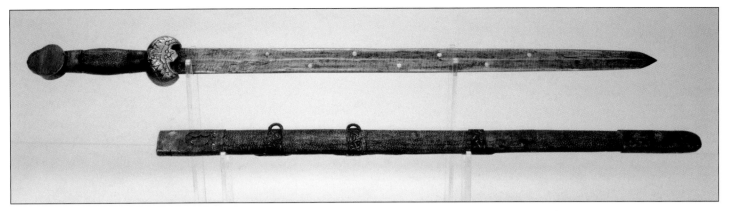

Fig. 11/13. Fantasy or genuine antique jian sword. The hilt is covered with yellow ray skin. A brass dragon's head decorates the hand-guard. The pommel is also made from brass and has elaborate incised decorations. Seven round brass dots are inlaid in the blade and there derives the name in Chinese of seven stars sword. An inscription with archaic characters is made from brass and inlaid in the blade. On the reverse side, instead of the inscription, a brass linear decoration in the shape of an ancient vessel (ting), is inlaid in the blade. The scabbard is covered with yellow ray skin and decorated with brass ornaments of annular shape. The scabbard's interior is lined with old wood, attesting to the old age of this sword. Blade's length: 25" (63.5 cm.). Sword's length: 32" (81.5 cm.). Estimated value: $850.

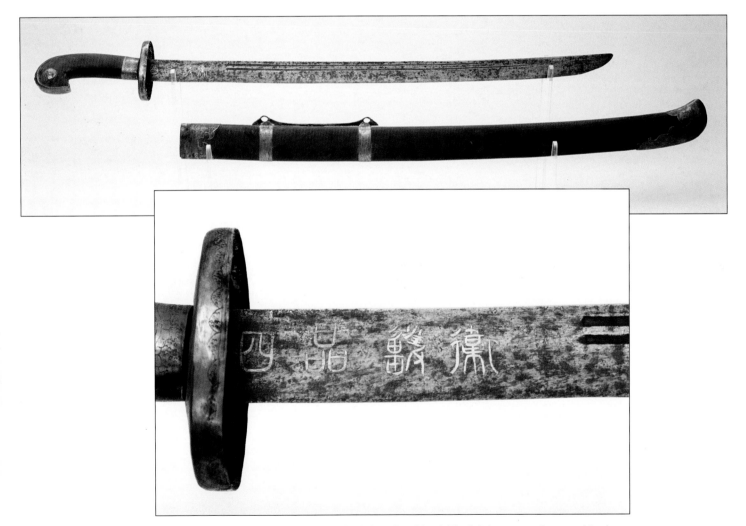

Fig. 11/14. Fantasy dao sword with wooden hilt and scabbard. The hilt has a round pommel in the shape of a bird's head. The hand-guard as well as the hilt and scabbard are adorned with hand-chiseled brass bands. Single-edged blade curves upward toward the point. Archaic characters are present on both sides of the blade. Two fullers are grooved into the blade. Blade's length: 27.8" (70.5 cm.). Sword's length: 36" (91.5 cm.). Estimated value: $700.

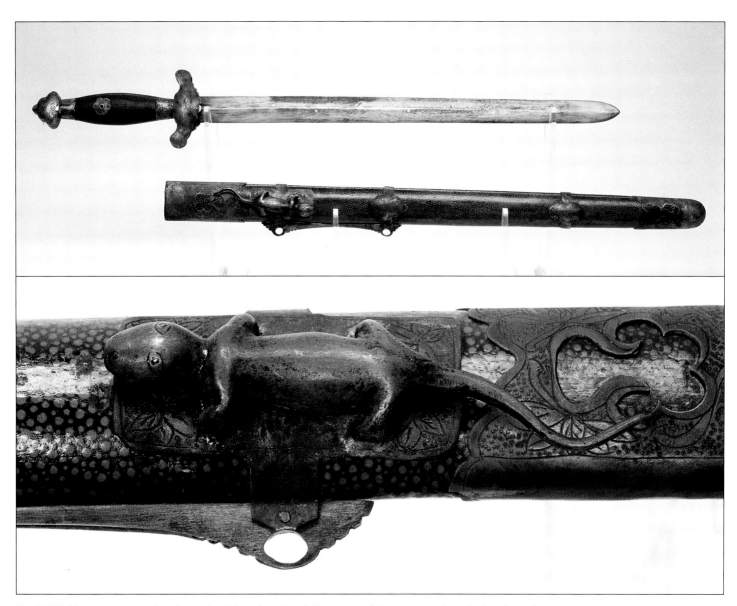

Fig. 11/15. Fantasy jian sword with wooden hilt and scabbard. Brass incised decorations adorn the hand-guard, pommel, and scabbard ends, as well as two annular brass bands that hold a two eyelet hanger. The scabbard is covered with ray skin and decorated with a brass lizard on the upper part. Double-edged blade with seven stars round brass decorations. The lining of the scabbard shows the wood to be aged. Blade's length: 20.8" (52.6 cm.). Sword's length: 31.8" (80.5 cm.). Estimated value: $450.

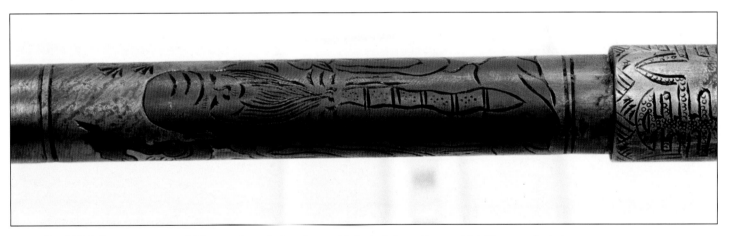

Fig. 11/16. Fantasy cane-sword. The cane is made from brass with incised decorations and inlaid copper featuring a figural design. The handle (pommel) has incised ornaments. Rectangular blade with one fuller on each facet. Blade's length: 19.8" (50 cm.). Cane's length: 34" (86.5 cm.). Estimated value: $450.

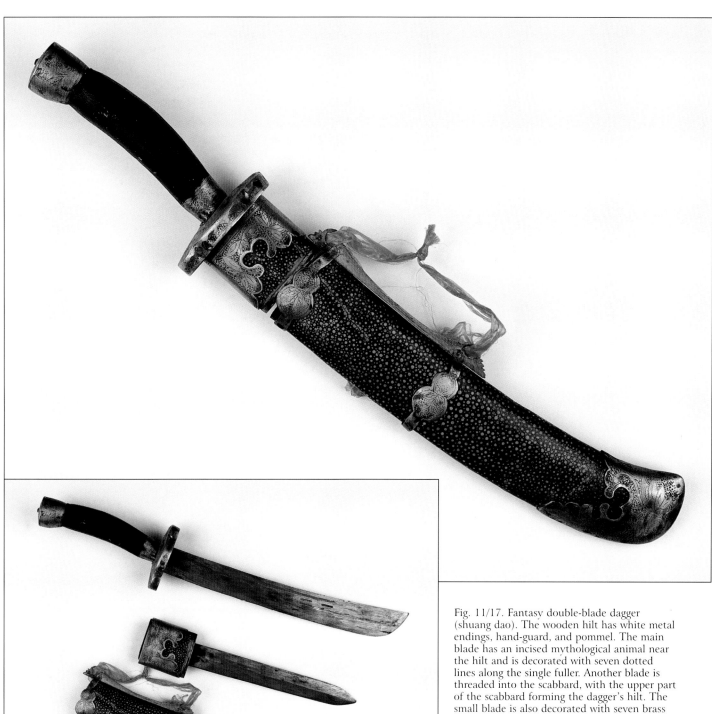

Fig. 11/17. Fantasy double-blade dagger (shuang dao). The wooden hilt has white metal endings, hand-guard, and pommel. The main blade has an incised mythological animal near the hilt and is decorated with seven dotted lines along the single fuller. Another blade is threaded into the scabbard, with the upper part of the scabbard forming the dagger's hilt. The small blade is also decorated with seven brass dots on both sides. The scabbard is covered with green ray skin. Large blade's length: 9.5" (24 cm.). Small blade's length: 6.5" (16.5 cm.). Estimated value: $800.

Japanese and Other
Fantasy Edged Weapons

Fig. 11/18. Japan. Showa period wakizashi sword. Silver hilt with elaborate decorations in high relief depicting samurai in battle scenes. The silver tsuba is rectangular in shape and decorated with a marine life design depicting fish, crabs, sting rays, etc. Kashira is made from silver with fish design. Silver fuchi with sea life. The scabbard is lacquered in black and red. On the other side, there is an inscription in a cartouche. This is a modern masterwork re-creating an Edo period sword. Blade's length: 17.5" (44.5 cm.). Sword's length: 27.3" (69.5 cm.). Estimated value: $2,000.

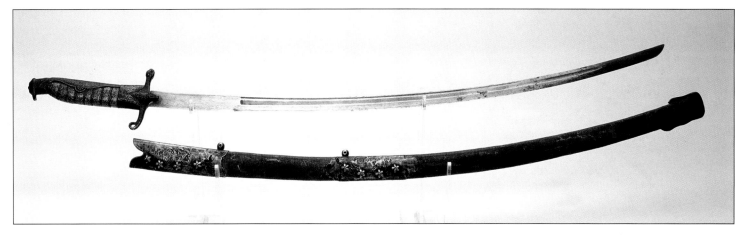

Fig. 11/19. Fantasy Japanese katana. Military sword, probably used for a cavalry officer. The yellow ray skin hilt is divided into horizontal bands by a metal wire grip. The hand-guard has two quillons, one ending in an animal head and the other in a central perforation. The back brass band is adorned with two chrysanthemums. Small pommel with perforation for hanging. Metal scabbard adorned with two wide brass bands having four stars surrounded by five leaves. Curved single-edged blade, without any decorations, has two fullers. Traces of lacquer are present on the scabbard. This sword apparently originates from a Manchurian arsenal that was de-accessed by Chinese authorities and could be dated as early as the end of 19th century. Most probably, it was manufactured by Chinese laborers. Blade's length: 36" (91.5 cm.). Sword's length: 45" (115 cm.). Estimated value: $975.

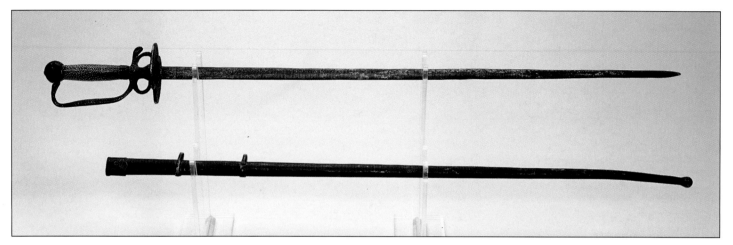

Fig. 11/20. Fantasy Japanese small sword with yellow ray skin hilt cover. The pommel is ball-shaped. A steel hand-guard with elaborate, pierced design has a bi-lobate shape and is placed below the two fingers grip, allowing for protection of the fingers. An incised decoration is present on the curved knuckle-bow that ends in a snake's head. A small quillon curves downward. Rapier type of blade for piercing purposes is double-edged with a sharp point. Steel scabbard with double hanger. This type of small sword is well described in the book *Swords and Hilt Weapons* by Michael D. Coe and associates (pages 66-69). This sword was apparently de-accessed from a Manchurian arsenal by the Chinese authorities. Blade's length: 25" (63.5 cm.). Sword's length: 32.8" (83 cm.). Estimated value: $975.

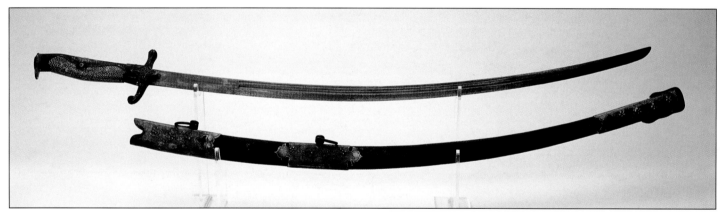

Fig. 11/21. Fantasy Japanese katana. This is a military sword decorated with four stars, probably denoting the rank of the officer. Yellow ray skin hilt has a brass plaque on the back decorated with one star surrounded by four leaves. The plaque ends with an oval pommel that has a perforation, apparently for hanging the sword. The hand-guard has two quillons, one with a perforation and the other in the shape of an animal's head. An unidentified decoration is in the center of the hand-guard. Single-edged blade with two fullers. The length of the blade leads me to believe that this was a cavalry sword. Metal scabbard adorned with three brass plaques. The distal two plaques have four stars embossed in the brass, while the proximal band has only three stars. The upper two bands have metal rings for the sword's suspension. Some rust and pitting corrosion are present on the scabbard. Apparently this sword, similar to the preceding ones, was de-accessed from Manchurian arsenals by Chinese authorities and made available for sale through private Chinese dealers. The origin is suspected as they were manufactured by Chinese workers as early as the end of 19th century. Similar swords were used by mounted Japanese police during the Meiji period. Blade's length: 36" (91.5 cm.). Sword's length: 45" (115 cm.). Estimated value: $950.

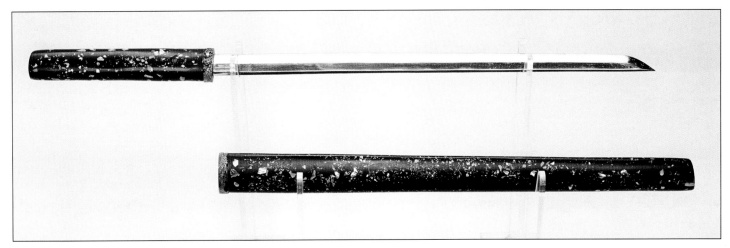

Fig. 11/22. Fantasy Japanese wakizashi sword. The hilt and scabbard are covered with heavy black lacquer inlaid with mother-of-pearl that gives an iridescent appearance. There is no hand-guard, but a brass edge ornament with shi-shi lions is present. The blade appears to be of a more recent manufacture, contrary to most of the genuine Japanese swords on the market. Nevertheless, the inner lining of the scabbard is made from aged wood, attesting to the antiquity of the sword. Apparently, this sword was de-accessed from a Manchurian arsenal for sale through Chinese dealers. Blade's length: 17.5" (44.5 cm.). Sword's length: 25.2" (64 cm.). Estimated value: $450.

Fig. 11/23. Fantasy Japanese katana sword. The hilt is made from bronze with relief braiding imitating textile braiding. Oval tsuba with four chrysanthemum flowers decoration. Greenish patina covers the metal. Single-edged blade with inscription on both sides. An archaic characters inscription coexists with a more modern age inscription on the opposite side, featuring two characters inscription, a flag with a star in the center, and the arsenal number 40101 engraved below. Brass scabbard with a dragon in the center on one side and an inscription with three chrysanthemum flowers on the other side. Single hanger with one ring is attached to the scabbard. This sword apparently was de-accessed from Manchurian arsenals for sale through Chinese dealers. Blade's length: 27" (68.5 cm.). Sword's length: 38" (96.5 cm.). Estimated value: $425.

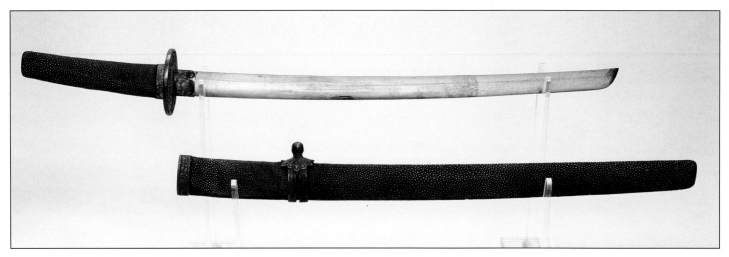

Fig. 11/24. Fantasy Japanese katana sword. The scabbard and hilt are covered with ray skin. Ornate oval tsuba decorated with floral design. Single suspension ring on the scabbard is decorated with paulownia flowers. This sword, probably made by Chinese workers, originates from a Manchurian arsenal and was distributed for sale by Chinese authorities. Blade's length: 20" (51 cm.). Sword's length: 29.8" (76 cm.). Estimated value: $400.

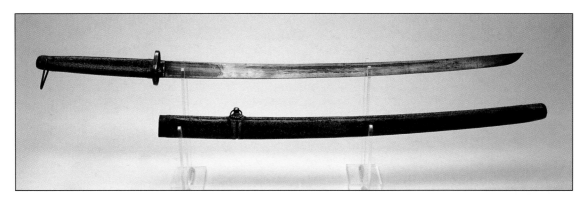

Fig. 11/25. Fantasy Japanese katana sword. The hilt and scabbard are covered with green ray skin. Single-edged blade with one fuller has an inscription on both sides of the blade. The arsenal number 46127 is also inscribed in the blade. The tsuba is oval-shaped, made from brass, and decorated with a bird. A brass annular ornament holds a suspension ring. Apparently, this sword was manufactured in Manchuria under the Japanese occupation. Blade's length: 27.8" (70.5 cm.). Sword's length: 37.8" (96 cm.). Estimated value: $375.

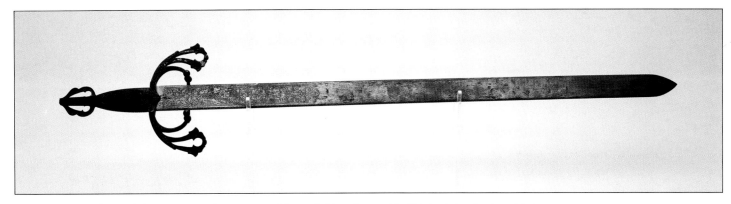

Fig. 11/26. Spanish sword that appears to be a ceremonial sword. Manufactured in Toledo, it has intricate blade engravings with a coat of arms swirled ornament. The obverse side has a turreted incised wall, while the reverse side has a three towers castle. Iron hilt with incised coat of arms and helmeted warrior's head. The quillons are curved downward with an incised high relief design. Blade's length: 35.5" (90 cm.). Sword's length: 42" (107 cm.). Estimated value: $900.

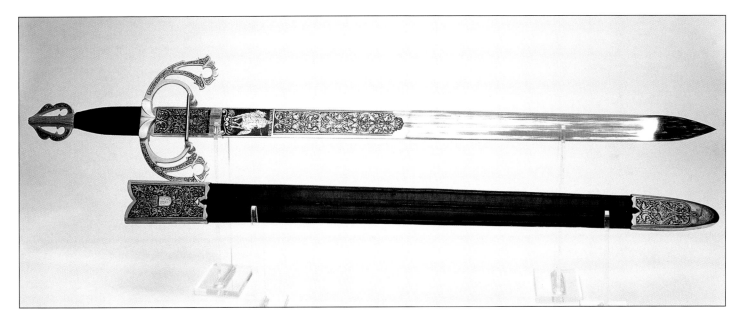

Fig. 11/27. Spanish presentation sword for ceremonial use. Braided textile hilt and leather scabbard with gilded metal endings, featuring on the proximal end a standing dragon with crown above. The blade has incised decorations of intaglio form, with the crevices filled with polychrome enamel. The proximal part of the blade has engraved a mounted warrior with the inscription of Tizona del Cid. Intaglio decorations are on the pommel, blade, quillons, and scabbard and feature polychrome enamel in the crevices. Blade's length: 35" (89 cm.). Sword's length: 41" (104 cm.). Estimated value: $850.

Glossary

Ankus (Ancus). Spear-axe used to train elephants. Hindi.

Bagh Nakh. Indian concealed weapon. Hindi.

Bahasa. National language of Indonesia and Malay peninsula.

Bairogi. Fakir concealed weapon. Hindi.

Baldric. Shoulder band for the sword attachment.

Bank. Concealed, curved Hindu knife.

Baselard. Swiss dagger originating from Basel.

BCE. Before common era.

Bhuj. Indian axe.

Bichaq. Turkish dagger.

Bichwa (Bichoa). Indian dagger.

Bidri. Inlaid decoration where the background is made from dark pewter. Hindi.

Bronze age. Started about 3500 BCE and followed the stone age.

Bronze d'oré. Gilded bronze. French.

CE. Common era.

Chape. Distal end of the scabbard.

Chilanum. Indian dagger. Hindi.

Cinnabar. Red lacquer containing a mercury amalgam.

Dao. Chinese curved sword or dagger.

Dapur bener. Straight blade of the kris dagger. Bahasa Indonesia.

Dapur luk (lok). Wavy blade of the kris. Bahasa Indonesia.

Dha. Burmese sword or dagger.

Falchion. European wide blade sword.

Firangi. Indian sword. Hindi.

Galar. Straight part of the scabbard. Bahasa Indonesia.

Ganja. Upper part of the blade. Bahasa.

Garuda. Hindu deity in shape of a bird, carrier of Vishnu.

Gladius. Roman short sword.

Grof. Hungarian nobleman.

Gupti. Cane sword. Hindi.

Hao. Central opening of a jade disk.

Hilt. Handle of the edged weapon.

Holbein. Small Swiss dagger.

Iron age. Started about 500 CE and followed the bronze age.

Jambiya. Islamic dagger.

Jian. Chinese straight sword.

Kard. Persian knife.

Kaskara. Sudanese sword.

Kastane. Sinhalese weapon. Sri Lanka.

Katar. Hindu edged weapon.

Khanda. Indian sword.

Khanjar. Islamic dagger.

Kilij. Turkish sword.

Kindjal. Turkish dagger.

Klewang. Malay sword.

Koftgari. Indian superficial inlay of precious metals.

Korambi. Malay concealed knife.

Koummiya. Moroccan dagger.

Kris. Indonesian dagger.

Longets. Downward extensions from the sword's hand-guard.

Mahratta. Hindu warriors from Southern India.

Majapahit. Medieval empire with the capital in central Java.

Menangkabou. Sumatra dagger.

Mendaq. The ring ferrule between the hilt and the blade of a kris dagger.

Mihrab. Altar decoration in a Masjid (Mosque).

Moghul. Mongol conquerors of Northern India.

Moorish. Muslim rulers of medieval Spain.

Navaja. Spanish switch-blade knife.

Neolithic period. Followed Paleolithic period and extended between 10,000 BCE to 3500 BCE.

Niello. Inlaid enamel decoration.

Paksi. Tang of a kris dagger. Bahasa.

Paleolithic period. The period between 19,000 BCE and 10,000 BCE.

Pamir. Meteoric iron in the blade of a kris dagger. Bahasa.

Pamor. Damascene design of kris dagger. Bahasa.

Panabas. Moro sword from Southern Philippines.

Pas d'ane. Sword guard below the quillons. French.

Pata. Indian gauntlet sword.

Pedang. Sumatra sword.

Pendaq. Scabbard's cover of the kris dagger. Bahasa.

Piha Khetta. Sinhalese weapon. Sri Lanka.

Pulomar. Curved blade Indian sword.

Quillon. Small ring dagger.

Quillons. Transverse bars below the sword's hilt.

Rechong. Acehnese dagger.

Repoussé. Embossed metal surface in relief. French.

Ricasso. Edgeless portion of the proximal part of the blade.

Sagittal. A section plane from the front to back (anterior to posterior).

Sanger. Processional Sinhalese spearhead. Ceylon (Sri Lanka).

Sarong. Scabbard. Bahasa.

Scabbard. The sheath covering the blade of an edged weapon.

Shamshir (Scimitar). Persian sword.

Shashka. Russian Caucasian sword, Islamic in origin.

Sinhalese. Ethnic group of Ceylon (Sri Lanka), speaking the Aryan dialect of Northern India Hindi.

Stupa. Buddhist temple with large terrace surrounding a central bulbous structure.

Takouba. Tuareg sword.

Talwar (Tulwar). Indian sword.

Tombak. Spear. Bahasa.

Ukiran. The hilt of a kris dagger. Bahasa.

Wedong. Southeast Asian dagger.

Wilah. Dagger's blade. Bahasa.

Wootz. Indigenous Indian steel-made.

Wrangka. Horizontal arm of the kris scabbard. Bahasa.

Yataghan. Turkish curved sword.

Note: Extensive Japanese terminology can be found in Chapter Six. In order to avoid duplication, this Japanese terminology has not been included in the Glossary.

Bibliography

Bull, Stephens. "An historical guide to arms and armor." *Facts on File,* 1991.

Coe, Michael D., Peter Connolly, Christopher Spring, Anthony Harding, and Frederick Wilkinson: *Swords and Hilt Weapons.* Weidenfeld and Nicholson, 1989.

Meltzer, Milton. *Weapons and Warfare: From the Stone Age to the Space Age.* Harper Collins, 1996.

Oakeshott, Ewart. *European Weapons and Armor: From the Renaissance to the Industrial Revolution.* Beinfeld Publishing, 1980.

Oakeshott, Ewart. *The Archeology of Weapons: Arms and Armour from Prehistory to the Age of Chivalry.* Dover Publications, 1994.

O'Connell, Robert L. *Soul of the Sword: An Illustrated History of Weaponry and Warfare from Prehistory to the Present.* Free Press. Distributed by Simon and Schuster, 2002.

Stone, George Cameron. *A Glossary of the Construction, Decoration and Use of Arms and Armor in All Countries and in All Times.* Mineola, New York: Dover Publications, Inc., 1999.

Wallace, John. *Scottish Swords and Dirks, An Illustrated Reference Guide to Scottish Edged Weapons.* Stackpole Books, 1970.

Weland, Gerald. *A Collector's Guide To Swords, Daggers & Cutlasses.* Secaucus, N.J.: Chartwell Books, 1991.

Wood, Michael. *Ancient Warfare: From Clubs to Catapults.* Runestone Press, 2000.